TEXTBOOK ON

JURISPRUDENCE

D0317217

TEXTBOOK ON

JURISPRUDENCE

Third edition

Professor Hilaire McCoubrey

Director of Postgraduate Affairs, University of Hull
Law School

and

Dr. Nigel D. White

Senior Lecturer in Law, University of Nottingham

OXFORD
UNIVERSITY PRESS

OXFORD
UNIVERSITY PRESS

Great Clarendon Street, Oxford OX2 6DP

Oxford University Press is a department of the University of Oxford.
It furthers the University's objective of excellence in research, scholarship,
and education by publishing worldwide in

Oxford New York

Auckland Cape Town Dar es Salaam Hong Kong Karachi Kuala Lumpur
Madrid Melbourne Mexico City Nairobi New Delhi Taipei Toronto
Shanghai

With offices in

Argentina Austria Brazil Chile Czech Republic France Greece
Guatemala Hungary Italy Japan South Korea Poland Portugal
Singapore Switzerland Thailand Turkey Ukraine Vietnam

Oxford is a registered trade mark of Oxford University Press
in the UK and in certain other countries

Published in the United States
by Oxford University Press Inc., New York

A Blackstone Press Book

© H. McCoubrey and N. D. White, 1993
Second edition 1996
Third edition 1999

British Library Cataloguing in Publication Data
Data available

Library of Congress Cataloging in Publication Data
Data available

ISBN-10: 1-85431-896-9
ISBN-13: 978-1-85431-896-1

9 10

Typeset by Style Photosetting Limited, Mayfield, East Sussex
Printed in Great Britain
on acid-free paper by
Biddles Ltd., King's Lynn, Norfolk

Contents

Introduction   xi

1 What is Jurisprudence?   1

1.1   The variety of jurisprudential issues   1.2   Some basic questions
1.3 Some points of method   1.4   Jurisprudence and its substantive context
1.5   What is the value of jurisprudence?

2 Classical Positivism: Bentham and Austin   11

2.1   Bentham's concept of jurisprudence   2.2   The command theory of
law   2.2.1   The command   2.2.2   The sovereign   2.2.3   The
attachment of sanctions   2.2.4   The Benthamite complete law   2.3   The
viability of command theory   2.4   The question of public international law
2.5 Bentham's censorial jurisprudence   2.6   Further reading

3 Modified Positivism: H. L. A. Hart   32

3.1   Hart's gunman and the critique of command theory   3.2   The
importance of rules   3.2.1   Obligation and the internal aspect of rules
3.2.2 The union of primary and secondary rules   3.2.3   The basis of the
rule of recognition   3.2.4   Legal systems and the importance of officials
3.3   Hart's argument on rule scepticism   3.4   Public international law in
Hart's theory   3.5   Hart and moral analyses of positive law   3.5.1   Abuse
of law: the debate between Hart and Fuller   3.5.2   The enforcement of
morality: Hart and Devlin   3.5.3   Hart's minimum content of natural law
3.6   The significance of Hart's theory   3.7   Further reading

4 Classical Naturalism   59

4.1   The central concerns of naturalist theories   4.2   The strands of classical naturalism   4.3   Classical Greek naturalism: Plato and Aristotle 4.3.1 Platonic idealism and legalism   4.3.2   Plato and the obligation to obey 4.3.3 The teleological analysis of Aristotle   4.4   The Judaeo-Christian impact: Augustine and Aquinas   4.4.1   Christian Platonism: St Augustine of Hippo 4.4.2   Christian Aristotelianism: St Thomas Aquinas 4.5   Transition to an age of reason?   4.5.1   Hobbes: a social-contractarian response to anarchy   4.5.2   Locke: social-contractarianism and bad government   4.5.3   Rousseau: a contract with society not government   4.6   The problem of objectivity   4.7   The standing of classical naturalism 4.8   Further reading

5 The Naturalist Revival   86

5.1   Lon L. Fuller and procedural natural law   5.1.1   Moralities of aspiration and of duty   5.1.2   The criteria of lawmaking 5.1.3   Procedural morality and the substance of laws   5.1.4   Is procedural naturalism actually naturalist? 5.2   John Finnis and the theory of natural rights   5.2.1   Finnis's defence of naturalism   5.2.2   The basic goods 5.2.3   The tests of practical reasonableness   5.2.4   From natural law to natural rights   5.2.5   The obligation to obey in Finnis's theory 5.2.6 The importance of Finnis's theory   5.3   Beyleveld and Brownsword: the moral nature of law   5.3.1   Law as a moral phenomenon 5.3.2   Obligation in a moral view of law   5.3.3 The place of Beyleveld and Brownsword in modern naturalism   5.4   The continuing role of naturalist jurisprudence   5.5   Further reading

6 Islamic Jurisprudence   106

6.1   The structure and sources of Islamic Law   6.1.1   *Sunnah* 6.1.2   *Ijma*   6.1.3   *Qiyas*   6.1.4   *Ijtahad*   6.2   The four Schools 6.3   Islam and the State   6.3.1   *Shari'ah* and secular law in Islamic States 6.3.2   *Shari'ah* and human rights   6.3.3   *Shari'ah* and the rights of non-Muslims   6.4   *Shari'ah* and international law   6.4.1   *Dar ul-Islam* and *Dar al-Harb*   6.4.2   *Jihad*   6.5   Further reading

7 Marxism and Post-Marxism   120

7.1   Classical Marxist theory   7.1.1   Law in classical Marxist theory 7.1.2 The transition from theory to practice   7.2   The development of Soviet legal theory   7.2.1   Law in Imperial Russia   7.2.2   The Soviet ordering of things   7.2.3   E. B. Pashukanis and early Marxism-Leninism

7.2.4   A. Ia. Vyshinsky and socialist legality   7.3   The development of Chinese legal theory   7.3.1   Law in the Imperial and Nationalist Chinese traditions   7.3.2 Law in the People's Republic of China   7.4   Developments in Western Marxist jurisprudence   7.4.1   Karl Renner and the contrast between form and function   7.5   The significance of Marxist legal analyses   7.6   Further reading

8   Pure Theory   144

8.1   In what sense a 'pure' theory?   8.1.1   Pure theory and the Kantian theory of knowledge   8.1.2   The meaning of 'purity'   8.2   The hierarchy of norms   8.2.1   The structure of norms   8.2.2   Validation in the hierarchy of norms   8.2.3   The *Grundnorm*   8.2.4   The problem of revolutionary transition   8.3   Concretisation and the substance of norms   8.3.1   The working of concretisation   8.3.2   The reality of concretisation   8.4   The official emphasis of Kelsenian analysis   8.5   The role of public international law in pure theory   8.5.1   Monism, dualism and the *Grundnorm*   8.5.2   The *Grundnorm* of public international law   8.6   The value of pure theory   8.7   Further reading

9   Dworkin and the Rights Thesis   157

9.1   Dworkin's criticism of positivism and pragmatism   9.1.1   Positivism   9.1.2 Pragmatism   9.2   The rights thesis   9.2.1   Objections to judicial decision-making on policy grounds   9.2.2   Entrenched rights   9.2.3   The consequentialist theory of rights   9.3   Judicial decisions and the common law   9.3.1   The 'one right answer' thesis   9.3.2   Integrity in practice   9.4 Judicial decisions and statutes   9.4.1   Settled and hard cases   9.4.2   Integrity in practice   9.5   The chess analogy   9.6   Democracy   9.6.1   The judge as protector of rights   9.6.2   The principle of equal concern and respect   9.7 Law and morality   9.7.1   Community morality   9.7.2   Morality and obligation   9.8   Further reading

10   Scandinavian Realism   178

10.1   Early psychological theorists: Petrażycki and Hägerström   10.1.1 Petrażycki and the theory of impulsions   10.1.2   Axel Hägerström: law and word magic   10.2   Vilhelm Lundstedt and the method of social welfare   10.2.1 The concept of social welfare   10.2.2   The importance of ideas of justice   10.2.3 The significance of Lundstedt's theory   10.3   Karl Olivecrona: independent imperatives   10.3.1   Olivecrona and legislative efficacy   10.3.2   Ideatum and imperantum: the binding quality of law   10.3.3   The problem of revolutions   10.3.4   Performatory imperatives and rights   10.3.5   The value of Olivecrona's analysis   10.4   Alf Ross and the judicial function   10.4.1 Validity and the chess analogy   10.4.2   Norms of conduct and of competence   10.4.3   Validity and the official viewpoint 10.4.4   Ross in the Scandinavian realist context   10.5   The message of Scandinavian realism   10.6   Further reading

11   American Realism   202

11.1   Major realist writers   11.1.1   Oliver Wendell Holmes   11.1.2   John Chipman   Gray   11.1.3   Karl Llewellyn   11.1.4   Jerome Frank 11.2   Major themes of American realism   11.2.1   Fact scepticism 11.2.2   Rule   scepticism   11.2.3   The   prediction   of   decisions 11.2.4   Judicial   reasoning   11.3   The   impact   of   realism 11.3.1   Jurimetrics   11.3.2   Judicial behaviouralism   11.4   Further reading

12   Critical Legal Studies   224

12.1   The critique of the liberal legal tradition   12.1.1   An attack on formalism   12.1.2   Critique of legal reasoning   12.1.3   Contradictions in the law   12.1.4   Deconstruction: trashing, delegitimation and dereification 12.1.5   The constitutive theory of law   12.2   A specific example of the critical approach   12.2.1   The critical approach to contract   12.3   Critical legal studies and feminist legal theory   12.4   The role of Roberto Unger 12.4.1   Contextuality   12.4.2   Empowered democracy   12.5   Further reading

13   Postmodern Legal Theory   250

13.1   A Critique of the Enlightenment   13.2   Lyotard and Foucault 13.3   Identity and the 'other'   13.4   Postmodernism and fundamental values   13.5   Derrida and deconstruction   13.6   Deconstruction and   justice   13.7   Deconstruction   and   the   liberal   constitution 13.7.1   Postmodern   constitutional   theory   13.8   Reconstruction 13.9   Conclusion   13.10   Further reading

14   The Economic Analysis of Law   275

14.1   The antecedents of the economic approach   14.1.1   Realism 14.1.2   Critical legal studies   14.1.3   Utilitarianism   14.2   Different conceptions   within   the   school   14.2.1   The   Coase   theorem 14.2.2   Efficiency   and   equity   14.3   Posner's   economic   analysis

14.3.1   The economic approach and legislation   14.3.2 The economic approach and the common law   14.3.3   Contract law   14.3.4   Criminal law   14.4   Wealth as a value   14.5   An assessment of the Chicago school 14.6   Further reading

15   Justice Theory   297

15.1   Perspectives upon justice theory   15.2   John Rawls and a liberal distributive theory of justice   15.2.1   The original actors and the veil of ignorance   15.2.2   Distribution and the thin theory of good   15.2.3   The principles of justice   15.2.4   Generational equity and the just savings principle   15.2.5   Application of the principles of justice   15.3   Robert Nozick and just entitlements   15.3.1   The idea of the minimal State 15.3.2 Minimalism, tax and the free market   15.3.3   The concept of just entitlements   15.4   Justice, individuals and society   15.5   Further reading

16   The Concept of Injustice   312

16.1   Law in the Third Reich   16.2   Post-1945 judicial consideration of Nazi law   16.3   Concepts of injustice in the post-war cases   16.4   Justice and injustice: the link   16.5   Further reading

Index   325

Introduction

The study of jurisprudence gives an opportunity to stand back a little from the detail of law in order to consider the nature, quality and functions of law. The nature of this enterprise and its value as an aspect of legal studies are outlined more fully in chapter 1. It will also rapidly become apparent that some different, or perhaps differently applied, techniques are required in studying jurisprudence than might be the case in other subject areas. These, again, are tackled in chapter 1. There is no reason why any of this should be thought 'difficult', on the contrary, jurisprudence affords a range of stimulating insights into what law and the legal enterprise are about.

It would be absurd to claim that without jurisprudence one cannot 'understand' law, but it may readily be claimed that a much fuller appreciation of law is conferred through the study of the underlying issues which inform the operation of law. This, in essence, is what jurisprudence is about.

This is intended to be a user-friendly book which provides a guide to the content, implications and problems of the major theories. The presentation is not simplified nor is it made needlessly obscure. Jurisprudence underlies much of legal activity; the authors hope that its study may not only be useful and informative, but also enjoyable.

H. McCoubrey
University of Hull
and
N. D. White
University of Nottingham

CHAPTER ONE

What is Jurisprudence?

The subject matter of jurisprudence, whether the discipline be classified as an art or a science, is the nature of law and its working. Within this broad classification there is some room for debate upon emphases and foci of interest, but to seek to confine the subject within too narrow a remit arguably subverts its central significance as a medium in which the nature and characteristics of 'legal' phenomena may be investigated. Jurisprudence offers a variety of perspectives upon law and to gain fully from the richness of the material offered it is important not to allow its nature to become obscured by limitations set by particular emphases which may well be important but which very rarely have the claims to exclusivity which are sometimes asserted on their behalf. The mid-19th century analytical positivist John Austin sought to define 'the province of jurisprudence' in the following terms:

> The matter of jurisprudence is positive law: law simply and strictly so called: or law set by political superiors to political inferiors. (J. Austin, *The Province of Jurisprudence Determined*, 1832 (London, Weidenfeld & Nicolson, 1955), p. 9.)

This seems at first sight a simple and effective statement of the parameters of legal study; it is, however, misleading when taken outside its original context. The same may be said, if anything to a yet greater extent, of the statement of the founder of American realist theory, Oliver Wendell Holmes, that:

> The prophecies of what the courts will do in fact, and nothing more pretentious, are what I mean by the law. (O. W. Holmes, 'The Path of Law' (1897) 10 Harv L Rev 457 at p. 461.)

This too has a 'common sense' simplicity which concords to a fair extent with the experience of legal practice. Not all, or even most, professional practice is directly concerned with litigation, but in advising a client upon, e.g., the drafting of a will, the ultimate viewpoint is whether the will, if challenged, can survive judicial scrutiny and effectuate the testator's stated intentions. There is nothing wrong with such essentially practitioner-oriented models of jurisprudence in themselves. Law is indeed a practical discipline, the focus of which is upon the pragmatic regulation of a variety of basic aspects of life in human society, and it follows that professional legal discourse is fundamentally concerned with the identification and application of legal rules and principles. It does not, however, follow that these are the only questions which can or should be asked about law. Indeed it may be thought essential that lawyers and others, but most especially, perhaps, those engaged in formal legal study, should take time to consider what law is, what are its purposes, what its limitations might be and what are the essential parameters of its application. Jurisprudence is ultimately a 'portmanteau' term which embraces the spectrum of these various questions and the responses which have been made to them. All of them have interest and importance in their proper context; none of them, it may be suggested, actually offers an exclusive and comprehensive 'truth' about the nature of law.

1.1   THE VARIETY OF JURISPRUDENTIAL ISSUES

It might be hoped that the simple statement that jurisprudence involves consideration of what the legal enterprise is about would not be controversial. It would, however, be an illusion to imagine that there is a simple answer to the question 'What is law?' or even to the question 'What is law about?' There are a great many questions which may be asked about law and its working and it should occasion no surprise that these questions, being different, invite different answers. Nor, as it is sometimes asserted, should it be thought that the difference between the various questions posed and the responses rendered implies that one response must be 'right' and the others in some sense 'wrong'.

It is more helpful to think of jurisprudence as a kind of jigsaw puzzle in which each piece fits with the others to produce a whole picture. The picture in this case would ultimately be a complete model of law. It may be doubted whether any such ideal solution to the questions of jurisprudence is practically attainable, but progress towards it necessarily involves the assimilation of many different theoretical insights which are not necessarily in conflict but which each make a contribution to the whole. In thus assembling a 'picture' of law each insight of theory must self-evidently be evaluated in its proper context if distortion is to be avoided. This sadly has not always been accepted in jurisprudential debate and some of the resulting distortions of analysis have had a most unfortunate effect upon the development of the subject. It is, for example, argued in this book that the so-called naturalist/positivist debate in legal theory arises precisely from a failure to realise that the two schools of thought are addressing quite distinct issues, both of which contribute to understanding of law but not in the same way or context. This is not, of course, to say that there are no genuine disagreements in jurisprudential scholarship. There are indeed occasions when different answers are given not to different questions but to the same one and then genuine debates and controversy will ensue. It can be suggested that a central task of jurisprudential study is to determine how the various insights of theory relate one to another and where the genuine incompatibilities lie and require to be resolved. It is only thus that the jurisprudential 'jigsaw' may be assembled into a satisfactory picture of law.

1.2 SOME BASIC QUESTIONS

This book takes a broad view of the remit of jurisprudential study, but the central question underpinning most of what follows is that of the very nature of law itself. Is law purely a formal concept, so that rules and principles created in a country through whatever constitutional mechanisms operate there are to be considered 'law' without qualification? This can, a little unfairly, be said to be the basic positivist position in which evaluations of the moral, ethical or even practical quality of rules or principles, according to some external criteria of reference, have no bearing upon their status as 'law'. Alternatively, is law a moral phenomenon, so that a law which is to a greater or lesser extent iniquitous may lose its 'law' quality in whole or part as a result? The difference between these propositions, thus crudely stated, has become the basis of an important 'debate' between positivist and naturalist legal theorists who have in many cases supposed that one of these approaches must necessarily exclude the other. In the light of what has been said above, however, it may be noticed that the basic positivist and naturalist propositions thus set out are framed in significantly different contexts. The key question is that of an obligation to obey law. Law is unequivocally normative, which is to say that it is founded upon 'ought' propositions which expect, indeed demand, compliance. English statutes do not request, they 'command', judges giving judgment never 'suggest' an answer or conclusion, they impose it, backed by all the power of the State. It is easy to assume that this evident normativity in law, summed up briefly by the statement of the late H. L. A. Hart that, '[Law's] existence means that certain kinds of human conduct are no longer optional, but in *some* sense obligatory' (H. L. A. Hart, *The Concept of Law*, 2nd ed., with postscript by P. A. Bulloch and J. Raz (Oxford, Clarendon Press, 1997), p. 6.), means that laws either satisfy set criteria of identification and are binding, or do not. In short, it may be, and commonly is, assumed that the normativity of law, its 'binding' quality, is a single unified quality which a given proposition either absolutely has or absolutely lacks. This is in fact clearly not the case. The existence and quality of an 'obligation' to obey law are products of a complex interaction of factors about which many different questions may be asked depending upon the context. It would plainly be pointless to argue before a court that a law which the court proposed to apply was invalidated because it or its consequences were morally repugnant. Courts, entirely properly, base themselves upon formal criteria of identification in determining what is the law. This is so even in countries in which the courts have a constitutional power to review legislation. The United States Supreme Court has the power to strike down legislative acts and executive decisions as 'unconstitutional' and does so on the basis of a constitution which is founded upon certain express moral and political assumptions. That constitution is itself, however, a legal instrument; the US Supreme Court does not in principle strike down legislation or decisions simply because it finds them morally objectionable quite apart from the constitution. If, however, a law the status of which is in the given State formally impeccable makes a demand upon a person which, according to one or another criteria of external evaluation, is clearly immoral, questions of moral obligation which may conflict with formal obligations may arise, as much for judges as for anyone else. This issue has arisen in extreme forms in 20th century totalitarian States, such as, for example, the Nazi Third Reich or Stalin's USSR. To be 'legal' in a given context is not necessarily to be 'moral' and in some situations may be so definitively not the case that claims to obedience may be overridden in any other than the most narrowly legalistic of senses.

One may also ask to what extent law is associated with force, especially the actual or potential deployment of coercive force by the State. There is unquestionably an important coercive element in the operation of law seen most clearly, but not only, in the functioning of criminal law. A number of legal theories, of very different types, have emphasised this aspect of law in their analyses. Classical positivism, Marxism and Kelsenian pure theory all do so to some extent. A law which cannot be enforced or which in practice is not enforced against those who wilfully choose to ignore or defy its requirements will ultimately, in practice if not in theory, lapse into redundancy and desuetude. The classical positivist theorists Jeremy Bentham and John Austin indeed argued that this coercive element, along with that of political 'sovereign' command, is ultimately the definitive characteristic of 'law' in distinction from the whole range of other influences upon human social conduct. Their view, which did not claim that law has no other important characteristics but merely that these are uniquely associated with it, has perhaps more in its favour than is sometimes admitted. Marxism, in contrast, sees force as part of the essence of law used as a blunt instrument for the maintenance of economic class domination. As a Christian-Aristotelian St Augustine also emphasised the coercive dimension of law, seeing it as an instrument for the suppression of vice and with little or no valid role beyond that. Again coercion may be seen as an important . aspect of the operation of law but to suggest that it transcends all other elements in significance is, at best, a distortion of reality.

Such questions do not constitute the totality of legal theory and jurisprudence, others of equal importance demand consideration. Some theorists are entirely sceptical about the substance and discourse of the variety of 'conventional' legal theories. The American realists, taking their inspiration from Oliver Wendell Holmes to whom reference was made above, emphasise a view, or rather some views, of law as essentially concerned with and defined by the working of courts. The Scandinavian realists, in contrast, treat law as essentially a psychological phenomenon. This school, having its origin in the work of Axel Hagerstrom at the beginning of the 20th century, argues broadly that the 'binding' effect of law results simply from the fact that people feel in some sense 'bound' by it, the interesting question being then how they are brought to do so. The modern critical legal studies movement which has to some extent intellectual roots in American realism, although it is quite distinct from it, suggests that the formal discourse and structures of law serve largely to conceal its real functioning and agenda. Critical legal scholars therefore adopt a variety of deconstructive strategies which are designed to undermine the conventional perception of law and to expose its 'real' operation. In this way and for this reason critical legal perceptions and methodologies have, for example, played an important part in the development of modern feminist legal theories in which the implicit and often unrealised 'male' orientation of much legal provision is highlighted in the context of failures to address women's concerns and requirements.

At a level of greater formalism the science or art of jurisprudence also needs to consider what might be termed the 'building blocks' of positive law. Does law consist simply of rules, whether legislative or judicial in origin, or are there broader structures within which 'rules' in a strict sense operate and are conditioned? Granted, in any event, the importance of courts in the legal system, how do they operate in applying and/or generating law? Law has indeed traditionally been seen as a body of rules of more or less fixed meaning and yet a simple observation of the working of English, or in fact United Kingdom, statutory interpretation indicates that, at a minimum, the linguistic certainty that so simple a view supposes is quite unreal. In an influential modern legal theory R. M. Dworkin addresses the problem of what happens when the rules run out. What, that is to say, happens where the legal rules do not actually supply a clear or even any answer in a given situation or case? Many theorists have pondered this and many, such as Bentham, have concluded that in such an event judges in effect invent answers in a process that comes close to unadmitted judicial 'legislation'. Bentham in particular denounced any such process as highly undesirable even if, in a given system, it was perhaps inevitable. Dworkin in his analysis of adjudication in 'hard cases' – those in which the rules do not give a ready answer – suggests that judges do not engage in disguised 'legislative' action but can find a 'right' answer to such cases through the application of 'principles' and 'policies' which co-exist with, but are different from, rules as such. The issue is one of considerable practical importance in assessing the actual operation of judicial decision-making in a context in which rules, however drafted, cannot in fact anticipate all the circumstances in which questions of application may arise.

Jurisprudence also develops concerns which properly reflect the social and political concerns of given times. Modern economic theories have had a significant impact upon a number of areas of legal theoretical concern. This is so in the context, e.g., of justice theory in which two of the most important modern theories, those of John Rawls and Robert Nozick, reflect quite different economic models of society and the role of the State. The Rawlsian model is a liberal distributive theory whereas that of Nozick is founded upon a model of broadly unconstrained acquisition and entitlements informed by advocacy of a minimalist role for the State. Modern economic thought has also generated distinct strands of jurisprudential enquiry in their own right, with especial emphasis in the period of the 1980s and 1990s.

1.3   SOME POINTS OF METHOD

Law students sometimes encounter a problem of method in jurisprudence which relates in part to the seemingly different structure and expectations of this subject in comparison with other areas of legal study. Most legal study involves in one way or another analysis of authorities – statutes, case decisions, statutory instruments, treaties and so on. One may be called upon to debate the meaning, application or practical consequences of, e.g., a statutory provision but in terms of formal legal analysis there can generally be no doubt about the authority of the statute as such. It often seems that there are no such secure mooring points in jurisprudence but merely a range of opinions, some of which appear to be mutually incompatible, and this can appear both troubling and frustrating from the viewpoint of conventional legal methods of study. Such an impression is, however, misleading. There are in fact authorities in jurisprudence, as indeed there are in almost any subject, but the nature of their authority differs from those which underpin substantive law. The writings of theorists present concepts and analyses of the various issues and questions within the wide remit of jurisprudential enquiry which are worthy of respectful consideration but which do not and cannot have any 'binding' quality upon those to whom they are addressed. It is possible to contend that a theorist is 'wrong' in a way that cannot be claimed of a statute in its own formal context, even if it may be argued from a policy viewpoint that it should be repealed or radically amended. Naturally in reaching conclusions either for or against a particular theoretical position some substantial and sustainable reason for the opinion advanced is necessary. Merely 'liking' or 'not liking' a given theory or argument cannot in itself be a foundation for analysis of its adequacy or lack thereof without support from supportable argument upon its substance.

A further, and often sadly neglected, point of jurisprudential methodology is the importance of context in developing an analysis of any given theory. The question of context may arise in at least two general forms. There must always be considered the question of the historical and cultural context in which a theory was originally advanced. The fact that a theory might have been advanced in a historically remote or very different social or political context from that which now exists by no means necessarily deprives the theory of modern relevance. It may, however, have a major impact upon its application and significance in the context of modern societies. Ancient writers such as Aristotle, or even writers of the 18th and 19th centuries, did not live in a world which operated according to the same assumptions and concerns as those which inform the modern world. It certainly does not follow that their work has therefore in some sense become redundant or irrelevant. It is however important to realise that in considering the detailed arguments and, even more so, the illustrative examples which may be given in the theories of earlier ages, some degree of cultural adjustment may be necessary in order to elucidate the implications of the argument for the present time. Where this is important in any of the following chapters of this book it is pointed out, but two instances of the problem to be addressed may be of value here. Both Plato and Aristotle have much to say of very great value in relation to the functions of law and the degree of 'obligation' which it is capable of imposing upon those to whom it is addressed. It is necessary, however, to remember that the ancient Greek city-states in the context of which they were writing were minute political units by modern standards, smaller in extent and population than many counties in the United Kingdom and vastly smaller than any US state. This has obvious significance for a modern view of, e.g., Plato's argument upon proper response to unjust demands made by the laws of a State, which essentially advances three options of obedience, argument to persuade the State to change its law, or removal to another more congenial State (see chapter 4). Adjustment of context is necessary before relating this argument to, e.g., the Third Reich. In his *Summa Theologica*, written in the 13th century, St Thomas Aquinas also addressed the question of the nature and extent of the obligation to obey law (see chapter 4). As part of this analysis Aquinas gives an example of a walled city under siege in which the authorities have, not surprisingly, ordered that the city gates be kept shut against the enemy. What, he asks, is to be done if a group of citizens fleeing from the enemy seek admittance to safe refuge in the city? (St Thomas Aquinas, *Summa Theologica* 1a2ae, 96, 6.) This example is remote even from modern military experience, and more so from that of most lawyers, but as an example of the potential for 'necessary' variation of the application of law in new and unanticipated circumstances it is clearly capable of translation into more familiar modern contexts. At the other end of the historical spectrum it is equally important to remember that modern theories are necessarily advanced, or certainly phrased, in the context of contemporary concerns and this fact needs to be taken into account in any assessment of their likely long-term impact. Thus, the concerns of modern economic theory clearly and properly relate to present and recent socio-economic experience. That experience is in itself not universal nor is it necessarily, or even probably, permanent, which is not to deny the import-ance of the theoretical insights but to counsel sensitivity in the assessment of their probable development and application.

The second methodological issue is of even greater importance and relates back to the fundamental issue of questions and answers raised above. In considering the work of any theorist or school of theorists it is essential always to start by enquiring, 'What question(s) is this theorist asking and for what purpose?' If this simple rule is followed much confusion may be avoided and, sadly, the consequences of its not being followed are all too evident in certain areas of jurisprudential debate. To state what should be, but is not always, obvious, different questions invite different answers and sometimes the same question may invite different answers in different contexts. To take a physical analogy, very different criteria will be applied in answering the question 'Is this a high temperature?' in relation, respectively, to a seaside holiday, a blast furnace or the interior of a distant star, the point being here that temperature in these sorts of contexts is essentially a relative term and everything will therefore depend upon the context of the particular usage. This relates directly to important strands of modern linguistic philosophy which tend to emphasise usage rather than 'absolute' meanings, as, for example, in the later work of Ludwig Wittgenstein. Similar points may be made about much jurisprudential debate. To refer back to issues raised above, a question such as 'Is there an obligation to obey law?' might seem to be a straightforward question inviting a simple answer. In fact it may be suggested that there is no singular 'obligation to obey' but rather a combination of factors which strengthen or weaken the 'normative' (i.e. the 'ought') quality of laws and which operate in somewhat different contexts. One must therefore ask in what context a theorist was or is asking the question in order both to assess the value of the answer and its relation to other 'answers' which may have been rendered. In this way the genuine debates in jurisprudence, meaning those arising from disagreement over the answer best given to the same or similar questions, can usefully be distinguished from those arising from the false assumption that the same question has necessarily been asked. In case this may seem to betoken an alarming degree of uncertainty and confusion, it may be pointed out that it is a prerequisite for useful discussion in any discipline that the participants should be in agreement as to the topic of the discussion, even if not necessarily upon the view they take of it.

Beyond the question of identification of issues and foci of concern there is also, of course, that of the inherent value or significance of particular questions and approaches. Just as different people may find some aspects of substantive law more engaging or interesting than others, this being indeed the bedrock of professional and academic specialism, so too they may find some aspects of jurisprudence far more rewarding than others. This in itself is hardly problematic, it is in fact inevitable. The matter becomes potentially problematic only when differentiation of emphasis or interest develops into a denial of the relevance or 'validity' of the issues which are not pursued or found interesting by a given person. It cannot be over-emphasised that the ultimate endeavour of the discipline of jurisprudence is to develop as full a picture as possible of the nature of law and its operations. In so doing there is much room for debate upon relative emphases and the proper placement of given questions and responses, but one should be cautious indeed in suggesting that a given question about law has actually no legitimate place in 'jurisprudence'. The distorting effects of such an approach can be seen in a number of instances, including the attempts of the late-18th and early-19th century positivists to define a severely circumscribed 'province of jurisprudence', to take John Austin's formulation. This led to an attempt to relegate a number of very important issues to some extra-jurisprudential dimension. It also involved an endeavour to elevate a particular form of analysis to a comprehensiveness inherently beyond it and in so doing distorted the presentation of the very important insights which that analysis could and does contribute.

1.4 JURISPRUDENCE AND ITS SUBSTANTIVE CONTEXT

Jurisprudence is by its nature a trans-national subject, its concerns relate in various ways to most if not all legal systems. All States have systems of law and, despite the variety of forms, the problems and questions arising tend to be very similar in their general nature. Books on jurisprudence are, however, naturally written in particular countries, in this case in the United Kingdom and specifically in England. As a result, the cases and legal provisions taken as examples at various points of the analysis tend commonly to be drawn from that jurisdiction. It would, however, be quite extraordinary to imagine that the debates and questions under consideration are themselves specific to any given system of law or to any particular jurisdiction. The theorists who are considered in this book come from a wide variety of nations, cultures and times and, by the very nature of that spectrum, the range of their argument and opinion cannot properly be confined to any one jurisdiction or tradition. Indeed a tradition of comparative study as between jurisdictions and traditions is one of the strengths of jurisprudential analysis which affords valuable insights into the implications and application of theoretical perceptions which might be obscured in a narrower focus of study.

1.5 WHAT IS THE VALUE OF JURISPRUDENCE?

Practising and practical lawyers — the two may be hoped to be found in combination but these are not simply synonymous categories — sometimes ask this question and it is one which does require address. It is of course true that no client is going to ask a legal practitioner whether a law is 'just' or what is the quality of the 'obligation' attaching to it, although the formal identification of applicable laws may be a question even if not phrased in quite that way. In the same way a patient seeking advice from a medical practitioner will want to know what is causing pain or other difficulties rather than seeking an exposition of medical ethics. The patient, and the lawyers' client, will, however, assume a background of professional ethics and a knowledge of the theoretical underpinning of the professional expertise which is being claimed.

The study of jurisprudence affords an opportunity to stand back a little from the detail of substantive law and to consider the purpose and operation of law as a whole, including fundamental questions relating what law is supposed to do and what it actually does in practice. Consideration of such issues is an important part of the study of law whether or not the person undertaking the study intends ultimately to engage in professional legal practice as such. Law is a practical discipline and its very practicality is based upon the adequacy of the theory upon which it rests, just as an aeroplane is a practical machine which works only if its design is based upon sound aerodynamic theory. The purchaser or user of a plane may not have much interest in aerodynamic theory but will be most displeased if the machine cannot in practice fly. The analogy with the role of jurisprudence in law is direct and those who ask 'What use is jurisprudence?' might more usefully ask 'What will happen to law without jurisprudence?'

CHAPTER TWO

Classical Positivism: Bentham and Austin

Positivist theories of law may briefly be described as those which concentrate upon a description of law as it is in a given time and place, by reference to formal, rather than to moral or ethical, criteria of identification. Such theories do not necessarily deny the possibility or relevance of moral analyses; they do, however, deny that criteria deriving therefrom can have any part in the identification of 'law' as such. These theories are commonly, if rather misleadingly, contrasted with the classical naturalist theories considered in chapter 4 which treat law as a prescription deriving its ultimate authority from a purposive morality, by reference to which its 'law' quality may be judged. This seeming conflict may to a considerable extent be resolved through the consideration that positivists and naturalists may not be asking the same questions about law, in which case the differences between their answers are hardly surprising. Be that as it may, the anti-naturalist origin of classical positivist thought has left a significant imprint upon the form and, to some extent, the substance of this school of theory.

Positivism has for much of the past one and a half centuries been the dominant school of jurisprudence from an Anglo-American viewpoint, and, indeed, the broad concerns and assumptions of positivism render it attractive as a 'practitioner jurisprudence'. Positivism is, however, like most schools of jurisprudence, subject to limitations which must be borne in mind when considering the application of the ideas being expressed. Some difficulties arise from the substantive arguments advanced but, it may be contended, the most serious arise from the very broad claims made for this school of theory by some of its proponents. These should not, however, be permitted to obscure the very real and valuable contribution which the positivist insight makes to the understanding of the phenomenon of law.

Analytical positivism has developed over time and taken forms quite distinct from its original base. The most important modern developments of this type are considered in the next chapter. In its classical, late 18th and 19th century, forms, positivist legal theory was developed through the work of Jeremy Bentham and John Austin, from whose concerns it took, for better or worse, a very particular coloration.

2.1   BENTHAM'S CONCEPT OF JURISPRUDENCE

The founder of classical positivist legal theory was Jeremy Bentham (1748–1832) whose ideas were later developed, some would say not entirely fortunately, by his disciple John Austin (1790–1859). Bentham set out to counter what he considered to be the errors of the conventional jurisprudence of his time, which was quasi-naturalist in type. In part he objected to a debased conventional naturalism, which actually bore little resemblance to classical naturalist legal theories. He took particular exception to Sir William Blackstone's uncritical account of the English constitution, making unsubstantiated appeals to natural rights in support of given practices, in the Introduction to his *Commentaries on the Laws of England*. Bentham also had a strong political objection to naturalist doctrine which was later confirmed by the events of the French Revolution. Bentham summed up this concern in the complaint that:

> the natural tendency of such [naturalist] doctrine is to impel a [person] . . ., by the force of conscience, to rise up in arms against any law whatever that he happens not to like. What sort of government it is that can consist with such a disposition, I must leave our Author [i.e., Blackstone] to inform us. (J. Bentham, *A Fragment on Government* (Oxford: Basil Blackwell, 1967), ch. 4, para. 19.)

This was to a considerable extent a misapprehension of the claims of naturalist theories, but a genuine difficulty in the conventional jurisprudence which Bentham attacked.

Beyond this Bentham attacked naturalism upon philosophical grounds. In some ways Bentham stood in a tradition of increasing 'secularisation' in legal theory which can be traced at least to the 17th century, for example, in the work of Thomas Hobbes (1588–1679) which is considered in chapter 4. Bentham's immediate philosophical inspiration, however, lay in the distinction between 'is' and 'ought', descriptive and normative, as exposed by David Hume. Hume wrote that:

> In every system of morality . . . I am surpriz'd to find, that instead of the usual [association] . . . of propositions, is, and is not, I meet with no

proposition that is not connected with an ought, or an ought not. . . . as this . . . expresses some new relation or affirmation, 'tis necessary that it shou'd be observ'd and explain'd; . . . for what seems altogether inconceivable [is], how this new relation can be a deduction from others, which are entirely different from it. (D. Hume, *A Treatise of Human Nature*, ed. L. A. Selby-Bigge and P. H. Nidditch (Oxford: Oxford University Press, 1978), 3.1.1.)

In other words it does not follow from the fact that a thing or condition 'is' that it 'ought' so to be. In fact it can be strongly argued that the classical naturalist arguments considered in chapter 4 do not fall foul of this criticism but the conventional quasi-naturalist jurisprudence attacked by Bentham was much more open to it.

In any event Bentham's broad aim was to establish a scientific jurisprudence which would clearly distinguish between the descriptive and the normative and deal with each upon its own appropriate level without confusion. To this end he made a division between 'expositorial' and 'censorial' branches of jurisprudence. Of these Bentham stated succinctly that:

To the province of the Expositor it belongs to explain to us what . . . the law is: to that of the Censor, to observe what he thinks it ought to be. (*A Fragment on Government*, Preface, para. 13.)

In short the existing state of the law should be considered without reference to intrusive moral or ethical criteria of identification, though thereafter, but only thereafter, its quality and any necessary improvements may be considered as a separate issue. Bentham had in fact a broad interest in law reform and made numerous suggestions for changes in legal substance and application both in England and abroad. His best-known scheme for an 'ideal' prison – the Panopticon – was ultimately rejected in the United Kingdom but was followed to a small extent in the United States. On the level of theory, Bentham's censorial jurisprudence is by no means without interest, but it is the expositorial jurisprudence which Bentham and Austin developed in their command theory of law which has left the greatest mark on Anglo-American legal theory.

2.2 THE COMMAND THEORY OF LAW

Bentham's definition of law is commonly summarised as 'the command of a sovereign backed by a sanction', although this is in fact an unduly simplified expression of his model. Bentham himself defined 'a law', and the singularity is important, as:

an assemblage of signs declarative of a volition conceived or adopted by the *sovereign* in a state, concerning the conduct to be observed . . . by . . . persons, who . . . are or are supposed to be subject to his power: such volition trusting for its accomplishment to the expectation of certain events . . . the prospect of which it is intended should act as a motive upon those whose conduct is in question. (J. Bentham, *Of Laws in General*, ed. H. L. A. Hart (London: Athlone Press, 1970), ch. 1, para. 1.)

We see here the elements of:

(a) 'command' – the will conceived by the sovereign is manifestly imperative,

(b) 'sovereignty' and,

(c) 'sanction', in the attachment of motivations to compliance in the form of anticipated consequences.

The relationships and the detail of these elements are manifestly more complex than the bald summary would seem to suggest. On first sight this definition is obvious. Law, whether statute or case, is never suggestive but always imperative in its expression. It is also clearly made either by government or by institutions acting under the authority of government. Compliance and failure of compliance are clearly attended by consequences which urge compliance. Consider the form of any English Act of Parliament, 'Be it enacted by the Queen's most Excellent Majesty . . .'. This is classically the language of sovereign imperation and is well known as such to any legal practitioner. However, this apparently simple model of law conceals major difficulties beneath its surface. In large measure these derive precisely from the simplicity of the model insofar as law is not a simple phenomenon readily capable of such containment. In order to understand properly the nature of the command model of law set up by Bentham and Austin, and the difficulties which were built into it, it is necessary to examine each of the elements separately before analysing its strengths and weaknesses as a description of a law.

2.2.1 The command

For Bentham, a command of the sovereign might be found in any declarative sign. He gave as an example a sovereign striking off the heads of the tallest poppies in a garden as a direction to execute popular leaders. There are a number of ancient references to actions of this kind, including the last ancient King of Rome (before the Republic and the Empire), Tarquinius Superbus, replying to his son Sextus by just this means (J. Bentham, *Of Laws in General*, ed. H. L. A. Hart (London: Athlone Press, 1970), ch. 13). Bentham admits, however, in the same passage that more conventional and readily recognisable forms of communication are desirable. Austin, as ever slightly more concrete, defines a 'command' as comprising:

> 1. A wish . . . by a rational being, that another . . . shall do or forbear. 2. An evil to proceed from the former, and be incurred by the latter, in case [of disobedience]. . . . 3. An expression or intimation of the wish by words or other signs. (J. Austin, *The Province of Jurisprudence Determined* (London: Weidenfeld & Nicolson, 1955), p. 17.)

The insistence upon the element of coercion is significant and may certainly be typical of commands, not least in a 'legal' context, but it may be questioned whether this is absolutely necessary. Whether or not implicit coercion may generally be an aspect of 'command' it is certainly not enough. It may be argued that the prerequisite is rather one of 'authority' which brings in much broader elements which have been differently addressed by other theorists, not least by modern positivists such as H.L.A. Hart, whose work is considered in chapter 3.

The principal difficulty of the Benthamite, and Austinian, concept of 'command' lies in the literality with which the concept is taken. Despite their acknowledgement that a 'sovereign' may be a body of persons rather than a single autocrat, indeed the 19th century English legal sovereign was clearly a collective body, Bentham and Austin seem to have become entrapped in a discourse of personal imperation. In part this followed from the expository nature of their jurisprudential enterprise in that a description of fact is not necessarily a very adequate vehicle for the analysis of a process. In the context of English law, and up to a point other common law systems, with equivalents in other legal systems, two particular problems arise in the interpretation of 'command' in the personalised form advanced in classical positivism. Laws commanded by long-dead members of the sovereign Crown in Parliament continue to be law although apparently not commanded by the current sovereign. Further, some species of laws may be made upon a delegated basis by subsidiary bodies, such as local authorities, acting within their appointed competences (i.e., *intra vires*) and, through the system of binding precedent (*stare decisis*) by judges. The former situation is conventionally explained by the idea of sovereign continuity (The King is dead, long live the King!) which is to say that although the personnel of the Crown in Parliament changes the institution is in continuous existence. Bentham disliked this type of idea as tending towards obfuscatory fiction. Lawmaking by judges, in particular, he considered a usurpation of the sovereign function, especially where precedent enshrines a restrictive interpretation of statutes. He wrote that:

> Applied in practice then, the effect of this language is, by an appeal made to the Judges, to confer on [them] . . . a controlling power over the acts of

the legislature. . . . Give to the Judges a power of annulling [legislative] . . . acts; and you a portion of the supreme power from an [elected] assembly . . ., to a set of men in the choice of whom [the people] . . . have not had the least imaginable share. (*A Fragment on Government*, ch. 2, paras 31 and 32.)

In the next paragraph, however, Bentham goes on to admit that 'repealing' or limiting a law is a much lesser power than that of making one even if one 'too great indeed for Judges'. Austin disagreed with Bentham upon this matter. Indeed he supported the opinion that judges properly exercise a 'legislative' function in filling in the gaps in prescription left by the legislature. Austin went so far as to claim that:

That part of the law of every country which was made by judges has been far better made than that part which consists of statutes enacted by the legislative. (*The Province of Jurisprudence Determined*, p. 191.)

This value judgment seems a little curious in its context and invites a wide ranging debate, but it is, uncharacteristically, a broadening of opinion in comparison with that held by Bentham.

Even so, an expositorial analysis of law cannot ignore the fact that laws made by past sovereigns continue in effect and that legal rules are made and established by subordinate authorities. Bentham explained these phenomena as acts of 'adoption' and tacit command. Such adoption was argued to take either of two forms: 'susception', when the mandate in question has already been issued, and 'pre-adoption', when it has not already been issued. Susception thus applies to the laws of former sovereigns and consists essentially of not repealing them and may, on the same basis, apply to prior acts of subsidiary bodies. Pre-adoption can only apply to the future acts of subsidiary bodies, consisting essentially of authorisation, since pre-adoption of the acts of a future sovereign would, on any analysis, be nugatory. At the extreme Bentham went much further in arguing that any transaction or claim to authority enforceable at law was a command of the sovereign by adoption. In a famous passage he remarked that:

Not a cook is bid to dress a dinner, a nurse to feed a child, . . . an officer to drive the enemy from a post, but it is by [the sovereign's] orders. (*Of Laws in General*, ch. 2, para. 6.)

The diversity of these examples, and others omitted, demonstrates the peculiarity of the proposition. The officer's orders rely upon a structure of superior authority and military law which ultimately derive from sovereign authorisation and, as Bentham interpreted the situation, the sovereign 'adopts' each successive level of 'command' by not countermanding it. Military orders, perhaps, fit reasonably well with a 'command' theory but the cook and the nurse, in more modern language we should perhaps refer more generally to 'employees', fit much more oddly into this scheme. It is true that a contract of employment may ultimately be enforced through legal proceedings, but to ascribe the arrangement itself upon this basis to sovereign command seems a contorted and needless nicety of interpretation. This is a point that emerges more clearly perhaps in the context of the application of 'sanctions' to facilitative laws such as provision for contract.

The idea of tacit, or adoptive, command has been much attacked, not least within the positivist tradition. H. L. A. Hart remarks that:

> The incoherence of the theory . . . may be seen most clearly in its incapacity to explain why the courts of the present day should distinguish between a Victorian statute which has not been repealed as still law, and one which was repealed under Edward VII as no longer law. Plainly . . . the courts . . . use . . . a criterion [of legal identification] . . . which embraces past as well as present legislative operations. (H. L. A. Hart, *The Concept of Law* (Oxford: Clarendon Press, 1961), p. 63.)

In short, legislation is a process the products of which are identified according to criteria of recognition without need for 'adoption' by the personnel of a given time. These criteria include, of course, due authority but this is not quite the same thing as a requirement for command by a presently extant individual or body. The idea of adoption of contracts and other similar arrangements, founded upon the notion that to permit is to command, seems to involve even more clearly a distortion of language. In general a permission is not a command: 'You may' is not synonymous with 'You must'.

It would seem to be that in avoiding one set of fictions Bentham fell into another. The discourse of imperation becomes distorting when it is followed too literally and too simple a model is imposed upon actually rather complex processes of authorisation. It is undeniable that laws are imperatively expressed and are in their effects both prescriptive and normative, but it does not follow from this that all laws are simply orders. Many laws are facilitative; for example, a contract or a will may only be made by following the instructions set out by law, but it hardly follows that one performing a contract or making a will does so at the *command* of the sovereign, even if the instrument does eventually fall to be interpreted by a court.

2.2.2 The sovereign

In view of his philosophical starting-point it is not surprising that Bentham was anxious in his definition of 'sovereignty' to avoid any suggestion of a right

to rule. True to his expository intention he was concerned simply to describe
the fact of rulership. Thus he defined a 'sovereign' as:

> any person or assemblage of persons to whose will a whole political
> community are (no matter on what account) supposed to be in a disposi-
> tion to pay obedience: and that in preference to the will of any other
> person. (*Of Laws in General*, ch. 2, para. 1.)

Several things are noteworthy about this definition. Its basis is a factual, or
supposed, habit of obedience on the part of those subject to the sovereign and
it is the fact rather than the cause which is important. The quality of the
sovereignty is unimportant and the habit of obedience might arise from any
cause from coercively induced fear through to moral admiration; most likely
it will combine a wide range of elements in varying degrees. The final clause,
the preferential habit of obedience, refers obviously to the primacy of the
sovereign, as compared with any subordinate power. Austin expressed this
more strongly by insisting upon not only a positive mark of sovereignty
(obedience by others) but also a negative mark:

> That [sovereign] is *not* in a habit of obedience to a determinate human
> superior. (*The Province of Jurisprudence Determined*, p. 194.)

Austin's point is seemingly obvious in that a person or entity which is
meaningfully sovereign is surely not subject to any other sovereign. The
addition of this negative mark can, however, be argued to be unduly
restrictive in the light of the political realities even of the 19th century, and
much more so of the turn of the 20th and 21st centuries.

Neither Bentham nor any other positivist has denied that a sovereign body
might, indeed undoubtedly will, be subject to political and practical limitations in the exercise of power. The sensitive questions arise rather in relation
to the imposition of formal or legal limitations upon sovereign power. Austin
dismissed this notion outright, stating that:

> . . . it follows from . . . the nature of sovereignty and independent political
> society, that the power . . . of a sovereign . . . in its . . . sovereign capacity,
> is incapable of *legal* limitation. A . . . sovereign . . . bound by a legal duty,
> [would be] . . . subject to a higher or superior sovereign [and] . . .
> [s]upreme power limited by positive law, is a flat contradiction in terms.
> (*The Province of Jurisprudence Determined*, p. 254.)

Constitutional laws which seek to limit sovereign power are seen as mere
'guides', a form of 'positive morality' which does not fall within the category
of 'laws properly so-called' from a positivist viewpoint. On Austin's logic this

would be unavoidable, because it is clearly absurd for a body to command itself and a still greater absurdity appears when the question of the attachment of sanctions to such law is addressed. Bentham, on the other hand, took a somewhat more flexible approach. He admitted limitations upon the exercise of sovereign power through a 'transcendent' law amounting to a self-denying ordinance by the sovereign and through a limitation of the 'habit of obedience'. The first of these was termed an 'express convention' and defined as:

> . . . the case where one state, has, upon terms, submitted itself to the government of another: or where the governing bodies of a number of states agree to take directions in certain specified cases, from some body or other that is distinct from all of them. (*A Fragment on Government*, ch. 4, para. 23, n. 1.)

Upon a Benthamite analysis the instruments establishing the European Communities would thus be express conventions in this sense. Bentham's account of such express conventions suggests that he considers them an enshrinement of a limitation of the habit of obedience. H. L. A. Hart remarks that:

> . . . in his [Bentham's] view the importance of an express convention in limiting the authority of a supreme legislature was derivative from what he takes to be the fundamental fact of the subjects' limited habitual obedience. (H. L. A. Hart, *Essays on Bentham* (Oxford: Clarendon Press, 1982), p. 231.)

Such express conventions would be by their nature inter-State; for reasons set out below the term 'international' is perhaps in this context to be avoided. Bentham also admitted, however, the possibility of some limitations of sovereign power within a State. The examples he gives of such a limited obedience are somewhat curious in terms of his stated purpose and relate to religious scruples. They include the instances that:

> The Jews would have done anything else for Antiochus, but they would not eat his pork. The exiled Protestants would have done anything else for Lewis [Louis XIV], but they would not go to mass. (*Of Laws in General*, ch. 2, para. 1, n. (b).)

These do not, however, seem to be evidence of any 'formal' limitation of obedience within the State but rather instances of resistance to the State. There seems to be a confusion between forms of 'constitutional' limitation and political resistance, deriving largely from an initially oversimplified doctrine of unlimited sovereignty.

Bentham was, however, willing to admit, reluctantly and with distaste, formal and 'legal' limitations upon prima facie sovereign power, in the form of laws *in principem*, which is to say laws directed to the sovereign (by the sovereign) as compared with more normal laws *in populum* (directed to the sovereign's subjects). In a 'command theory' such laws are profoundly problematic. How can a sovereign (or any other body) meaningfully 'command' itself or, indeed, its *ex hypothesi* unlimited 'successors'? Bentham gives a complex explanation of these 'laws *in principem*' which he terms *pacta regalia*, stating that:

> When a reigning sovereign then in the tenor of his laws engages for himself and for his successors he does two distinguishable things. By an expression of will which has its own conduct for its objects, he enters himself into a covenant: by an expression of will which has the conduct of his successors for its object, he addresses to them a recommendatory mandate. (*Of Laws in General*, ch. 4, para. 16.)

Bentham was unwilling generally to admit that such *pacta regalia* would truly equate with 'laws' in the normal sense and considered that they would be maintained only by 'auxiliary sanctions' such as political or religious pressure. Where they actually are maintained by courts of law he considered that sovereignty must be held to be shared between the political leadership and the courts, which would evidently be the Benthamite analysis of the United States' constitution, a situation which, however, he felt to be highly undesirable in the light of his disapprobation of judicial incursions upon sovereign action.

The classical positivist analysis of limitations upon sovereignty, formal and otherwise, involves a number of devices which appear, and to some extent are, markedly contorted. Much of this may be argued to have been unnecessary in that the problem derives not from anything fundamental to the approach adopted but from the insistence upon a misleading personal analogy for sovereignty. Bentham and Austin were fully aware of the corporate nature of the British sovereign and yet the personal language ('he' and 'his') is both noteworthy and significant. Clearly for an individual meaningfully to command him or herself is difficult and to issue binding instructions to another individual who will occupy the same place is similarly problematic. The analogy is, however, dubious in that the sovereignty, whether individual, group, autocratic, totalitarian or democratic, is in one way or another the expression of a process which is at once the head and part of a legal order. This lack of distinction between authoritative process and pure imperation is perhaps the great lacuna in the classical positivist analysis and one which formed an important plank in the revised positivism advanced by H. L. A. Hart.

2.2.3 The attachment of sanctions

The attachment of a sanction to legal prescription as the motivation for compliance is an important aspect of the classical positivist definition of 'law'. It is the recognition of a characteristic of which H. L. A. Hart later wrote:

> The most prominent general feature of law at all times and places is that its existence means that certain kinds of human conduct are no longer optional, but in *some* sense obligatory. (H. L. A. Hart, *The Concept of Law* (Oxford: Clarendon Press 1961), p. 6.)

In short the central issue is that of the nature of the obligation to obey law. Bentham states that:

> Nature has placed mankind under the governance of two sovereign masters, *pain* and *pleasure*. (J. Bentham, *An Introduction to the Principles of Morals and Legislation*, ed. J. H. Burns and H. L. A. Hart (London: Methuen, 1982), ch. 1, para. 1.)

This is the fundamental basis of the principle of utility upon which Bentham founded his 'censorial jurisprudence' but in the context of 'sanctions' the idea is that the 'obligation' to obey law consists simply of the anticipation (primarily the fear) of consequences attached to non-compliance, or, to a lesser extent, of consequences following from compliance. The motive for obedience to law, meaning the factors upon which it relies to secure its intended effects rather than the general, and much more variously derived, 'habit of obedience' to the sovereign, thus becomes in Bentham's terms:

> . . . the expectations of so many lots of pain and pleasure, as connected in a particular manner in the way of causality with the actions with reference to which they are termed *motives*. When it is in the shape of pleasure . . . they may be termed *alluring* motives: when in the shape of pain, *coercive* [motives]. (*Of Laws in General*, ch. 11, para. 1.)

Bentham actually admitted that there may be several types of motivation for compliance with law, including 'physical', 'political', 'moral' and 'religious' sanctions, but the apparent concession to a 'naturalist' form of analysis is misleading. Neither Bentham nor Austin ever denied the existence of factors affecting law beyond their defined 'province of jurisprudence'. Within that province, however, it is clear that Bentham envisages only a political sanction, one imposed by the sovereign, as a definitive characteristic of 'law'.

There are several points to be noticed in Bentham's basic statement upon the motivation for compliance with law. The first is that this is a probabilistic concept of obligation. There can be no absolute certainty that a given sanction will be effective in a given case. The person who gets away with an illegal act has patently evaded the applicable sanction and, indeed, the obligation to obey has failed in this situation. The motivation acts through the expectation of entailed consequences rather than through the certainty of them. Secondly, the motivating consequence, the 'sanction', is connected in a particular manner by way of causality with the action, or forbearance, to which it is directed. The unpleasant, or pleasant, consequence is not the product of a random association but is itself an imposition by the sovereign. Clearly, under Bentham's basic definition it is a part of 'a law' and as such 'legal' in nature. Finally Bentham admits two forms of sanction: coercive (i.e., negative) sanctions which threaten an unpleasant consequence for disobedience and, with less emphasis, 'alluring' sanctions which promise a beneficial consequence in case of compliance. Provisions supported by an 'alluring sanction' were termed by Bentham 'praemiary laws' and were clearly considered to be the exception rather than the rule.

Austin was not prepared to make this concession and followed the logic of a discourse of 'sanctions' to its apparent ultimate conclusion. He stated that:

> It is the power and the purpose of inflicting eventual *evil*, and *not* the power and the purpose of imparting eventual *good*, which gives to the expression of a wish the name of a *command*. (*The Province of Jurisprudence Determined*, p. 17.)

In fairness to Austin it is important to consider this seemingly inflexible statement in its proper context. Although Austin here expressly disagreed with Bentham, he conceded that a promised 'reward' might well be a motive for compliance. His point was rather that if 'law' is to be categorised as 'command' then the associated sanction can only be negative in nature. In short, orders do not derive their particular quality from promises of benefit (even though these may be offered) but from, at least, an implicit threat of coercion. Within the immediate logic of a command theory this is not as negligible an argument as has sometimes been suggested, its defect lies rather in an unduly precise insistence upon that logic. Illustrative examples are not hard to find. The legal requisites for the making of a will have been set out by legislation from the Wills Act 1837 onwards and failure to satisfy these requirements may lead to the failure of the will. This, on Austin's analysis, is the negative sanction, the fear of failure, which motivates compliance on the part of a testator. Such a logic may certainly be imposed on the process but it may clearly be seen to be an imposition. The aim of the testator is to ensure the posthumous disposition of his or her property in a particular way. If the formalities are not correctly observed, who is 'punished'? Certainly not the testator, at least from any viewpoint of earthly relevance. The primary 'victims' are surely the 'innocent' beneficiaries. A more credible analysis would seem to be that the formalities of testamentation are essentially a set of 'instructions' for the attainment of a given objective, in this case the disposal of property after death in accordance with one's wishes. In a similar way the instructions accompanying self-assembly furniture are, one hopes, an accurate guide to the assembly of the piece concerned. If the person assembling, e.g., a chair does not correctly follow the instructions and, when sat upon, the chair falls apart this might be considered a 'penalty' for failing to follow the instructions. It would, however, more realistically be considered a natural, if unfortunate, consequence of incompetence and a failure to gain an anticipated 'reward'. The distortion of usage imposed by Austin's insistence upon a narrow 'command' model, ironically inspired precisely by a desire to avoid distortion of descriptive language, relates, again, back to the omission from consideration of the factor of 'authority' as a factor in lawmaking. The legal formalities of testamentation are facilitative; they enable a convenient and socially necessary process to be performed; they entail a promise that the State will, by virtue of its authority, enable the will thus expressed to be implemented. A person who fails to observe the formalities is not truly, or at all, punished but rather fails effectively to take advantage of the recognised facility offered. In this context Bentham's admission of alluring sanctions attached to praemiary laws may be contended to have allowed within the command theory a degree of flexibility which is in practice much more realistic than the seemingly stricter descriptive logic adopted by Austin.

The sanctions element of the classical command theory emphasises its basis in a 'social realist' analysis of lawmaking as a power relation, defined, if not entirely characterised, by the potential for the application of coercive force. The application of a sanction must, however, be seen in its proper context as an element of a 'complete law' (see 2.2.4) rather than as an isolated, and possibly overemphasised factor.

2.2.4 The Benthamite complete law

The elements of the command theory are brought together by Bentham in his model of a 'complete law'. It is important to realise that this is not a reference to a statute, or statutory provision, as in 'section 55 of the Town and Country Planning Act 1990' (the basic definition of 'development' requiring planning permission), but a model of all the requisites for the operation of a given legal command. It is worth reiterating that Bentham defined 'a law' as:

> . . . an assemblage of signs declarative of a volition conceived or adopted by the *sovereign* . . . concerning . . . conduct [and supported by a sanction]. (*Of Laws in General*, ch. 1, para. 1.)

This assemblage includes, obviously, not only the substantive direction for conduct in question but also a host of associated elements without which it cannot be implemented. These will include many administrative and operational factors e.g., provision for the organisation of courts and the application of sanctions, which will be focused upon the implementation of the 'command' in question but which will also apply to many other commands. Such operational factors may also, of course, be diffused amongst a wide range of particular legal provisions. The complete law is thus concerned not with legal provisions in a narrow sense but with the focus of factors by and through which a legal directive is made operative.

Bentham presented his complete law as comprising two main parts, the second of which is divided into two subparts. The divisions are:

(a)   the direction, comprising the principal law which is the sovereign's direction as to conduct which is in question; and
(b)   the prediction, which is divided into: (i) the proximate subsidiary law and (ii) the remote subsidiary law.

The proximate subsidiary law sets out the sanction attached to secure compliance with the principal direction. The remote subsidiary law then sets out all the necessary administrative machinery for implementation.

This, then, is intended as a social realist description of law in operation as a bundle of elements focused upon a direction for conduct of a particular type qualifying as 'legal'. As a model it transparently ignores numerous factors actually bearing upon the operation of law, including a diverse range of moral, ethical, political and practical questions. These are dismissed not as irrelevant in themselves but as falling beyond the proper province of expository jurisprudence.

2.3   THE VIABILITY OF COMMAND THEORY

In modern legal theory, including modern positivism, the command theory is much criticised. The modern positivist H. L. A. Hart comments upon the dissimilarity between a mere coercive command backed by threats, which, by its nature, implies an immediate and temporary relationship, and the creation of a general obligation to compliance such as that associated with law. He also points out the difficulties of accommodating the complexities of law within the constraining command model. Hart concludes, before presenting his own revised positivist theory, which is discussed in chapter 3, that:

> The root cause of failure is that the elements out of which the theory was constructed, viz. the ideas of orders, obedience, habits, and threats, do not include, and cannot by their combination yield, the idea of a rule, without which we cannot hope to elucidate even the most elementary forms of law. (H. L. A. Hart, *The Concept of Law* (Oxford: Clarendon Press, 1961), p. 78.)

The idea of law as 'rules' is itself open to criticism (see chapter 9) but Hart's criticism is surely valid insofar as it emphasises the inability of a simple command theory to account adequately for the authority of law and the general obligation associated with it. The command analysis of law as coercively enforced orders cannot, in short, account for the normativity of law. That which one is forced to do is by no means necessarily the same as that which one recognises as proper to do, yet in most societies most of the time obedience to law is considered right and if it ceases to be so its continuing viability may be seriously in question. By the same token the probabilistic element of the Benthamite, and still more the Austinian, sanction is doubted by Hart, who remarks that:

> . . . the relevant connection between disobedience and punitive sanctions is not the likelihood of the latter, given the former, but that the courts should recognise disobedience as a reason according to law for its punishment. (H. L. A. Hart, *Essays on Bentham* (Oxford: Clarendon Press, 1982), p. 135.)

The probabilistic element is in Hart's view not a definition of the obligatory characteristic of 'law' but a statement of its 'force' in given cases.

There must also be raised, again, the question of the exclusion from expository jurisprudence of moral and ethical criteria of obligation. Clearly in the making and, up to a point, the implementation of law such factors do play a part, even without going into the question of the claim in conscience of an unequivocally abominable 'law'. Bentham's objection to such 'naturalist' thinking has been argued above to have been founded upon a misapprehension of the actual nature of classical naturalist argument (as to which in detail see chapter 4). It must also be remembered that Bentham did not deny the possibility of moral argument upon law, merely its appropriateness as a part of a 'scientific' expositorial description of 'law as it is'. In this context it may be pointed out that Austin stated that:

> The Divine laws, or the laws of God, are laws set by God to his human creatures. As I have intimated already, . . . they are laws or rules, *properly* so called. (*The Province of Jurisprudence Determined*, p. 34.)

He went on, not surprisingly, to distance divine from human laws and 'religious' from 'political' sanctions but the point is nonetheless worth making that the iconoclasm of Bentham and Austin's work should not be unduly emphasised.

If the implications of this thought had been followed through in classical positivist theory it would have had fewer difficulties. The perceived, and in many cases real, defects in the command theory may be argued to arise not so much from the ideas advanced as from the claims made on their behalf.

Bentham and Austin intended their scientific expositorial jurisprudence to be an accurate and complete description of positive law which might provide the springboard for a censorial jurisprudence proposing rational improvements. Unfortunately, and rather obviously, the command model does not and cannot afford an all-embracing model even of law 'as it is'. The basic points made are by no means exceptionable. Is positive law generally an imperatively expressed direction issued by or on behalf of sovereign authority? Consider, again, an Act of Parliament or a case decision, and the appearance is obvious. Are positive legal directions supported by sanctions, negative or, perhaps, positive? Criminal law certainly is and if fitting civil and, especially, facilitative laws into this pattern involves some strain it is worth pointing out that in some cases at least judicial determinations of rights and liabilities may ultimately be enforced through the sanction of contempt of court. Is the Benthamite complete law a rational model? The application of any particular legal provision clearly does involve the operation of a large mass of other associated legal provisions, or part provisions, and procedures.

If all this is accepted, where, then, lies the essence of the problem? Quite simply in that the description and explanation are unavoidably incomplete, even if convenient for certain purposes of legal discourse. Laws are much more complex than simple orders, a sovereign body is not just a glorified sergeant-major and in particular the whole question of lawmaking as an authoritative process must be considered. Threatened, or even promised, sanctions are not the only, or even the primary, motivation for obedience to law; there must also be considered the recognition of authority and, with but beyond that, the moral and ethical context in which positive law is made and considered. The distortions which are so evident in aspects of classical expositorial positivism arise not from the omission of these factors but from the attempt to treat the model as a complete analysis.

Classical expositorial positivism, in short, describes one important aspect of law, its imperative sovereign expression and its coercive maintenance, both of which are significant, but emphatically not complete, diagnostic features. In that limited context Bentham and Austin's expositorial work offers much of value even to the modern legal theorist. When extended beyond its proper context it rapidly strays into bizarre paths inviting originally undeserved ridicule.

2.4   THE QUESTION OF PUBLIC INTERNATIONAL LAW

A somewhat sterile controversy has resulted from the conclusion of Austin that public international law is not 'law' but a form of 'positive international morality'. He wrote that:

Grotius, Puffendorf, and the other writers on the so-called law of nations, have fallen into a . . . confusion of ideas: they have confounded positive international morality, or the rules which actually obtain among civilised nations, . . . with their own vague conceptions of international morality as it *ought to be*. (*The Province of Jurisprudence Determined*, p. 187.)

This statement appears in part to misunderstand what Grotius, Puffendorf and many others actually claimed, but its essential conclusion was almost inevitable granted the assumptions upon which Austin based his theory. There was in the 1830s, and is now, no international sovereign which commands public international law. Some sanctions are available to the international community, now primarily, although not only, through the United Nations, ranging from economic sanctions through to military action authorised under chapter VII of the United Nations Charter such as that undertaken by the Coalition Powers in the 1990–1 Gulf Conflict, but these are hardly based upon the model intended by Austin. It has interestingly been argued that even upon his own criteria Austin may have assumed too readily that international law is not 'law'. W. L. Morrison argues that:

. . . if he had been prepared to investigate whether a particular sovereign with whom he was concerned recognised the system of international law generally, or whether numbers of them did, he might have been led to a much more standard view of the basis of authority of international law than the snap conclusion he made. (W. L. Morrison, *John Austin* (London: Edward Arnold, 1982), pp. 99–100.)

This may be so but it must be conceded that considerable obstacles would have to be overcome in order to force public international law into the pattern prescribed by Austin. If public international law did not in the 1830s and probably does not, even now, satisfy what is basically an 'institutional' test set by Austin, that failure is not necessarily definitive of the issue. D. J. Harris remarks that:

Although international 'law' is still not law according to Austin's test, most international lawyers would at least dispute that test is more helpful than certain others by which international law could be said to be 'law'. (D. J. Harris, *Cases and Materials on International Law*, 4th ed. (London: Sweet & Maxwell, 1991), p. 6.)

International law is undeniably much more 'open textured' than municipal (i.e., national) law and in a variety of ways derives from the agreement of States, rather than from sovereign imposition. The formal sources of law, from the viewpoint of international judicial determination, are set out by art.

38 of the Statute of the International Court of Justice and are: (a) general or particular treaties establishing rules recognised expressly by states in dispute, (b) international custom, (c) general legal principles accepted by civilised nations and (d) as subsidiary sources, judicial decisions and the teachings of 'highly qualified publicists'. (For analysis of these 'sources' see M. Dixon, *Textbook on International Law* 3rd ed. (London: Blackstone Press, 1996), Chapter 2.) All of these sources, as applied in the international context, are means of determining, in one or another form, a consensus amongst the community of nations in a manner clearly related to customary law, which, as indicated above, Austin also did not consider to be law 'properly so called' in its own right. This has led some commentators to compare public international law with so-called 'primitive law', meaning the law of certain low technology societies. Some of the legal-anthropological assumptions which underlie this argument might be questioned but it may reasonably be argued that the appropriate test to be applied, in both cases, is not one of institutions but one of function. In short, does public international law serve the same ends in the community of nations that positive law, Austin's laws 'properly so called', plays in a nation State? If, as it is here contended, the answer to that question is yes, it would seem that public international law has in its context a good claim to be termed 'law'. Austin's exclusion of such law from his category 'properly so called' would then seem to be a product of an unduly narrow definitional focus.

2.5 BENTHAM'S CENSORIAL JURISPRUDENCE

The expositorial command theory advanced by Bentham and developed by Austin was intended as the basis for a 'censorial jurisprudence' which was to examine a rational programme for the improvement of law, this being the separate examination of positive law as it 'ought to be' called for upon the logic of Hume's division between descriptive and normative propositions which has been considered above. Bentham was no mute admirer of law 'as it is', or more accurately 'as it was' in his day. He was, on the contrary, deeply contemptuous of many aspects of English common law as he observed it, considering it to be in many cases illogical and badly administered.

The basis for Bentham's improving censorial jurisprudence was the principle of utility, which he defined as follows:

> . . . that principle which approves or disapproves of every action whatsoever, according to the tendency which it appears to have to augment or diminish the happiness of the party whose interest is in question. (J. Bentham, *An Introduction to the Principles of Morals and Legislation*, ed. W. Harrison (Oxford: Basil Blackwell, 1967), ch. 1, para. 2.)

He added that:

An action . . . [conforms] to the principle of utility . . . when the tendency it has to augment the happiness of the community is greater than any it has to diminish it. (Ibid., ch. 1, para. 6.)

This is often reduced to a criterion of the tendency to promote the 'greatest happiness of the greatest number'.

In practice, few actions, legislative or otherwise, have unmixed tendencies and for the operation of a 'principle of utility' as a criterion of evaluation it is obviously necessary to have some means of assessing the overall, or average, tendency of a given action. The polar opposites in this instance are, of course, those of 'pleasure' and 'pain' which have already arisen in the expositorial context of the motivation to compliance with law. It is important here to stress that these ideas do not simply signify frivolous enjoyment or physical hurt, although they might include both. A more felicitous rendering in a modern context might be found in a terminology of 'benefit' and 'detriment'. In order to determine the tendency of an act Bentham advanced the idea of a 'felicific calculus' as a balancing of the beneficial and detrimental tendencies of any given action.

The detrimental balance was termed by Bentham a 'mischievous' tendency, an illustration of the weakening of the force of some words over time. He gave as a principal example the effects of a highway robbery, or, in modern conditions perhaps a mugging. (See *An Introduction to the Principles of Morals and Legislation*, ch. 12.) He categorised the resulting 'mischiefs' as falling into 'primary' and 'secondary' divisions. Here the primary mischief comprises (a) an 'original' element, the actual robbery, and (b) a 'derivative' element, e.g., the inability of the victim to pay creditors (who are thus also 'victims') as a result of the robbery. The secondary mischief comprises (a) an 'alarm', here the fear of other people who hear reports of the crime that they too may be robbed or mugged, and (b) a 'danger', that people may actually be robbed or mugged, not least if deterrent action fails. Against these weighty 'mischiefs', it may be added, the presumed 'pleasure' derived by the robber or mugger from the successful robbery or mugging is readily outweighed in the felicific calculus in determining the overall tendency of the action to be 'mischievous'.

This analysis is related to the evaluation of legislative action. Under the principle of utility Bentham states that:

. . . the happiness of the individuals, of whom a community is composed, that is their pleasures and their security, is the end and the sole end which the legislator ought to have in view. (*An Introduction to the Principles of Morals and Legislation*, ch. 3, para. 1.)

Thus, the quality, as compared with the expositorial identification, of 'law' is to be determined by its tendency to promote the greatest happiness of the greatest number. Here it may be noted that punishment, one of the obvious forms of sanction attached as a motive for compliance, is in itself a mischief. Bentham remarks of this that:

> . . . all punishment in itself is evil. Upon the principle of utility, if it ought at all to be admitted, it ought only to be admitted in as far as it promises to exclude some greater evil. (*An Introduction to the Principles of Morals and Legislation*, ch. 13, para. 2.)

Such 'greater evil' comprises the harm or injury done to all or any of the members of the community which is done or threatened by the conduct to be penalised. In chapters 13 and 14 of *Principles of Morals and Legislation*, Bentham offers a detailed analysis of the appropriateness of punishment and the proportionality of punishment to offence. Some of this analysis is, it must be admitted, strikingly mechanistic even if it does genuinely attempt to advance a purposive penology divorced from a doctrine of severity as an end in itself, in marked distinction from the practical penology of Bentham's own day. In this, as in other areas of thought, Bentham acknowledged a clear debt to the earlier work of Beccaria (see in this context H. L. A. Hart, 'Bentham and Beccaria' in *Essays on Bentham* (Oxford: Clarendon Press, 1982), p. 40 at pp. 45–7).

The 'good of the greatest number' is not, in the model of Bentham or Austin, truly a communal good. Bentham indeed considered the 'community' to be a fiction encompassing what is no more than an aggregation of individuals. The idea is rather that the efficient pursuit of individual goods on a utilitarian basis will benefit the aggregation of individuals. Austin remarks concisely that:

> . . . since the general good is an aggregate of individual enjoyments, the good of the general or public would diminish with the good of the individuals of whom that general or public is constituted or composed. (*The Province of Jurisprudence Determined*, p. 107.)

The achievement of the greatest happiness of the greatest number (of individuals) might, of course, involve the misery of the few. Bentham was certainly prepared to contemplate very savage penal measures, if considerably less savage in many cases than those actually inflicted in his day.

The immediately obvious difficulty with the principle of utility as a basis for a censorial jurisprudence lies, in particular, in a rather mechanistic balancing of pain and pleasure and, more generally, in the failure to recognise the Aristotelian principle that human beings are 'political animals' (*politikon zōon*), meaning social creatures (as to this see chapter 4). If this is accepted there follows an inevitable tension between individual wishes and collective needs, one of the functions of 'good' law being then to balance these distinct, but by no means necessarily conflicting, polarities. Perhaps inevitably the difficulty may be argued to be of the same type as that arising in classical positivist 'expositorial' jurisprudence. The principle has a valid point to make, and certainly had in the context of the practice of the late 18th and early 19th centuries. To claim, as Bentham did, that the principle of utility is a complete and perfect answer to all the questions of 'expositorial' jurisprudence must appear a bizarrely exaggerated claim.

Ultimately, Bentham and Austin's legal theory in both its 'expositorial' and 'censorial' aspects presents important analyses of some of the questions of jurisprudence. It does not present a complete or perfect answer to all of them and is rendered occasionally bizarre not by its own substance but by attempts to fit issues into its format which in reality have no true relation to it. Modern positivism, notably that advanced by H.L.A. Hart, has attempted to address some of the resulting apparent infelicities in a recasting of positivist concerns. These ideas are the subject-matter of chapter 3.

2.6 FURTHER READING

Austin, J., *The Province of Jurisprudence Determined* (London: Weidenfeld & Nicolson, 1955).

Bentham, J., *A Fragment on Government* (Oxford: Basil Blackwell, 1967).

Bentham, J., *Of Laws in General*, ed. H. L. A. Hart (London: Athlone Press, 1970).

Hart, H. L. A., *Essays on Bentham* (Oxford: Clarendon Press, 1982).

Hart, H. L. A., *The Concept of Law* (Oxford: Clarendon Press, 1961), chs 2, 3 and 4.

Moles, R. N., *Definition and Rule in Legal Theory* (Oxford: Basil Blackwell, 1987), chs 1 and 2.

Postema, G. J., *Bentham and the Common Law Tradition* (Oxford: Clarendon Press, 1986), chs 5 and 7.

CHAPTER THREE

Modified Positivism: H. L. A. Hart

The command theory advanced by Bentham and Austin (see chapter 2) is subject to a number of difficulties when presented as a complete description of the operation of positive law. The legal theory of H. L. A. Hart was founded upon a critique of a form of the classical command model which led to a revised 'positivist analysis' founded not upon a combination of command and force (or sanction), but upon the combination and operation of rules in a 'legal system'. Hart commences from the basic proposition that:

> The most prominent general feature of law at all times and places is that its existence means that certain kinds of human conduct are no longer optional, but in some sense obligatory. (H. L. A. Hart, *The Concept of Law* (Oxford: Clarendon Press, 1961), p. 6.)

The key words are, of course, 'in *some* sense' and Hart denies that the classical positivist model of law, as an implicitly coercive expression of political power, sufficiently accounts for the character of law as an obligation-imposing social phenomenon. Hart also argues that an equation of the obligatory characteristic of positive law with moral obligation is equally inadequate and thus rejects naturalist theory (see chapter 4) on the ground that it insufficiently distinguishes the particular character of *legal* obligation.

Analysis of both naturalist and classical positivist theories suggests that their claims may have greater strength, when viewed in their proper context, than Hart appears willing to concede. Most naturalist writers do not deny the difference between what a government might in practice do and what it has a moral entitlement to do. This distinction is clearly one that divides force or political power from moral claim in a context of legal validity. On the other hand Bentham and Austin clearly did emphasise command and sanction as definite characteristics of law but they did not suggest that law was uncomplicated by other features, including the possibility of a convergence of multiple motivations for compliance with positive law. However, the questions addressed by Hart are of central jurisdictional significance and are not as such analysed in detail by either classical positivists or naturalists. Hart himself expressed the goal of his theory as:

> an improved analysis of the distinctive structure of a municipal legal system and a better understanding of the resemblances and differences between law, coercion, and morality, as types of social phenomena. (*The Concept of Law*, p. 17.)

This 'improved' analysis is essentially a revised positivism which is presented as building upon the 'failure' of classical positivism but which stands in its own right as a distinct account of the jurisprudential character of positive law.

3.1 HART'S GUNMAN AND THE CRITIQUE OF COMMAND THEORY

Hart commences from a very simple instance of a coercive order, that made by an armed bank robber, the 'gunman', to a bank clerk to hand over money upon immediate pain of being shot (*The Concept of Law*, p. 19). This example parallels the reference by St Augustine of Hippo, in a very different naturalist context (see chapter 4), to a captured pirate brought before Alexander the Great. When asked how he dared to rob ships at sea, the pirate replied that he had only one ship and was condemned as a pirate whereas Alexander had many and was acclaimed an Emperor, making the point that power as such does not confer legitimacy (St Augustine, *De Civitate Dei*, 4.5.4). Hart's point is narrower and is simply that the bank robber has no *authority* over the clerk. The obvious contrast is with a tax demand made pursuant to law by the Inland Revenue or an equivalent agency. This too is superficially a demand with menaces but, although defaulters are certainly threatened with penalties, the demand is made with authority. Further, the obligation to pay is general to all relevant persons in receipt of taxable income and exists whether or not enforcement is immediately practical. Upon this basis Hart makes a clear distinction between the situations of 'being obliged' and being 'under obligation', the former involving the actual or predictable application of compulsion, the latter involving a concept of duty whether or not any sanction can reasonably be expected to be applied.

Hart emphasises the obligation element and he argues that the command model, however it may be elaborated or distorted, cannot adequately account for this in the complex structures of a real society. In the concluding summary of his critique of command theory Hart lists four principal defects in the analysis (*The Concept of Law*, p. 77). These are:

(a)   Law, even a criminal statute, is, notably unlike the coercive demands of a gunman, addressed generally rather than to a particular person and applies even to those enacting it.

(b)   Some laws do not impose duties but rather create powers, whether public or private, e.g., delegated legislative authority or the capacity to initiate legal relations, and these cannot readily be forced into a model of coercive orders.

(c)   Not all legal rules emerge from a command process at all, an obvious example being those deriving from custom. It may be added here that Hart has, of course, dismissed any Benthamite explanation in terms of a tacit command evidenced by enforcement in the courts as a rationalising distortion.

(d)   The idea of unlimited sovereignty which is free of all legal constraint fails to take account of the continuity of law which is an obvious feature of a modern legal system, without reference, again, to a distorted explanation of tacit command.

Hart emphasises that these failures are, in his opinion, not incidental but fundamental, in that the basic components of command theory are incapable of any combination which will give an account of what he argues to be the essential element of law, the combination of rules in the definition of formal social prescription. Thus he states that:

What is most needed as a corrective to the model of coercive orders or rules, is a fresh conception of legislation as the introduction or modification of general standards of behaviour to be followed by the society generally. (*The Concept of Law*, p. 43.)

This involved a fundamental remoulding of positivist concerns as the foundation of quite a different form of legal theory.

3.2   THE IMPORTANCE OF RULES

The existence and the interaction of rules are fundamental to Hart's legal theory and appear to be obviously the substance of law. Whether one considers statutes, case decisions or even customary law – from s. 57(1) of the Town and Country Planning Act 1990 ('Subject to the following provisions of this section, planning permission is required for the carrying out of any development of land') to the rule in *Rylands* v *Fletcher* (1868) LR 3 HL

330 (dealing with the liability of those who accumulate dangerous things upon land which are liable to do damage and which escape and in fact cause damage) – the law appears to consist of rules. The rules form a normative regulatory structure which exists as a system rather than as a pattern of discrete commands. They apply to anyone in the relevant situation, e.g., considering the development of land or accumulating dangerous things upon it. They are also not temporally limited in operation. *Rylands* v *Fletcher* was decided by judges who are no longer capable of wielding a judicial authority which itself derived from the authority of a Crown in Parliament comprising persons now dead. Seen in this light the importance of rules as a basic building block of law can hardly be doubted, although a number of modern theorists cast doubt upon the exclusive importance of rules in the structure of law. A prominent example is found in the work of R. M. Dworkin (see chapter 9) who contends that law consists not only of rules but also of policies and principles, most especially the latter, which come into play in discerning the 'right answer' in 'hard cases' to which the naked rules afford no clear outcome. Dworkin nonetheless concedes the importance of Hart's analysis of rules (R. M. Dworkin, *Taking Rights Seriously* (London: Duckworth, 1977), p. 20).

The underlying theme of Hart's analysis of law as rules may be suggested to be precisely that concept of lawmaking as authoritative process which, it has already been suggested, was the major weakness of classical positivism as a complete explanation of positive law in operation (see chapter 2).

3.2.1 Obligation and the internal aspect of rules

Legal rules are not optional prescriptions; they create obligations which are characteristic in type. Hart distinguishes the 'obligation' associated with positive law from mere convergent habit and also from any psychological experience of 'feeling bound'. He argues that not all rules are necessarily obligation-imposing, but that those which are so are distinguished by one primary and two subsidiary characteristics (see *The Concept of Law*, pp. 84–5). The primary characteristic is one of 'seriousness of social pressure' for conformity. The two subsidiary characteristics are, first, that the rule is thought to be important because it maintains some significant element of social life and, secondly, that the conduct required may conflict with the wishes of the person(s) to whom the rule applies. The combination of these factors is suggested to inform the meaning of statements about 'obligation' in social context. Thus, the obligatory characteristic of positive law may be taken to involve rules requiring patterns of conduct, which are not necessarily those desired by those subject to them, which support some perceived plank of social relations and which are the subject of significant pressure for conformity.

This analysis informs Hart's idea of an 'internal aspect' of rules. He states that:

> What is necessary is that there should be a critical reflective attitude to certain patterns of behaviour as a common standard, and that this should display itself in criticism (including self-criticism), demands for conformity, and in acknowledgements that such criticisms and demands are justified, all of which find their characteristic expression in the normative terminology of . . . 'right' and 'wrong'. (*The Concept of Law*, p. 56.)

The 'critical reflective attitude' manifests itself in acceptance of the existence of rules constituting in themselves a justification for criticism of deviant conduct. Thus whilst from an 'external' viewpoint one might be able to predict the consequences of given action or inaction, and even to live satisfactorily in the society concerned, one would lack understanding of a vital element in the operation of the prescription. As Hart expresses it:

> . . . the external point of view, which limits itself to the observable regularities of behaviour, cannot reproduce . . . the way in which the rules function . . . in the lives of those who normally are the majority of society. . . . For them the violation of a rule is not merely a basis for the prediction that a hostile reaction will follow but a *reason* for hostility. (*The Concept of Law*, p. 88.)

This model of 'obligation' which is claimed to be distinct from the classical positivist emphasis upon a coercive 'obliging' and from the naturalist emphasis upon moral aspiration raises a number of important questions.

Although Hart does not use the term, the method of analysis which he adopts has, as MacCormick points out, a distinct hermeneutic element (N. MacCormick, *H. L. A. Hart* (London: Edward Arnold, 1981), in particular at pp. 38 and 59). Hermeneutic method has antique roots, most particularly, although not only, in Protestant approaches to Biblical exegesis, but is primarily concerned with the interpretation and understanding of the language of texts and materials viewed in their contextual continuity. A methodology of this type is clearly of value but the results which Hart derives from it are open to some question. One objection is that ideas and applications of 'obligation' are in practice various and do not readily lend themselves to the singular categorisation attempted by Hart. MacCormick remarks that:

> Rather than lumping the different notions together as Hart does, we should explicate their differences and show how they severally relate to the central idea that in morals and in law we have to do with . . . 'requirements' of right conduct, marking the line drawn between what is wrong and what is, at least, acceptable. (*H. L. A. Hart*, p. 59.)

Paradoxically it might be argued that in seeking to expose and expunge the errors of classical positivism Hart himself may, to some extent, have fallen victim to a problem which in large part underlay those very infelicities, that is to say the adoption of a definitional aspiration which assumes that the 'obligatory characteristic' of positive law is capable of uniform categorisation.

The extraordinary contortions necessary to display the command theory as a 'complete' account have been considered above (see chapter 2). Hart's 'rules of obligation' are not made subject to distortions upon such a scale, partly because they are not deployed over so wide a front. Hart admits the possible role of coercive sanctions as a subsidiary obliging agency in relation to law. What, oddly from a hermeneutic viewpoint, he does not appear to consider is that whilst his categories of 'being obliged' and being 'under obligation' are different, their significance for legal theory may vary according to the context in which they are considered. There are, of course, a considerable range of possible analyses of the obligatory characteristic of law beyond the positivist spectrum. Naturalist analysis emphasises moral criteria of evaluation (see chapters 4 and 5), some of the Scandinavian realist theories stress the psychological experience of 'feeling bound' which Hart denies and, indeed, denounce both naturalism and positivism as subject to an 'imperative fallacy' (see chapter 10). From rather different perspectives both Marxist and critical analyses tend to treat concepts of legal obligation as artificial constructs which conceal different, and not necessarily beneficial, agendas (see chapters 7 and 12). It has already been suggested in chapter 1 that the interpretation of such divergent views rests to some extent upon assessment of the question which is being asked in each case. Without claiming that all disagreements can thus be reasoned out of existence, it would seem reasonable to argue that legal obligation is by its nature a many-sided phenomenon, each aspect of which must be analysed and distinguished in its own right, without selective exclusion. Unfortunately attempts to treat given conclusions as answers to questions to which they are not properly addressed is a recurring defect in the discipline of jurisprudence. However, the problems resulting from overextended applications of particular theoretical perceptions should not necessarily be taken to devalue a theory within its proper context. The particular context appropriate to Hart's rules model is ultimately made obvious by his analysis of the nature of a legal system.

3.2.2 The union of primary and secondary rules

The idea of rules imposing obligations is not held out by Hart as a sufficient basis for the establishment of a legal system. Hart argues that such primary duty-imposing rules cannot, at any level of organisation beyond the extremely simple, exist satisfactorily in isolation. He sets out three principal defects which would exist in a society which sought normative regulation through primary rules alone. These are:

(a)   The primary rules may be 'uncertain' in application, that is to say that no procedures would exist for their interpretation and the determination of their scope where this was not intrinsically clear.

(b)   The rules would be 'static' with the only mechanism for change being the very slow processes of developing customary practice.

(c)   The maintenance of such rules will be 'inefficient' granted the lack of mechanisms for determination of disputes about their application.

Hart argues that these difficulties are resolved by the addition of 'secondary rules', which:

> . . . specify the ways in which the primary rules may be conclusively ascertained, introduced, eliminated, varied, and the fact of their violation conclusively determined. (*The Concept of Law*, p. 92.)

The types of secondary rule which meet the defects of a structure of primary rules alone are described by Hart as comprising a 'rule of recognition', 'rules of change' and 'rules of adjudication'. The first affirms the claim of purported rules to command support; it is, in short, a criterion of identification. In most legal systems there will not be one simple rule of recognition operating as a criterion of identification for legal rules but, rather, a more or less complex structure of rules which will collectively perform the function of identification. Such rules, which may both define and limit legislative capacity within a given system, may also be suggested to solve the problem of constitutional limitations upon sovereign power (see 3.2.3) which was a cause of difficulty for both Bentham and Austin. The second category is related to the first in that it provides a mechanism whereby new rules may be introduced and old rules may be changed or abolished. The third type is obvious in its functions both in its most formal context in law courts and in lesser adjudicatory bodies acting under formal authority.

Hart contends that a 'legal system' properly so called is the product of the combination, or 'union' of these two types of rule. The rule of recognition, as the criterion of identification, is fundamental to the system, but the form and function of 'secondary rules' in general raise a number of important issues.

A peripheral consideration arises from Hart's legal anthropology. Hart gives as the type of a society governed by primary rules alone:

> . . . primitive communities . . . where the only means of social control is that general attitude of the group towards its own standard modes of behaviour in terms of which we have characterised rules of obligation. (*The Concept of Law*, p. 89.)

In practice the identification of 'standard modes of behaviour' indicates the existence of some form of 'secondary rule' mechanism and many so-called 'primitive' societies demonstrate very sophisticated means of identification, interpretation and application of norms. It may also be thought that qualities of stasis, in the sense of inhibiting rigidity, and uncertainty would to a large extent be mutually exclusive. However, Hart suggests that such 'primitive' societies, lacking developed secondary rules would be 'pre-legal' since they appear to lack the institutional base and rules necessary for a recognisable 'legal system'.

In practice there is good reason to think that many so-called 'primitive' societies have sophisticated means of identifying, interpreting and applying their social norms. Modern legal-anthropological thought would certainly not necessarily concur with a dismissal of the 'legal' usages of 'primitive', meaning not high-technology, societies. Simon Roberts remarks that:

> While there may be some room for argument as to what constitutes legislative and adjudicative organs, or centrally organised sanctions, Hart appears simply wrong [in arguing that societies without such institutions are difficult to imagine beyond the very smallest scale]: many societies *have* existed without them and [legal anthropology examines] how order is secured in such societies. (S. Roberts, *Order and Dispute: An Introduction to Legal Anthropology* (Harmondsworth: Penguin, 1979), p. 25.)

The key words here are perhaps 'what constitutes' the legal-systemic institutions in any given case. Anthropological scholarship tends to suggest that the relevant tests are not so much institutional as functional, i.e., how are tasks performed appropriately in their given context, not what institutional similarities with advanced systems can be discerned. Indeed thought of this general type can be found in work done in the late 1930s by K. N. Llewellyn and E. A. Hoebel (see Llewellyn and Hoebel, *The Cheyenne Way* (Norman, Okla: University of Oklahoma Press, 1941); as to Llewellyn's general legal theory see chapter 11). Viewed in this light it may be questioned whether any structure of legal norms, however 'primitive', is actually 'uncertain', 'static' or 'inefficient' in the senses of these terms used by Hart. Indeed, the defects of uncertainty and stasis, in the sense of constraining rigidity, have the appearance of mutual incompatibility. The issue is properly that of the solutions found to these various defects in different contexts rather than a search for a particular category of solution as a criterion for a legal system as such. The doubt which may reasonably be cast upon the anthropological base of the description of the need for secondary rules does not, however, deny the importance of the case being made in relation to the operation of legal systems in developed States.

Within such a legal system the operation of secondary rules will, as Hart suggests, be much more complex than a simple categorisation of them might seem to suggest. It has already been suggested that rules of recognition act in a much more complex fashion than a simple single rule. Similar points may be made about other types of secondary rule. Power conferring 'rules of change' may operate at a variety of levels in government and other public administration, but may also be argued to operate in the 'private' sector. Making a will or entering into a contract alters the legal position of the parties concerned and may be seen as a creation of a form of local legal regime for them. Hart refers to the work of Hans Kelsen (see chapter 8) in support of a quasi-legislative analysis of the creation of, e.g., contractual relations (see *The Concept of Law*, p. 94). It may be added that this type of thought is more familiar in civilian jurisdictions than in the common law tradition. Rules of adjudication can also be seen to involve a large and complex body of procedural provision but may extend into many much less formal areas of dispute resolution than litigation.

The model of law as system is perhaps Hart's most important contribution to positivist legal theory and it undoubtedly deals far better with a number of issues to which the command theory of Bentham and Austin was inappropriately addressed. There are, however, a number of points which remain open to question. These primarily focus upon the crucial questions of validation, interpretation and application which lie at the heart of a legal system.

3.2.3   The basis of the rule of recognition

The establishment of a critical reflective standard is an important aspect of the attachment of obligation to law but it is not necessarily a uniquely legal phenomenon and Hart does not claim it to be so. In order to find a foundation for the legal rules which are to be understood internally it is evidently necessary to discover a criterion by reference to which those rules which are legal can be identified. The problem is that identified by Hart as 'uncertainty' and the solution offered is the 'rule of recognition'. Hart illustrates the operation of such a rule by reference to the very simple legal and political context of a hypothetical Rex dynasty. Rex I is presented as an autocratic monarch originally established in power more or less by force who, after suppression of early resistance, is in practice generally obeyed. Rex I is thus, in effect, a crowned gunman who has established power in a political society without any necessary connotation that obedience is right, although some of the aspects of early Rexite government might be considered in some basic sense legal. If, however, Rex I dies and, in Hart's example, is succeeded by his eldest son Rex II who continues to be obeyed, a very simple rule of male primogeniture (succession by eldest son) would seem to have developed as a criterion of legislative authority. That is to say that Rex II has legislative capacity not, or not only, because he originally wielded effective force but because a rule confers a formal legislative authority upon him. In the simple system of the Rex dynasty this rule will then establish a critical reflective standard according to which the word of Rex II, and Rex III, will be law. It is noteworthy that, after the initial establishment in power of Rex I, this is not a system that relies upon a Benthamite *realpolitik* but upon a form of right to rule which Bentham and Austin were anxious to avoid. Note also, however, that this is not a moral but a formal right to rule, whether Rex I, Rex II or Rex III are in any way good rulers is not at this point brought into question.

The rule of recognition established by the hypothetical Rex dynasty is as simple as can be imagined, involving nothing more than the proposition that the person who is the eldest child of the previous autocrat inherits legislative capacity. In reality, even in an autocratic monarchy or dictatorship, rules of recognition are, generally, considerably more complex than this. The model of such rules also solves the problem of constitutional law which proved so difficult to incorporate in Bentham and Austin's command theory. With the appreciation of legislative capacity as a feature of an authorised system comes the idea that the identifying rule can both define and limit without any question of sovereignty as such arising. The rule of recognition is, in Hart's terms, clearly a 'secondary rule', but it is in very significant ways quite unlike any other such rules.

Legislative and other legal decision-making powers are validated by rules, and subordinate powers, such as that of a local authority to make by-laws, rest upon some statutory authorisation. However, the proposition that in the United Kingdom the Crown in Parliament possesses legislative authority represents the end of this line of reasoning. As Hart puts it:

> . . . we have reached a rule which, like the intermediate statutory order and statute, provides criteria for the assessment of the validity of other rules; but it is also unlike them in that there is no rule providing criteria for the assessment of its own legal validity. (*The Concept of Law*, p. 104.)

The rule of recognition is thus an 'ultimate rule'. It is a criterion of validity which cannot itself be validated since validity is an internal statement made within a system, the functioning of which depends upon the supposition of the rule of recognition itself. The question is not one of validation but whether the particular rule is accepted by the courts or not.

The rule of recognition in Hart's model has an obvious and close relationship with the *Grundnorm* in Hans Kelsen's pure theory (see chapter 8). The *Grundnorm* in Kelsen's theory is the foundation of a hierarchy of norms each of which is validated by a prior norm until, finally, the *Grundnorm* itself is reached. This is validated by no other norm and is essentially the root assumption of the existence of the legal system. In both Hart's and Kelsen's theories the basic rule or norm may reasonably be taken as the point at which the legal theory plugs into political reality. It may also be suggested that the practical acceptance of a given rule of recognition as the ultimate criterion of validity for a legal system must involve consideration of a number of 'external' factors. Indeed the fountain of internality cannot itself derive 'internally'. N. E. Simmonds remarks that:

> The significance of [propositions about legal validity] can only be clarified by reference to [a] . . . context . . . involving the ascription of authority to certain sources of norms. . . . legal discourse is linked to law as a fact without itself being reducible to factual, descriptive discourse. (N. E. Simmonds, 'Practice and validity' [1979] CLJ 361 at p. 364.)

In a very general sense the 'rule of recognition' may be taken as the means whereby the divide between descriptive and 'legal' discourse is bridged. Hart does not deal with the question of the selection of a rule of recognition, nor perhaps should he be expected to do so in his chosen context. The issue is, however, one of importance and is dealt with, under different terminology, in other areas of legal theory.

Once established, such an authorising rule may, of course, fail or be changed by various forms of political discontinuity. This point may reasonably be considered in the context of the 17th-century crisis in English, and United Kingdom, constitutional development.

The political, economic and religious conflicts which fuelled the Civil War led to the overthrow and execution of Charles I and, after various political shifts, to the installation of Oliver Cromwell as Lord Protector in 1653. Cromwell may be taken, in very much more complex circumstances, as a rough equivalent of Rex I (he was in fact offered, but declined, the throne on several occasions). His son Richard Cromwell followed him as Lord Protector but, unlike Rex II, proved unable to sustain the position in the face of political uncertainties and the ambitions of a variety of warlords and was overthrown in May 1659. In what is now a somewhat antique text, G. M. Trevelyan makes the telling point that:

> Oliver [Cromwell] . . . had striven ever more earnestly, if not successfully, towards constitutional growth. But the generals . . . each [strove] . . . to realize by force his own personal ambition, or some visionary reign of Christ. In its last stage the military rule contained no power of evolution or principle of settlement. (G. M. Trevelyan, *England under the Stuarts* (1904), (London: Methuen, 1965), p. 314.)

The 'rule' establishing the Puritan 'Commonwealth' thus failed and in 1660 the 'Restoration' of Charles II took place upon the initiative of General Monk with the agreement of a 'free Parliament'. The situation restored was, however, hardly that once claimed by Charles I and was in a number of respects clearly 'upon terms', despite the Royalist pretence that no legally significant interregnum had occurred between 1649 and 1660.

The constitutionally decisive move occurred with the Glorious Revolution of 1688. At that time James II was overthrown and a body claiming 'Parliamentary' status and comprising peers and MPs, although they had not been duly summoned to sit in Parliamentary session, invited James's daughter Mary and her husband William, Prince of Orange, jointly to assume the throne as William III and Mary II. This invitation was expressly upon limiting terms recited in the 1688 Declaration of Right and the 1689 Bill of Rights and in a number of respects these measures represented the decisive shift of power from monarch to Parliament and the foundation of the subsequent model of the Crown in Parliament. It was this era which called forth the social-contractarian theories of John Locke (see chapter 4) as an explanation of limited government. It is, however, also arguable that in these events there may be discerned a complex shifting of 'rules' conferring legislative authority in a manner quite consistent with Hart's analysis.

The question of a changing 'critical reflective attitude' and the perceived 'rightness' of obedience in changing circumstances may also be illustrated from this period of history. The Restoration government of the 1660s introduced a variety of legal measures against some, although by no means all, of the Cromwellian Commonwealth factions, but there were relatively few treason trials. Those that did take place principally involved the regicides who had been involved in the trial and execution of Charles I and in this context defences which might loosely be termed 'superior orders' were sought to be advanced. They were rejected by the court largely upon the basis of the opinion that obedience to a treasonable order is itself treasonable. In the case of the major regicides it is perhaps not surprising that a defence founded essentially upon the power of the revolutionary regime of which they were members failed. In the case of Sir Harry Vane, not one of the regicides, in relation to obedience to the regime after 1649, the rejection of this form of plea in relation to obedience to the Cromwellian Commonwealth must, however, seem to have been not only harsh but even technically dubious. Much later, in 1846, Lord Campbell wrote that in Vane's case:

No satisfactory answer could be given to the plea that the Parliament was then *de facto* the supreme power of the State, and that it could be as little treason to act under its authority as under the authority of an usurper on the throne, which is expressly declared by the statute of Henry VII not to be treason; and it was miserable sophistry to [argue] . . . that, as there was no one else acknowledged as King in England, Charles II, while in exile, must be considered King *de facto* as well as *de jure*. (J. Campbell (Baron Campbell), *The Lives of the Lord Chancellors*, vol. 3 (London: John Murray, 1846), p. 195.)

The question of obedience in a context of revolutionary change in the rule validating legislative capacity inevitably raises the issue of the relevance of the efficacy of a legal system. Hart argues that whilst, generally, an internal statement about the validity of rules supposes the external fact of the efficacy of the system concerned, this is not necessarily the case. Thus adherents of an overthrown regime will commonly cling to its legal criteria of validity in the hope of its eventual restoration. The reasoning of the English Restoration judges would afford an example of this hope when gratified. The ultimate test in Hart's view is the conduct of officials and especially of judges in relation to a given system of rules but he denies that the concept of validity rests simply upon an external prediction of what judges will in fact do. Hart argues, rather, that:

> [A judge's] statement that a rule is valid is an internal statement recognising that the rule satisfies the test for identifying what is to count as law in his court, and constitutes not a prophecy of but part of the *reason* for his decision. (*The Concept of Law*, p. 102.)

In this context the role of the judge is of evident practical significance, but in a broader context the emphasis placed by Hart upon the 'official' viewpoint raises important questions.

3.2.4   Legal systems and the importance of officials

The official standpoint is of crucial importance in Hart's model of a legal system. The point is made plainly in his statement that:

> There are . . . two minimum conditions necessary and sufficient for the existence of a legal system. . . . rules of behaviour which are valid according to . . . criteria of validity must be generally obeyed, and . . . its rules of recognition . . . and its rules of change and adjudication must be effectively accepted as common public standards of official behaviour by its officials. (*The Concept of Law*, p. 113.)

As Hart then adds, this is:

> . . . a Janus-faced statement looking both towards obedience by ordinary citizens and to the acceptance by officials of secondary rules as critical common standards of official behaviour. (*The Concept of Law*, p. 113.)

He thus contends essentially that whereas 'primary rules' are addressed to all citizens, including officials in their personal capacities, 'secondary rules' are contrived for official rather than 'private' consumption. The basis for this argument is partly that the necessity for a detailed understanding of the system and its criteria of validity is largely confined to those who in practice operate it, which is to say officials. It would perhaps be more accurate to refer to those who are 'officially' engaged within the legal system, including judges and the practising legal profession, as well as those who are 'officials' in the narrower context of current linguistic usage. In any event the 'Janus-faced' analysis of the 'official' and 'general' understanding of rules poses an important issue.

It may first be said that as a matter of fact it is clearly the case that lawyers in particular, but also a variety of other 'officials', will have a more detailed and technical familiarity with what Hart terms 'secondary rules' than will most people. This is to say no more than that, in medical equivalence, a doctor would be expected to have a more technical view of the patient's condition than the patient, which is not to say that the latter will not be aware of being ill. Hart's proposition is, admittedly, not that the general public are actually unaware of secondary rules, it is merely that their need for detailed awareness is not the same as that of officials. Even accepting this caveat it might still seem that general public awareness plays a more vital role in the operation of law than Hart concedes.

The overwhelming proportion of daily legal activity proceeds without any need for official intervention. The average person will undertake a number of legal transactions on most days, for example, entering into contracts for the purchase of goods or services. Statistically the likelihood of any of these being considered by a court is so vanishingly small as to be discountable, but there will, nonetheless, be a consciousness to some extent that a potentially justiciable obligation is being created. By the same token a failure by someone to do a promised favour might be rude and might occasion resentment, but it would hardly raise thoughts of litigation. Such practical judgments require all participants in the legal system, not just specialist officials, to have some critical consciousness of its criteria and application, even if the latter do have a more detailed knowledge. Brendan Edgeworth remarks that:

> One is presented . . . with the professional's world-view as the yardstick of reality. But all levels of society produce, apply and interpret 'the law', and its social existence cannot be identified in totality without examining the entire range of hermeneutical forms associated with it. (B. Edgeworth, 'Legal positivism and the philosophy of language: a critique of H. L. A. Hart's "descriptive sociology"' (1986) 6 LS 115 at p. 138.)

Although, in another context, Hart denies that he is a formalist his general analysis of legal validity and obligation is clearly formal in nature. This, it may be suggested, is the basic reason for the importance of the official view in his theory.

H. L. A. Hart's pre-eminent contribution to positivist legal theory is the understanding of law as a formal system, and the obligation with which he is concerned is that which is recognisable according to the formal criteria adopted within the system. In cases of doubt or dispute the question can only effectively be determined by a court and in this context the formal cognition of judges and officials is decisive. The argument, in short, properly addresses not understanding as such, but authoritative understanding. Viewed in this light the official emphasis is comprehensible, but any implication that general public understanding, at some level, is somehow an optional extra, discounts a major practical aspect of law in operation.

3.3   HART'S ARGUMENT ON RULE SCEPTICISM

Rule scepticism, and its more extreme companion fact scepticism, are fundamental to the discourse of American realist legal theory (see chapter 11). Their broad implication is that, in the first case, perceived rules are little more than rationalisations of what courts have done concealing the real business of legal practice, which is to predict what courts will do in the future. The second approach goes further and suggests that the fact basis of cases is in reality the product of judicial interpretation rather than objective observation. Such views must seem prima facie to be opposed to a rule-based theory such as Hart's. The opposite viewpoint of formalism, on the other hand, is seen as seeking to confer upon rules a certainty in application which they in many cases lack. Hart himself takes a view, suspicious of both types of approach, founded upon the proposition that:

> Formalism and rule scepticism are the Scylla and Charybdis of juristic theory; they are great exaggerations, salutary where they correct each other, and the truth lies between them. (*The Concept of Law*, p. 144.)

The starting-point for Hart's analysis of this point is found in the 'open texture' of law.

Hart argues, incontrovertibly, that language, including legal language, is by its nature often uncertain and therefore leaves room for choices in interpretation and application. Indeed, modern linguistic philosophy, from the later work of Wittgenstein, has tended to emphasise contextual usage rather than core meaning in the analysis of language. In a common law system, not only does statutory language demand the making of choices in its application but the application of case precedents involves a yet wider scope of choice. It is this factor which Hart treats as the 'open texture' of law.

Hart concedes that there is an area of judicial discretion in which judges do in effect have to make choices, at which point some element of rule scepticism may reasonably be adopted. But, Hart also argues that these are 'fringe' instances and that, as for the scope of discretionary decision making by a scorer, referee or umpire in a game, the overwhelming preponderance of cases will in practice be settled by and according to a rule. Thus:

> We are able to distinguish a normal game from the game of 'scorer's discretion' simply because the scoring rule, though it has, like other rules, its area of open texture where the scorer has to exercise a choice, yet has a core of settled meaning. (*The Concept of Law*, p. 140.)

Similarly, Hart argues, the application of law is normally settled by rules even if, in a few atypical cases, the matter falls to judicial discretion. It is important for Hart's theory that the uncertainty implied by judicial discretion should be minimised because it otherwise threatens to subvert the rule-based model which is being advanced. Thus, he states that:

> at the fringe . . . we should welcome the rule sceptic . . . [whilst not being blinded] to the fact that what makes possible . . . striking developments by courts of the most fundamental rules is, in great measure, the prestige gathered by courts from their unquestionably rule-governed operations over the vast, central areas of the law. (*The Concept of Law*, p. 150.)

Hart thus concedes, whilst marginalising, the role of judicial discretion.

Such a position attracts criticism from a number of directions. The American realist 'rule-sceptical' tradition takes, by its nature, a significantly different approach (see chapter 11), albeit with a variety of levels of 'scepticism'. In countering the more extreme forms of scepticism, Karl N. Llewellyn argued that at least at the higher levels of adjudication a form of judicial professionalism introduces a 'reckonability' which somewhat defuses unbounded discretion (K. N. Llewellyn, *The Common Law Tradition: Deciding Appeals* (Boston, Mass: Little, Brown and Co., 1960)). Ronald Dworkin, in contrast, denies that even in 'hard cases', to which rules do not supply a ready answer, judges do not have a 'strong' or absolute 'discretion', but are guided, in particular, by 'principles' which are a foundation for 'rights' (see chapter 9). Having said this, there may in one respect at least be contended to be rather more scope for judicial discretion than either Hart or Dworkin might willingly concede. The point may be illustrated by reference to the rather striking case of *Attorney-General* v *Prince Ernest Augustus of Hanover* [1957] AC 436.

The case turned upon an antique statute, the Princess Sophia Naturalisation Act 1705 (4 & 5 Anne c. 16 also known as 4 Anne c. 4). The 1705 Act, which was repealed and superseded by the British Nationality Act 1948, provided that:

Princess Sophia, Electress and Duchess Dowager of Hanover, and the Issue of her Body, and all Persons lineally descending from her, born or hereafter to be born, be and shall be, to all Intents and Purposes whatsoever, deemed, taken, and esteemed natural-born Subjects of this Kingdom.

The political context was simple. Queen Anne was evidently going to die childless, her heir being thus the Princess Sophia who was the granddaughter of James I and whose son, George I, ultimately succeeded to the throne. The purpose of the Act was to ensure that the next monarch would be British. Prince Ernest August of Hanover was a distant descendant of Princess Sophia but had no proximate connection to the British throne. He claimed under the terms of the Act that he had, immediately prior to the passage of the British Nationality Act 1948, been entitled to British nationality under the 1705 Act and therefore retained it under the 1948 Act. The case passed through the High Court, Court of Appeal and House of Lords. There were only two possible outcomes, either he was or was not entitled to British nationality. In the course of the case two rules of statutory interpretation were applied. The High Court applied the 'literal rule' and held that, as a descendant of the Princess Sophia, the Prince was entitled to nationality. The Court of Appeal applied a form of the 'golden rule' and held that such an outcome would be absurd and that the Act was not intended to apply to a person such as the prince. Before the House of Lords it was pointed out that if all descendants of the princess were entitled to British nationality this would by the 20th century have covered most European royalty, including Kaiser Wilhelm II of Germany. The House of Lords shared the view of the High Court and, applying the 'literal rule', upheld the claim of the prince to British nationality. Whatever view may be taken of this case and its outcome it would appear that there was a choice to be made within an open-textured provision.

It is, perhaps, uncontroversial that the bulk of legal disputes and, certainly, day-to-day legal administration can be settled straightforwardly according to rules. It is also clear that there is some room for choices to be made. Hart, Dworkin and others disagree as to how choices are in fact made where the rules do not supply an answer. Hart's model of discretion and partial concession to rule scepticism are not necessarily a decisive answer but, as he himself states, such cases are on the fringe of his primary concerns. As such they may reasonably be left as an issue better dealt with in another context, notably those of American realist thought and the rights thesis of Dworkin.

3.4 PUBLIC INTERNATIONAL LAW IN HART'S THEORY

It will be recalled that the status of public international law as 'law' was denied by Austin, who preferred to relegate it to a sphere of 'positive morality' (see 2.4). This has led over the years to, arguably rather sterile, debate within positivist theory and amongst public international lawyers.

Hart commences by restating the classical doubt that public international law has a sufficient institutional base realistically to be considered 'law', adding that:

> The absence of these institutions means that the rules for States resemble that simple form of social structure, consisting only of primary rules of obligation, which . . . we are accustomed to contrast with a developed legal system. (*The Concept of Law*, p. 209.)

This refers back to an anthropological argument which has been suggested above to be doubtful (see 3.2.2), but it also refers to a conventional, if again doubtful, comparison between public international and 'primitive' law. This is not, however, the basic thrust of Hart's argument. His concern is rather with the 'binding' or obligatory effect of public international law. Hart argues that whilst the command theory fits international law no better than municipal law, the contention that public international law is no more than a form of moral claim does not, either, fit the usage or discourse of international law. In the end, however, he is constrained to deny that the public international legal system possesses any true rule of recognition which provides general criteria of validity for its rules. He finally notes the argument that some multilateral treaties may bind States which are not expressly party to them and, thus, have a form of 'legislative' effect. This, Hart concedes, may be an element of a nascent rule of recognition. He suggests, therefore, that:

> . . . international law is at present in a stage of transition towards acceptance of this and other forms which would bring it nearer in structure to a municipal system. (*The Concept of Law*, p. 231.)

He adds that although at present the analogy between public international and municipal law may be one of content rather than form:

> . . . no other social rules are so close to municipal law as those of international law. (*The Concept of Law*, p. 231.)

This is an ambivalent position to take and it would appear that public international law fits a little awkwardly into Hart's analysis of legal systems. Quite clearly the standard statement of the sources of public international law, for the purposes of the International Court of Justice, in art. 38 of the Statute of the Court, is not a rule of recognition for Hart's purposes, although the language used implies an assumption of the existence of some such rule. The later form of Kelsenian pure theory (see chapter 8) takes a reverse position from that of Hart and accepts international law as the foundation for the existence of municipal law systems. It is not necessary to go to quite such lengths, however, to wonder whether Hart's doubts about the status of public international law create a difficulty for his theory which might easily be avoided.

The problem appears essentially to be one of institutional comparison, in much the same form as that which arises in the context of Hart's legal anthropology (see 3.2.2). Quite obviously the formal structure and context of application of the norms of public international law are significantly different from those of municipal law, this, in a more extreme form, having been also the root of John Austin's concern in this area (see 2.4). If, however, a functional analysis is adopted, examining not institutional similarities or divergences, but the purpose and operation of norms in the municipal and international norms in their respective contexts, a much stronger case may be made out for the 'legal' nature of the latter. This, perhaps, tips the balance of argument in that it may be contended that public international law is not in a state of transition to something more like a municipal legal system as Hart suggests (*The Concept of Law*, p. 231), but, rather, performs the same function differently but appropriately in the context of a different type of community, that of nations.

3.5   HART AND MORAL ANALYSES OF POSITIVE LAW

The relationship between law and morality, or more accurately between legal validity and moral quality, has posed major questions for jurisprudence over the centuries. The moral criteria for the evaluation of positive law and the implications of their application are the particular concern of 'naturalist' theories (see chapters 4 and 5) but have at various times troubled positivists also. Debate in this context has taken a variety of forms. There has been some concern with the role, if any, which moral criteria of evaluation, or identification, ought to be permitted. This question arose with particular urgency in the earlier part of the 20th century in the particular context of totalitarian abuses of positive law, notably in the Nazi Third Reich and in the former USSR under Stalin. There has also arisen the question of the extent to which positive law may properly be used to enforce moral propositions for their own sake. H. L. A. Hart has made very significant contributions to both of these areas of contention from a positivist perspective.

3.5.1   Abuse of law: the debate between Hart and Fuller

The oppressive or tyrannical use of positive law by a variety of political regimes has not, unfortunately, been confined to any particular historical era. However, the use of law and the legal system in the Nazi Third Reich undoubtedly raised the issue in a very stark and extreme form. Whether or not the Third Reich was a *Rechtsstaat*, in effect a State subject to a rule of law, is a question which raises a number of fundamental jurisprudential issues (see also 5.1.3 and chapter 16). After the Second World War and the collapse of the Third Reich through military defeat, an immediate practical problem was faced in the question of the rectification of specific decisions embodying abuses of legal process under the former regime. In this context a major debate took place between H. L. A. Hart and the procedural naturalist Lon L. Fuller (see 5.1) upon the question of the validity of some or all Nazi laws and legal decisions.

The immediate focus of the debate was one of the so-called 'grudge cases' reconsidered in 1950 (an account of the case is given in H. O. Pappe, 'On the validity of judicial decisions in the Nazi era' (1960) 23 MLR 60). Grudge cases were broadly those in which persons living under Nazi jurisdiction had made use of oppressive laws and procedures for the settlement of personal grudges or ambitions.

The first defendant had in 1944 wished to eliminate her husband, a German soldier, and had to this end reported to the authorities critical remarks which he had made about Hitler whilst on leave from the army. He was charged under laws of 20 December 1934 and 17 August 1938 with making statements critical of the Reich and potentially impairing its defence. He was convicted and condemned to death but was 'reprieved' and sent to the Eastern front. In the event he survived and after the war his wife and the judge who had tried his case were brought to trial upon charges under the 1871 German Criminal Code, para. 239, relating to unlawful deprivation of liberty. The postwar (West) German court found the judge not to be guilty because the decision had been made under a then existing, albeit oppressive and cruel, law. The woman who had reported the victim was, however, found guilty because she had acted from personal malice in a way which was contrary to conscience and thought immoral at the time. The court expressly stated that its decision was not founded upon any idea that the laws under which the victim had in 1944 been convicted were invalid on moral grounds.

Regrettably the argument between Hart and Fuller was founded upon a brief and misleading report of the case ((1950–1) 64 Harv L Rev 1005) which seemed to give the impression that the postwar court had decided that the laws in question were formally invalidated by their immoral substance. For this reason the debate between Hart and Fuller concentrated upon this issue, which forms no part of classical naturalist argument (see chapter 4) and ignored some of the more interesting issues arising from the postwar treatment of grudge cases.

Hart's argument (see H. L. A. Hart, 'Positivism and the separation of law and morals' (1958) 71 Harv L Rev 593) was broadly that the laws made in Nazi Germany, however oppressive or immoral, concorded with the rule of recognition (this was of course prior to the publication of Hart's exploration of such rules in *The Concept of Law*) then applicable and must be considered to have been 'law'. Hart admitted that the actions of grudge informers may well have deserved punishment, but concluded that it would be better in the particular circumstances to enact straightforwardly retrospective penal legislation than to rely upon an invalidating effect of immorality. Fuller on the other hand (Lon L. Fuller, 'Positivism and fidelity to law: a reply to Professor Hart' (1958) 71 Harv L Rev 630), argued that the formalistic conception of the duty to obey law embodied in positivism attempts to isolate legal obligation from all other forms of obligation. In the post-Nazi context, judges, according to Fuller, had no choice but to consider moral questions in their attempt to rebuild a viable legal order.

These arguments are not without interest and importance, but a more useful analytical reference point can be found in a subsequent decision upon very similar facts (an account may be found in H. O. Pappe, 'On the validity of judicial decisions in the Nazi era' (1960) 23 MLR 260 at p. 264). Here the defendant in the postwar trial was charged with unlawful deprivation of liberty and attempted homicide. After an initial acquittal the case went to the West German Federal Supreme Court which quashed the decision and referred the case back to the lower court. The Supreme Court made two fundamentally significant points. First, if the proceedings were improper then the presiding judge was as guilty as the informer who had initiated them. Secondly, there was no need to consider the validity of the Nazi laws in question since even upon their face they had not been correctly applied. The law concerned 'public' statements and if this meant anything at all it must imply a distinction from 'private' statements which would surely include the conversation between spouses here in question. Secondly, even if this point were not well taken, the court had a broad sentencing discretion and to apply the death penalty (later commuted) in a case of this type amounted to a culpable abdication of responsibility.

Thus, the wartime proceedings had been procedurally improper and both the defendant and the judge had a case to answer. The defendant had had, through malicious misuse of process to encompass injury, the *mens rea* of crime which found its *actus reus* in the improper proceedings to which she was an accessory. This line of argument has surely much to commend it in that it relies upon procedural abuses for the resolution of the 'formal' question and these are far from hard to find in Nazi jurisprudence. It is much to be regretted that Hart and Fuller, granted the interest of each in legal systems, did not address the issue at this level.

3.5.2   The enforcement of morality: Hart and Devlin

The use of positive law to enforce moral propositions for their own sake has at various times been a source of controversy. In 1859 John Stuart Mill argued that society has no 'right' to enforce its moral perceptions where their violation would not cause objectively perceptible 'harm' to others (see J. S. Mill, *On Liberty*, ed. G. Himmelfarb (Harmondsworth: Penguin, 1974)). He argued that, in the absence of 'harm', diversity is a positive factor in society which is dangerously inhibited by 'moral' repression. This issue endures in modern debate (see, for example, Stuart Hampshire, 'Public and private morality', in *Public and Private Morality*, ed. Stuart Hampshire (Cambridge: Cambridge University Press, 1978). There remained, however, the difficult question of what precisely constitutes 'harm' for this purpose. Mill's proposition was questioned by Sir James Fitzjames Stephen (J. F. Stephen, *Liberty, Equality, Fraternity* (London: Smith Elgard and Co., 1874)), who argued that society could not safely be precluded from enforcing its morality at 'need', even if it should not always do so.

Hart and Devlin's 'debate' resulted from the publication of the Wolfenden Report (*Report of the Committee on Homosexual Offences and Prostitution* (Cmnd 247) (London: HMSO, 1957)) which recommended that male homosexuality between consenting adults and prostitution, subject to protection of minors, should not be criminal (female homosexuality was anyway not criminal). This recommendation was in due course followed. In his 1958 Maccabean Lecture on Jurisprudence, Lord Devlin took exception not to the Committee's conclusion but to the form of supporting argument it adopted (see P. Devlin (Baron Devlin) *The Enforcement of Morals* (London: Oxford University Press, 1965), especially chs 1 and 6). This was essentially an application of the Millsian 'harm principle' arguing that there are private areas of morality into which the law should not intrude. In response to this Devlin contended broadly that society rests upon the base of a shared morality which is in itself a 'seamless web' and which can be legally defended exactly as society may be defended from subversive action (*The Enforcement of Morals*, pp. 13–14). Like Sir James Fitzjames Stephen before him, Lord Devlin did not argue that society should always enforce all aspects of its moral code, but he did urge that society must always be able to defend itself against a threat to its moral structure felt to be intolerable.

For Devlin the 'morality' in question is a 'jury-box' morality, that of the average 'right-minded' citizen (*The Enforcement of Morals*, p. 15). Devlin admits the obvious potential tension between private inclinations and the 'public' demands of a society and suggests three basic principles in attaining a balance between them. These are: (a) maximum freedom compatible with social integrity, (b) the law should, however, be slow to change its 'moral' stance lest the moral social base be subverted, and (c) privacy should to the greatest possible extent be respected.

This position is in some respects stronger than Hart allows or represented. It is, however, subject to at least two major questions. There is an obvious danger in relying on a simple 'popular' morality as a basis for legal intervention which might simply lead to persecution of the unpopular. Beyond this,

Devlin's argument for moral enforcement actually rests upon an analogy with 'subversion', in particular with treason, which is surely a refined form of 'harm' principle.

In response to Lord Devlin's argument, Hart defended the libertarian position (see H. L. A. Hart, *Law, Liberty and Morality* (London: Oxford University Press, 1963)). He criticises a tradition of 'judicial moralism' (*Law, Liberty and Morality*, p. 7) citing the early remark of Lord Mansfield in *Jones v Randall* (1774) Lofft 383, at p. 385, that:

> Whatever is *contra bonos mores est decorum*, the principles of our law prohibit, and the King's court as the general censor and guardian of the public manners, is bound to restrain and punish.

He cites *Shaw v Director of Public Prosecutions* [1962] AC 220 as an example of the same principle. There a charge of 'conspiracy to corrupt public morals' had been upheld in a case involving publication of what amounted to a directory of prostitutes. In more recent times some of the views expressed by the Court of Appeal in *R v Brown* [1992] QB 491, a case involving charges of assault in relation to consensual acts of homosexual sado-masochism, seem to proceed from a somewhat similar base of moral disapprobation as such.

Hart proceeded to distinguish between 'moderate' and 'extreme' varieties of the moral thesis, suggesting that Stephen represented the latter and Devlin the former. He identified moderation with emphasis upon the value of morality as a 'social cement' and extremism with the enforcement of morality as an end in itself. It must, however, be doubted whether Stephen could fairly thus be categorised as 'extreme'. Hart's central criticism of Devlin's position is, however, much more soundly based. He attacks the populist model of morality partly upon the basis of the importance of minority rights. Thus:

> The central mistake is a failure to distinguish the acceptable principle that political power is best entrusted to the majority from the unacceptable claim that what the majority do with that power is beyond criticism and must never be resisted. (*Law, Liberty and Morality*, p. 79).

Devlin did not actually quite claim this. However, the question of the morality to be enforced is a serious one and the peril suggested by Hart does seem to lurk within the model of popular morality.

Finally, Hart recognises the need for enhanced legal protection of those who are too young, ill or otherwise hindered from fully voluntary decision-making to protect themselves effectively. This is not, however, a moral argument as such, merely an admission of a special application of a harm principle. In particular, Hart denies, with Mill, any right to protection from being shocked.

There is clearly a major distinction between the foundations of Hart's and Devlin's arguments upon this issue. However, one may reasonably ask whether the practical applications of moderate moralism and Hart's qualified liberalism would in most cases be far divergent. A final question arises in the problem of whether acts tending to degrade human beings, even voluntarily, might justifiably be constrained (see R. Dworkin, 'Is there a right to pornography?' (1981) 1 Oxford J Legal Stud 177 and T. R. S. Allan, 'A right to pornography?' (1983) 3 Oxford J Legal Stud 376). In answer to this conundrum one might turn to Immanuel Kant's 'principle of right', in effect that humanity should always be respected for its own sake and not used as a means to some other end (see 4.6).

3.5.3   Hart's minimum content of natural law

Neither Hart nor any other mainstream positivist denies that important moral questions may be asked about positive law and its application. However, insofar as positivism claims to be able to supply a comprehensive account of law the impact of moral questions upon the assessment of 'law' quality causes difficulty. Hart seeks to resolve this issue by introducing a 'minimum content of natural law' into his positivist theory, avoiding what he perceives as the errors found in the adoption of moral criteria of validation. He states that:

. . . some very obvious generalizations – indeed truisms – concerning human nature . . ., show that as long as these hold good, there are certain rules of conduct which any social organisation must contain if it is to be viable. Such rules do in fact constitute a common element in the law and convention morality of all societies [which distinguish them] as different forms of social control. (*The Concept of Law*, p. 188.)

It would be difficult to dissent very strongly from this proposition. In most, if not all, countries fundamental moral norms are enshrined in law, e.g., as basic criminal taboos. The proscription of murder is an obvious example and it would, indeed, be difficult to imagine a viable society in which murder was compulsory rather than forbidden. It may be added that many such provisions not only seek to penalise deviance but, equally importantly, to reaffirm the moral base of the social order. This point leads back to some extent to Lord Devlin's argument upon the enforcement of morality through law (see 3.5.2).

Hart's 'minimum content of natural law' rests, as Hart puts it, upon:

The general . . . argument . . . that without such a content laws and morals could not forward the minimum purpose of survival which men have in associating with each other. (*The Concept of Law*, p. 189.)

Hart suggests five 'truisms' which underlie the content of any viable set of legal rules. These are:

(a)   Human vulnerability, which dictates the proscription of the major crimes of violence.

(b)   Approximate equality, meaning that although human beings have different capacities no person is so overwhelmingly powerful as to be able to sustain permanent dominance by individual effort. Thus, there is a need for a 'system of mutual forbearance and compromise which is the base of both legal and moral obligation' (*The Concept of Law*, p. 191). This is clearly a recasting of the basic social contractarian model of Thomas Hobbes (see 4.5.1).

(c)   Limited altruism, which makes rules of mutual forbearance necessary to secure a balance between altruistic and selfish inclinations in a social pattern of life.

(d)   Limited resources, which, since necessities are not infinitely available and can be won only through labour, demands some system of entitlement to property.

(e)   Limited understanding and strength of will, which tempt individuals into deviant or antisocial conduct for short-term personal gain and render sanctions necessary. Hart is, however, careful to make clear that these sanctions are not the source of obligation but merely a defence against atypical deviance.

The significance which Hart attributes to the satisfaction of these basic requirements is considerable. He states that:

> If the system is fair and caters genuinely for the vital interests of all those from whom it demands obedience, it may . . . retain [their] allegiance . . . for most of the time, and will accordingly be stable. [But] . . . a narrow and exclusive system run in the interests of the dominant group . . . may be made continually more repressive and unstable with the latent threat of upheaval. (*The Concept of Law*, p. 197.)

This is a pragmatic argument to the effect that laws which fail to serve their basic social function(s) will ultimately cease to be viable and will, in one way or another, be displaced.

This leaves the question of the relation between moral or ethical judgment and the law at any given time. In a broader context R. W. M. Dias suggests that the answer lies in 'time-frames', i.e., that positivism provides an explanation of the immediate identification of valid law but that naturalism supplies an element which may in the longer term act to vitiate bad laws, through political processes or otherwise (see R. W. M. Dias, *Jurisprudence*, 5th ed. (London: Butterworths, 1985), p. 500). This, however still leaves open the question of the relation of naturalist criteria to legal definition at the point when, and if, they finally do operate. Hart approaches the matter differently and distinguishes between 'wide' and 'narrow' views of the matter. He identifies the former with the view of a bad provision that 'This is law but too iniquitous to obey or apply' and the latter with the conclusion that 'This is in no sense law' (*The Concept of Law*, p. 205). Not surprisingly, the narrow view is rejected by Hart in preference for the wide alternative. However, the narrow view as Hart describes it appears to be a caricature of the arguments of classical naturalism (see 4.1), which actually tend much more towards Hart's wide model. It may strongly be argued that naturalist moral or ethical criteria apply not to the assessment of formal validity and the formal obligations that go with it, but to the moral quality of formally valid law and the extent to which moral obligation may, or may not, also be associated with it. The resolution of that issue rests upon the interaction of a great many factors which cannot be bound within the narrow limits of legal formalism.

Hart's naturalism is indeed a minimum and is founded in its essentials upon a limited form of social-contractarianism, although not relying upon overt social-contractarian rhetoric. The truisms upon which it rests are in themselves unexceptionable but it may be doubted whether they are sufficient to answer the actual range of naturalist questions. Ultimately it may be asked whether the minimum content of natural law is actually necessary in the context of the positivist theory which Hart advances. It seems to deal with issues which are separate from the main concerns of the theory and to do so in a very summary form. This is not a criticism of the admission of the existence of moral questions, merely a doubt that the minimum content adds much to the theoretical context in which it is set. This in turn leads to a more general view of the place of Hart's concept in general legal theory.

3.6   THE SIGNIFICANCE OF HART'S THEORY

H. L. A. Hart set out to produce a modified and improved positivist legal theory. The theory which he in fact advances undoubtedly makes a very important and helpful contribution to legal analysis, but, like all theories, should be understood and applied in its proper context. It was suggested at the outset that the infelicities which Hart identifies in the classical positivist theories of Bentham and Austin largely result from a mistaken endeavour, on their part, to force the phenomena of positive law into their format as a comprehensive model of jurisprudence. The idea of coercive sovereign command, which is the basis of classical positivism, forms one rather obvious element of law. There are, however, many other elements which go to make up what Hart properly identifies as the vitally important obligatory characteristic of law.

Hart's model brings out and analyses the equally important element of what may be termed 'formal obligation', those obligations which are detected and implemented actually or potentially through courts. A viable legal system will, in one way or another, include both elements. The internal aspect identified by Hart and the official interpretation of law in practice are essential, but so too is the potential for coercion of the deviant, as Hart concedes in setting out his 'truisms'. A system in which it was accepted that contracts are always observed unless one of the parties finds it convenient to default would obviously harbour a very serious defect.

Beyond this there is also the question of moral obligation. Was Pastor Niemöller in Nazi Germany right to defy the unconstrained power of the State, leaving aside, for the moment, the question of the legality of the provisions concerned. This is not an issue which can be answered either formally or by reference to the coercive, or rewarding, potential of the State. It is, in short a moral or ethical question falling within the concern of naturalist theories in their own right rather than as an adjunct to a positivist theory. In conclusion, it may be suggested that Hart sets out a model of law which deals with a very important aspect of the operation of law and which is in that context both constructive and helpful. It does not, any more than did the work of Bentham and Austin, supersede other areas of jurisprudence, it should rather be read in parallel with them in building up a model of the unavoidably complex realities of law.

3.7 FURTHER READING

Devlin, P., *The Enforcement of Morals* (London: Oxford University Press, 1965).

Fuller, Lon L., 'Positivism and fidelity to law: a reply to Professor Hart' (1958) 71 Harv L Rev 630.

Hart, H. L. A., *The Concept of Law* (Oxford: Clarendon Press, 1961).

Hart, H. L. A., *Law, Liberty and Morality* (London: Oxford University Press, 1963).

Hart, H. L. A., 'Positivism and the separation of law and morals' (1958) 71 Harv L Rev 593; also in Dworkin, R. M. (ed.) *The Philosophy of Law* (London: Oxford University Press, 1977), ch. 1.

MacCormick, N., *H. L. A. Hart* (London: Edward Arnold, 1981).

Moles, R. N., *Definition and Rule in Legal Theory* (Oxford: Basil Blackwell, 1987), chs 3 and 8.

CHAPTER FOUR

Classical Naturalism

The positivist theories of law which were predominant in conventional Anglo-American jurisprudence for much of the past 150 years, and to a considerable extent still remain so, are broadly characterised by an insistence upon the autonomy of law and legal phenomena. In particular, laws are held to be recognised only according to formal criteria and not by reference to moral or ethical criteria of identification or to the satisfaction of social expectation. The separation of 'is' and 'ought' emphasised by David Hume and developed in the context of legal theory by Jeremy Bentham, considered in chapter 2 above, is held by many positivists to be a fatal flaw in classical naturalist arguments. The group of theories termed 'naturalist' contend, in a variety of ways, that law is to be identified by reference to moral or ethical, as well as formal, criteria of identification and in this are criticised for confusing the categories of 'is' and 'ought to be'. The thrust of this argument was most graphically stated by Austin, who remarked that:

> The most pernicious laws . . . are continually enforced as laws by judicial tribunals. Suppose an act [that is] innocuous . . . be prohibited by the sovereign under the penalty of death; if I commit this act, I shall be tried and condemned, and if I object . . . that [this] is contrary to the law of God . . ., the Court of Justice will demonstrate the inconclusiveness of my reasoning by hanging me up, in pursuance of the law of which I have impugned the validity. (J. Austin, *The Province of Jurisprudence Determined* (London: Weidenfeld & Nicolson, 1954), p. 185.)

From this type of view there has developed a so-called 'naturalist–positivist debate' which may be, and is here, contended to be a sterile argument founded upon a simple misunderstanding.

The root of the misunderstanding lies in the idea that the two forms of theory are advancing different answers to the same question about the nature of law. When it is argued that naturalism and positivism are, unsurprisingly, giving different answers to different questions, the so-called 'debate' can be seen as a distraction from the consideration of much more genuine questions about the nature and operation of positive law.

4.1 THE CENTRAL CONCERNS OF NATURALIST THEORIES

Naturalist thought covers a vast historical spectrum from the Old Testament to the present day, but in its classical forms up to the late 18th century, which underlie the modern revival of this type of theory, certain central concerns may readily be identified. By reference to the work of the great 13th-century theorist St Thomas Aquinas, it has been remarked elsewhere that naturalist thought:

> . . . implies not that 'bad' laws cannot be made and imposed but that such laws are defective in being wrongly made and are thus limited or even entirely lacking in their claim to be obeyed as a matter of conscience. This is in fact a concern with the moral nature of the power to make laws rather than with the formal identification of State prescription. (H. McCoubrey, *The Development of Naturalist Legal Theory* (London: Croom Helm, 1987), p. xii.)

Naturalist argument is thus not directed to the formal identification of positive law by courts, but to the limits of the right of governments to make laws and the implications for the degree of the obligation to obey associated with law, especially when such limits are ignored. In somewhat more modern terms, the twin pillars of naturalist argument may be said to be, on the one hand, a 'proper purposes' doctrine in lawmaking, and, on the other, the nature and limitations of the obligation to obey law. Austin was right: he might indeed be punished for an innocuous or even beneficial act pursuant to 'law' recognisable, in a positivist context, as such. That observation is not contradicted by the proposition that the law concerned was improperly made, defective in the obligation it imposed, and ripe for change. The problem which naturalists must address is, of course, that of the limits of their argument. Jeremy Bentham stated the dangers in 1776 in an attack upon the Introduction to Sir William Blackstone's *Commentaries*. He wrote of naturalism that:

> the natural tendency of such doctrine is to impel a man, by the force of conscience, to rise up in arms against any law whatever that he happens not to like. (J. Bentham, *A Fragment on Government* (Oxford: Basil Blackwell, 1948), p. 93.)

Naturalist argument in fact goes to some length to avoid any such counsel of anarchy and, although classical arguments were set down in eras remote from our own, their basic concerns are in very many respects thoroughly 'modern'. For this reason they continue to merit close attention.

4.2 THE STRANDS OF CLASSICAL NATURALISM

Over the long development of classical naturalist thought a wide variety of theory and context may be found, but two principal categories of approach are immediately obvious. These relate to the perceived source of the moral or ethical evaluation of positive law being addressed. Some theorists have sought criteria of evaluation in perceived or revealed higher sources of morality, religious or otherwise. Others have found the model for 'good law' in rational observation of human society. There is, of course, no necessary contradiction between these two ideas, indeed some theorists have incorporated both elements, including, for example, St Thomas Aquinas. Nonetheless these two elements are an important factor in considering the range of theories. For present purposes it is convenient to concentrate upon three broad strands in the development of classical naturalism, these being (a) the classical Greek theories of law, (b) the Judaeo-Christian approaches, notably the technical development in legal theory of the High Middle Ages, and (c) the developments of the 18th-century Age of Reason which related in a variety of ways to both (a) and (b) and also look forward to much more recent developments.

In dealing with all these theories it is important to bear in mind that although the context in which they were advanced was, to varying degrees, distanced from our own, the problems they addressed are still with us. Walled cities and modern suburbs have, from the viewpoint of legal theory, more in common than might at first be thought.

4.3 CLASSICAL GREEK NATURALISM: PLATO AND ARISTOTLE

For the present purpose the most important contributions to classical Hellenistic legal theory were made by Plato (c. 427–347 BC) and Aristotle (384–322 BC). The latter was the pupil of the former, who had, in turn, been taught by Socrates. Their views differed in certain important respects and this difference was to be reflected also in much later developments in legal theory. Both were, however, generally rationalist in their approach in that they considered 'good' and 'bad' laws, and the appropriate reactions to them, to be discoverable by rational observation. The ultimate source of concepts of good and evil, whether divine or the product of the 'natural' forces acting upon the human condition, was not a matter of importance in their legal theory.

4.3.1 Platonic idealism and legalism

Plato was an 'idealist' who taught that the real world should be moulded to conform to a better 'ideal' reality which is open to the understanding of human reason. Plato did not speculate upon the source of this higher ideal, nor did he consider it to be open to the understanding of people generally. Instead, he considered that it could be understood only by persons of suitably trained ability. In the *Republic* he set out a model for the perfect society which he founded not upon a rule of laws but upon a form of 'benevolent dictatorship' through the government of a 'philosopher king'. This Utopian ruler was to be a person able to perceive and comprehend the ideal reality in order to relate it to the actual State, having:

> . . . a list of characteristics, which all go together, and which the mind must have if it is to have a sufficiently full apprehension of reality.
>   . . . good memory, readiness to learn, breadth of vision and grace, and be a friend of truth, justice, courage, and self-control. (Plato, *Republic*, 486–7, transl. D. Lee, 2nd ed. (Harmondsworth: Penguin, 1974), p. 280.)

Such rulers were to be trained through a rigorous, if less than wholly practical, education and would then proceed upon the rationally perceived dictates of ultimate virtue. Their rule would thus not be encumbered by legal forms but moulded by wisdom and accepted through the very evidence of its excellence. Law as such was conceded little or no role, being considered a crudely inflexible means of transmitting the requirements of virtuous reason. The viability of this programme must be doubted in practice and many have urged that the argument of the *Republic* should not be taken as a practically intended manifesto. Trevor J. Saunders remarks that:

> It makes much better sense to think of the *Republic* as an extreme statement, designed to shock, of the consequences of an uncompromising application of certain political principles – in fact, as an *un*attainable ideal. (T. J. Saunders, 'Introduction' in Plato, *Laws* (Harmondsworth: Penguin, 1975), p. 28.)

Plato did in fact undertake some attempts to give rulers philosophical training, notably in the case of Dionysius II of Syracuse, who, although he respected Plato, showed little evident aptitude for idealised philosopher-kingship. A distant political parallel may here be drawn between Platonism and Confucian thought. Confucius (K'ung-Fu-tzu, 551–479 BC) also taught that rulers should mould their conduct to a perceived virtue and thereby acquire for their rule the 'mandate of heaven' and emphasised example and the dictates of *li* (rites), rather than the coercive demands of *fa* (positive law). He commented upon the legendary ruler Yao that:

Sublime, indeed was he. 'There is no greatness like the greatness of heaven', yet Yao could copy it. (Confucius, *Analects*, 8.19, transl. A. Waley (London: Unwin Hyman, 1988).)

The Confucian scholar Mencius (Meng K'e) wrote later that:

> . . . only the benevolent man is fit to be in high position. For a cruel man to be in high position is for him to disseminate his wickedness among the people. (Mencius, *Mencius*, transl. D. C. Lau (Harmondsworth: Penguin, 1970), 4A, 1.)

There is here more than a slight echo of the Platonic philosopher-king, the more so when it is borne in mind that when, some time after Confucius's death, Confucianism was adopted as the official ideology of Imperial China by the Han dynasty, law was relegated to a subordinate position as a means for the punishment of malefactors rather than for the guidance of the well-intentioned. Confucius himself had disparaged law as a means of dispute resolution, remarking that:

> I could try a civil suit as well as anyone. But better still to bring it about that there were no civil suits! (Confucius, *Analects*, 12.13, transl. A. Waley.)

Official Confucianism was, however, compromised by a number of other influences which introduced more than a slight element of harsh reality to Imperial Chinese government.

Plato himself advanced a more practical model in the *Laws*, which purports to set out a code for the fictional Athenian colony of Magnesia. As a means of virtuous instruction, a legal code was obviously seen by Plato as a second best in comparison with the rule of the, elusive, philosopher king. None the less the laws are advanced as a form of regulation which although authoritarian should not be tyrannical, indeed they are presented as being as much didactic as coercive. Plato urges therefore that laws should not only compel but also persuade, commenting that:

> . . . no legislator ever seems to have noticed that in spite of its being open to them to use two methods . . ., compulsion and persuasion . . ., they . . . never mix in persuasion with force when they brew their laws. . . .
>
> It seems obvious . . . [that the reason for the legislator giving a] persuasive address was to make the person to whom he promulgated his law . . . [have a] greater readiness to learn. (Plato, *Laws*, 722–3, transl. T. J. Saunders, revised reprint (Harmondsworth: Penguin, 1976), pp. 184–5.)

The laws are then considered a vehicle not only for coercive control but also for education in virtue. It is thus presumed that the laws themselves will be 'good', in inculcating a rationally perceived model of virtuous living, which leads to the question of the appropriate response when the laws are not in fact so designed or administered.

4.3.2 Plato and the obligation to obey

Plato considered this question at length, in the context of the trial and execution of his own teacher Socrates (469–399 BC), in the works which have been collected and published in English as *The Last Days of Socrates*. The teaching of Socrates was offensive in a number of respects to the Athenian establishment of the day and he was eventually charged with impiety and corruption of youth, in effect sedition, and brought to trial. He was convicted and condemned to death but execution was delayed upon ritual grounds during the ceremony of the 'mission to Delos', with the implication that if Socrates, a well-known philosopher, were to escape and flee into exile he would at once relieve Athens of the irritation of his teaching and the odium of bringing about his death. In *The Last Days of Socrates*, Plato purports to present statements and conversations of Socrates relating to law and the duty of obedience. In fact he is setting out developed 'Socratic' arguments upon these points in the form of a monologue and three dialogues in the setting of Socrates's trial and execution. Two sections are of immediate interest, the *Apology*, which is an idealised representation of Socrates's contentions before the Athenian tribunal, and the *Crito*, which is represented as a dialogue between Crito and Socrates, who is imprisoned and awaiting execution, upon the arguments for escape which Socrates rejects in an analysis of the nature and extent of the duty to obey positive law. Both sections deal explicitly with the problem of obligation in relation to a 'bad' law, or a law 'badly' administered.

In the *Apology*, Socrates is represented as arguing that the State has no right to demand that a person commit evil, and where this is in fact demanded the only honourable course is refusal. He gives as an example an order given to him and others during the oligarchic rule of the '30 tyrants' to arrest Leon of Salamis in order that he might be unjustly executed. Socrates alone refused and argued that had not the '30 tyrants' then been overthrown he would himself have been put to death (Plato, *Apology*, 31D–33B, transl. H. Tredennick, in *The Last Days of Socrates*, revised reprint (Harmondsworth: Penguin, 1969), p. 65). One may argue about the formal status of particular instructions by the State (see A. D. Woozley, *Law and Obedience. The Arguments of Plato's* Crito (London: Duckworth, 1979), pp. 55–8), but it would seem clear that Socrates denies the right of the State to command injustice and it is difficult to imagine that the formal context of the command would be sufficient to create such a 'right'. Socrates does not, however, deny that the State can in practice wreak injustice – Leon of Salamis was, after all, executed. The point of the argument is made clear by Socrates's statement after his own condemnation that:

> . . . the difficulty is not so much to escape death; the real difficulty is to escape from doing wrong. . . . When I leave this court I shall go away condemned . . . to death, but [my accusers] will go away convicted by Truth herself of depravity and wickedness. (Plato, *Apology*, 38A–39D, transl. H. Tredennick, in *The Last Days of Socrates*, p. 73.)

If, upon Socrates's argument in the *Apology*, there can be no ethical obligation to do wrong at the behest of the State, a clear distinction is drawn between such a case and the obligation which arises where the State, through its law, does not command wrong of an individual but actually does wrong to him or her. That is to say, where the individual is not sought to be made an actor in 'legal' wrongdoing, but is the victim thereof. This is the subject of the dialogue in the *Crito*.

In the *Crito* three grounds for an obligation to comply with the law are set out in the course of an argument presented as a hypothetical discussion between Socrates and the personified laws of Athens. These arguments have a considerable social-contractarian element and may be seen, in some respects, as precursors of 17th and 18th-century thought and, indeed, of certain modern theories. The first is an overtly paternalist argument, making a clear comparison between the relationship of parent and child and that of State and citizen (Plato, *Crito*, 50E–51C, transl. H. Tredennick, in *The Last Days of Socrates*, p. 91). In essence the individual is argued to have an obligation to obey arising from gratitude for the law maintaining a system in which he or she has chosen to reside, thereby acknowledging its authority. This argument falls somewhat oddly upon modern ears, but there is also advanced a more general social-contractarian argument founded upon voluntary residence in a State. As the personified laws are made to contend:

> . . . whoever . . . stays [in the State] . . ., seeing the way in which we decide our cases in court and the other ways in which we manage our city, we say he has thereby, by his act of staying, agreed with us that he will do what we demand of him. (Plato, *Crito*, 51D–E, transl. A. D. Woozley, in A. D. Woozley, *Law and Obedience. The Arguments of Plato's* Crito (London: Duckworth, 1979), p. 152.)

This is a frequently encountered form of argument in favour of an obligation to obey the law. It rests upon the assumption that the individual is free to depart to some other State, and legal system, but having not done so and continued to take the benefits of the system in question, he or she is properly taken to have accepted an obligation of obedience. A. D. Woozley draws a parallel with one response to protestors against the Vietnam War in the USA under the Johnson and Nixon presidencies, 'America – love it or leave it' (*Law and Obedience. The Arguments of Plato's* Crito, p. 81). The most severe form of argument in this part of the *Crito* is that by disobeying, in Socrates's case by escaping, an individual attempts to destroy both the law and the social fabric which it supports and which – by remaining in the State – that individual must be taken to have accepted whilst it was of benefit to her or him. Thus the personified laws of Athens are made to ask Socrates straightforwardly:

> Do you intend anything else by this [disobedience] . . . than to destroy both . . . the laws and the entire city – at least as far as you can? Or do you think it possible for that city to exist and not be overthrown in which the decisions of the courts . . . are set aside and made ineffective [by private citizens]? (Plato, *Crito*, 50B, transl. A. D. Woozley, in A. D. Woozley, *Law and Obedience. The Arguments of Plato's* Crito, p. 150.)

This is, of course, closely parallelled by Bentham's denunciation of the tendencies of naturalist argument in general, to which reference has been made above.

These arguments leave open to the individual residing in a State of whose laws he or she does not approve only three permissible options. These are (a) to persuade the State to amend the law or laws in question, (b) to move to some other, and more acceptably governed, State, or (c) to remain in the territory and obey (Plato, *Crito*, 51D–52A). In short, options of persuasion, departure or obedience. The departure referred to is one admitted by the state and not an illegal 'escape' such as Crito is made to urge upon Socrates.

Such conclusions rest upon two important assumptions about the nature of the State in question. It is firstly assumed that some form of 'persuasion', whether by personal contention or through participation in a political process, is possible. Secondly, it is presumed that 'legitimate' departure to some other State is possible. The first condition will almost certainly not be met by modern totalitarian States, whose laws are likely to be most particularly objectionable. The second will, in any modern setting, present greater difficulties than Socrates would have encountered in moving to some other neighbouring small city-state. Whether or not Socrates's arguments for obedience are weakened or even vitiated by the absence of these conditions is not specified in the text of the *Crito*. It would seem, however, curious to argue that the potential victim of genocide, e.g., in the Third Reich, who can manifestly neither persuade nor depart should therefore submit willingly to slaughter.

There is an apparent inconsistency in the argument for disobedience found in the *Apology* and that for obedience found in the *Crito* (this is explored in

A. D. Woozley, *Law and Obedience. The Arguments of Plato's* Crito, pp. 17–27). However, it is arguable that this may be resolved by drawing the distinction between a duty to do no wrong to others and a duty to accept an unjust infliction pursuant to an obligation already accepted. Plato's argument denies the right of the State to command evildoing, but it also denies the right of an individual to refuse submission when wrongful acts are commanded by the law to be done to him or her, subject, perhaps, to the availability of the options of persuasion and (prior) departure.

4.3.3 The teleological analysis of Aristotle

Although Plato emphasised the importance of the didactic element of positive law, he ultimately considered humankind to be perversely inclined and in need of authoritarian guidance from a philosopher king or, at least, an enlightened legislator who, by reason of superior wisdom and rigorous training, had a privileged insight into the ideal condition. Aristotle, in contrast with Plato, taught that human beings have an inherent potential for good, the achievement of which it is the proper function of the State to facilitate. In this he saw properly conceived laws as a better instrument for the inculcation of virtue than any realistically probable form of autocratic or oligarchic rule. This idea of the proper purpose of law derives from a teleological analysis of the human condition. Aristotelian teleology teaches that all things have a potential for development specific to their nature, the achievement of which is its particular 'good'. Thus, the 'good' of an acorn is to develop into an oak tree. Anything which assists this process is 'good' for the acorn, anything which is a hindrance thereto is 'bad' for it. The case of humankind is, of course, more complex, primarily by reason of the attribute of rationality which confers powers of choice which may be exercised for good or ill. In the *Politics*, Aristotle argued that one of the products of reason is the nature of the human being as a *politikon zōon* (Aristotle, *Politics*, 1253a.7), a 'political animal', combining for mutual life in societies of which the highest and most complex is the State. A 'good' law is then one which enables its subjects, as social creatures, to achieve their maximum potential appropriate development and in this, as for Plato, there is clearly a large element of moral education. The legislators who are to draft such laws will clearly require extensive training, much in the manner of their Platonic counterparts, even if the substance of perceived virtue is much more accessible in the Aristotelian model.

Interestingly, in the *Nichomachean Ethics*, Aristotle appears to concede the existence of a morality higher than that embodied in 'good' laws. This is expressed as a distinction between universal justice and that embodied in particular provisions. Aristotle indicates that this is not a different order of justice but an equitable standard which the law itself should reflect but which may also be used to correct difficulties which may arise from the unfairness of particular applications of rules which are 'good' as general provisions. Thus it is stated in the *Nichomachean Ethics* that:

> . . . equity, although just, and better than a kind of justice, is not better than absolute justice only than the error due to generalisation. . . . it is a rectification of law in so far as law is defective on account of its generality. (Aristotle, *Ethics*, transl. J. A. K. Thomson, revised H. Tredennick (Harmondsworth: Penguin, 1976), p. 200.)

The question of obligation and the associated problem of the 'bad' law is little considered by Aristotle, which is not, perhaps, surprising in a work primarily concerned with the identification of the 'proper' uses of law and legislative power. In the Aristotelian scheme, however, it would seem that the citizens were to be educated in the constitutional structures of their State whatever its moral qualities, leaving, in case of bad, or badly administered laws, only the resorts admitted by the arguments advanced by Plato, through Socrates.

We must also remember that some of the, to modern eyes, seeming curiosities of Platonic and Aristotelian analysis arise from the political context in which they were advanced. The ancient Greek city-states were, by modern standards, extremely small political units, which were yet further reduced, for present purposes, when it is borne in mind that the politically enfranchised citizen body constituted a relatively small proportion of the total population. In such contexts, arguments of individual persuasion and relatively free departure to a more congenial State have more practical merit than they might in a large modern democracy, to say nothing of a modern totalitarian State.

Confrontation with problems of scale and diversity of traditions within larger political groupings were forced upon the ancient Hellenistic world by the massive military expansion undertaken by Alexander of Macedon, Alexander the Great, whose tutor had been Aristotle. One fruit of this development was the rise of Stoic philosophy, which taught that there is a rationally observable higher order, a cosmic reason, which may be appreciated by all peoples, not just a privileged 'civilised' few, and that 'good' local laws made by any particular State should conform to this wisdom in order to guarantee, or establish, the natural and rational order of human social life.

The apparent universalism of this theory held obvious attractions for the Roman Empire with its vast and diverse territories and was the foundation for the work of the most important pre-Christian Roman legal theorist, Cicero (106–43 BC). Cicero saw law as a rational ordinance governing human conduct which at the level of positive enactment, termed the *lex vulgus*, was essentially an exercise of political power which might or might not be appropriate in terms of the advancement of its proper purposes. As in earlier theories, in their different ways, understanding of such 'proper purposes' was to be derived from insight into a higher rationality insofar as it relates to the human condition. For Cicero, such cosmic reason, the *lex caelestis*, was a divine law but one accessible in its relevant parts to the human mind, through rational insight and enquiry. Such perceptions were then considered 'natural law', the *lex naturae*, and it is this which Cicero advances as the proper model for the making of laws (Cicero, *De Legibus*, 1.56).

It was, significantly, accepted that the *lex naturae* might find different applications in the practical circumstances of different peoples, leaving, nonetheless, a common structure of basic principle. In Roman practice this idea found expression, rather literally, in the concept of a *ius gentium*, thought to be a body of legal principles common to all peoples, as compared with the *ius civile* which was the particular law of a given State, especially of the Roman Empire. The moral quality and claims of all the practical variants would, however, rest upon concordance with the *lex naturae*. The *lex vulgus* might, of course, in all too many cases be, in varying degrees, questionable upon this evaluation. For Cicero, as for other classical writers, the judgment thus made was an assessment of quality which might have important implications for individual action but would not compromise the claim of the *lex vulgus* to any formal status as positive law.

In many ways this final phase of development of classical Graeco-Roman legal theory was readily adaptable to the revolution in thought which followed inevitably from the adoption of Christianity as the official religion of the Roman Empire by the Emperor Constantine the Great in AD 312. This policy change necessitated a fusion between the apparently very different Judaeo-Christian and Hellenistic traditions of jurisprudence, which continues, directly and indirectly, to have a marked influence today.

4.4   THE JUDAEO-CHRISTIAN IMPACT: AUGUSTINE AND AQUINAS

The ancient Judaic tradition of jurisprudence appears to be much more absolute in its claims than any of the Hellenistic approaches. The law stated in the Pentateuch, the first five books of the Old Testament, is not represented as some higher standard by reference to which the quality of positive legal enactments might be evaluated. The written law, the Torah, is represented straightforwardly as a statement of substantive law authorised by the will of God stated to Moses on Mount Sinai (Exodus 20:1 to 21). A very detailed legal code is set out in Exodus 21:1 to 22:17. The law set out in the Old Testament was not, of course, wholly static, it represents the developing needs of a people engaged in the extended processes of settlement and urbanisation. It is important also to notice that, whilst the moral authority of this law is attributed to divine origin, it is not represented merely as an external or arbitrary imposition but, on the contrary, as a prescription offered to, and accepted by, the people. In Exodus 24:3 we are told (in the Authorised Version) that:

> . . . the people answered with one voice, and said, All the words which the Lord hath said we will do.

The argument is thus, in effect, that an 'offer' was made by God and 'accepted' by the people, leading to an analysis which might, with many qualifications, be described as a form of 'social contract' with God. This is, however, quite different from the Platonic contractarian argument considered above in two vital respects. First, the higher law is accepted once and for all as a conscious submission to authority. Secondly, the higher law is not seen merely as a standard of evaluation but as a concrete divine prescription, violation of which would constitute an abomination. It is clear from various incidents recounted in the Old Testament that disaster was considered potentially to follow both for those enacting abominable human laws in defiance of the Torah and also for those obeying them. It may be added in parenthesis that an attempt is made in Judaic jurisprudence to circumvent the inherent inflexibility of holy laws – divine prescription can hardly be subject to revision – through the use of the body of scholarly interpretation in the Halacha. This is said, ingeniously if not wholly satisfactorily, to have the same authority as the Torah, because a right interpretation is, by definition, inseparable from the original proposition to which it relates. There is an interesting distinction between this and the way in which this issue is sought to be resolved in Islamic jurisprudence (see chapter 6).

Judaic jurisprudence undergoes significant change in a Christian context, by reference, in particular, to the doctrine of grace, but this falls beyond the remit of the present discussion. The idea of concrete and divinely authorised standards remains, nonetheless, a central concept. Christianity's change in AD 312 from intermittently persecuted sect to official religion rendered imperative an accommodation between the moral teaching and tradition of the Church and the secular institutions of the Empire by which it had now been embraced. This initiated a process which was completed only in the High Middle Ages, long after the fall of the Roman Empire in the West. The conclusions reached formed the basis of Western legal theory until the upheavals of the 16th and 17th centuries and retain an important, if less overt, influence even at the present time.

The early stage of the process of fusion is best represented in the work of St Augustine of Hippo, and the later, medieval, phase by that of St Thomas Aquinas. The distinction between the two theories rests in part upon the classical models with which they worked. At the time of St Augustine the works of Aristotle had been lost, so he adopted an approach of Christian Platonism. When Aquinas wrote, many of the works of Aristotle had been rediscovered, allowing in a number of respects a more subtle Christian adaption of classical theory.

4.4.1 Christian Platonism: St Augustine of Hippo

St Augustine (345–430), the Bishop of Hippo near Carthage in North Africa, had, before his conversion to Christianity, been a teacher of rhetoric in Milan and was therefore well qualified to attempt the reconciliation of Christian and Hellenistic thought.

In his greatest work, *De Civitate Dei* (the City of God), St Augustine portrayed the human condition as torn between the attractions of good and evil, with the perfect state being one of voluntary submission to the will of God, which is here functionally equivalent to the Platonic ideal. The will of God is then seen as the highest law, the *lex aeterna* (eternal law), for all people, playing something of the role of Stoic cosmic reason. Positive law, the *lex temporalis*, is for St Augustine relegated to an even less honoured place than its equivalent had been for Plato. It is presented as a means for the coercive discouragement of vice, which represents the abuse of freedom of will through bad choices. For the right-choosing people who act in accordance with the relevant and knowable aspects of the *lex aeterna*, positive law is not relevant.

This opens the broad question of laws which are not 'good' in the Augustinian scheme of things, those which encourage or even command vicious conduct. It is here that certain statements of St Augustine, taken well out of context, have served to fuel the naturalist–positivist debate. The best known of these statements is the seemingly dramatic assertion that '*lex iniusta non est lex*', an unjust law is no law (*De Libero Arbitrio*, 1.5.33; an accessible version of this work will be found in St Augustine, *On the Free Choice of the Will*, transl. A. S. Benjamin and L. H. Hackstaff (Indianapolis, Ind: Bobbs-Merrill, 1964)). The idea that a State cannot in practice make and enforce unjust regulations would be absurd as a matter of observation, without need for theoretical analysis, and this was certainly no less the case in St Augustine's day than at present. What St Augustine actually meant is shown by the statement that nothing which is just is to be found in positive law (*lex temporalis*) which has not been derived from eternal law (*lex aeterna*) (St Augustine, *De Libero Arbitrio*, 1.6.50). Thus, an unjust law is one which does not concord with the higher (divine) reason and which is thus conceived, or directed, for an improper purpose. A positive law so devised might, of course, be coercively enforced but could not be argued to have any moral force, especially in forcing vice (sin) upon the virtuous. The argument, in short, relates to the moral obligation attaching to law rather than the ability of a

State actually to do wrong through its laws. Augustine considered that the authority of governments rested not upon their coercive power but upon the purposive propriety of their actions. In *De Civitate Dei* unjust governments are equated with criminal gangs. Citing Cicero, Augustine describes a pirate condemned to death by Alexander the Great who, when asked by Alexander how he dared to be a pirate, replied that whilst Alexander had a vast navy and was called an Emperor, he had just one ship and was denounced as a pirate (St Augustine, *De Civitate Dei*, 4.5.4).

One further point must be made about Augustinian legal theory. St Augustine imposed upon the idea of law a very narrow definition of terms according to which positive law (but not eternal law) is limited to the role of coercive discouragement of vice (sin). Other roles are more or less arbitrarily excluded from the positive-legal sphere. Such limitations are by no means an exclusively Augustinian phenomenon. The classical Marxist idea of law is similarly constrained by definitional limitations. This may, however, reasonably be argued to have a distorting effect upon the argument when applied to modern, or even late Roman, society wherein positive law manifestly serves, well or otherwise, much broader functions. This possible weakness in the Augustinian analysis may be considered to have been cured in the much later Thomist (referring to St Thomas Aquinas) analysis of law.

4.4.2   Christian Aristotelianism: St Thomas Aquinas

Although in his great work, the *Summa Theologica*, St Thomas Aquinas (1225–74) refers to St Augustine with great respect, the analysis of positive law which is advanced in it differs dramatically from the Augustinian model. The impact on Aquinas of the works of Aristotle which had been rediscovered by the 13th century is obvious. Like Aristotle, and unlike St Augustine, Aquinas considered that positive law plays a proper and 'natural' part in the political and social life of human beings, which is not constrained or defined by a sole concern with sin. In the introduction to the volume of the *Summa Theologiae* (*Summa Theologica*) dealing primarily with questions of law, the Dominican editors state that:

> The subject [law] is . . . freed from a current Augustinism which stressed the minatory role of law. . . . [Aquinas] brings out the *potestas directiva*, relegating the *potestas coactiva* to a secondary office of positive law, and one not called for if citizens are truly lawful. In brief, law has a dignity greater than that of a remedy *propter peccatum*. (St Thomas Aquinas, *Summa Theologiae*, general ed. T. Gilby (London: Blackfriars with Eyre and Spottiswoode, 1966), vol. 28, 1a2ae, 90 to 97, Introduction, pp. xxi to xxii.)

In the Thomist analysis, therefore, law may take its current coercive elements from the fact of vice, but the punishment of vice is not its only or primary aim, it is also admitted to have the capacity to set out guidance for 'good' living in the community, irrespective of vice as such.

The Thomist definition of 'law' (all law, not just positive law) is worth pausing over. It is stated that law:

> nihil est aliud quaedam rationis ordinatio ad bonum commune, ab eo qui curam communitatis habet, promulgata. (St Thomas Aquinas, *Summa Theologica*, 1a2ae, 90.4.)

That is to say that 'law' is nothing but a rational regulation for the good of the community, made by the person(s) having powers of government and promulgated. By reference to what has been said in chapters 2 and 3 it will at once be noticed that there are both 'naturalist' and 'positivist' elements in this definition. Starting with the latter, the last two requirements, essentially enactment and promulgation by a sovereign would not look remarkably out of place even in the work of Jeremy Bentham. These requirements of sovereignty and promulgation are extended by Aquinas to the eternal law (*lex aeterna*), the will of God, in particular as it relates to human actions, as well as to human positive law making. A legislative will (from whomsoever it may emanate) must clearly be both identifiable and known if it is to have any practical viability as a prescription for conduct. The first two elements of the Thomist definition, rationality and intent for the good of the community, are the 'naturalist' components. Both of these requirements relate directly to the Thomist notion of the 'good law'. Such a law must be rational because, it is presumed, virtue is derived from reason, here, ultimately, the reason of God in the *lex aeterna*. It must also be directed to the good of the community, or the 'common good', rather than for the particular benefit of a specific person, such as the legislator. Obviously a provision for the common good will benefit particular individuals. The law of contract is a convenience for individuals desiring to enter into contractual relations, but it is expressed generally and embraces all who may, individually, find themselves in the given situation. As to the general nature of 'goodness' for this purpose, Aquinas essentially adopts the teleological analysis of Aristotle. F.C. Coplestone remarks that:

> . . . moral law is for [Aquinas] . . . one of the ways in which creatures are directed towards their several ends. He sees the moral life in the general setting of the providential government of creatures. . . . the moral law . . . is a special case of the general principle that all finite things move towards their ends by the development of their potentialities. (F. C. Coplestone, *Aquinas* (Harmondsworth: Penguin, 1955), pp. 119–20.)

Assuming the existence of the higher rationality of the *lex aeterna* governing the potential for 'good' of human beings, the next obvious question is the means by which it can be known. This is an important issue for any form of naturalist argument, since, upon any analysis, an objective concept of what is right must be distinguished from the subjective wishes of the commentator or legislator. Without this the 'is/ought' distinction of David Hume would indeed be violated.

In the Thomist scheme ultimate reason is accessible to human beings through two principal media. These are (a) the *lex divina* (divine law) which is presented essentially as scriptural revelation, and (b) the *lex naturalis* (natural law), which is the fruit of rational human observation of an order which itself, by definition, rests upon the *lex aeterna*. Human positive law, the *lex humana*, will be 'good' in so far as it rests upon these foundations and 'bad' in so far as it does not.

For Aquinas, very clearly, a provision of positive law which facilitates or serves a teleologically good purpose will be binding upon the consciences of those to whom it is addressed, as well as being enforced by agencies of the State. This may readily be seen in modern societies also. As was suggested in chapter 2, many laws are in practice recognised as having a force far beyond their potential for coercive enforcement. The reason that the overwhelming majority of people do not commit murder is not fear of arrest but recognition that murder is wrong. Indeed that recognition clearly antedates the legal rule. In Thomist terms the rule is founded, in this case, upon indications of both the *lex divina* and *lex naturalis*. Any viable society must place strict limits upon interpersonal violence, although these may vary somewhat, otherwise it will inevitably tear itself apart. Other laws may be morally neutral, even if, once a decision has been made, for example, as to the particular formalities associated with conveyancing, social morality and the imperatives of cohesion demand compliance. There remains, however, the problem of the bad law.

For Aquinas, a provision of positive law might be bad in two ways, it might contravene the *lex aeterna*, and would then be abominable, or it might be humanly 'unfair'. It might, of course, be both. The basic Thomist reaction to bad laws merits quotation and is that:

> . . . lex tyrannica cum non sit secundum rationem non est simpliciter lex sed magis est quaedam perversitas legis. (A tyrannical law made contrary to reason is not straightforwardly a law but rather a perversion of law.) (St Thomas Aquinas, *Summa Theologica*, 1a2ae, 92.114.)

In this context it should be noted that 'tyranny' refers to lack, or abuse, of sovereign authority, but not necessarily with the modern connotation of cruelty. In the Thomist scheme the obligation to obey such a perverted law will rest upon the nature of its error. If it is actually contrary to the higher reason of the *lex aeterna* there can be no moral obligation to obey attached to it. If, on the other hand, it is badly conceived and humanly unfair the extent of any moral obligation to obey would depend on the circumstances. The practical examples offered here by Aquinas are not particularly helpful in that they relate principally to exceptions of necessity where in a particular case obedience would be manifestly inappropriate and official dispensation cannot be sought. In the more general context of bad law Aquinas argues that the moral obligation to obey fails in the case of a, humanly, bad law unless greater 'scandal' would result from disobedience (St Thomas Aquinas, *Summa Theologica*, 1a2ae, 96.4; also 2a2ae, 104.6). The point is spelt out by Aquinas in *De Regimine Principum* (Of the Government of Princes) in which it is urged that some degree of unjust government should be tolerated for fear of bringing on a worse state of things by rebellion or disobedience, but that there are limits to this. Tarquinius Superbus, the last king of ancient Rome, and the Emperor Domitian are cited as examples of properly deposed tyrants (St Thomas Aquinas, *De Regimine Principum*, 6.44). The essential point is that governmental authority has a moral base which may be weakened or lost through abuse of power. This must, again, emphatically be distinguished from any idea that an unjust government cannot coercively impose its laws: the argument relates to its right to do so and the quality of the moral obligation to obey, if any, which will result from such an attempt. The idea of government as a morally defined activity is, of course, far from being limited to the theories of medieval European scholasticism. In responding to the question of the permissibility of tyrannicide, the Confucian scholar Mencius (Meng K'e) stated in an ancient Chinese context that:

A man who mutilates benevolence is a mutilator, while one who cripples rightness is a crippler. He who [does such things is] . . . an 'outcast'. I have indeed heard of the punishment of the 'outcast [King] Tchou', but I have not heard of any regicide. (Mencius, *Mencius*, 1.B.8, transl. D. C. Lau (Harmondsworth: Penguin, 1970), p. 68.)

Despite the vast differences of context the functional parallel is obvious.

It should also be said that in the medieval political structure the Church, and in particular the Pope, were seen as having an authority to denounce iniquitous rulers and to authorise their deposition. It was not, however, presumed that particular representatives of the Church would necessarily occupy the moral high ground. It was rather intended, as formally stated by the doctrine of the two powers approved by Pope Gelasius I (492–6), that each has a part to play within the unified cause of the attainment of truth and justice. Thus A. P. D'Entrèves states that:

St Thomas does not conceive of a relation between two different societies, between State and Church . . . but of a distinction of functions. . . . We are entirely on the lines of . . . the Gelasian doctrine . . . of the distinction and interrelation of two great spheres of human life. (A. P. D'Entrèves, *Aquinas, Selected Political Writings* (Oxford: Basil Blackwell, 1959), p. xxi.)

This mechanism of determination and application is no longer workable in modern society, but this, like much of the tone of Thomist analysis should not be allowed to confuse. The essential concern of the argument, the limit of the moral authority, as compared with the coercive capacity of government, recurs in every historical context. The insights of the Thomist analysis of law have much to say of modern abuse of positive law, once the appropriate cultural transitions have been undertaken.

4.5   TRANSITION TO AN AGE OF REASON?

The certainties, doctrinal and political, of the medieval world order in which Aquinas wrote dissolved in the 16th and 17th centuries. The rise of the modern nation State as the primary European political unit was not a sudden development of the Renaissance era but it was one which reached an important stage of fruition at that time. Following slightly after, the Protestant Reformation, in various forms in different places, terminated the universal authority of the medieval Western Church and with it some of the instrumental, although not necessarily the substantive, elements of theories such as that of Aquinas. The impact of both these influences is neatly illustrated in the case of England by the preamble to the 1532 statute for the restraint of ecclesiastical appeals (24 Hen 8, c. 12) forbidding ecclesiastical appeals from the English Church to the Pope. The preamble states that:

> Where by divers sundry old authentick Histories and Chronicles, it is manifestly declared and expressed, that this Realm of England is an Empire, and so hath been accepted in the World, governed by one . . . King, having the Dignity and Royal Estate of the Imperial Crown of the same . . . with plenary, whole, and entire Power, Preeminence, Authority, Prerogative and Jurisdiction . . .

The reference to 'Empire' does not imply colonialism but derives from the standard political discourse of the medieval Holy Roman Empire which originated in the Carolingian Empire established by Charlemagne. The term implies in this context entire political independence. The idea was by no means uniquely English, or even Protestant, and clearly signalled a change which could not be ignored in the development of legal theory. The change was neither immediate nor dramatic. Protestant theologians, such as John Calvin, actually remained, not very surprisingly, close to the medieval position upon the quality of law and obligation, on matters of principle if not on details of application.

However, in the longer term the ending of certain universalist assumptions in a context of increasing secularism led to a recasting of the purposive naturalist analysis of law in forms of revived social-contractarianism. Three writers, addressing very different circumstances in the 17th and 18th centuries, merit particular attention in the present context: Hobbes, Locke and Rousseau. These theorists all sought to base a view of the purpose and authority of law upon a social contract in some ways reminiscent of that advanced by Plato, but more concretely conceived in terms of a surrender of the power of individuals to a State organisation, the 'sovereign'. The central question then became that of the terms upon which this surrender was made and, thus, the expectations which the people legitimately hold of law. Of course, no literal social contract was entered into in the distant past and for most, if not quite all, of the social-contractarians, the 'contract' itself was a rhetorical device used to explore questions of expectation and obligation arising in much more complex social and historical conditions. A different, if indirect, insight into the rational analysis of the quality of law is afforded by the moral theory of Immanuel Kant. This, indeed, may be considered of general importance for the implementation of naturalist analyses.

4.5.1 Hobbes: a social-contractarian response to anarchy

Thomas Hobbes (1588–1679) lived during the troubled period in England of the reign of Charles I, the Civil War, the Cromwellian Commonwealth and, later, the Restoration. His principal work, *Leviathan*, was published in 1651 and, hardly surprisingly, reflected a concern with the maintenance of peaceable order and the avoidance of civil collapse. Hobbes argued that the proper purpose of government and law was primarily to guarantee peace and order. In support of this, *Leviathan* gives a celebrated, and bleak, description of the human condition without a surrender to governance and order:

> Whatsoever therefore is consequent to a time of Warre, . . . the same is consequent to the time, wherein men live without other security, than what their own strength . . . shall furnish them withall. In such condition, there is . . . no Society; and which is worst of all, continuall feare, and danger of violent death; And the life of man, solitary, poore, nasty, brutish, and short. (T. Hobbes, *Leviathan*, ch. 13, ed. C. B. Macpherson (Harmondsworth: Penguin, 1968), p. 186.)

The value of government is thus presented as having the advantage of a power so far exceeding that of any individual that it may compel peace, and therefore a security of life otherwise lacking. In more detail, this contractarian model of government is said to rest upon two basic principles: (a) that all should strive for peace but may resort to force in self-defence when the endeavour proves impossible, and (b) the people should be satisfied with as much liberty as they are willing to allow to others. (T. Hobbes, *Leviathan*, ch. 14, ed. C. B. Macpherson, p. 190.)

This introduces a fundamentally important aspect of social-contractarian thought. The perception of the human being as a social or political creature living in groups, Aristotle's *politikon zōon*, inevitably raises a tension between individual desires and collective needs. The castaway completely alone on a desert island is not subject to any objective restrictions on noise making, but the appearance of more castaways will at once produce a society in which the rights of the others occasionally to rest or sleep will have to be balanced against the individual right to sing or shout. Hobbes's second 'natural law' states this precisely: social living involves compromise between individual and collective claims (which are the claims of a group of individuals). It is one of the more evident functions of law to draw a balance between these claims. The way in which this is done relates closely to certain ideas of justice which are considered in chapter 15, as also to the idea of human fairness found in the work of St Thomas Aquinas.

Hobbes does not, however, emphasise or develop this aspect of social contractarian theory. In ch. 30 of *Leviathan* it is admitted that a sovereign is bound in conscience to support and maintain the contentment, as well as the mere security, of the people, but this is commended as a moral duty rather than as a contractual duty owed to the people themselves. The question of abuse of power by the sovereign to whom (or which) individual power is surrendered was largely dismissed by Hobbes in the comment that those who complained about their governments failed to consider:

. . . that the estate of Man can never be without some incommodity or other; and that the greatest, that in any forme of Government can possibly happen to the people in generall, is scarce sensible, in respect of the miseries, . . . that accompany a Civill Warre; or that dissolute condition of masterlesse men, without subjection to Lawes. (T. Hobbes, *Leviathan*, ch. 18, ed. C. B. Macpherson, p. 238.)

Hobbes's primary concern is again obvious in this argument, in effect, that almost any government is better than none. There is here no Thomistic claim that government is itself a morally constrained enterprise. In Hobbes's scheme one may hope for good government but the only irreducible expectation is the warding off of the perils of anarchy. For Hobbes, the obligation to obey results from nothing more than the implicit election for submission deriving from the fact of life in society, and even this lacks the voluntarism advanced by Plato in *The Last Days of Socrates*.

In ch. 21 of *Leviathan*, however, Hobbes does briefly explore circumstances in which a sovereign might lose the claim to be obeyed. After an extremely limited concession of rights which might now be considered forms of human rights, Hobbes concedes four broad cases in which the obligation to obey the sovereign might cease. The first, and most obvious, is essentially breach of the social contract. Where the sovereign fails to maintain the order which is the fundamental term of the social contract, the individual right of self-defence will be restored and will abrogate the duty of obedience owed to the ruler. The other circumstances conceded by Hobbes in which such duty might end, such as abdication or cession of sovereignty to another body by treaty, are clearly different and technical in character, not bearing upon the primary issue.

4.5.2 Locke: social-contractarianism and bad government

John Locke (1632–1704) lived a generation on and in circumstances very different from those which had troubled Hobbes. Locke's writings provided the theoretical accounting for the 1688/89 'Glorious Revolution' in which James II was overthrown and replaced, jointly, by William III and Mary II, broadly upon terms set by Parliament, or, more technically, a body acting as Parliament. This was a fundamentally important event in English and United Kingdom constitutional and Parliamentary development and Locke's theories also strongly influenced the drafters of the United States constitution in some respects.

Locke's starting concern was not with the perils of ungoverned anarchy but with what he, and his patron the Earl of Shaftesbury, considered to be the 'tyrannical' government of James II. In the *Two Treatises on Government*, published in 1690, Locke re-examines the 'pre-contractual' state of nature from a perspective differing markedly from that of Hobbes. It is seen as a condition in which there are already 'natural rights' vested in all individuals in relation to the 'property'. From a modern viewpoint this idea needs to be treated with some caution. For Locke 'property' included the modern senses of land, material goods and financial accumulations, but it also extended to personal rights. The latter included a 'property' held by people in their own skills and work (J. Locke, *Two Treatises on Government*, bk 2, ch. 5), which can be argued to generate an entitlement to proportionate remuneration for labour undertaken.

> This can be seen as an argument of economic individualism which reflects the developing capitalist economy of England in Locke's time. It is in fact a basic 'bourgeois' theory of economic relations. (H. McCoubrey, *The Development of Naturalist Legal Theory* (London: Croom Helm, 1987), p. 70.)

In fact, it reflected the circumstances of Locke's time exactly as Hobbes's approach had reflected its historical context and as Rousseau's was to.

According to Locke the defect of the hypothetical state of nature was that the even and effective protection of natural property rights in a state of nature would be uncertain and unsatisfactory. The function of government and civil society in Locke's scheme is thus that of providing a sufficiently powerful means of protecting natural rights which exist independently of it. The idea entered into contemporary conventional jurisprudence and can be found overtly stated in, e.g., the remark of Pratt CJ in *Entick* v *Carrington* (1765) 19 St Tr 1029 at p. 1060, that:

> The great end for which men entered into society was to secure their property.

The function of the State as thus conceived is much more detailed than that advanced by Hobbes; it also suggests a much more complex structure of obligations as between governments and peoples. Locke sets out various circumstances of change in government which may amount to, or bring on, its dissolution, but then sets out the important general principle that:

> . . . it can never be supposed to be the will of society that the legislative should have a power to destroy that . . . for which the people submitted themselves to legislators of their own making: . . . Whensoever, therefore, the legislative shall transgress this fundamental rule . . . and . . . endeavour to grasp . . . absolute power . . ., by this breach of trust . . . the people . . . have a right to resume their original liberty, and by the establishment of a new legislative . . ., provide for their own safety and security, which is the end for which they are in society. (J. Locke, *Two Treatises on Government*, bk 2, ch. 19 (London: Dent, 1924), p. 229.)

This could hardly be stated more clearly and it is at once evident that the social contract is, for Locke, breached not only by complete failure of government but also by bad government. It is also worth emphasising that the residual popular 'right' is not one that is seen only as being 'resumed' *ex post facto*. It is remarked by von Leyden that Locke contends that:

> . . . a supreme power remains with the people to remove or change [government] . . . if it governs contrary to its position of trust. . . .the community [also] 'perpetually retains' a supreme power to save themselves from any attempt at oppression. (W. von Leyden, *Hobbes and Locke: The Politics of Freedom and Obligation* (London: Macmillan, 1982), p. 156.)

In deference to Bentham's fears of a counsel of individualism leading to anarchy, it should be pointed out that this right of withdrawal of obedience appears to be a group rather than an individual right. The idea of government as a 'trust power' capable of revocation in case of breach, or possibly when the commission of breach has become evident, moves considerably beyond the limited model of Hobbes. This approach too, however, failed to meet the circumstances of France under the *ancien régime* and a more radical form of social-contractarianism thus developed, exemplified by the work of Rousseau.

4.5.3 Rousseau: a contract with society not government

Jean-Jacques Rousseau (1712–78) was born in Geneva but was primarily influential in France, not least through his best-known work, *Du Contrat Social*, published in 1762. Although manifestly a social-contractarian, Rousseau treated this form of analysis quite differently from Hobbes and Locke. Rousseau's concern was not specifically with either the avoidance of anarchy or the constitutional imperfections of given forms of government, but with the possibility of 'any legitimate and sure principle of government, taking men as they are and laws as they might be' (J.-J. Rousseau, *The Social Contract*, introduction to bk 1, transl. M. Cranston (Harmondsworth: Penguin, 1968), p. 49), in short, the classical concern with the construction of a good social order. The incidental separation of 'is' and 'ought' in this statement is also worth noticing in passing. For Rousseau the hypothetical 'state of nature' was a pre-social condition in which human beings, as social creatures, would have been deprived of any context for the development of their moral potential. Equally, real societies, such as France under the pre-revolutionary *ancien régime*, were far from conducive to any such development. Thus, at the outset of *Du Contrat Social*, Rousseau makes the well-known declaration that, '*L'homme est né libre, et partout il est dans les fers*' (human beings are born free but are everywhere in chains) (J.-J. Rousseau, *Du Contrat Social* (Paris: Garnier Flammarion, 1966), p. 41). The social contract is then advanced as the basis upon which human beings 'agree' to combine in society and which is founded precisely upon the facilitation of the development of potential.

It is important to notice that the hypothetical 'surrender' of individuals is not here to a sovereign or even to a given form of government but to the idea of political society as such. The controlling power is then the general will of the members of society, the *volonté générale*. People living subject to this will are argued not to be made subject to power, nor to remain deprived of developmental potential in a pre-social condition, but to be under a collective obligation founded upon the general will which facilitates 'free' development through the provision of a necessary moral framework.

This model presents some difficulties at the level of actual application. The first is the question of the nature and content of the general will itself. If this will is no more than majority opinion, Rousseau's scheme would seem to threaten a manipulative tyranny of the majority of the sort feared and denounced by J.S. Mill in the 19th century. In another context Mill wrote that:

The will of the people . . . practically means the will of . . . the majority
. . .; the people, consequently, *may* desire to oppress a part of their number,
and precautions are as much needed against this as against any other abuse
of power. (J. S. Mill, *On Liberty*, ed. G. Himmelfarb (Harmondsworth:
Penguin, 1974), p. 62.)

This, however, was not Rousseau's intention. Far from being 'popular
opinion', if indeed such a coherent canon of thought exists, Rousseau's
general will is carefully distinguished from the will of all individuals, dismissed as a mere *'somme de volontés particulières'* (J.-J. Rousseau, *Du Contrat
Social*, bk 2, ch. 3, Garnier Flammarion, ed., p. 66), a summation of
individual wills. It is presented instead as a will focused upon the general
good rather than upon individual benefits, whilst taking account of the
diversity of actual human interests thus:

From the deliberations of a people properly informed, . . . the great number
of small differences will always produce a general will and the decision will
always be good. (J.-J. Rousseau, *The Social Contract*, bk 2, ch. 3, transl. M.
Cranston, p. 73.)

This 'will', unlike popular opinion, cannot in Rousseau's opinion be misled
and is, in effect, the hypothetical opinion which a wise and well-informed
people would hold. There is an obvious analogy with the wise insights
required by Platonic or Aristotelian arguments but there are also, unfortunately, much more sinister analogies to be drawn. In the Third Reich a
Volksgeist, will of the people, which was in fact, of course, the will of the Nazi
Party, was much referred to as a jurisprudential standard. It may fairly be
assumed that Rousseau, who considered compliance with the general will to
be true freedom, would have been appalled by the legal abuses of the Third
Reich. Indeed it is strongly implied by Rousseau that the wisdom informing
good lawmaking pursuant to the general will derives ultimately from a divine
or higher rational source (J.-J. Rousseau, *Du Contrat Social*, bk 2, ch. 7).
Despite this there must still be thought to lurk an implicit danger of
totalitarian abuse beneath the concept of the general will.

Since, for Rousseau, the social contract is made with society rather than
with a given form of government, the dissolution of the obligation owed to a
government and its legal order does not involve any renegotiation of the
contract. In *The Social Contract* it is stated that:

. . . when . . . the people institutes a [form of] . . . government, . . . it does
not enter into any undertaking; . . . [the government] is simply a provi-
sional form that it gives to the administration until such time as it pleases
to arrange it differently. (J.-J. Rousseau, *The Social Contract*, bk 3, ch. 18,
transl. M. Cranston, pp. 146–7.)

The French Revolution of 1789, which overthrew the incompetent regime of Louis XVI, presented no analytical difficulty in the context of the contractarian analysis advanced by Rousseau. It would not, however, follow that the post-revolutionary regimes should necessarily be accepted as having concorded with the general will. Social-contractarianism, like other naturalist analyses, prescribes critical evaluative criteria of assessment but cannot guarantee that any particular mechanism for change will produce desirable results.

4.6   THE PROBLEM OF OBJECTIVITY

Any naturalist analysis rests upon the application of moral or ethical criteria of evaluation to the quality of the making and implementation of positive law. Any such analysis must claim to distinguish between fundamental moral propositions and other more subjective criteria, such as mere prejudice, if the generality and objectivity of its application is to be maintained.

This issue was addressed, in a much broader context than legal theory, by Immanuel Kant (1724–1804) in two principal works, the *Groundwork of the Metaphysic of Morals* of 1785 and the *Critique of Practical Reason* of 1788. It is unnecessary for present purposes to address the complete detail of Kantian moral theory but the broad structure of the argument is of evident relevance. For Kant a 'moral' action is one which is the product of 'good will', 'goodness' being for this purpose an inherent quality rather than a pragmatic judgment of success or failure in given cases. It is defined by the concordance of the 'maxim' upon which the decision to act is founded with the 'duty' deriving from universal reason. The basic test set out by Kant ties in the categorical imperative, that one should 'act as if the maxim of your action were to become through your will a universal law of nature' (I. Kant, *Groundwork of the Metaphysic of Morals*, ch. 2, p. 52, transl. H. J. Paton in *The Moral Law* (London: Hutchinson, 1948), p. 84). The point is illustrated by Kant through instances of 'bad' maxims for action, for example, one who borrows money not intending to repay it would act upon a maxim which, if made applicable to all, would subvert the whole concept of 'borrowing' (I. Kant, *Groundwork of the Metaphysic of Morals*, ch. 2). The categorical imperative would apply as much to legislative action as to any other form of action. S. Korner suggests an analogy between Kant's analysis in terms of conformity with universal reason and Rousseau's general will, despite the vagueness in detail of the latter (S. Korner, *Kant* (Harmondsworth: Penguin, 1955), pp. 139–40). Indeed, there is an obvious connection with the general rationale of human social existence which underlies all naturalist legal theories. It should be emphasised that the Kantian categorical imperative does not imply that all States should enact precisely the same positive laws. A wide variety of cultural practices might be held compatible with a universal principle, thus the idea that *pacta sunt servanda*, agreements are to be performed, makes no precise specification for the particular formalities of contract to be adopted by a legal system.

Kant also considers the morality of the ends sought by action and advances a principle of right, that humanity should always be respected as an end in itself and never utilised simply as a means to some end (I. Kant, *Groundwork of the Metaphysic of Morals*, ch. 2). It may from this be taken that laws calculated to exploit some group in society without reference to their own humanity would thus be 'immoral', a law maintaining serfdom or slavery would, for example, be insupportable in a modern view.

It has been stated elsewhere that in the light of Kantian moral theory:

> . . . positive law . . . should concord with the categorical imperative and should tend to the furtherance of humanity in accordance with the principle of right. . . . A law which does not meet these criteria is without rational justification and is morally insupportable. (H. McCoubrey, *The Development of Naturalist Legal Theory* (London: Croom Helm, 1987), pp. 80–1.)

Such a test does not conflict with any substantive doctrine advanced within the body of classical naturalism and is a useful analytical instrument in the application of most of them.

4.7 THE STANDING OF CLASSICAL NATURALISM

Classical naturalism was argued by the early positivist theorists to breach the distinction between 'is' and 'ought', descriptive and normative, propositions by claiming that only good law is 'law'. No such claim is made by the theories here considered in that their analysis is directed to the quality and propriety of lawmaking, not to the ability of the State in practice to impose regulation. A different question potentially arises, however, from the proposition that law may be evaluated by reference to standards deriving from the fact of human nature. That is to say that what law 'ought' to be is judged according to what human nature, in some sense, 'is' in fact or in potential. This would, however, be a false question. Positive law defines a minimum framework for human social order and thus surely 'ought' to be beneficial in terms of the nature of its subjects, as that 'is' found to be.

If this is accepted any conflict between positivism and naturalism is seen to be apparent rather than real. Classical naturalism then provides the theoretical base for analysis of legitimate expectations of the processes of making and administering positive law. In the modern world post-positivist thought has revived interest in analysis of the moral and ethical quality of law and consequent development in theory has built upon the classical naturalist tradition.

4.8 FURTHER READING

Aquinas, Thomas, Saint, *Summa Theologiae* (*Summa Theologica*), 1a2ae. 90–97, Dominican ed. (London: Eyre and Spottiswoode, 1966).

Aquinas, Thomas, Saint, *Selected Political Writings*, transl. J. G. Dawson, ed. A.P. D'Entrèves (Oxford: Basil Blackwell, 1959).

Augustine of Hippo, Saint, *On the Free Choice of the Will*, transl. A. S. Benjamin and H. Hackstaff (Indianopolis, Ind: Bobbs Merill, 1979).

D'Entrèves, A. P., *Natural Law*, revised ed. (London: Hutchinson, 1970).

Hobbes, T., *Leviathan*, ed. C. B. Macpherson (Harmondsworth: Penguin, 1968).

McCoubrey, H., *The Development of Naturalist Legal Theory* (London: Croom Helm, 1987).

Plato, *The Laws*, transl. T. J. Saunders, revised reprint (Harmondsworth: Penguin, 1976).

Rousseau, J.-J., *The Social Contract*, transl. M. Cranston (Harmondsworth: Penguin, 1968).

Von Leyden, W., *Hobbes and Locke* (London: Macmillan, 1981).

Woozley, A. D., *Law and Obedience: The Arguments of Plato's* Crito (London: Duckworth, 1979).

CHAPTER FIVE

The Naturalist Revival

In Anglo-American jurisprudence and much of the spectrum of common law legal thought, classical naturalist ideas were, from the middle of the 19th century onwards, largely overshadowed by the varieties of positivist legal theory (see chapters 2 and 3). This also happened in other jurisdictions although to varying degrees. The reasons for this were various and related to the general culture of the period as well as to matters of a specifically jurisprudential nature. An implicitly 'positivist' notion of law is still typical of professional legal discourse, and, indeed, the concerns of positivism well fit it for this purpose. In this, as in many other contexts, the assumption that any particular form of analysis renders an exclusive or comprehensive analysis of positive law and its operation produced the distortions which have been considered in chapters 1 and 2 when positivist argument was applied to aspects of law to which it was entirely unsuited.

The resulting tensions of theory became particularly apparent in the earlier part of the 20th century, most particularly in the 1930s as the emergence of modern totalitarian States, of a variety of ideological colourings, posed moral and ethical questions about the operation of law which, if hardly new, had emerged in varied and stark forms. This was the case in different ways in the fascist States and in the former USSR under the Stalin dictatorship. The questions were rendered both practically and ethically unavoidable when the full scope of legal abuse under the Nazi Third Reich in Germany between 1933 and 1945 was unambiguously exposed in the aftermath of defeat in the Second World War (see also chapter 16). These concerns raised doubts about the adequacy of formalist legal theories, emphasising a descriptive analysis of formal criteria of legal identification. In short, how can an analysis concerned essentially with what law 'is' deal with the problem of a law which, upon civilised criteria, manifestly 'ought not' to be as it 'is', or 'was'? Positivism does not strictly deny the importance of the moral, ethical or even political quality of law, but the relegation of these issues to a realm beyond jurisprudence increasingly seemed to exclude matters from consideration which were not peripheral but central to the nature of law in the modern world. The result was a revival of interest in naturalist jurisprudence and this has had a marked effect upon modern developments in theory from the middle of the 20th century to the present time.

A number of theories have been developed in the context of modern naturalism, but three of somewhat different emphasis, merit particular attention. These are, in order of time, the 'procedural naturalism' advanced by Lon L. Fuller, the theory of 'natural rights' advanced by Finnis and the moral analysis presented by Beyleveld and Brownsword.

5.1   LON L. FULLER AND PROCEDURAL NATURAL LAW

Lon L. Fuller, professor of general jurisprudence at Harvard University from 1948 to 1972, was immediately concerned with the problems raised by the totalitarian abuse of law in the 1930s and 1940s and advanced a theory of law which he categorised as 'procedural naturalism' in an effort to set out the minimal requirements for a recognisable 'legal system'. The basis for this analysis was the perceived weakness of law in the Third Reich and the extent to which it could realistically have been considered to have been 'law' in any meaningful sense. It is possible to debate in some detail whether the Third Reich actually was a *Rechtsstaat*, one governed by a 'rule of law' (see 16.1.1). Fuller himself specifically debated this issue with H. L. A. Hart (see 3.5.1), unfortunately upon the basis of a misleading report of the case which was the focus of debate. However, the theory which Fuller advanced was not specifically tied to the question of the use of law in the Third Reich but sought to make a much more general point about the nature and functions of a legal system. As its usual description suggests, Fuller's theory was not founded upon the substantive content of legal provisions but upon the procedural structure of a legal system. It is open to some question whether this approach is correctly termed 'naturalist' (for discussion of this see 5.1.4), it cannot, however, be denied that the analysis raises issues of profound importance for the understanding of law.

In *The Morality of Law*, Fuller addresses the problem of the interface between law and morality with particular regard to the fact that in the general legal theory of the time:

There is little recognition . . . of a much larger problem, that of clarifying the directions of human effort essential to maintain any system of law, even one whose ultimate objectives may be regarded as mistaken or evil. (Lon L. Fuller, *The Morality of Law*, rev. ed. (New Haven, Conn: Yale University Press, 1969), p. 4.)

Consideration of this larger issue forms the bulk of the work, but as a preliminary to this Fuller analysed the nature of the morality to which law is to be related. At this basic level too he considered contemporary jurisprudential debate to have become confused and, thus, urgently to require clarification.

5.1.1 Moralities of aspiration and of duty

Fuller considered that debate upon the morality of law had become confused in part through a failure adequately to distinguish between two levels of morality which he defined as moralities of 'aspiration' and of 'duty'. Fuller states the distinction between the two moralities in terms of the level of the demand imposed:

> The morality of aspiration . . . is the morality of the Good Life, of excellence, of the fullest realisation of human powers. . . . Where the morality of aspiration starts at the top of human achievement, the morality of duty starts at the bottom. It lays down the basic rules without which an ordered society is impossible, or without which an ordered society directed toward certain specific goals must fail of its mark. (Lon L. Fuller, *The Morality of Law*, pp. 5–6.)

The essential difference is indicated by Fuller's choice of terms. The morality of 'aspiration' is a goal of excellence, or even perfection, closely related, as Fuller points out, to the Platonic ideal. It is in a sense a maximum goal. The morality of 'duty' on the other hand is a minimum standard which must be attained before the enterprise can be recognised to have the identity which it claims at all. One may aspire to excellence but the standard of 'duty' is the minimum required for a viable social order so that failure to achieve it is not merely, in some sense or to some degree, a lapse but is actually a wrong.

Fuller contends that the division between these two moralities is not a gulf separating polar extremes, but a point upon a graduated scale. Thus:

> . . . we may conveniently imagine a . . . scale . . . which begins . . . with the most obvious demands of social living and extends upward to the highest reaches of human aspiration. Somewhere along this scale there is an invisible pointer that marks the dividing line where the pressure of duty leaves off and the challenge of excellence begins. (Lon L. Fuller, *The Morality of Law*, pp. 9–10.)

Fuller argues that, wherever that pointer might be fixed, the appropriate standard of evaluation in the analysis of law, in terms of its claim to be 'law', is one of 'duty' rather than 'aspiration'. This relates partly to a view of the basic function of law. It is implicit in Fuller's analysis that it is not the business of law to prescribe for excellence but rather to ensure the minimum baseline from which development towards excellence might move.

In so far as, to express the point in somewhat different terms, law cannot make people 'good' but rather establish a base for the inhibition of 'badness' from which a good life may develop, this rather minimalist moral analysis of the comparative standard for law may be accepted. It does not, however, state the limits of the moral questions which may be asked about law. Beyond the establishment of the base for a viable society, it does not seem unreasonable to suggest that law may also facilitate, or hinder, aspiration towards higher social conditions, even accepting the validity of the distinction between 'aspiration' and 'duty'. This indeed figures prominently amongst the concerns of some of the classical naturalist theories considered in chapter 4. The analysis of moral criteria and their relationship with law advanced by Fuller is important in itself but also to a large extent informs the nature of his general legal theory. Ultimately this goes to the root of the question which may be raised upon the claim of the theory fully to fit into a naturalist context.

5.1.2 The criteria of lawmaking

The major part of Fuller's argument concerns the essential requirements for the making of recognisably 'legal' norms within the context of a 'morality of duty'. He commences this analysis by considering the reign of a hypothetical King called Rex. Unlike Rex I, the founder of the dynasty of Rexes in H. L. A. Hart's analysis (see 3.2.3), Fuller's Rex is a hereditary monarch succeeding to a well-established dynasty with, unfortunately, a lamentable record in matters legal. The attempts of the well intentioned but incompetent Rex to improve matters are then used as a hypothetical model of the ways in which the enterprise of lawmaking might be rendered ineffectual or, indeed, vitiated altogether.

The subject of this analysis is termed by Fuller 'the morality that makes law possible' (Lon L. Fuller, *The Morality of Law*, ch. 2). The product is essentially a set of minimum criteria for recognisable legislative, or other 'legal', activity, which Fuller expresses in the form of eight negative criteria which would, to varying extents, individually and cumulatively indicate failure in lawmaking. Some of these negative criteria require further comment, but the list may usefully be set out as such. The more or less fatal defects are set out by Fuller as 'eight ways to fail to make law' (*The Morality of Law*, pp. 33–41). The summarised list (see *The Morality of Law*, p. 39) is:

(a)   failure to establish rules at all, leading to absolute uncertainty;
(b)   failure to make rules public to those required to observe them;
(c)   improper use of retroactive lawmaking;
(d)   failure to make comprehensible rules;
(e)   making rules which contradict each other;
(f)   making rules which impose requirements with which compliance is
impossible;
(g)   changing rules so frequently that the required conduct becomes
wholly unclear;
(h)   discontinuity between the stated content of rules and their administration in practice.

Any of these would manifestly pose a problem, whether all would be
absolutely fatal defects in an endeavour to make law raises somewhat more
complex questions. A system which failed to make rules at all would clearly
be only very dubiously a recognisable legal system. Similarly a rule with which
compliance would be impossible might be recognised by a court as law,
indeed there are examples of such rules being applied, but, equally, they
would be, and have been, of very dubious quality indeed. An obvious example
would be a law penalising people on the basis of an inherent quality such as
their racial identity. The Nuremberg race laws of the Nazi Third Reich which
in practice, if not quite in form, made it illegal to be Jewish, were an especially
stark example of precisely this.
   Some of the listed defects would, whilst being objectionable in general, not
necessarily be unacceptable in all cases. Retroactivity would be a good
example. One might reasonably consider that for a law to be made retroac-
tively so as to cure a failure in the existing law would not only be unobjectionable but highly desirable. Fuller counsels against this as a general
conclusion, citing the Roehm purge of 1934 under the Third Reich as a
warning instance. Hitler had come to consider the SA faction led by Roehm
as a threat to his position and therefore descended upon the group at one of
their meetings and ordered the summary shooting of some hundred persons.
Subsequently a retroactive decree was enacted converting these murders into
lawful 'executions', informed by Hitler's claim that he himself was the
'supreme court' of the German *Volk* (see *The Morality of Law*, pp. 54–5).
   This seems a rather curious example with which to illustrate the point. In
the first place it may be questioned whether the Third Reich was a *Rechtsstaat*, a state ruled by law, at all, a question of which Fuller was well aware
(see 3.5.1). Secondly, this use of law to validate a patently political purge
which was wholly devoid of legal process is subject to so many other
objections, even in terms of Fuller's procedural criteria, that the question of
'retroactive cure' seems at most a peripheral issue. There are, of course,
numerous objections to retroactive legislation, or judicial precedents, and

Fuller gives a number of examples. One may none the less suggest that if a law which is reasonable in itself failed to take account of some situation in which people are greatly and improperly prejudiced by its application, then retroactive relief for those people would seem justifiable. The important point to be emphasised is the element of 'relief' which should also require that the action does not unfairly prejudice other people who relied upon the law as it stood. Such instances may be rare, may indeed be hoped to be so, but the possibility should not be ignored.

Similarly complex arguments may be raised about the practical implications of a number of Fuller's negative criteria. It may, however, be accepted that most of them most of the time would be severely deleterious in their effects and that a 'legal system' subject to all of them would hardly be recognisable as such. Beyond this, however, there arises the vital question of the practical operation and impact of the procedural criteria.

In particular it must be asked to what extent failure in relation to the negative criteria will vitiate the claim of a purported 'legal system' to be such. Is failure in all eight required before this point is reached, or will failure in just one suffice? The answer would seem to be that this is not truly an 'eight-point test' with some 'passmark' which a candidate legal system must attain. It would seem that all the negative criteria represent defects but that these are cumulative in effect. A system which at all times failed in all eight regards would clearly be entirely unacceptable. A system which failed occasionally in one or two would not. The issue of possibly acceptable retroactive action may again be referred to in this context. Fuller states that:

> The citizen's predicament becomes more difficult when, though there is no total failure in any direction, there is a general and drastic deterioration in legality.
> . . . there can be no simple principle by which to test the citizen's obligation. . . . . A mere respect for constituted authority must not [however] be confused with fidelity to law. Rex's subjects . . . remained faithful . . . [but] not faithful to his law, for he never made any. (*The Morality of Law*, pp. 40–1.)

In short the procedural criteria represent a slippery slope, the point at which a given system actually plunges to conceptual perdition must be left as a matter of fact and degree in the actual situation.

5.1.3 Procedural morality and the substance of laws

An equally important question arises in the relation of Fuller's procedural morality to the substantive content of laws. For Fuller the negative criteria which he sets out reflect an 'inner morality' of law, that is to say 'the morality that makes law possible' (the heading of ch. 2 of *The Morality of Law*). This is throughout a procedural morality which is concerned with the capacity of a system to produce norms which are recognisably 'legal' at all. The possibility of procedurally adequate enactment of substantively iniquitous laws is to a large extent ignored. Fuller himself remarks that:

> In presenting my analysis of the law's internal morality I have insisted that it is, over a wide range of issues, indifferent toward the substantive aims of law and is ready to serve a variety of such aims with equal efficacy. (*The Morality of Law*, p. 153.)

It would indeed be expected that a procedural morality might admit and encompass a broad range of substantive enactment. The analysis would be open to criticism were it not so. This still, however, leaves open the problem of procedurally adequate iniquity.

What, for example, if in a totalitarian State it were to be enacted that any person who expressed disagreement with any publicly stated opinion of the dictator upon any matter would, from the date of the enactment, be shot; further, that this rule contradicts no other rule and is then applied rigorously and to the letter at all times. The 'law' is a rule, it is public, not retroactive, comprehensible, not contradicted by other rules, not impossible to obey, not subject to change, and applied exactly as it is stated. In short, it satisfies perfectly Fuller's procedural criteria but is still profoundly objectionable as a use of law according to many of the classical naturalist legal theories. It might well, for example, from the viewpoint of the Thomist analysis be considered classically a 'tyrannical' law and thus a perversion or abuse of law (*perversitas legis*, see 4.4.2).

Fuller claimed that procedural naturalism to some extent set up barriers to the imposition of substantive iniquity. He remarks expressly that:

> . . . I treated what I have called the internal morality of law as itself presenting a variety of natural law. It is, however, a procedural or institutional kind of natural law, though . . . it affects and limits the substantive aims that can be achieved through law. (*The Morality of Law*, p. 184.)

Some forms of substantive iniquity clearly could not be imposed in a manner compliant with Fuller's procedural criteria, but it would seem an exaggerated claim to suggest that 'good' procedures preclude 'bad' law. Fuller does not actually make such a claim. Indeed the basic distinction between the moralities of 'aspiration' and of 'duty' from which he commences his argument tend against any such proposition. The limits of the substantive impact of a procedural morality are suggested in Fuller's comment that:

. . . an acceptance of this [internal] morality is a necessary, though not a sufficient condition for the realisation of justice, . . . this morality is itself violated when an attempt is made to express blind hatreds through legal rules, and . . . the specific morality of law articulates . . . a view of man's nature that is indispensable to law and morality alike. (*The Morality of Law*, p. 168.)

In response to this one must ask why it would be procedurally impossible to express 'blind hatreds' through 'law' – many States seem to have achieved this feat with ease – unless, of course, a substantive morality is to be smuggled into the procedural criteria.

In addressing this issue Fuller is very critical of Hart's 'minimum content of natural law' (see 3.5.3) and starts from the proposition that, whereas the morality of duty is a requirement, the morality of aspiration is a source of 'counsel' only. He does, however, admit one 'imperious' tenet of substantive naturalism in the maintenance of 'channels of communication' between people, and peoples (*The Morality of Law*, p. 186). In so far as this rather minimalist conception seems to imply a recognition of common humanity it may be accepted as an essential tenet of naturalism. It is hardly, however, sufficient. In the light of Fuller's criticism of Hart it is perhaps curious that his very limited substantive naturalism seems to be appended to his procedural model as a rather awkward addition, much as Hart's 'minimum content of natural law' appears to be attached incongruously to his central positivist argument (see 3.5.3). Ultimately it may be suggested that an attempt to absorb a substantive naturalism into a procedural argument is yet another instance of the inappropriate extension of a concept into areas well beyond its proper remit. Beyond this there arises the question of whether Fuller's approach is truly to be considered 'naturalist' at all.

5.1.4 Is procedural naturalism actually naturalist?

Fuller clearly considered his procedural criteria to represent an 'internal morality' of law and properly to be categorised as a naturalist analysis (see *The Morality of Law*, p. 184). His theory was also evidently a response to the inadequacies of strict positivism as a vehicle for the consideration of the abuse of law by 20th-century totalitarian regimes. The procedural emphasis of the analysis, however, raises some doubt as to the strength of its naturalist claims. Robert S. Summers comments that:

Fuller devoted more sustained thought to legal processes than to any other facet of law. But . . . he did not stress the necessarily moral value of certain legal processes. Yet he arrived at this idea even earlier (1949) than he did his views on the moral value of his principles of legality. (R. S. Summers, *Lon L. Fuller* (London: Edward Arnold, 1984), p. 40.)

Fuller criticises the essentially amoral stance of positivist theory, arguing that Hart's concept of an identification of rules through the operation of a rule of recognition (see 3.2.3) does not actually distinguish law from mere coercive demands. Fuller traces this failure to an omission of any concept of 'reciprocity', by which is meant an idea that recognition and compliance on the part of the citizen body imports defined expectations of the State, default in which would be in some sense wrongful. This idea of legitimate expectation by the subjects of law, as compared with the mere identification of rules, is significant. It may, indeed, be accepted as distinguishing the central arguments of Fuller from those of Hart, subject to the latter's 'minimum content of natural law'.

Ultimately, however, the procedural naturalism advanced by Fuller is less purposive than its author claims and the issues of the proper use of law which are central to classical naturalism are largely ignored in the analysis. It has been suggested elsewhere that:

> . . . Fuller may fairly be said to have contributed an interesting and important critique of positivist formalism from a quasi-naturalist viewpoint but his theory must none the less be considered somewhat peripheral from the viewpoint of the mainstream of naturalist thought. (H. McCoubrey, *The Development of Naturalist Legal Theory* (London: Croom Helm, 1987), p. 179.)

In its historical context Fuller's work may be seen as an important, and insightful, contribution to the later 20th-century criticism of the over-extension of the formalist analyses of positivism. In its significant divergence from mainstream naturalist concerns, however, the theory would perhaps be more appropriately categorised as a post-positivist analysis than as a naturalist theory *stricto sensu*.

5.2 JOHN FINNIS AND THE THEORY OF NATURAL RIGHTS

Unlike Fuller's concept of procedural natural law the theory of 'natural rights' advanced by John Finnis falls unequivocally into the category of 'naturalist' theory. Indeed in presenting his case Finnis places considerable emphasis upon the analysis advanced by St Thomas Aquinas (see 4.4.2).

Finnis's contribution to modern naturalist jurisprudence may be argued to be important in two quite different ways. It is not unique in its broadly Thomist base but its development from that base is both innovative and distinctive in a manner different from modern restatements of Thomism such as that advanced by John C. H. Wu (see J. C. H. Wu, *The Fountain of Justice* (London: Sheed and Ward, 1959)). Finnis's core concern with theory of rights sets classical naturalist concern with the moral or ethical and purposive nature of law into a modern discourse of 'rights' which is firmly rooted in fundamental preoccupations of the modern legal and political world. Secondly, Finnis's theory moves away from the still essentially formal concerns of post-positivist analyses, such as that of Fuller, and adds a modern naturalist voice to jurisprudential debate. This serves the interest of a diversification of the range of analyses which may be seen as a prerequisite for the adequate address of the broad issues arising from the operation of law in the modern world.

5.2.1 Finnis's defence of naturalism

Finnis commences his analysis with a defence of naturalist jurisprudence from the conventional criticism that it somehow violates the distinction between descriptive and normative, 'is' and 'ought', propositions classically set out by David Hume and taken up in the jurisprudence of Bentham (see 2.1). Finnis addresses this basic issue in the form in which it is pressed by Julius Stone, and offers a decisive response to the standard positivist critique:

> 'Have the natural lawyers shown that they can derive ethical norms from facts?' . . . the answer can be brisk: They have not, nor do they need to, nor did the classical exponents of the theory dream of attempting any such derivation. (J. M. Finnis, *Natural Law and Natural Rights* (Oxford: Clarendon Press, 1980), p. 33, referring to J. Stone, *Human Law and Human Justice* (London: Stevens and Sons, 1965), p. 212.)

Finnis contends that classical naturalist argument does not improperly derive 'ought' propositions from the simple observation of human conduct, a descriptive 'is' proposition. He argues instead that people understand their individual aspirations and nature from an 'internal' perspective and that from this there may be extrapolated an understanding of the 'good life' for humanity in general. Thus a general 'good' may be derived from particular experiences or appreciations of 'good', which is not to say that what people in fact want they always 'ought' to have. To take a very crude example, the self-perceived 'good' of a serial killer is manifestly incompatible with the 'good' of other people and cannot, thus, form any part of the general human 'good'. In contrast, an individual's wish for personal security can be something of general application and thus symptomatic of such general human 'good'. The point can be related to basic Kantian argument (see 4.6). Finnis explains this form of derivation of the concept of 'good', by reference to St Thomas Aquinas:

> The basic forms of good grasped by practical understanding are what is good for human beings with the nature they have. Aquinas considers that

practical reasoning begins . . . by experiencing one's nature . . . from the inside, in the form of one's inclinations. . . . by a simple act of non-inferential understanding one grasps that the object of the inclination . . . is an instance of a general form of good, for oneself (and others like one). (*Natural Law and Natural Rights*, p. 34.)

As an analysis of the derivation of human 'good' this has much to commend it since such 'good' necessarily relates to human nature, without making any assumption that what people 'want' is necessarily what 'ought' to be.

A somewhat distinct point may, however, be made here. Positive law sets out basic prescriptions for the conduct of human society and in so doing it may reasonably be argued that it ought to serve the needs which arise from human nature. If that nature were different, so too, no doubt, would be human expectations of law, assuming such an institution to be relevant to the hypothetical circumstances. Human nature as it is cannot, according to Hume's basic dictum, found an 'ought', i.e., the fact that people are that way does not necessarily mean that they ought to be so. The 'is' of law is not the same as the 'is' of human nature and granted that law operates in human society there is no breach of Hume's argument in stating that what law is ought to conform to requirements dictated by what human nature is. The issue is one of the relation of legal function to the external parameter of human need. If this is accepted one can then proceed to Finnis's essential contention upon the determination of what need, or needs, law is to serve.

5.2.2 The basic goods

In order to determine what are the basic goods which human beings, by reason of their nature, value, Finnis advances certain generalisations about human societies which lead to a model of what things most people in most societies may be considered to think important. Finnis argues that despite the very considerable cultural diversity of human societies, there are certain basic concerns which are preponderantly found in a survey of the literature of anthropological investigations. On the basis of these general concerns Finnis sets out a model of seven 'basic forms of human good'. These are:

(a) Life, meaning not merely existence but also the capacity for development of potential. Within the category of life and its preservation Finnis includes procreation.

(b) Knowledge, not only as a means to an end but as a good in its own right which improves life quality.

(c) Play, in essence the capacity for recreational experience and enjoyment.

(d) Aesthetic experience, in some ways related to play but not necessarily so, this is broadly a capacity to experience and relate to some perception of beauty.

(e) Sociability or friendship, occurring at various levels but commonly accepted as a 'good' aspect of social life. One might add that this 'good' would seem to be an essential aspect of human conduct as social creatures, *politikon zōon* as Aristotle put it.

(f) Practical reasonableness, essentially the capacity to shape one's conduct and attitudes according to some 'intelligent and reasonable' thought process.

(g) Religion, this is not limited to, although it clearly includes, religion in the formal sense of faith and practices centred upon some sense of the divine. The reference here is to a sense of the responsibility of human beings to some greater order than that of their own individuality.

These goods are set out concisely (see *Natural Law and Natural Rights* pp. 86–9). A number of important questions may be asked both about this list and its particular components.

The first and most obvious question is the claim of the list to be comprehensive. Might not other goods be set out and listed? Finnis argues that:

> . . . there are countless objectives and forms of good. But . . . these . . . will be found, on analysis, to be ways or combinations of ways of pursuing (not always sensibly) and realising (not always successfully) one of the seven basic forms of good, or some combination of them. (*Natural Law and Natural Rights*, p. 90.)

One of the great obstacles to any satisfactory compilation of lists of goods, or indeed rights in a general context, lies in the lurking danger of cultural specificity. What is accepted as appropriate in one culture may well not be in another. The basic goods advanced by Finnis are categoric rather than specific in form and might obviously find particular application in a variety of ways.

A more complex question, perhaps, arises when it is asked how choices are to be made as between basic goods should any two or more of them prove incompatible in a given situation. Each good is advanced by Finnis as fundamental and of equal importance with each of the others: there is no hierarchic ranking amongst them.

In order to determine how the goods are to be applied as criteria of evaluation in the context of the operation of a real society it is obviously necessary to set up a structured scheme of assessment. This is done through the medium of tests of 'practical reasonableness' which may provide guidance as to what, in practice, is to be considered right or wrong in applying the basic goods.

5.2.3 The tests of practical reasonableness

The basic aim of the tests of practical reasonableness is related by Finnis to the broad methodology of classical naturalist thought in relating moral and ethical criteria to action and consequences. Thus:

> . . . [these] requirements . . . express the 'natural law method' of working out the (moral) 'natural law' from the first (pre-moral) 'principles of natural law'. . . . [This concerns] the sorts of reasons why (and thus the ways in which) there are things that morally ought (not) to be done. (*Natural Law and Natural Rights*, p. 103.)

The actual tests which Finnis sets out (*Natural Law and Natural Rights*, pp. 103–26) are:

(a)   A coherent life plan, meaning a set of 'harmonious' intentions and commitments by reference to which one intends to arrange one's life.

(b)   No arbitrary preferences are to be made amongst values, that is to say that a person may not individually choose to aspire to a particular good but that confers no entitlement to regard that good as devalued, e.g., in reference to the wishes of others. In this context Finnis is extremely critical of Rawls's 'thin theory of good' (see 15.2.2), claiming that it unduly restricts the range of goods to be considered.

(c)   There must be no arbitrary preferences amongst persons. This requires little comment in a modern context. The test would manifestly exclude, e.g., the varieties of irrational discrimination upon bases of race, gender or other such criteria.

(d) and (e)   Proper senses of both 'detachment' and 'commitment', meaning, in effect, a sufficient degree of flexibility to respond appropriately to changes in one's own circumstances and to the changing needs of others.

(f)   The significance of efficiency within reasonable limits, meaning that the efficient pursuit of goals, and avoidance of harm, is a real factor in the application of moral considerations but it cannot be treated in itself as a supreme or central principle. Taken beyond its proper limits, indeed, the pursuit of efficiency for its own sake may become both irrational and immoral.

(g)   Respect for every basic value in every act, meaning ultimately that no choice should be made which directly contravenes any 'basic good'.

(h)   Consideration for the common good. Finnis treats this as more or less obvious, and, indeed, such a requirement would seem inseparable from an assessment of moral relations within a social context.

(i)   People should follow the dictates of their conscience, even if that conscience is, unbeknown to the actor, in error. Finnis, following Aquinas, argues that a wrong conscience should be respected as an aspect of the full personhood of the individual concerned since in contravening its dictates that person would, in his or her own terms, act irrationally or immorally. One must conclude, however, that the second, third and eighth tests, at least, would seem to set some limits to this. A person who felt 'conscientiously' committed to participate in genocide could hardly on that basis be admitted to do so.

Finnis argues that the tests of practical reasonableness in combination with the basic goods represent the structure of a 'natural law' analysis.

This model is indeed much more clearly a mainstream naturalist argument than, e.g., the procedural natural law advanced by Lon L. Fuller (see 5.1). Finnis argues also that the combination of the basic goods and the tests of practical reasonableness would enable a society to obviate gross injustice and that they also provide a model of basic rights.

5.2.4   From natural law to natural rights

The generation of absolute rights from the practical morality embodied in his naturalist analysis is based by Finnis upon the proposition of practical reasonableness that:

> . . . it is always unreasonable to choose directly against any basic value, whether in oneself or in one's fellow human beings. . . . Correlative to the exceptionless duties entailed by this requirement are . . . exceptionless . . . human claim-rights. (*Natural Law and Natural Rights*, p. 225.)

The argument is thus essentially that it will always be wrong to make a choice directly contravening any of the basic goods and that the duty to respect these goods thus generates human rights to which there can be no exceptions.

The rights which are thus derived from the basic goods (*Natural Law and Natural Rights*, p. 225) are:

(a)   not to be deprived of life as a direct means to an end,
(b)   not to be deceived in the course of factual communication,
(c)   not to be condemned upon charges which are known to be false,
(d)   not to be denied procreative capacity, and
(e)   to be accorded 'respectful consideration' in any assessment of the common good.

There have been, and are, numerous assessments of the rights and their nature in various international treaties, such as the 1948 Universal

Declaration of Human Rights, and in a variety of academic treatments of the theory of rights, such as the rights thesis advanced by Ronald Dworkin (see chapter 9). All such endeavours, including that of Finnis, raise a variety of questions, according to their particular context. Lists of rights are inevitably specific expressions of more general principles and it might be argued that they are not truly autonomous but simply reflections of a moral or ethical climate in given situations. Those situations may of course change and threats may be posed to areas of life not formerly considered and this in turn may generate senses of new rights deriving from the basic moral climate. It may not be the case that all rights are concerned with defence of perceived entitlements from harm, but it may strongly be argued that the phrase 'I have a right to . . .' would come most naturally where someone seeks to deny the proposition.

One may readily accept that Finnis's 'exceptionless claim rights' are properly derived from their given context and are in themselves by and large unexceptionable. It would, however, be rash to take them as an exhaustive list or even one which leaves no questions open. The exceptionless claim-right not to be deprived of life as a means to an end may be considered as a particularly stark example. A person in Finnis's scheme may of course choose to undertake actions which place his or her own life at risk, e.g., in attempting to rescue another person from danger. Can people be required so to act? If the 'claim-rights' are 'exceptionless' presumably they may not. Here however one encounters the always difficult interface between individual and community expectations. To avoid the military examples one might consider a small community faced by an uncontrolled forest fire. Fighting the fire may well be a life-threatening activity for the fire-fighters (i.e., potentially all the physically fit persons in the community), not fighting the fire may also be life threatening (for everyone in the community). The answer here lies in the criteria of practical reasonableness but its discernment may well present considerable difficulties in some cases.

5.2.5   The obligation to obey in Finnis's theory

Finnis's analysis of the obligation to obey law is in many ways more subtle than the approach adopted in many theories of law, and certainly more so than that found in classical positivism (see chapter 2). He identifies four types of obligation which may be associated with law. These are: sanction-based obligation, 'intra-systemic' formal obligation, moral obligation and a distinct 'collateral' moral obligation (see *Natural Law and Natural Rights*, p. 354). The first three may broadly be seen, respectively, in the classical positivism of Bentham and Austin (see chapter 2), the later positivism of H. L. A. Hart (see chapter 3) and in the spectrum of naturalist theories (see chapter 4 as well as this chapter).

In a direct comment upon the views of John Austin, Finnis remarks that the dismissal of some of these senses to other disciplines or even, as for John

Austin, their denunciation as 'nonsense' is an 'unsound jurisprudential method' (see *Natural Law and Natural Rights*, p. 354). In this Finnis is surely correct. It may be argued very strongly that the idea of 'obligation' which is associated with law is not a singular phenomenon but, rather, a combination of different obligatory factors which have been variously explored by different schools of jurisprudence. The coercive, formal and moral elements in the obligatory characteristic of law may readily be seen. Jurisprudence has suffered, it may be argued, from trying to choose between these elements. It is not one but all of them in combination which will define the issue of legal obligation.

Finnis's division between moral and 'collateral' moral obligation is interesting. In effect he suggests that in disobeying a law, even a bad law, a person places at risk the whole legal system and that there may therefore be a 'collateral' moral obligation to obey such a law, notwithstanding its immorality, because of the damaging incidental effects of disobedience (see *Natural Law and Natural Rights*, pp. 361–2). This may be questioned insofar as the question of collateral damage can be seen as part of the question of moral obligation in general (see, e.g., the Socratic argument in Plato's *Crito*, analysed in 4.3.2). The internal morality of law, in contrast, is bound up in its formal dimension, which necessarily supposes the uniform obligation, subject to any explicit or implicit formal exceptions, to obey the law. This is perhaps a quibble, but it may be suggested that the tripartite categorisation of legal obligation into coercive, formal and moral elements has much to commend it. Finnis doubts the value of the coercive element, in the light of its predictive uncertainty. It may, however, still be suggested that coercion remains an element in the equation even if not a perfectly satisfactory one.

Finnis sets out the reasoning of the good citizen, based upon practical reasonableness, in relation to the duty to obey as a three-stage process (*Natural Law and Natural Rights*, p. 316). The stages are:

(a) The common good demands compliance with law.

(b) Where conduct is stipulated by law compliance can only be rendered by observing such conduct.

(c) Therefore the conduct so stipulated as obligatory must be performed.

The first stage will generally be assumed, leaving only the second and third stages open to discussion in a given case. However, in appropriate circumstances, the first stage may be reclaimed allowing choices to be made amongst variously 'moral' but universally 'valid' (in a formal sense) legal provisions.

There is for Finnis, as for St Thomas Aquinas (see 4.4.2), a 'weighting' in favour of obedience in most cases. Thus:

. . . the reasons that justify the vast legal effort to render the law . . . impervious to discretionary assessments . . . are reasons that also justify us in asserting that the moral obligation to conform to legal obligations is relatively weighty. (*Natural Law and Natural Rights*, p. 319.)

The 'justification' is of course precisely the uniformity of law as a general public prescription.

5.2.6 The importance of Finnis's theory

The theory of law advanced by Finnis is clearly one that fits centrally into the spectrum of naturalist thought. It relates at many points closely to the thinking of St Thomas Aquinas but also offers an original approach which speaks very clearly to the modern age. This is particularly the case in its analysis of essential naturalist issues in terms of a modern discourse of rights. This is a highly significant contribution to the modern naturalist revival, not as an abolition or denial of other schools of jurisprudence but rather as a redress of an imbalance which existed in conventional jurisprudence from the middle of the 19th century to the latter part of the 20th century.

5.3 BEYLEVELD AND BROWNSWORD: THE MORAL NATURE OF LAW

In *Law as a Moral Judgment* (London: Sweet and Maxwell, 1986), Deryck Beyleveld and Roger Brownsword offer a somewhat different modern naturalist analysis from that advanced by Finnis. As any naturalist thesis must be, the argument advanced by Beyleveld and Brownsword is founded upon the concept of law as a moral phenomenon and upon the contention that no violation of the dichotomy between descriptive 'is' propositions and normative 'ought' propositions arises from that view (see *Law as a Moral Judgment*, pp. 18–23). From this point they proceed to advance a view of law founded directly upon morality and, in particular, to attack the 'difference' between laws and morals asserted in much positivist argument.

5.3.1 Law as a moral phenomenon

Beyleveld and Brownsword argue that it is broadly common ground between the naturalist and positivist approaches that there is an intimate link between the concepts of obligation and validity. They deny, however, the central positivist thesis that law and morality are inherently separate phenomena and are to be treated as such. Thus:

> . . . our target . . . is the thesis that the concept of law is morally neutral, which involves *inter alia* the claim that the *de facto* [formal] criteria of legality are decisive. . . . The central contention . . . is that this thesis is wrong. (*Law as a Moral Judgment*, p. 4.)

Beyleveld and Brownsword argue that the entire enterprise of legal regulation is an endeavour to deal with problems of social order through a structure of rules. The working of such an enterprise is then suggested to be capable of satisfactory explanation only by reference to conditions of human social order, which presupposes a moral base to the order which is thus to be maintained. What justification, otherwise, could there be for maintaining it?

By reference to the arguments of Alan Gewirth (in *Reason and Morality* (Chicago, Ill: University of Chicago Press, 1978)), Beyleveld and Brownsword accept the argument that any rational person who undertakes an action must, by virtue of rationality, do so by reference to a supreme moral principle with specific content, termed the 'principle of generic consistency' (for detailed discussion of this see *Law as a Moral Judgment*, pp. 127-45).

The argument is then advanced that there exists an 'ideal typical' model of social order, which provides an evaluatory standard for the assessment of the actual operation of law. This view is underpinned by the argument that:

> . . . when the view that practical reason presupposes moral reason is placed in the context of . . . [a] claim about the constellation of facts and interests needed to define a problem of social order, then we have a necessary connection between law and morality. (*Law as a Moral Judgment*, p. 145.)

This model of law as a regulatory mechanism founded upon a moral view of society is obviously related to the core of naturalist thought. It may also be accepted that the argument for an essential link between law and morality is strongly supported by Beyleveld and Brownsword's argument. It is, however, perhaps unfortunate that this model is advanced as necessarily antagonistic to positivist thought as such, rather than to the conventional presentation of much positivist thought. If it is accepted that positivism is primarily concerned with the formal analysis of law (see chapter 3), including to some extent its command and coercive aspects (see chapter 2), then a different type of difference principle may be suggested. That is to say that law may indeed be a moral phenomenon and one properly considered in those terms, but it has also, internally, a formal dimension which is open to analysis in its own terms. Properly considered, such analyses may be argued to be complementary in any complete understanding of law and not seen as opposing contentions about identical questions.

5.3.2 Obligation in a moral view of law

For Beyleveld and Brownsword the duty to obey law relates directly to its moral quality. Thus:

> Laws, for us, are morally legitimate prescriptions under the [principle of generic consistency], and they straightforwardly generate legal-moral obligations. (*Law as a Moral Judgment*, p. 325.)

The model of obligation advanced is obviously morally based, but also admits the systemic aspects of formal identification.

A law which is both moral and formally identified will clearly carry full obligation. If it fails in some particular, however, there may still remain some degree of obligation. Beyleveld and Brownsord set out four possibilities (*Law as a Moral Judgment*, p. 373). There may be:

(a) an internal collateral obligation to obey a 'provisionally legal' prescription,

(b) similarly an internal obligation to obey a 'subjectively legal' rule believed by an official to be valid until its standing has been formally determined,

(c) an external collateral obligation to obey lest disobedience injure the social structure, and

(d) an 'external synthetic collateral obligation' to obey where compliance would better promote the legal and moral order than would disobedience.

Internality and externality are by reference to the 'principle of generic consistency' polity.

The problems of subjectivity, which may be levelled at notions of justifiable disobedience, or qualified obedience, are countered by Beyleveld and Brownsword by reference to ideas of 'accountability' and 'restraint' (*Law as a Moral Judgment*, pp. 295–304 and 368–78). The first of these is essentially a concept of the trusteeship of governments in the exercise of powers and their answerability therefor. The second is concerned with the question of the desirability of stability of norms even where, up to a point, injustice may result in a particular case. These elements are found in varying forms in much naturalist theory and have been referred to in relation to, e.g., the work of St Thomas Aquinas (see 4.4.2) and J. M. Finnis (see 5.2.5). The provision of some such mechanism(s) may be considered essential if the charge of an invitation to subjectively selective obedience is to be avoided.

5.3.3 The place of Beyleveld and Brownsword in modern naturalism

The moral analysis of Beyleveld and Brownsword is clearly in the mainstream of naturalist legal theory. It presents law as a moral phenomenon and indeed as one which can only properly be understood in moral terms. The argument might be seen in some ways as a more extreme thesis than those found in the classical naturalist spectrum or, indeed, that set out by Finnis. A number of questions may be asked about this approach. In particular the dismissal of the positivist analysis as wrong in itself, rather than tending to advance excessive claims, and the exclusive claims made for the form of naturalism advanced may be doubted. The analysis does, however, address the broad issues of the naturalist agenda from a rather different perspective and as such makes a substantial contribution to modern debate upon the moral nature of law.

5.4   THE CONTINUING ROLE OF NATURALIST JURISPRUDENCE

The revival, or continuation, of the moral and ethical analyses of positive law represented in the spectrum of naturalist jurisprudence brings forward vitally important questions about law. It has been emphasised in this and the previous chapter that there is essentially no choice to be made between naturalism and positivism, or other schools of thought. Neither a moral and ethical nor a formalist analysis can reasonably be held out as rendering any complete picture of the complex phenomenon of law as a means of social regulation. Nor can such forms of analysis usefully be treated as a mere adjunct of other, differently directed, thought. Naturalist, positivist and many other schools of thought contribute to the totality of legal theory. The presentation of fundamental, and often very ancient, naturalist concerns within the context of modern legal and social discourse must, for this reason, be considered a most positive development.

5.5   FURTHER READING

Beyleveld, D., and Brownsword, R., *Law as a Moral Judgment* (London: Sweet & Maxwell, 1986).

Coulson, N. J., *Conflicts and Tensions in Islamic Jurisprudence* (Chicago, Ill: University of Chicago Press, 1969).

Finnis, J. M., *Natural Law and Natural Rights* (Oxford: Clarendon Press, 1980).

Fuller, Lon L., *The Morality of Law*, rev. ed. (New Haven, Conn: Yale University Press, 1969).

Fuller, Lon, L., 'Positivism and fidelity to law: a reply to Professor Hart' (1957–8) 71 Harv L Rev 630.

MacCormick, N., 'Natural law reconsidered' (1981) 1 Oxford J Legal Stud 99.

CHAPTER SIX
Islamic Jurisprudence

Islamic jurisprudence is both a very important and a frequently misunderstood and misrepresented view of the nature and working of law. It is also a model of law of vast importance in the modern world, not only in that substantial number of countries in which it is the sole or dominant tradition but also more generally through international and trans-national interactions, as, for example, in the distinctive character of Islamic commercial law in the area of international trade. Islamic law is a religious law, founded upon the *Qu'ran* revealed to the Prophet Muhammad. As with any anciently established system of religious law, its jurisprudence is called upon to deal with two basic structural issues. The law was revealed, by definition, at a given point in history and it has therefore been necessary to develop modes of interpretation to enable the application of legal rules and principles in social circumstances in some ways very significantly different from the context in which they were first received. This is not, of course, an issue in itself unique to Islamic law – any ancient prescription must necessarily deal with this issue – but the structure of this law and its particular relation to the social structures which it moulds and guides render these processes in the present case of especial importance both in legal theory and practice. There is then also the question of relations with 'secular' provision, which is to some degree permitted in Islam. This too has parallels with other perceptions although the Islamic understanding is very clearly distinct in its nature.

From the viewpoint of a general textbook upon jurisprudence a preliminary question arises as to the basic character of Islamic legal theory. Is it to be considered a form of 'naturalism' as its religious base and ethical structure must seem strongly to suggest, or is it better considered to be *sui generis* in its character and essentially outside such categorisations? The first point to be understood is that the Islamic theory of law is not, as most western naturalism is, a theory *about* law upon the basis of which comparisons and evaluations may be made about its substance. On the contrary, Islamic law, the *Shari'ah*, in the Muslim concept quite simply *is* the law. In this sense Islamic jurisprudence should not strictly be seen as either 'naturalist' or 'positivist' in character since these categories have little real meaning in a Muslim context. However, whilst this is true in principle, the reality is, inevitably, somewhat more complex. In practice Islamic States, and multi-cultural States in which Islam is the dominant faith tradition, do have 'secular' law-making institutions and indeed do so by necessity. The *Shari'ah* lays down both highly specific rules and broad principles and the latter at least require implementation in given, and mutable, social circumstances which may differ in a number of regards from those which obtained in the lifetime of the Prophet. To take an obvious example, the *Shari'ah* makes no direct provision for the regulation of modern vehicular traffic and by reason of historical fact could not realistically have done so. Basic principles of social responsibility within the law, however, indicate clearly what sort of measures are required and these can be translated into specific rules by a 'secular' legislative process. In many Islamic States there will be one or another form of Religious Council which advises the government upon the *Shariat* rectitude of its 'secular' legislation. Such constitutional mechanisms come close at least to certain aspects of historical naturalism and would not have seemed incomprehensible to such figures as, e.g., St. Augustine of Hippo in the tradition of Christian naturalism (see 4.4.1), although such institutions were never precisely replicated even under the so called 'Doctrine of the two Powers' (see 4.4.2)

6.1   THE STRUCTURE AND SOURCES OF ISLAMIC LAW

The *Shari'ah* is considered a holy law revealed by Allah through the Prophet Muhammad. The matter of divine origin is fundamental to Islamic jurisprudence and the bedrock and primary source of Islamic law is the text of the *Qu'ran* received by the Prophet between the ages of 41 and 63 over a period of 22 years, 2 months and 22 days. As suggested above, the *Qu'ranic* texts of course required and require interpretation and application and in these processes lie much of the Islamic 'science' of jurisprudence. One possible source of confusion is immediately obviated in that only the classical Arabic text is accepted as authentically the *Qu'ran* – translations are permissible but are not in themselves authoritative. All other 'sources' of the *Shari'ah* are thus not in any way conceived as alternatives to or variations of *Qu'ranic* norms but rather as parts of the process of *Tafsir* – interpretation and clarification. The accepted hierarchy and significance of these other 'sources' was established by one of the greatest of early Islamic jurists, Muhammad ibn-Idris ash-Shafi'i, to whom much credit is due for the systematisation of 'scientific'

Islamic jurisprudence at a time when there was a real danger of fragmentation. A significant amount of customary Arabian practice was almost certainly ingested into the *Shari'ah* which came thereby to have attributed to it the authority of God. This is less dramatic in its implications than is sometimes suggested. Although Muslims refer to the period before the Prophetic revelation as 'the time of ignorance' it was never suggested that everything which had gone before should *ex hypothesi* have been abandoned. The point, which is worth emphasising in the present context, is that the development of Islamic jurisprudence has been by no means so simple as some of its adherents and its opponents seem to wish to suggest.

The most important of the sources of the *Shari'ah* beyond the *Qu'ran* itself is treated in effect as a supplementary, but not alternative, primary source and is the *Sunnah* – the life and teaching of the Prophet. The secondary interpretative sources are then *ijma* – the consensus of the Muslim community, *Qiyas* – understanding by analogy, and *Ijtahad* – understanding by personal reasoning, supposedly ended with the early 'closing of the gates of *ijtahad*' but possibly reopened in the 13th/14th centuries AH (i.e., 19th century AD). In the present context it is important to note that the interaction, especially, of the various secondary sources may be seen as a means of solving one of the fundamental problems of any system of religious law. The point at which the law is received is necessarily in some fixed historical era and whilst general principles may hold good for all time, detailed applications will need to be considered in the light of social changes which will almost certainly become more radical as the time of accepted revelation becomes more remote. This is not a problem unique to Islam, it is found in one way or another in most faiths, certainly all those with significant normative content. The processes of jurisprudential adaptation in the context of Christianity have been considered in 4.4, those adopted within Islamic jurisprudence are different in kind but also of great significance and interest. Islam shares with other faiths the need both to conserve the purity of foundational doctrine whilst also finding effective application in, sometimes radically, changing historical circumstances. This was exacerbated in the case of Islam by the early 'closure of the gates of *ijtahad*' (human interpretative development) which sought, in theory if not quite in practice, to set the law in a definitive interpretation for all time. More recently the need has in fact been felt for an increase in the moulding of application to changing circumstances which has led in some sense to a reopening of *ijtahad*. N. J. Coulson remarks of this that:

These recent developments have given to Islamic law a new historical perspective. *Shar'ia* [*Shari'ah*] doctrine, which grew to maturity in the first three centuries of Islam and which then remained essentially static for a period of ten centuries, appears now in the course of further evolution.

(N. J. Coulson, 'Islamic Law' in J. Duncan M. Derrett, *An Introduction to Legal Systems* (London: Sweet & Maxwell), 1968, p. 54 at p. 55.)

The means by which Islam deals with this basic issue of anciently received religious laws is one of primary jurisprudential interest and importance.

6.1.1 Sunnah

Sunnah is in essence the understanding gained from the life and practice of the Prophet, including what amounted to judicial decisions made by him as the first leader of the Muslim community. The *Sunnah* is founded upon reports of the particular Prophetic decisions and actions known as *hadith*. Two points require immediately to be made. The first is that the Prophet himself is not being presented as an alternative to the *Qu'ranic* revelation. The argument is rather that since the Prophet was the one through whom the *Qu'ran* was revealed and who in his life lived closely in understanding of its precepts, his life and practice may be accepted as a revealed elucidation of the holy text. The second, and very important, point is that of the authenticity of the tradition relied upon – in short the degree of confidence which may be reposed in the accuracy of the reports of Prophetic speech and actions. Initially, authenticity was established by an absence of challenge from those who had actually heard the utterance or witnessed the action. Abdur Rahman I. Doi cites as an example the settlement of an inheritance claim brought by Fatimah, the Prophet's daughter, upon the basis of unchallenged recollection of a Prophetic statement (*Shari'ah: The Islamic Law* (London: Ta Ha Publishers, 1984), p. 50).

Over the years collections of *hadith* were built up and after the lifetimes of the original Companions of the Prophet, who had personally witnessed his words and actions, a tradition of critical *hadith* scholarship developed by necessity for the testing of the authenticity of claimed traditions. Six canonically accepted collections of *hadith* were made by the end of the 3rd century AH (9th century AD) upon the basis of the techniques of *isnad* according to which the authority of any claimed *hadith* could be assessed. *Isnad* rested in broad outline upon establishing a reputable chain of report back to a known original witness, or ideally a group of witnesses. The latter was of especial importance where the *hadith* comprised an event rather than a reported Prophetic statement. Equally obviously, a purported *hadith* which was clearly contrary to *Qu'ranic* statement or to another better established *hadith* would necessarily be rejected as inauthentic.

6.1.2 Ijma

The concept of *ijma* is basically that of the scholarly consensus of the Islamic community (the *Ummah*). As a source of law it is clearly derivative in distinction from the *Qu'ran* itself and from the traditions of the *Sunnah*, but is nonetheless accepted as an authority upon the basis of an interpretation or understanding which the Islamic community as a whole, or at least its expert jurists, agree is exceedingly unlikely to be erroneous. This is a view supported by a Prophetic utterance to the effect that the Islamic community could not agree upon error. *Ijma* is not, however, viewed as an independent source but as a means of ascertaining reliable Islamic opinion upon the meaning and interpretation of the primary sources – the *Qu'ran* and the *Sunnah*. There is some debate as to who can actually establish *ijma*: it is certainly not simply a test of popular opinion. In practice the matter seems to rest to some degree upon the gravity of the issue in question and it is also accepted that even a fairly small body of scholarly opinion will suffice to establish *ijma* if no protest is voiced by others, in a manner clearly analogous with the tradition of *hadith* scholarship.

6.1.3   *Qiyas*

This is a process of reasoning by analogy from existing principles or understandings to find solutions to categorically similar problems which are not otherwise precisely addressed. The process is one commonly found where it is required to apply a fixed prescription to new or altered circumstances not specifically covered; it was found, for example, in classical China as a juristic technique in the face of the overly specific and inflexible provisions of the successive Imperial Codes. It was specifically established by Abu Hanifah, the founder of the Hanafi School of jurisprudence (see 6.2), in part as a way of curbing the development of a speculative jurisprudence which, as the Islamic community expanded, was feared to threaten a 'corruption' of Islamic juristic understanding and may as such be seen as a product of the work of ash-Shafi'i (see 6.2). Some Islamic scholars nonetheless oppose the idea of *qiyas* as a potential dilution of *Qu'ranic* and *Sunnah* authority, but the more general view appears to be that, so long as *qiyas* is applied only where there is no unequivocal guidance from either the *Qu'ran* or *Sunnah*, the practice is acceptable and, indeed, necessary.

6.1.4   *Ijtahad*

Ijtahad was the process of independent reasoning and interpretation and as such represented the contribution of human reasoning *stricto sensu* to the development of the *Shari'ah*. It fell within the scheme of ash-Shafi'i's juristic analysis and was supposed to commence from the *Qu'ran* and the *Sunnah* and in this sense to be an interpretative application rather than a process of justice in its own right. Nonetheless in the 4th century AH (10th century AD) the Islamic community reached the conclusion that the phase of this form of development had come to an end and that there had consequently occurred a 'closure of the gates of *ijtahad*', closing this mode of development off until at least the 13th century AH (19th century AD). Some modern Islamic writers have questioned whether this permanent closure of the gates of *Ijtahad* represented genuine *ijma* or, if it did, whether it was actually intended to be 'permanent'. Thus, Abdur Rahman I. Doi suggests that the 'closure' was more in the way of a temporary response to the Mongol conquest of Baghdad, the seat of the Caliphate (*Shari'ah: The Islamic Law*, pp. 68–9 and 81) and the threat posed thereby to the cohesion of the Islamic community. Another view is presented by N. J. Coulson who points out that the 'closure' appears to have developed before the Mongol incursion and suggests that the move actually represented an internal force of doctrinal conservatism. He writes that:

> The point had been reached where the material sources of the divine will – their content now finally determined – had been fully explored. An exaggerated respect for the personalities of former jurists induced the belief that the work of interpretation and expansion had been exhaustively accomplished. (N. J. Coulson, *A History of Islamic Law* (Edinburgh: Edinburgh University Press, 1964/78), p. 81.)

It is of course possible that both these views are correct and that the 'closure' resulted both from a movement of internal conservatism and from an apprehension of external threat. However that may be, in the modern age there has developed a practice of *neo-ijtahad*, founded partly upon evident need and partly upon doubts as to the nature and finality of the 4th century AH 'closure'. The need to 'reopen the gates of *ijtahad*', if indeed they had ever strictly been 'closed', arose from the self-evident need to apply *Shari'at* principles in new and in some respects radically altered circumstances to which existing modes were not wholly addressed. For this effectively to be done a scholarly process was necessary which was close to, if not actually historically continuous with, that of the classical *ijtahad*. This development may be seen as one of the processes of adaptation necessary for the application of an ancient law established at a given, and remote, historical era according to which well accepted principles may find necessarily new applications.

6.2.   THE FOUR SCHOOLS

The four established Schools of Islamic jurisprudence, the Hanifi, Maliki, Shafi'i and Hanbali, emerged from the post-Prophetic development of Islamic jurisprudence and are in essence the survivors of a phase of expression which generated a great many 'schools' of jurisprudence, primarily resulting in the development of local practices and understandings by *Qadis* (judges) which was perhaps inevitable as the Islamic community expanded well beyond the point of origin in the Hijaz (the region of the Hijaz). This diversity of juristic opinion, however, posed a further threat to the cohesiveness of the Islamic consensus which was suppressed through the development of a more rigorous, but also more conservative, *Shari'at* scholarship and out of this process the four canonically orthodox Sunni Schools emerged in their present forms.

The relationship between the four Schools requires some explanation. They do not as such represent divergent opinions upon the central substance of Islam but do represent somewhat divergent approaches to understanding and application, in particular in relation to so-called 'minor', if sometimes important, issues of interpretation and application which remain within canonical orthodoxy. The four Schools are still to a degree geographically based, the Hanafi being dominant in the Middle East and the sub-Continent, the Maliki in much of Muslim Africa, the Shafi'i in Malaysia, Indonesia and some of the Gulf States, whilst the highly conservative Hanbali is the principally accepted School in Saudi Arabia. The distinctions are not of course solely geographical, there are also significant substantive distinctions. The Hanafi and Maliki Schools, which predate the work of ash-Shafi'i, essentially accepted his stricter formulation of *Shar'at* scholarship, but also retained much of their existing understanding and practice which they reconciled with the implications of ash-Shafi'i's reforms. The Shafi'i School follows directly the work of ash-Shafi'i himself, its founder, the Hanbali school was originally much the most conservative of the Schools and sought to reject the role of human reason in Islamic jurisprudential development altogether. Later, however, the Hanbalis accepted the validity of *Qiyas*. The end result is that, whilst the four Schools retain certain clear distinctions of both understanding and interpretation, there is a consensus upon fundamental elements of the law. In much of the Islamic world elements of each of the four Schools may be resorted to for guidance in the application of *Shari'at* principle. They thus represent to some degree a spirit of flexibility at least upon peripheral matters which can be, and has been, used as a means of legal development and reform of practice. There are, however, limits to this flexibility and it was partly for this reason that the practice of *neo-ijtahad* developed in the modern age (see 6.1.4).

6.3 ISLAM AND THE STATE

The post-Prophetic expansion of the Islamic community from the original small community in Medina naturally led to the development of formal structures of State. The central element of the historical structure was the office of Caliph. The *Caliph ul-Islam*, Commander of the Faithful, was in a loose sense seen as the successor of the Prophet as leader of the community but not as a recipient of divine revelation. After the immediate successors of the Prophet, the Ummayad Caliphs in Damascus and later the Abbasid Caliphs in Baghdad were of variable quality, some were notable contributors to the Islamic community, others were ornaments neither to their faith nor their political structures. The Ottoman Sultans of Turkey of the House of Othman, having murdered their final predecessor, were the last to claim the Caliphate which endured after the Sultanate itself, being finally suppressed by Kemal Ataturk in the 1920s. The validity of the Ottoman claim was, naturally, uncontested within the Ottoman Empire, but whether the claim represented a genuine expression of *ijma* within the non-Ottoman *Ummah* may at least be doubted. The office of Caliph is also the root of the division between *Sunni* and *Shi'ite* Islam. The *Shi'a* accept the validity of the Caliphate only in the era immediately following the life of the Prophet and have since that era relied on the authority of leading Imams, which in its most significant modern expression may be seen in the position of the Iranian Ayatollahs following the overthrow of the regime of the Shah. It may be added in parenthesis that there is not really a distinction of fundamental doctrine between *Sunni* and *Shi'a* Muslims, although there is also not infrequently considerable political bitterness – exemplified in an extreme form by the persecution of the *Shi'ite* Marsh Arabs in Southern Iraq.

Inevitably, the expanding Islamic community ceased to be a politically unified entity and as a result Islamic States developed. In the Middle East these mostly, at least notionally, acknowledged the suzerainty of the Ottoman Sultans and Caliphs but the extent to which the writ of Istanbul actually ran in these territories varied very considerably. Often, authority was effectively farmed out to local administrators who for all practical purposes conducted themselves with sovereign dignity in the territories concerned. Naturally enough, the political authority of the Ottoman Sultan was never acknowledged, e.g., in Mughal India or by the Malay Sultans.

In practice, there were collisions between political and religious authority in Islamic States in a way parallel with, if different in manner from, those encountered in other faith communities. This, not surprisingly, raises the same questions, again in somewhat different forms, which are raised by the broad 'Naturalist' tradition – with certain interesting conclusions.

6.3.1 *Shari'ah* and secular law in Islamic States

The relationship between the *Shari'ah* and secular law in Islamic States is obviously a key jurisprudential question. It was remarked at the beginning of this chapter that the *Shari'ah* does not operate in the manner of, for example, Christian naturalism as an external overview of the quality of secular law and the obligation imposed by it. The assumption is rather that it *is* the law and that no derogation from it is in any wise possible. In practice the situation is rather more complex. Islamic States are by no means theocracies in the sense of a political regime which claims for itself divine authority in the manner of the pre-modern, and in some cases rather more recent, European notion of a 'divine right of Kings'. Secular government and legislation are recognised as necessary by Islam, not least because by its nature the *Shari'ah* does not and could not provide a completely comprehensive prescription down to minute details of regulation. *Shari'at* prescription is indeed variable in the rigour of its assertion. There are matters which are either compulsory or forbidden, the well-known ban upon the consumption of alcohol would be an example of the latter. There are also, however, matters which are rather more ambiguously defined as either recommended or unrecommended but not actually mandated in either direction. There are then also some matters for which the *Shari'ah* does not actually prescribe at all. In these latter categories from a *Shari'at* perspective the State is free to give legislative direction and may even be required to do so, so long as such legislation does not contravene fundamental principles of *Shari'ah*. At this level something much more like a classic 'naturalist' position begins to develop. In many of the Gulf States, for example, a *Shura* Council, literally a Consultative Council, has been set up in which Islamic experts advise the government upon the *Shari'at* rectitude of legislation and other government decisions. How these Councils are structured and what practical impact they have is, obviously, somewhat variable but it would be an unwise Islamic government which overtly flouted the *Shari'ah* or expert advice upon it. Nonetheless conflicts have arisen between governments and religious opinion in a number of States which has taken a variety of forms. Some care is needed in categorising such clashes and extreme examples such as the occasional conflicts, e.g., between so-called 'fundamentalists' and the government in Egypt are an extreme example which are not in fact necessarily informed by strictly 'Islamic' opinion.

In this context it should be explained in parenthesis that the term 'fundamentalist' is actually inappropriate. In its proper context it is a term used to describe Christians who take Biblical texts literally without need for interpretation. The *Qu'ran* is a rather different type of book from the Bible in the sense that it is a fairly straightforward set of injunctions which, although they may require interpretative application, can only be taken literally. In this sense all Muslims are by definition fundamentalists in a proper analogical application of the term. The term has however come to be used not in a context of textual understanding but to refer to certain extremist political movements within Islam whose conduct is by no means necessarily concordant with *Shari'at* injunctions.

In countries in which Islam is the dominant but not the sole national religion a somewhat more complex situation naturally arises. Thus in Malaysia, for example, in which Islam is the national religion but where there are also very significant Buddhist, Taoist, Hindu and Christian populations, the *Shari'ah* is applied to Muslims along with the secular law of the land but not to followers of other faiths. Wu Min Aun remarks that:

> According to the Federal Constitution, the power to administer Muslim Law is primarily that of the states comprising the Federation. . . . The jurisdiction of the State and the *Syariah* courts in [relevant] . . . matters is subject to certain federal laws. For instance, the punishment of offences by the *Syariah* courts is limited to those professing the religion . . . (Wu Min Aun, *The Malaysian Legal System* (Petaling Jaya: Longman Malaysia, 1990), pp. 38–9).

This, it may be added, is wholly concordant with Islamic understanding which is in principle far more tolerant of populations of other faiths than is commonly supposed, both within and beyond the Islamic world.

6.3.2   *Shari'ah* and human rights

In much western writing Islamic law is taken to be essentially antithetical to ideas of human rights. This is in fact by no means necessarily the case. It must first be said that the Islamic world is not monolithic in its social structures and practices. Thus, to take the important question of the status of and opportunities for women in Islamic societies, in some Islamic countries women are in practice accorded almost no enforceable rights whilst in others the practical opportunities for women to attain important public positions are at least as good as in many western states. The *Shari'ah* is a law directed to a community and as such includes highly significant provision for human welfare. At the same time the underlying concepts are commonly communitarian rather than individualistic and this raises the important question of the supposed division between 'Eastern' collectivism and 'Western' individualism. This supposed dichotomy is at best questionable. In essence it represents an arguably false division between rights and duties which are in fact different views of the same normative phenomenon. One person's right may be seen as the duty of another, without entering into the more subtle debates of Hohfeldian analysis. Human beings are also social creatures destined to live in one way or another in community with others, as theorists from Aristotle onwards (see 4.3.3) have acknowledged, and in this sense collective rights are actually in principle protections of the individuals comprising the society. In practice there is manifestly a proper balance to be drawn between individual expectations and collective entitlements and this is one, although not the only, foundation of the human rights concept. In the development of this understanding neither traditional Islamist perception of the West as drug obsessed and limitlessly promiscuous nor the common western vision of Islam as oppressive and harshly restrictive is very helpful. There clearly are dangerously licentious elements in western society, there are no less clearly elements of Islamic society in which self-seeking elites have imposed a regime contemptuous of disadvantaged individuals and taken unto themselves the authority of God for so doing. Both positions are false – liberalism and licence are not synonymous nor does the *Shari'ah* inherently involve oppression, quite the contrary. Some Muslim writers have made the point that human rights in Islam are a religious duty laid upon all Islamic States whereas, e.g., the UN Universal Declaration of Human Rights is often not observed by States (see, e.g., Abdur Rahman I. Doi, *Shari'ah: The Islamic Law*, pp. 422–3). The UN Declaration is indeed all too often ignored, but to claim that all supposedly Islamic States actually observe the human rights embodied within the *Shari'ah* would at best be an overstatement. Both modern western traditions and the modern practice of Islam have much to learn and reform in their practice and in so doing may find that the supposed divisions are actually less wide than is often supposed, or at least this may be hoped.

6.3.3 *Shari'ah* and the rights of non-Muslims

In principle non-Muslims in an Islamic State enjoy the protection of the *Shari'ah* and have their rights protected no less than Muslims. Abdur Rahman I. Doi remarks that:

> Since the Dhimmis [non-Muslims under Muslim rule] are under Dhimmat-Allah, they enjoy complete religious, administrative and political freedom – a right guaranteed to them in return for their loyalty and the payment of a reasonable tax called *Jizyah* which will be utilized in the defence and administration of the state. (*Shari'ah: The Islamic Law*, p. 427.)

This principle is well-established and in some places is scrupulously observed, in others, however, it is not. Religious persecution is certainly not a uniquely Islamic phenomenon, most religions have perpetrated, many in some cases continue to perpetrate, such cruelties, but Islam is no more free from this malpractice than any other faith, or indeed ideological, community. As writers such as Dworkin have pointed out (see chapter 9), the granting of rights to unpopular minorities is one of the key tests of a rights-based society – the granting of rights by a majority to themselves reflecting their given predilections can hardly be judged to be significant in this context. The commitment to the rights of people of other faith traditions is anciently and broadly rooted in Islam, but the practice in the modern world is variable and the comments made above in relation to the human rights of Muslims in Islamic States apply with no less force in the present context.

6.4   *SHARI'AH* AND INTERNATIONAL LAW

International law, *Al Siyah*, has an important role in Islam and took shape at an early stage in the development of the *Shari'ah*. It must here be said that international law in general had a much earlier origin than its supposed genesis in the 1648 Peace of Westphalia which in fact marked only the inauguration of its Western, early modern form. In reality, wherever there are States, or equivalent political entities, some form of 'international law' will develop – as is evidenced by the rediscovered ancient clay tablets containing diplomatic correspondence between the Pharaohs of Egypt and the Kings of the Hittites. It is recorded that the Prophet himself was insistent that agreements entered into with foreign, non-Muslim States should be faithfully performed – an instance of the basic international legal doctrine that *pacta sunt servanda*, which is the foundation, *inter alia*, of modern treaty law. In practice there is very little conflict between the *Shari'ah* and modern public international law and the issue is not a large one in Islam. It is, however, important that with the changing shape of relations within the Islamic community, the concept of *Al Siyah* which first defined relations between the Muslim community and non-Muslim community, now also deals with relations between Islamic States *inter se*.

Clearly there would be serious difficulty if provisions of international law were to conflict with the *Shari'ah*, but this is unlikely so far as general international law is concerned since this law develops essentially in a consensual fashion and could not do so in the face of the determined opposition of Islamic States. The question of human rights referred to above (see 6.3.2) has caused some debate, but this is not so much a matter of fundamental principle as one of interpretation and application – fundamentally important as the issues may be in given cases.

6.4.1   *Dar ul-Islam* and *Dar al-Harb*

From an Islamic perspective the world is divided into two communities, or 'houses', the *Dar ul-Islam* (House of Faith) and the *Dar al-Harb* (House of War). Some commentators suggest that this means that there is thus a duty laid upon Muslims to fight against those of other faiths and to secure their conversion by force. In an eschatological vision there may be an element of this in the view taken of the *Dar al-Harb*, but it is not the view taken in the present time frame; indeed in principle, if by no means always in practice, Islam is supposed to be remarkably tolerant of other faiths. In this sense the *Dar al-Harb* is supposed to be seen not necessarily as an object of Islamic hostility so much as a potential source of hostility to Islam: that is to say a 'House' from which war may come rather than a community against which war is necessarily to be waged. This division is fundamental to the Islamic view of international relations, according to which relations within the Islamic community, the *Ummah*, can never be the same as those with non-Muslim countries or entities.

One particular question arises for Muslims as regards the *Dar al-Harb* and that is the nature and extent of the obligation which Muslims living in non-Islamic States are subject to. Islam does not excuse Muslims from compliance with the laws of non-Islamic States, but still less does it excuse them from compliance with the *Shari'ah*. In minor matters, concerning things which are merely recommended or unrecommended, rather than prescribed or proscribed, it may be that some accommodation not dissimilar from that advanced, e.g., by St Thomas Aquinas in a Christian context (see 4.4.2), that is to say that a dutiful citizen must pay some, although not an unlimited, price in dubious law for social stability. This, however, could hardly apply where fundamental contravention of the *Shari'ah* was demanded by a system of non-Islamic law. As from the early days of extensive Arab trading networks, in which this problem arose on a number of occasions, the rule is essentially that, faced with such a situation, the earliest possible return to the *Dar ul-Islam* should be sought. Of course this is hardly an answer where a State will neither allow freedom of religion nor freedom of movement as, for example, in the former USSR. In such a case there would of course be a violation of the international law of human rights but again the basic question of enforcement arises.

6.4.2 *Jihad*

The idea of *Jihad* is much misunderstood outside the Islamic world and, to some extent, even within it. Referring back to the relation between the *Dar ul-Islam* and the *Dar al-Harb* (see 6.4.1), *Jihad* is not a concept of 'holy war' enjoining aggression against non-Islamic States, it is rather an idea of a 'war of necessity' coming close to the concept of collective self-defence now embodied in Article 51 of the United Nations Charter. It has its origins in the *Hijiah*, the flight of the Prophet from the hostility of the Meccans to refuge in Medina and is an idea of struggle against the enemies of faith. Upon the basis of a comment made by the Prophet when returning to Medina from battle, the greater *jihad* is seen as a Muslim's own spiritual struggle for purity of faith and contention for the observance of Islamic standards in Islamic society. The lesser *jihad*, armed struggle against external enemies, is a carefully limited concept which is concerned strictly with defence of the Muslim community if it is attacked. The key *Qu'ranic* text for the present purpose is found in Chapter 9:123 which in translation reads:

O you who believe, fight the unbelievers who gird you about, and let them find firmness in you: and know that Allah is with those who fear Him.

In this sense the lesser *jihad* is quite simply a system of Islamic collective security.

Confusion arises from two sources, from outside and from within the Islamic community. Externally, Islamic division of the world into the categories of the *Dar ul-Islam* and the *Dar al-Harb* has led some to imagine that Islam actually enjoins holy war against all non-Muslims, which is not the case. The concept of *jihad* has also, however, been the subject of corruption and misapplication within the Islamic world with rulers attempting to place a cloak of religion over what were simply secular conflicts. The Ottoman Sultan, in his capacity as Caliph, attempted to declare the First World War a general *jihad* against the non-Muslim Allied powers, a curious proposition granted that the Ottoman Empire was in alliance with the non-Muslim German and Austro-Hungarian Empires. The attempt fell to the ground when the purported proclamation of *jihad* was denounced by the Sherif of Mecca who was fighting against Ottoman forces on the Allied side. More recently President Saddam Hussein attempted to declare the 1990–91 Gulf War a *jihad*, an almost impossible proposition since the Iraqi invasion of Kuwait was an act of aggression by one Islamic state against another.

6.5 FURTHER READING

Coulson, N. J., *Conflicts and Tensions in Islamic Jurisprudence* (Chicago: University of Chicago Press, 1969).
Coulson, N. J., *A History of Islamic Law* (Edinburgh: Edinburgh University Press, 1964).
Doi, Abdur Rahman I., *Shari'ah: The Islamic Law* (London: Ta Ha Publishers, 1984).
Fyzee, A. A. A., *Outlines of Muhammadan Law*, 4th ed. (Delhi: Oxford University Press, 1974).

CHAPTER SEVEN

Marxism and Post-Marxism

The dramatic changes which took place in the former Soviet Union after the adoption of policies of glasnost and perestroika by the Gorbachev administration, followed by the collapse of Soviet and East European communism, has clear implications for the continuing significance of Marxist thought in the development of jurisprudence. It would, however, be an error to imagine that that effect has simply been one of abolition. It must be remembered that 'Marxism' has never simply been synonymous with the various forms of Marxism-Leninism practised in the former Soviet Union and also that the Marxist-derived ideology and jurisprudence of the People's Republic of China continues to raise most important questions in both theory and practice. It is inevitable, and entirely proper, that the consideration of Marxist jurisprudence should involve study of its forms of application in, *inter alia*, the former Soviet Union and in China. However, the starting-point is not one of practical political and legal history but rather one of theory.

Marxist theory in one way fits rather awkwardly into the corpus of jurisprudence because the very idea of legal theory is to a significant extent alien to Marxist thought. This thought is founded upon an economic and political analysis to which legal theory is, at most, an adjunct. This basic fact must be appreciated from the outset if either the nature of the Marxist argument or the Marxist-derived practices of law are to be understood. Once this is accepted, both the theory and its practical derivatives become much more clear in their implications. For the present purpose it may be sufficient to outline the broad appreciation of law in classical Marxist thought, with some consideration of the practical experience of the former Soviet Union and of China, leading to an assessment of the future relevance of these forms of Marxist-based jurisprudential thinking.

7.1   CLASSICAL MARXIST THEORY

What is now considered classical Marxist theory was developed by Karl Marx (1818–83) and Friedrich Engels (1820–95). Marx and Engels rejected what they viewed as the naïve idealism of contemporary European thought and sought instead a 'scientific' analysis of the processes of social development. The solution which they advanced lay in the concept of dialectical materialism which was a radically adapted form of an argument advanced by G. W. F. Hegel. Hegel (1770–1831) had proceeded from the proposition of Immanuel Kant, that every thesis has a contrary antithesis, to argue that the contradiction between thesis and antithesis can be resolved to reveal a higher reality termed a 'synthesis'. The resolution of thesis and antithesis into synthesis was then conceived as a continuing process resolving contradictions in the attainment of higher states of knowledge until a condition of absolute understanding would be reached. According to this Hegelian dialectic social development is also seen as a continuing resolution of contradictions leading to a final synthesis in the achievement of the optimum conditions of human life. For Hegel the primary vehicle for this process of development was the State which, consequently, he emphasised as an entity greater than the sum of its parts and having an importance which transcends the interests of its individual members. In the Hegelian State the individual finds fulfilment in playing a proper role in the State, a view which conformed neatly with the State ideology of Prussia and, after 1870, of Imperial Germany, and underlay much political thought of the period.

Marx did not accept the statism of the Hegelian dialectic but advanced a varied form of analysis, dialectical materialism, which emphasised not the State but economic class relations as the engine of social development. In classical Marxist thought society rests upon an economic base and all other social and political phenomena are seen as a 'superstructure' which rests upon it and takes its form at any given time from the nature of the developing economic relations within the base. It is in this sense that Marxist thought is said to be 'materialist'. It claims to be founded upon 'real' economic relations in the processes of production and exchange rather than upon 'ideal' hypotheses about society. Social understanding is then seen as an ideological perception of the economic relations existing at a given time which will change as the underlying economic relationships alter. For the classical Marxist such change will not be gradual or evolutionary but spasmodic and more or less violent. It is this perception which informs the Marxist concern with revolutionary change.

In Marxist analysis it is argued that starting from an economically undifferentiated state of society in which all means of production and exchange are held in common, the increasing complexity of developing economic activity will produce clearly distinct classes defined by their role in the economic structure. It is then argued that diversification and class orientation in economic activity concentrate ownership and control of the means of production in a dominant class which will then subject subordinate classes to its interests. Out of this will come the class antagonism which is a hallmark of Marxist political theory. Social development is then perceived as following the development of relations in the economic base, as real economic power shifts and previously subordinate classes successively seize a dominant role with the passage of time. The change is marked by revolutionary episodes and in this respect Marxism may be seen as a form of catastrophe theory.

Classical Marxists contend that as the economic base and the balance of power relations within it change, ideological perceptions and the superstructural institutions will lag behind. The pressure created by the divergence between economic reality and the ideology and institutions will eventually prove unsustainable and at that point there will be a sudden revolutionary realignment forcing the ideology and social superstructure to reflect the new order of the economic base. Successive revolutions are then argued to occur as dominant classes are superseded by formerly subordinate classes and power passes through monarchic and 'feudal' periods of control to the domination of a 'bourgeois' merchant class in the capitalist phase of development. Upon a Marxist analysis this bourgeois revolution occurred in the United Kingdom during the traumas of the 17th century, sealed by the constitutional settlement of 1689 when William III and Mary II were put on the throne, upon terms, in place of James II in the foundation of the more or less modern idea of the Crown in Parliament (for a different analysis of this process see 3.2.3). At this point the proletariat becomes the last remaining subordinate class and when, inevitably, according to the Marxist model, the proletarian revolution takes place it will be the final stage of revolutionary development simply because there are no further subordinate classes to continue the process. This ending of class conflict is then supposed to lead more or less directly to the withering away of the superstructural instruments of class domination, including the State and positive law, and their replacement by a vaguely defined communistic ordering of things. Marx gave little detail of this final anticipated social order, primarily because his immediate concerns were with the political and industrial conditions of the later 19th century in what he saw as the crisis of late capitalism in the immediate prelude to proletarian revolution.

The Marxist dialectical materialist analysis is presented as a 'scientific' model of social development founded upon 'real' phenomena and rejecting the unprovable assumptions of 'idealist' theories. Marxist theory can, however, be argued itself to be implicitly value-laden. The treatment of institutions as reflecting deeper social realities and changing in reflection of their condition from time to time as part of some form of dialectical process may readily command some support. The selection of economic relations and associated class conflicts as the fundamental social determinant is, however, evidently a selective presentation of data. In fairness, Marx and Engels did not deny the incidental importance of other factors and even conceded that matters such as constitutions and legal forms might even determine the forms of historical development at given times (see Engels's letter to J. Bloch of 21 September 1890, quoted in M. Cain and A. Hunt, *Marx and Engels on Law* (London: Academic Press, 1979), p. 56). However, this emphasis tends towards a dubious 'class reductionism' in which the entire analysis may become contorted in order to conform to the apparent dictates of the selected base. As has been argued elsewhere:

> Into [social] interactions go such matters as culture, ethical or other beliefs and inherited concepts of solidarity as well as purely economic factors. To concentrate solely upon economics as the base factor is severely to limit the analysis and to interpret all other factors in its light actually involves a distortion. (H. McCoubrey, *The Development of Naturalist Legal Theory* (London: Croom Helm, 1987), p. 109.)

It is also noteworthy that the revolutionary process is seen not only as a 'scientifically' inevitable phenomenon but also as something to be desired and worked for. The historical explanation for this may be evident enough in the case of Marx's own writings, but there would still seem to be an implicit breach of the distinction drawn by David Hume between descriptive and normative, 'is' and 'ought', propositions (see 2.1).

7.1.1   Law in classical Marxist theory

In Marxist analysis positive law is an element of the social 'superstructure' the form and use of which at any given time will be a reflection of the condition of the economic base. This fundamental point leads to the important insight of Marxist jurisprudence that law is not an autonomous phenomenon and to the argument that the implicit assumption of much formal legal discourse that it is so is a form of 'legal fetishism'. That positive law is not a free-standing phenomenon but one intimately related to a range of political, ethical, moral, social and economic factors should be obvious enough. Indeed the point is part of a range of theories, including, for example, the moral analyses of classical naturalism. Marxism itself may, indeed, be open to criticism for its exclusive emphasis upon the importance of economic factors but the emphasis upon the non-autonomy of law is, nonetheless, important. It may be convenient in professional legal discourse to speak 'as if' law operated in isolation from 'external' influences but there is a severe danger of distortion in a professional habit of mind which forgets that this is a convenient mental shorthand rather than an accurate description. This element of Marxist jurisprudence may serve as a valuable reminder of what is sometimes a damaging weakness in conventional formal legal analysis.

As an element of the social superstructure positive law is seen as an instrument of class domination used by a ruling class to maintain and advance its interests. It is argued by Marxists to be present in all phases of class domination prior to the proletarian revolution but not to carry equal emphasis in all stages of development. Thus, law is perceived as having a relatively minor role in the phase of feudal domination but as coming into its own during the bourgeois phase, not least because of its close relationship with institutions of private property. The bourgeois State is seen as expressing itself through legal forms, typified by ideas such as a Diceyan 'rule of law' which Marxists perceive as a deceptive cover for the operation of bourgeois economic and industrial power. Engels expressed this view clearly in remarking that:

> . . . law is sacred to the bourgeois, for it is . . . enacted . . . for his benefit. . . . Because the English bourgeois finds himself reproduced in his law . . . the policeman's truncheon . . . has for him a . . . soothing power. But . . . [t]he working man knows . . . that the law is a rod which the bourgeois has prepared for him; and when he is not compelled to do so he never appeals to the law. (F. Engels, 'The condition of the working class in England' [1842], in K. Marx and F. Engels, *Collected Works* (London: Lawrence and Wishart, 1975), p. 514.)

Again, in its immediate context Engel's statement was not unsupported, but when elevated into a tenet of orthodox doctrine the determination to explain all law in such terms may well lead to distortions of analysis.

This possibility may be seen on at least two levels. On the one hand 'reforming' legislation such as some of the Victorian Factories Acts tends to be dismissed in classical Marxist analysis as designed simply to maintain the larger interests of the dominant class by staving off the discontent of subordinate classes through marginal concessions. Beyond this, it is interesting to note that the rather vague communist ordering of things would seem to include a considerable range of activities which, upon other definitions, might be considered legal but which are excluded because they are not acts of class domination. There is here an obvious comparison with the limiting definition of law adopted, in a very different context, by St Augustine of Hippo (see 4.4.1). St Augustine considered law, even when properly conceived and used, to be simply the *poena et remedium peccati*, the penalty of and remedy for sin. For him any regulation not conceived for the coercive repression of sin, both in the contemporary and the future state of things, fell into a category other than that of law. Ultimately such arguments turn almost entirely upon particular selections of definition and those, variously, chosen by St Augustine and Karl Marx were very limiting. If a theory excludes certain matters from its consideration that may, in its context, be a legitimate choice, but it should not be forgotten in considering the theory and its implications that a selective choice has been made.

7.1.2 The transition from theory to practice

The view of law taken in classical Marxist theory is clearly anti-legalistic and it was not anticipated that 'law', as defined, would have any long-term future role after the termination of class conflict by a proletarian revolution. The October 1917 Revolution in Russia was, perhaps, not entirely in accordance with Marxist teaching. The Revolution nonetheless established in power a regime which set out to operate in line with Marxist theory. When put to the test in practice both the model of law and the predicted outcome proved somewhat problematic. As a result the legal theory and practice of, as principal examples, the former Soviet Union and of the People's Republic of China diverged very significantly from orthodox Marxist expectation.

7.2 THE DEVELOPMENT OF SOVIET LEGAL THEORY

In the course of a troubled political history of rather more than 70 years, Soviet legal theory underwent dramatic changes which require examination. The Soviet idea of law did not, of course, develop in a vacuum and before its development can usefully be assessed a brief consideration of the pre-Revolutionary Russian legal tradition is necessary.

7.2.1 Law in Imperial Russia

As in Western Europe Russian law developed by a suffusion of 'barbarian' practice with Roman principle and structure. In Russia the influences were the East Roman (Byzantine) Empire and the Eastern Orthodox Church. For a variety of reasons, amongst which the medieval Tartar conquest tends to be overemphasised although it was not unimportant, the Muscovite tsardom from which modern Russia developed had a very weak legal tradition. The early tsardom was a personal autocracy in which little or no distinction was made between 'law', administration and personal instructions. Added to this the late development and long endurance of serfdom in Russia rendered law irrelevant to a large proportion of the population. Serfs were chattels rather than persons at law and whilst they might, in theory, have had rights these were of little value in the absence of any *locus standi* to seek remedies for their breach. Within peasant communities there was, of course, a strong framework of customary norms and communal means of dispute resolution, but there was little protection from arbitrary seigneurial whim. In an extraordinary, and perhaps exceptional, instance as late as 1763 the brutal regime imposed by Countess Saltykova sufficiently appalled neighbouring magnates that she was brought to trial, degraded from the nobility and banished to a convent. For the unfortunate serfs, however, relief came, even insofar as it did, only through the unpredictable, and indeed unlikely, action of other landowners, not through any recourse available to the victims themselves.

At the opening of the 19th century the state of Russian law and the legal system had become a national scandal. Under Nicholas I (1825–55), a legal code, the *Svod Zakonov Rossiiskoi Imperii*, was published in 1832, with effect from 1835, the first Russian code of any significance since 1649. Nicholas I himself recognised that serfdom was a blockage to further reform and that it would sooner rather than later have to go. In practice, however, the government was unwilling to confront the landowners over the issue at this time.

The major era of Imperial law reform came, with much else, in the 1860s under Alexander II (1855–81). Law reform was rendered inevitable by the liberation of the serfs in 1861, a measure which conferred legal personality and *locus standi* upon a vast number of people with whose judicial requirements the existing antiquated and corrupt system was manifestly unable to cope. It was recognised that the need was not for reform but replacement. A sweeping measure of judicial reorganisation was enacted in 1864. Modern courts of first instance and appellate jurisdiction were set up. Further a modern legal profession was created with independence of action and speech in the courts. It is noteworthy that when policies of repression were restored from the later 1870s the courts of law remained one of the few places where freedom of speech remained. It is not insignificant that both Kerensky and Lenin were lawyers by profession. Two English elements imported by the 1864 reforms merit emphasis. Jury trial was adopted and at the lowest level a 'peace jurisdiction' was set up which was closely modelled upon the English magistracy (for a general account of the reforms see H. McCoubrey, 'The reform of the Russian legal system under Alexander II', *Renaissance and Modern Studies*, vol. 24 (1980), pp. 115–30).

The reforms were resisted, for different reasons, by both reactionaries and revolutionaries. Amongst the former the jurist Konstantin Pobedonostsev savagely attacked the institution of jury trial and the idea of judicial independence. Revolutionaries, on the other hand, often dismissed the scheme as a 'feudal' or possibly 'bourgeois' plot. Both harked back to a highly idealised notion of traditional dispute resolution suggesting that the formalities of law were in some sense alien and 'un-Russian'. It is worth dwelling upon this for a moment since something of this attitude fed into aspects of later Soviet jurisprudence. The evidence is strong that the Russian people had no hesitation in making use of modern courts once such institutions had been made available. D. Mackenzie Wallace, travelling in Russia in the early 1870s, commented that:

In Moscow the authorities calculated that under the new system the number of cases would be more than doubled [to about 1,000 cases per magistrate per annum]. . . . The reality far exceeded their expectations: each justice had an average 2,800 cases. In St Petersburg and other large towns the amount of work . . . was equally great. (D. Mackenzie Wallace, *Russia* (London: 1877), p. 74.)

In this context the confusion of unavailability with unwillingness to use in a 'Russian' tradition has more the ring of ideological convenience than of objective analysis.

In the period of reaction from the later 1870s to 1905 the reformed legal system did not emerge unscathed but on the whole survived surprisingly well. There continued, however, the problem that the government, or certain sections of it, failed to appreciate that a rule of law is not simply a rule 'by law' but also a constraint upon government action. The problem continued even after the establishment of the 1906 constitution which, in the political aftermath of the Russo-Japanese War, theoretically established an Imperial *Rechtsstaat* including the institution of a duma (parliament). Marc Szeftel remarks that:

the eleven years of the duma period [1906–17] represented at once the time of maximum freedom, in spite of all its modesty, in the history of the Russian Empire, and the period of maximum possibilities that Russia might have been on its way to becoming a pluralist society with a full-fledged constitutional system in the not too distant future. (M. Szeftel, *The Russian Constitution of April 23, 1906* (Brussels: Les Éditions de la Librairie Encyclopédique, 1976), p. 17.)

There is much to be said for this view, but that major obstacles beset this path can be seen in the scandalous Beilis case in 1911 (see S. Kucherov, *Courts, Lawyers and Trials under the Last Three Tsars* (New York: 1953), pp. 243–68). Mendel Beilis, a Jewish janitor, was charged with the murder of Andrei Yuschinsky on straightforwardly racist grounds and, despite a complete lack of evidence and the intense scepticism of the prosecuting and judicial authorities, was put through a trial process of some two and a half years. The trial was marked throughout its long duration by the racially inspired political interference of the Minister of Justice, Shcheglovitov. Ultimately Mendel was acquitted, an inconceivable outcome 20 or so years later under Stalin, but the incident illustrates powerfully both the strength of the developing legal system in late Imperial Russia and the serious political obstacles which it still faced.

Despite the very short period of social democratic rule under the Mensheviks between February and October 1917 the traditional refusal to countenance legal restraint upon the State carried forward into the Soviet era.

In a sense it fitted well with classical Marxist analysis, although the more positive aspects of the 1864 reforms and the 1906 constitution did not. The use made of law by the Soviet government became, however, less and less Marxist as time went on.

7.2.2 The Soviet ordering of things

The economic and military strains of the First World War brought about the collapse of the Imperial system and ultimately revolution. Nicholas II was forced to abdicate by the army and power was seized by the Mensheviks led by Kerensky in the February 1917 Revolution. A social-democratic republic was set up under the nominal presidency of Prince Lvov but with Kerensky as premier. Kerensky attempted to keep Russia in the war, in faith with its Allies, but this was by now beyond Russian capacities and the resulting continuation of crisis gave Lenin and the Bolsheviks, with some facilitation (the famous 'sealed train') by Germany, to seize power in the October 1917 Revolution.

The October Revolution was not strictly a Marxist occurrence. Russia at this time was seen as emerging from a feudal condition into an era of bourgeois economic dominance and the orthodox next step from a Marxist perspective would have been the Menshevik rather than the Bolshevik revolution. Having seized power, however, Lenin and the Bolsheviks were faced with problems of post-Revolutionary government which Marx and Engels had largely ignored.

Lenin doubted that the unaided proletariat would actually set up the communist society envisaged by Marx and therefore concluded that a more or less extended time of party rule would be necessary to eliminate class enemies and contrary ideologies and also to educate the proletariat itself for a communist future. This period was described as a 'dictatorship of the proletariat'. It was more accurately a dictatorship of the party on behalf of the proletariat. Whatever form this took it manifestly required institutions of party government which Marx had expected rapidly to wither away, and these included, up to a point, the institutions of positive law.

The underlying attitude to such institutions, including the law, was in the first place that they were essentially disreputable bourgeois relics for which the new proletarian society found a temporary use in the suppression of its enemies. In other words they were inherently instruments of class domination which were used for a final time whilst the proletariat exercised dominance over its surviving opponents. When this task had been completed the 'bludgeon' seized from the pre-Revolutionary regime would in theory be discarded. This remained the theoretical position until 1937 and was summed up succinctly in 1927 by P. I. Stuchka, then president of the Supreme Court of the USSR. He stated that:

Communism means not the victory of socialist law, but the victory of socialism over any law, since with the abolition of classes with their antagonistic interests, law will die out altogether. (Quoted by H. J. Berman, *Justice in the USSR*, rev. ed. (Cambridge, Mass: Harvard University Press, 1963), p. 26 citing, P. I. Stuchka (ed.), *Entsiklopediia Gosudarstva i Prava*, vol. 3 (Moscow: 1927), p. 1594.)

This basic policy endured through the first three phases of Soviet political development, 'war communism', the 'new economic policy' and the first two 'five year plans', covering the period of Lenin's rule from 1917 to 1923 and the early Stalin years from 1923 to 1937. The first idea had been to retain certain elements of public law, suitably amended, as an instrument of party government whilst immediately abolishing most private law as useful only to a bourgeois economy. Under the new economic policy, however, it was decided that the stage of bourgeois development could not entirely be omitted and therefore, under strict party control, certain elements of a mixed economy were revived and this included aspects of private law. In 1928 this more gradualist policy was abandoned in favour of a direct approach to a classless single economy through stages determined by successive five-year plans, of which the second terminated in 1937. The attitude to law, as an instrument of class domination having a significant but clearly temporary utility in the new order, remained under the first two five-year plans roughly the same as it had been under the new economic policy.

In 1937 there occurred a profound change. Many of the early Bolsheviks, including in particular Leon Trotsky, had expected that the Russian Revolution would spark other proletarian revolutions and that progress towards world communism would not be long delayed. Lenin's successor as Soviet leader, Joseph Vissarionovich Dzhugashvili who took the name Stalin, favoured instead a policy founded upon the idea of 'capitalist encirclement'. The idea, broadly, was that a Soviet Union surrounded by ideologically unfriendly States, including both the Western democracies and, during the 1930s, the fascist countries, had no choice but to retain a strong State structure because without this it would be overwhelmed. This was in part merely practical, but the idea of a continuing State by no means necessarily implied the actual forms which the Stalin dictatorship took. Further, the State was not now to be a temporary, and rather disreputable, expedient but a valid and indeed vital part of the post-Revolutionary order. This extended also to the law and in explanation of this Stalin's principal jurist, A. Ia. Vyshinsky, developed the idea of 'socialist legality' upon the basis that the Soviet State could have its own ideologically appropriate form of positive law as much as could a bourgeois State. It is a paradox that this idea of socialist legality informing a long-term 'stability of laws' was adopted and maintained during the period of the Stalinist 'show trials' involving purges and political massacres on a scale not seen in Russia since the 'oprichnina' tyranny of Ivan the Terrible in the 16th century.

After the death of Stalin in 1953 his personal dictatorship was denounced as a betrayal of socialist legality and a major policy change was announced by his successor, Nikita Khrushchev. At the 22nd Communist Party Congress of the USSR in 1961 it was declared that the dictatorship of the proletariat had ended and been succeeded by a 'State of all the people'. With this there was a revival of ideas of a withering away of law in accordance with Marxist precept in favour of communal dispute resolution and group pressure to conformity. This never happened on a large scale though the ideas were represented by some movement towards less formal proceedings in minor cases before 'comrades' courts' and the use in minor criminal cases of techniques of 'shaming', e.g., display of offenders' names and photographs in public places. However, the law continued to be seen very much as a State ideological instrument with political education by no means the least of its functions. After the fall of Khrushchev the emphasis under the Brezhnev, Andropov and Chernenko administrations returned to a somewhat more formalist view, although without massive changes of emphasis. Writing before the break-up of the Soviet Union, W. E. Butler remarked that:

> Socialist legality eventually evolved into a standard by which excesses of the Stalinist period came to be condemned and legal reforms to be effectuated in the post-Stalin era.
>
> . . . there is some indication that the human rights discussions of the 1970s have made Soviet legal theorists aware that citizens' rights cannot always be reliably protected by the State, but must be protected against the State. (W. E. Butler, *Soviet Law*, 2nd ed. (London: Butterworths, 1988), pp. 35 and 37.)

What hope this may have held must now, of course, remain a matter for speculation.

The adoption by the Gorbachev administration of policies of glasnost and perestroika and of reforming initiatives in response to the massive difficulties faced by the centralised economy of the Soviet Union in the 1980s led to massive change. The USSR and central party rule collapsed to be replaced by the much more loosely knit Commonwealth of Independent States (CIS) with a diversity of political and legal structures amongst its various members. Amongst the former Soviet republics the pattern appears highly diverse. In the liberated Baltic republics a more or less 'Western' pattern seems to be developing. In some of the central Asian republics it seems likely that the law will be strongly influenced by Islamic jurisprudence, whether or not *Shari'ah* law is ultimately adopted in full. In the Russian Republic itself the political structure remains at the time of writing in some doubt, but the existing Soviet legal institutions appear to have taken on a distinctly 'Westernising' colouring in their initial development at least.

The various phases of development of Soviet law and practice involved changes, sometimes very violent changes, of informing theory. As with the rest of Soviet legal activity the development of theory cannot be distinguished from the political background: many of the theorists would indeed have denounced an attempt so to do as 'legal fetishism'. That said, the endeavour of Soviet legal theorists to accommodate themselves to the radically changing perspectives of Marxism-Leninism in the USSR was an important aspect of Marxist, or perhaps neo-Marxist, considerations of law. Two theorists in particular, E. B. Pashukanis and A. Ia. Vyshinsky, require comment as, more generally, does the shape of post-Stalinist legal theory.

7.2.3 E. B. Pashukanis and early Marxism-Leninism

Evgeny Bronislavovich Pashukanis was the leading Soviet jurist and ultimately vice commissar for justice of the period of the new economic policy and the first two five-year plans. He failed to make the transition to later Stalinism and was liquidated as an ideological 'wrecker' in 1937. His basic legal theory is set out in *Law and Marxism: A General Theory*, transl. B. Einhorn (London: Ink Links, 1978). For Pashukanis there could not be such a thing as truly socialist, still less communist, law. Law was for him, as for all mainstream early Marxist-Leninists, a bourgeois phenomenon expressing class domination which had no more than a temporary use as a weapon against remaining enemies during a period of transition from the old to the new order. The general nature of Pashukanis's view of law is made clear by the statement that:

> . . . in our transition period, the legal form as such does not contain within itself those unlimited possibilities which lay before it at the birth of bourgeois capitalist society. On the contrary, the legal form only encompasses us within its narrow horizon for the time being. It exists for the sole purpose of being utterly spent. (*Law and Marxism: A General Theory*, p. 133.)

Law is thus seen as an inherently bourgeois phenomenon and one which could have no permanent or long-term role in the new order.

Pashukanis, in accordance with orthodox Marxist doctrine, considered that legal forms reflect the state of the mechanisms of production and exchange and the ideology of the ruling class at any given time. It cannot, therefore, be studied as an autonomous structure of rules, but only as a superstructural element reflecting the real economic relations which it is used to express. As a typical element of a bourgeois capitalist social order law was argued by

Pashukanis to rest upon the structure and relations of a market economy. This factor is evident from any viewpoint in, e.g., the structures of the law of contract or of company law, but Pashukanis argued that the market base of law informs areas of legal provision far removed from anything that would normally be considered commercial. Thus, he relates even constitutional law to market concepts, whilst denouncing it as a cover for the reality of class domination in a bourgeois State. He stated that:

> The constitutional State (*Rechtsstaat*) is a mirage, but one which suits the bourgeoisie very well, for it . . . conceals the fact of the bourgeoisie's hegemony from the eyes of the masses. . . . Power as the 'collective will', as the 'rule of law', is realised in bourgeois society to the extent that this society represents a market. (*Law and Marxism: A General Theory*, p. 146.)

The point of this remark lies largely in the social-contractarian analyses (see 4.5) in which, from a Marxist viewpoint, the idea of a bargain between State or society and people actually conceals the maintenance of the interests of the dominant class at the expense of subordinate classes.

The expression of commodity exchange relations through legal norms, according to Pashukanis, treats human beings as 'subjects', meaning legal persons, in a manner which can only have meaning in a market structure. Thus, once the market has gone, the law in all its dimensions will wither away since, to pursue the Marxist terminology, the superstructure will have lost its base or foundation.

Such a view was completely in conformity with the ideas of war communism, the new economic policy and, to a somewhat lesser extent, the first two five-year plans. It was, however, wholly incompatible with the ideas of the later Stalin dictatorship and for this reason both the theory and its author were eliminated. Pashukanis's ideas were never readopted in the Soviet Union, although after the fall of Stalin the injustice of his personal fate was recognised. In Western Marxist debate upon law, however, Pashukanis continues to exert a significant influence.

7.2.4   A. Ia. Vyshinsky and socialist legality

A major policy change took place in the Soviet Union based upon Stalin's idea of capitalist encirclement (see 7.2.2). The consequent acceptance of the Soviet State and its law as satisfactory elements of the post-Revolutionary order, rather than disreputable expedients, clearly demanded a change in legal theory. The liquidation of Pashukanis was largely organised by his successor, A. Ia. Vyshinsky, who became Procurator General and the leading Stalinist jurist. His legal theory is set out in *The Law of the Soviet State*, transl. H. W. Babb (New York: Macmillan, 1954), which is vituperative in the extreme in its consideration of all opposing views and often unclear or even contradictory in its statements of theory. The essentials of Vyshinsky's theory of law and certainly its impact are, however, clear enough.

Whereas for Pashukanis, Stuchka and other early Marxist-Leninist jurists the law was an inherently bourgeois relic of the old order which could never truly be part of a socialist society, Vyshinsky argued that a socialist society could develop socialist law, to exactly the same extent as a bourgeois society could develop bourgeois law. Such a law would fully embrace a socialist ideology and serve its ends. This concept was expressed by Vyshinsky as one of 'socialist legality' and was stated to inform a new era of 'stability of laws'. It is important to understand the limitations of this idea which in no way imported notions of a rule of law or of any restraint upon the leading role of the Communist Party. The new socialist legality envisaged by Vyshinsky was in many ways double-edged. For those inside the system, people who embraced the ideology of the State and party, socialist law was to be a benign and educative, in the sense of indoctrinatory, force accurately reflecting the new social order. For those outside the system, however, class enemies and adherents of contrary ideologies, socialist law remained a bludgeon and an instrument of class domination, used by the party on behalf of the proletariat to strike down their enemies. It has been remarked elsewhere that:

> Law, whether or not inherently 'socialist', [was] in the Soviet system . . . subject to . . . ideological override which follow[ed] from the very idea of 'socialist legality'. . . . Soviet courts were . . . [enjoined] to enforce rules of law not as neutral directions . . . but in the light of ideology and overtly for the achievement of ideological ends. (H. McCoubrey, *The Development of Naturalist Legal Theory* (London: Croom Helm, 1987), p. 117.)

There was, thus, to be no 'rule of law' but there was to some extent to be a rule 'through' law.

This theory goes some way to explain, although not to excuse, the immediately obvious legal paradox of the Stalin years. On the one hand legal norms which had been seriously undermined under the theory advanced by Pashukanis were restored and some return to a recognisable due process was established through the Judiciary Act of 1938. On the other hand, the opening era of socialist legality was characterised by sweeping political purges achieved through the mechanism of show trials which in most cases amounted to little more than judicial murder. As Berman put it:

> Vyshinsky in 1938 wrote with utter frankness that alongside 'suppression and the use of force', which are 'still essential' so long as worldwide communism does not exist, it is necessary to have 'also' due process of law. . . . Where the stability of the regime is threatened, law goes out the

window. . . . opposition . . . is dealt with by 'suppression and the use of force'. (H. J. Berman, *Justice in the USSR*, rev. ed. (Cambridge, Mass: Harvard University Press, 1963) p. 57.)

The opposition thus dealt with in the Stalinist show trials were for the most part not the pre-Revolutionary opponents for whose extirpation Lenin had conceived the dictatorship of the proletariat, but primarily Bolsheviks, such as Pashukanis, who had not with sufficient rapidity or enthusiasm made the jump into the Stalinist order. The imputations of 'wrecking' and of 'fascist' allegiance routinely made at the trials were for the most part transparently absurd.

After the death of Stalin and the abandonment of the personal dictatorship, the show trials and other overt forms of State terrorism were denounced as incompatible with the concept of socialist legality. While the idea of socialist legality was itself retained and there was no move to return to the immediate anti-legalism of Pashukanis, legal formalism did for a time become tainted by association with the abuses of the Stalin years. The formal abolition of the dictatorship of the proletariat in 1961 fuelled renewed debate upon the form and role of law in the Soviet Union with an introduction of less formal modes of adjudication at least in lesser cases. With variations of emphasis the debates in Soviet legal theory swung between formalism and relatively informal popular justice until eventually the Soviet Union was dissolved. The shape of law in the variety of former Soviet Republics (see 7.2.2) will certainly be diverse. They will no doubt, however, diverge far from the varieties of experience of Soviet law and legal theory. It was, perhaps, inevitable that Soviet concepts of law should over the course of some 80 years have moved a very considerable distance from the classical Marxist starting-point. The interesting question is rather whether the particular forms of the divergence were significant or merely products of historical and cultural chance. In considering this question an interesting comparison may be found in the experience since 1949 of the People's Republic of China.

7.3 THE DEVELOPMENT OF CHINESE LEGAL THEORY

The proclamation of the establishment of the People's Republic of China on 1 October 1949 by the Chinese Communist Party led by Mao Tse-tung (Mao Zedong) and the withdrawal of the Nationalist Kuomintang led by Chiang Kai-shek to Taiwan, exposed Marxist theory to a culture and context in many ways quite different from that of pre-Revolutionary Russia. China was, up to a point, traditionally anti-legalist, meaning in reality that the functions of law were very narrowly conceived and entirely limited to coercive control by the State. Although the terminology is somewhat inappropriate, it was also the case that law in Imperial China was considered to have a deterrent didactic effect in the service of State ideology. Although the substance of both the Imperial legal tradition and the Nationalist law which had replaced it was, inevitably, rejected by the Communist State, the preceding tradition in some ways was by no means incompatible with a Marxist-Leninist idea of law.

Initially China closely followed the model of the Soviet Union under Stalin. Indeed the very severe deterioration of Sino-Soviet relations in subsequent years was in part related to the abandonment of Stalinism by later Soviet regimes. The Stalinist model was, however, very radically modified in China also, most notably in the period of the Cultural Revolution. This originated in Chairman Mao's concern that if the post-Revolutionary social order were allowed to become stabilised this would in itself generate 'class' interests and antagonisms. He therefore announced a policy of continuing revolution in which there would be permanent struggle against recurring class enemies and contrary ideologies. In practice massive purges took place, large numbers of people were sent to the countryside to learn 'correct' attitudes from the rural communities and in many places, especially the larger cities, a virtually unaccountable rule by Red Guards was established.

This period involved the virtual abandonment of legal forms and savage persecution of any who were deemed not to support the Cultural Revolution. At the local level 'popular justice' was instituted which frequently involved little more than the hounding of unpopular people by the Red Guards. After the death of Chairman Mao many of the abuses of the Cultural Revolutionary period were blamed upon the radical group which was given the name 'Gang of Four' and had been headed by Chiang Ch'ing (Jiang Qing), who was married to Mao. The trial of the Gang of Four in 1976 marked a return to ideas of socialist legality and, although the outcome of the trial was at no point in doubt, there was a trial in which process was observed.

Subsequent development in China has largely turned upon wide-ranging economic reforms accompanied by very great caution in political developments. The Tienanmen Square incident in which pro-democracy demonstrators were swept away by military action illustrated very pointedly the extreme sensitivity of these questions. In general it may be said that the use of law in China as between those who, ideologically, are 'inside' the system, even if erring, and those who are 'outside' it may be considered by no means dissimilar from at least certain strands of former Soviet practice. It may be added that the outcome of the policies of perestroika and glasnost adopted by the Gorbachev administration in the closing years of the former USSR may reasonably be thought to have been noted by the authorities and policy-makers in Beijing.

7.3.1 Law in the Imperial and Nationalist Chinese traditions

The classical Chinese view of law resulted from the combination of two philosophical approaches, one overt the other implicit. The official philosophy of Chinese dynasties from the Han dynasty (206 BC to 220 AD) to the (Manchu) Ch'ing dynasty (1644 to 1912) was founded upon Confucian teaching (see comments in 4.3.1) which took a limiting, and rather disparaging, view of positive law. Confucius taught that human beings are fundamentally inclined towards virtue. Even if the attainment of the ultimate condition of sagehood may be an unrealistic general aspiration, nobility of character is a reasonable goal attainable by following the 'way' (*tao, dao*) of benevolence, righteousness, proper conduct and wisdom. In this context, observance of traditions of proper conduct termed *li* were emphasised as the route to virtue. Positive law, *fa*, on the other hand was seen as a punitive prescription designed to deter and punish those who were obdurately antisocial or simply wicked. *Fa* was thus an unfortunate necessity rather than a social institution much to be admired.

The disapprobation of resort to law, in many ways seen as a mark of bad citizenship in the developed Imperial legal tradition, can be seen at a very early stage in the view of Confucius (K'ung-Fu-tzu, see also 4.3.1) that:

> I could try a civil suit as well as anyone. But better still to bring about that there were no civil suits! (Confucius, *Analects*, 12.13, transl. A. Waley (London: Unwin Hyman, 1988), p. 167.)

Under the Imperial Chinese legal tradition there were in fact no civil suits because positive law was conceived entirely in criminal terms. An action for what might in a Western tradition be considered breach of contract could only be brought as an accusation of culpable wrongdoing.

In actual court proceedings the idealism of Confucianism was distinctly compromised by the covert survival of elements of quite a different political philosophy, that of legalism. This very harsh philosophy was adopted by the first, if short-lived, Imperial dynasty, the Ch'in, established by the first Emperor, Ch'in Shih Huang-ti in 221 BC. It involved rigorous control of the population by minutely detailed regulations enforced by savage penalties in any case of default. It was, in principle, based upon an opposite view of human nature from that taken by Confucius and, later, Mencius (Meng K'o) and assumed human inclination to evil which could only be suppressed by the fear and actuality of severe punishment for all default. The Han and succeeding dynasties officially spurned legalism but much of its spirit actually survived in court proceedings. In court both plaintiff and defendant were treated equally as persons in trouble. The proceedings could only conclude in a confession of wrongdoing by one, or both, parties and these could, if necessary, be secured by physical coercion. In this respect, there were limits upon the powers of magistrates who were themselves subject to strict control by the elaborate civil service bureaucracy. Even so, the procedure and the ultimate penalties were expressly designed to intimidate and severely to discourage resort to litigation by private citizens. Derk Bodde and Clarence Morris remark that:

> [Legalist] influence probably explains . . . the continuing penal emphasis found in all the imperial codes, and . . . their treatment of even . . . noncriminal matters [in] . . . a standard formula: 'Anyone who does x is to receive punishment y'. . . . Despite this . . . the really spectacular phenomenon of imperial times is . . . the incorporation of the spirit and sometimes the actual provisions of the Confucian *li* into the legal codes. (D. Bodde and C. Morris, *Law in Imperial China* (Philadelphia, Pa: University of Pennsylvania Press, 1973), pp. 28–9.)

This combination of methods strongly influenced by legalism in the service of an official Confucian ideology (much elaborated under what may be termed 'Mencian' influence) gave a very particular flavour to Imperial Chinese law and legal practice.

It may be added that law was at all except the very highest levels of the Imperial bureaucracy no more than one aspect of administration. A legal profession in the sense of counsellors or representatives of litigants not only did not exist but was forbidden, on the basis that such people would stir up trouble and needless wrangling amongst citizens. A late flavour of this view can be seen in a Ch'ing dynasty 'casebook', the *Hsing-an-hui-lan*, citing an Imperial edict received by the Board of Punishments from the Emperor Chia-ch'ing in 1820. The emperor stated that:

> The multiplication of lawsuits among the people brings much harm . . . and the machinations of the litigation tricksters are what produce all the inconsequential verbiage going . . . into these accusations. These rascally fellows entrap people for the sake of profit. (See D. Bodde and C. Morris, *Law in Imperial China*, p. 416.)

The emperor went on to require that such tricksters be diligently sought out and severely punished, whereas those who had been tricked into litigation by them might be treated more leniently. The only litigation advisers who were officially permitted were close relations of the parties, this exception resting upon Confucian ideas of familial obligation. Some interesting comparisons between this anti-legal tradition and the more legalist traditions of the West have been advanced (see, e.g., V. H. Li, *Law without Lawyers: A Comparative View of Law in China and the United States* (Boulder, Colo: Westview Press, 1978)).

After the traumatic internal and external events of the later 19th century the Imperial administration was overthrown in a Nationalist revolution in 1911 with Dr Sun Yat-sen, the leader of the Kuomintang Party, as first president. The last emperor, P'u-yi, later became 'emperor' of the Japanese puppet state of Manchukuo and much later, as an instance of political re-education, a member of the Chinese People's Congress. Despite the Nationalist rejection of much of the Imperial tradition, the Ch'ing dynasty law code, the *Ta Ch'ing Lu Li*, was basically retained in its last revised form, as of 1910, but with the introduction of many foreign rules and principles. These were to a large extent German or Japanese, the latter itself being much influenced by German practice. The end result, illustrated by the civil code ultimately issued in 1923–9 (see *China Civil Code* (Peking: Commission on Extraterritoriality, 1923)) was in many ways a sinicised version of European civilian practice. Law had thus become much more a respectable part of official consciousness but involvement with law for many Chinese people carried, and continues to carry even beyond the People's Republic, a very distinct social stigma.

In 1949, with the establishment of Communist power throughout mainland China, the Nationalist system was largely abandoned in favour of a Marxist-Leninist model. This was, however, not a simple absorption of Soviet practice, bearing in mind that Chinese culture embodied a much stronger, even if very narrowly focused, legal tradition.

7.3.2 Law in the People's Republic of China

Not surprisingly the initial view of law taken after 1949 was somewhat similar to that taken in the former Soviet Union after the fall of Pashukanis (see 7.2.4) and included the idea of a genuinely 'socialist' legality. Phillip M. Chen comments that:

> The courts were to be guided by the decrees of the workers' and peasants' government and the judges' own 'socialist revolutionary conscience'. (P. M. Chen, *Law and Justice: The Legal System in China 2400 BC to 1960 AD* (New York: Dunellen, 1973), p. 108.)

The pattern of a stable system which was on the one hand ideologically didactic but on the other severely coercive had a clearly Soviet resonance.

This pattern, along with many others was, however, severely disrupted by the policies of the Cultural Revolution which lasted from 1966 to 1976. The basis for these policies in a wish to prevent a separation of 'classes' in a settled society led to a massive assault upon many social institutions, including the legal system which Mao considered to be alienated from popular consciousness. The courts were closed and legal personnel were dispatched to re-educative labour in the countryside. 'Justice' became in theory a matter for decision by the people in general, in practice for infliction by the Red Guards. Folsom and Minan comment upon this period that:

The Red Guards, with Mao's blessing, freely searched houses without legal process, arrested anyone, investigated anything, and sentenced, imprisoned, and frequently executed. There were no legal procedures to constrain the Red Guards, no time-limits, no prohibitions on torture – rape to humiliate was a common occurrence. (R. H. Folsom, and J. H. Minan, *Law in the People's Republic of China* (Dordrecht: Nijhoff, 1989), p. 12.)

All of this ended with the death of Mao and the arrest of the dominant political faction of this era, the Gang of Four and their associates.

The return to the idea of socialist legality was clearly stated by art. 5 of the constitution promulgated on 4 December 1982, providing that:

The State upholds the uniformity and dignity of the socialist legal system. ... No organisation or individual may enjoy the privilege of being above the constitution and the law. (*Constitution of the People's Republic of China*, English translation (Beijing: Foreign Languages Press, 1983).)

The practice had been symbolised by the trial of the Gang of Four themselves, involving 10 defendants led by Jiang Qing. The preface to the official account of the trial, written by one of the judges, Professor Fei Hsiao Tung, concisely stated the new, or more accurately revived, view of the law. He stated that:

The years of lawlessness ended with the arrest of the Gang of Four in 1976. ... It was recognised that socialist legality must prevail . . . the National People's Congress enacted a series of important laws . . . [coming] into force in 1980. . . . there was a nationwide movement to familiarise the people with the rule of law and to impress on all that everyone is equal before the law. (Fei Hsaio Tung, 'Preface' to *A Great Trial in Chinese History* (Beijing: New World Press, 1981), p. 9.)

The 'rule of law' is not, of course, that conceived in a Western tradition but rather the application of norms in a context of socialist legality. The trial of the Gang of Four and their adherents in 1980 to 1981 clearly had a didactic intention but rules of process were observed and, although convictions were inevitable from the outset, the sentences imposed were in no case capital, except that Jiang Qing and Chang Ch'un-ch'iao (Zhang Chunqiao) were sentenced to death with a two-year reprieve and permanent deprivation of political rights. The reprieve was in essence designed to assess the progress of political re-education.

The consequences of the policies of perestroika and glasnost in the former Soviet Union have undoubtedly had an impact in China and have engendered very considerable caution in matters of political, as compared with economic, reform. The political sensitivity of the situation in the light of late Soviet developments was shown in the very severe response to the protests in Tienanmen Square. In the late 1990s the return of Hong Kong to China, with the proposition of 'two systems in one country', has created a co-existence of a Western and Marxist-Leninist legal system in different parts of one State. How, if at all, the two may in time influence each other remains at the time of writing to be seen. The pattern for the next several years would seem to be, however, one of emphasis upon socialist legality with both the inward and outward faces considered, in extreme degree, in the Soviet context (see 7.2.4).

7.4 DEVELOPMENTS IN WESTERN MARXIST JURISPRUDENCE

Western Marxist thought upon law has in many ways been influenced by the Soviet and Chinese experience, and by experience in other communist States, but has not been exclusively shaped by them. In a brief review no more than a sample can be offered but a significant variety of thought may nonetheless be illustrated, ranging from the early thinking of Karl Renner to the more modern approaches of Hugh Collins and Zenon Bankowski.

7.4.1 Karl Renner and the contrast between form and function

Karl Renner was one of the first Marxists to seek to develop a legal theory as such. In his major published work, *The Institutions of Private Law and their Social Functions*, transl. A. Schwarzschild (London: Routledge & Kegan Paul, 1949), Renner sought to relate the seeming stability of legal norms to the Marxist analysis of shifting power relations within the economic base. He argued that although the outward form of a legal norm might appear to remain stable, its function, meaning its use, would change in reflection of the shifting patterns of class interest and domination in the economic base. Thus:

> the economic substratum dislocates the functions of the norm, . . . it reverses them; but the norm itself remains indestructible. (*The Institutions of Private Law and their Social Functions*, p. 300.)

For Renner, therefore, the substantive concern of jurisprudence was not so much the forms of law as the shifting economic uses to which they were put. He emphasised that a legal concept such as 'property' might virtually reverse in function as a result of this type of historical process. Property, notably in land, was, in Renner's view, originally a badge of independence in control over the means of crop raising and subsistence, a simple and explicit relation of form and function. With the increasing complexity of economic organisation and the diversification of economic activity, however, this simple relationship changed. Renner argued that in a developed capitalist economy, property, through investment ownership, comes to represent not independence but control over the economic activities of others and, of course, an instrument of domination. Similar arguments are deployed in respect of other legal concepts. Thus, contract becomes not truly an open bargain but rather a form of unequal power relationship, notwithstanding the use of the language of market bargaining.

Renner's Marxism has been questioned because of his concession of a stability of legal forms. This seems, however, to be founded upon a misunderstanding. Renner did not claim that the law actually was unchanging, merely that it 'appeared' to be so. The emphasis upon the importance of the 'real' economic base was thoroughly in tune with classical Marxist thought.

More recently Hugh Collins has rejected the crude class instrumentalism of some forms of classical Marxist argument, contending that such a model would require an implausibly cohesive view on the part of a dominant class. He also suggests that the law in general does not display the basic discontinuities which the shifting demands of such a class-instrumentalist model would seem to suggest. Collins suggests that it may rather be the case that legal reasoning is, internally, a coherent exercise but one conducted in a context which is shaped by the currently dominant ideology. Thus:

> Instead of lawyers and judges serving as the lackeys of the dominant class . . ., doctrinal development is . . . an anxious search for rules which correspond to common-sense ideas of right and wrong based upon the dominant ideology. . . . but our understanding of those phenomena no longer coincides with . . . the thesis of the autonomy of law. (H. Collins, *Marxism and Law* (Oxford: Clarendon Press, 1982), p. 73.)

Collins also makes the point that the classical Marxist definition of law as inherently an instrument of class repression is very limiting in its effects and that while, in that use, 'law' might wither away, there is no reason to deny that the subsequent ordering of things might, on a different definition, be considered 'legal' (see *Marxism and Law*, p. 106).

In contrast Bankowski and Mungham focus upon, and strongly criticise, social welfare law and other forms of law purporting to assist the materially disadvantaged in modern society (see Z. Bankowski and G. Mungham, *Images of Law* (London: Routledge & Kegan Paul, 1976)). They suggest that such laws deceive people into believing that a transformation of the capitalist condition can be achieved by law, a view which any Marxist would reject. They also suggest that the proliferation of such forms of law in the late 20th century actually represents the self-interest of lawyers, i.e., it creates more, profitable, work for them. Ultimately they consider that the law will indeed wither away along with the capitalist conditions which it reflects. They also suggest, however, that in the new and consensual ordering of things some new form of legality will develop in order to resolve 'clashing diversities' in a free but still complicated society (see *Images of Law*, p. 31). This has all the appearance of a redefinition of 'law' which a number of modern Marxists have found necessary. This is especially interesting in the light of the view taken of norms such as those of social welfare law which are fitted essentially into a mould of class repression.

In varying ways most modern Western Marxist writing upon law wrestles with the concepts of law and legal systems and their definition in terms of class repression. Varying answers are given to what, from a Marxist viewpoint, is a conundrum. Commonly, however, some form of analysis is found necessary in which a class-repressive use of law is distinguished from qualitatively different legal institutions in a society without class conflict. This particular tension, along with the developing conceptions of socialist legality in present and former communist States, suggests that the class reductionism of classical Marxist analysis may, whatever view is taken of its basic premises, have oversimplified the role of law.

7.5   THE SIGNIFICANCE OF MARXIST LEGAL ANALYSES

The Marxist analysis of the role of law, together with its various derivatives, is founded upon a very particular view of the nature of socio-political development. Its economic emphasis and class instrumentalism impose a limited definition of 'law', in contrast with a vague post-proletarian revolution 'ordering of things'. This has been found unsatisfactory in communist States and to some extent in Western Marxist thought. This has resulted in developments which, to varying, and sometimes considerable, extents, diverged from the classical Marxist view. If Marxist analyses are in themselves open to broad criticism on the basis of a narrowly exclusive definition of 'law' and a greatly excessive class reductionism, there are also some useful insights to be found. In particular, the perception of the non-autonomy of law is an important counterpoint to the implicit assumptions of much formal legal discourse. This does not mean that it is appropriate to replace legal formalism with a simple economic fundamentalism, but the relationship of positive law with economics and ideology, as well as morality, ethics, creed and culture is an inescapable aspect of law in general which formalist analyses often unwisely ignore. In its exploration of this element there is perhaps to be found the most positive contribution of Marxist thought to general jurisprudence.

The distant expectation of a consensual 'ordering of things' which remains an element of some aspects of Marxist thought rests upon an assumption that conflict is simply a product of divergent class interests. Such a view of human nature is, in one way, perhaps very optimistic. The equivalence of this to the

Augustinian concept of law as a mere *potestas coactiva* (coercive power) directed simply to the problem of sin has been suggested above. The evidence for this basic Marxist suggestion seems presently, at most, weak.

7.6 FURTHER READING

W. E. Butler, *Soviet Law*, 2nd ed. (London: Butterworths, 1988).

M. Cain and A. Hunt, *Marx and Engels on Law* (London: Academic Press, 1979).

H. Collins, *Marxism and Law* (Oxford: Clarendon Press, 1982).

R. H. Folsom and J. H. Minan, *Law in the People's Republic of China* (Dordrecht: Nijhoff, 1989).

V. H. Li, *Law without Lawyers: A Comparative View of Law in China and the United States* (Boulder, Colo: Westview Press, 1978).

E. B. Pashukanis, *Law and Marxism: A General Theory*, transl. B. Einhorn (London: Ink Links, 1978).

P. Phillips, *Marx and Engels on Law and Laws* (Oxford: Martin Robertson, 1980).

CHAPTER EIGHT

Pure Theory

Hans Kelsen (1881–1973) advanced a highly distinctive theory of law which has had a significant influence upon the development of modern jurisprudence, even if its perspective may now seem to be subject to important limitations. Kelsen considered himself a 'positivist' and stated unequivocally that:

> The pure theory of law is a theory of positive law. As a theory it is exclusively concerned with the accurate definition of its subject-matter. It endeavours to answer the question, What is the law? but not the question, What ought it to be? It is a science and not a politics of law. (H. Kelsen, 'The pure theory of law', transl. C. H. Wilson (1934) 50 LQR 474 at p. 477.)

This is manifestly a positivist agenda, both in its emphasis upon what law 'is' and in its claims to 'scientific' analysis. However, the theory cannot simply be equated with the English tradition of legal positivism associated with Jeremy Bentham, John Austin and H.L.A. Hart (see chapters 2 and 3). The pure theory was advanced in a different context and was to a significant extent influenced by rather different considerations from those which shaped the English positivist tradition. Kelsen's work originated in the intellectual climate of post-1918 Vienna. This was a period of dramatic change. The dismemberment of the Austro-Hungarian Empire after the First World War and the transition from imperial centre to the capital of a much reduced republic enhanced a critical 'scientific' tradition which already had deep roots in pre-war Austria, seen, e.g., in the psycho-analytical work of Sigmund

Freud. Both the strengths and the weaknesses of this general tradition may be seen to advantage in Kelsen's legal theory.

Like all positivists Kelsen was concerned with what law 'is', but he was not directly concerned with the substantive norms of any particular legal system. His interest was instead in the nature of the building blocks out of which a legal system, any legal system, is constructed. The model which he advanced is one of a hierarchy of norms, each of which is validated by a preceding norm until, finally, an ultimate source of authorisation is reached in a basic norm termed the *Grundnorm*. This model is essentially abstract and Kelsen never suggested that actual legal systems are expressly formulated in this way. It is, rather, suggested that this is how a legal system, whatever its mode of expression, actually works.

8.1   IN WHAT SENSE A 'PURE' THEORY?

Kelsen termed his legal theory 'pure', implying some lack of contamination. By this he meant that the theory excluded from consideration all factors which could not be regarded as of the essence of 'law'. These included a wide range of considerations which other schools of jurisprudence incorporate in their models of law and its operation, for some of which Kelsen manifested an unmistakable contempt. This endeavour to establish a pure theory rested upon a concept of knowledge which owed much to the work of Immanuel Kant (1724–1804).

8.1.1   Pure theory and the Kantian theory of knowledge

Immanuel Kant argued that in acquiring knowledge human beings impose a framework of categorisations upon their impressions of the world beyond themselves. The impressions thus processed in the cause of understanding therefore have imposed upon them a structure which is not necessarily inherent in the objective phenomena observed. This might be found, for example, in interpretations of causality or even appreciations of time. It should be emphasised that this is not to assert a condition of error or falsity, it is simply to advance an analysis of the way in which impressions are processed and structured into a form of understanding acceptable to human mentality.

In a similar way Kelsen's scientific model of law seeks to set out a formal structure through which the nature of law and legal systems may be known, even though the analytical structure may be far removed from the overt substance of any given legal system. Thus, for Kelsen, although jurisprudence is to be considered a science it should not be treated as a natural science which is concerned with the observation of facts and analysis of causal relations. Instead, Kelsenian jurisprudence seeks to discover a logical structure underlying an objective reality.

The pure theory is a science of norms, one concerned with 'ought' propositions and not the study of factually descriptive 'is' propositions. Lest it be thought that there is here a conflict with the claimed positivism of Kelsen's theory it should be emphasised that these are not, e.g., the moral or ethical 'oughts' with which naturalist theories are concerned. The point is rather that law is by its nature normative: it is concerned precisely with what people 'ought', or 'ought not', to do. Of course, people do not always actually do what they ought to, or, indeed, always avoid doing what they ought not to do. For Kelsen legal norms take the general form, if condition x applies then consequence y ought to follow. The effect of such a norm is essentially to validate, i.e., render 'legal', the actions or decisions which in any given case comprise consequence y. Again it must be stressed that this is a model of how the law works and not a description of how it is stated. In English law the Town and Country Planning Act 1990 does not, quite, state that 'if development is undertaken without planning permission, then an enforcement notice ought to be served upon the developer'. There is a certain degree of local planning authority discretion in this respect. The process is seen by Kelsen as one of authorisation. Thus the local planning authority is authorised by the summary norm stated above to serve enforcement notices in appropriate cases, but not, of course, in inappropriate cases.

8.1.2 The meaning of 'purity'

Kelsen's theory is represented to be 'pure' in the sense that it carefully excludes from consideration all factors and issues which can be considered not to be strictly 'legal'. These include all the moral, ethical, sociological and political factors and values which are commonly advanced in explanation or pleaded in justification of law. Kelsen explained that:

> The pure theory of law . . . establishes the law as a specific system independent even of the moral law. It does this not . . . by defining the legal norm . . . as an imperative, but as an hypothetical judgment expressing a specific relationship between a conditioning circumstance and a conditioned consequence. ('The pure theory of law', transl. C. H. Wilson (1934) 50 LQR 474 at pp. 484–5.)

Such 'conditioned circumstances' arising in the application of positive law are not, of course, denied to have moral, political or sociological effects, but their analysis is relegated to disciplines other than that of jurisprudence.

The purity of Kelsen's theory inevitably, and intentionally, distances it from real legal systems. The model is a blueprint for the operation of legal systems in general rather than any particular legal system. The logic behind the purity of the model is clear enough, but it must be asked whether such an attempt to isolate the essence of 'law' from all other factually associated factors may not tend to distort the analysis.

8.2 THE HIERARCHY OF NORMS

The Kelsenian model of a legal system is one of a hierarchy of norms in which each norm is validated by a prior norm until the point of origin of legal authority is reached with the basic norm, the *Grundnorm*. In order to comprehend this system it is necessary to appreciate the nature of the norms in question and the function of the hierarchic relationship existing between them. Both these questions raise a number of important, and in some ways problematic, issues.

8.2.1 The structure of norms

The nature of the norms which form the Kelsenian hierarchy is determined by the intended purity of the analysis. The pure theory excludes not only moral, political and sociological values but also ideas of the purpose, in the sense of legislative or judicial intention, of law. Such ideas are considered themselves to rest upon, e.g., political or sociological values. The pure theory is concerned with the active function of legal norms, that is to say, how they actually work. Interpreting norms should be left to moralists, politicians and sociologists.

According to Kelsen the key function of law in this sense is one of coercion. He argued that all legal norms are concerned with force, either with a response to unilateral use of force, for its suppression, or in the threatened or actual use of legal force to secure compliance with lawful orders and directions. The second category, of course, embraces the first insofar as, e.g., a tortfeasor or criminal may be confronted with legal force in order to terminate the wrongful conduct in question. Thus the normative formula, if condition x is satisfied then consequence y ought to follow will take the concrete form, if the specified situation occurs then the stated sanction ought to be applied.

The emphasis upon coercion is superficially reminiscent of the classical positivist model of law as the 'command of a sovereign backed by a sanction' (see 2.2). The comparison would, however, be somewhat misleading, in that Bentham and Austin saw the application of sanctions as a predictive element accounting for the working of legal obligation. Kelsen's norms, in contrast, are not supposed to be factually predictive. It is simply being stated that a sanction ought to be applied in a given case, not that it actually will be applied. The difference is fundamental and rests ultimately upon the Humean dichotomy between descriptive, 'is', and normative, 'ought', propositions.

The Kelsenian norm, therefore, states the conditions for the application of sanctions, always bearing in mind that these are hypothetical norms

concerned with the way in which positive law acts rather than with the forms
in which it may be stated. In effect, the norms are summaries of authorisations admitting the taking of given action in response to the occurrence of
given events. Within the Kelsenian model the next, and vital, question is that
of the relationship between the norms and the manner of their validation.

8.2.2 Validation in the hierarchy of norms

The Kelsenian norms are not represented as being equal in status. Their
relationship is vertical rather than horizontal. Kelsen stated that:

> The legal order is not a system of coordinated norms of equal level, but a
> hierarchy of different levels of legal norms. Its unity is brought about by
> . . . the fact that the validity of a norm, created according to another norm,
> rests on that other norm, whose creation in turn, is determined by a third
> one. (H. Kelsen, *Pure Theory of Law*, transl. M. Knight (Berkeley, Calif:
> University of California Press, 1967), pp. 221–2.)

Thus, upon the Kelsenian model, the norm that the judge hearing a case
orders the payment of damages by the defendant then damages ought to be
levied (under coercion if need be), follows from the prior norm that, if the
conduct of a defendant falls within the stated category then the judge ought
to make an award of damages, and so on up to a legislative enactment or (in
a common law system) an original judicial precedent. Behind this, ultimately,
there lurks the *Grundnorm* itself. Such a linear example is a little simplified in
that, although a line of norms may be traced from the *Grundnorm* through
legislation down to the enforcement of a particular judgment, there will in
practice be several lines of norms involved. They will include norms of
judicial appointment leading to the conclusion that, if the judge has been duly
appointed to office then judgments made within the scope of his or her
authority ought to be enforced. The point relates to the contrast between the
authorised demands of the Inland Revenue and the unauthorised demands of
the gunman cited in H. L. A. Hart's analysis (see 3.1).

The structure of these norms is also dynamic rather than static. It is not
the substantive content of norms which is here in question but the manner
of their authorisation, and such authorisations clearly include the possibility
of authorised changes.

The formalist nature of Kelsen's analysis of the hierarchy of norms is
striking. The quality of a judgment, or even of legislation, is irrelevant. All
that matters is that an unbroken chain of normative authorisation 'validates'
the final decision or action, whatever that may be. All of this supposes an
existing and stable legal order, but some means must be found to identify
what, in a given case, that order actually is. In Kelsen's theory the answer to
that question is found in the basic norm termed the *Grundnorm*.

8.2.3 The *Grundnorm*

The *Grundnorm* is the starting-point of any chain of legal norms, the apex of a normative pyramid which, through a long line of connections, authorises the decisions and actions taken in the system at ground level, i.e., in the determination of particular issues and cases. What then is the *Grundnorm*? According to Kelsen:

> . . . the basic norm . . . must be formulated as follows: Coercive acts sought to be performed under the conditions and in the manner which the historically first constitution, and the norms created according to it, prescribe. (In short: One ought to behave as the constitution prescribes.) (*Pure Theory of Law*, transl. M. Knight, pp. 200–1.)

A number of points arise from this definition. Most obviously it must be asked whether the *Grundnorm* is identical with the 'constitution' and why the 'historically first' constitution should be selected, rather than that which is currently operative.

In terms of professional legal discourse it would be tempting to identify the *Grundnorm* with the constitution, especially in a State such as the USA which, unlike the United Kingdom, has a written constitutional document. This would not, however, be quite correct, because the constitution itself is a norm, the effect of which might crudely be summarised in the form: if a decision or an action is constitutional then it ought to be permitted. The *Grundnorm* operates one step further back and does not define the constitution but instead validates it. It is, in short, the presupposition of the validity of the constitution, or the constitutional order, of the State in question, without which the whole legal edifice dependent upon it must crumble. In the pure Kelsenian concept no assumptions are made about the substance of the constitution and certainly not that it should be democratic or involve any balance of powers or any other such concepts. A constitution to the effect that 'if the autocrat gives an order, then it ought to be enforced' would be sufficient for this purpose, apart from the all too evident difficulties in attempting to found a functioning *Rechtsstaat*, a State governed by law, upon such a minimalist basis.

The reference to a 'historically first' constitution involves a chain of constitutional validations in which constitutional evolution, through processes of amendment or other procedures not involving a revolutionary discontinuity, lead back to a first accepted constitution. The 'historical first' is thus the starting-point of the current constitutional order and not necessarily whatever arrangement originally obtained in the country concerned. From this point of view the historically first English constitution would be the Revolutionary settlement of 1689 and not the arrangements of William the

Conqueror, or Edward the Confessor. In the United States it would be the independence constitution and not the arrangement of colonial government under George III. The Kelsenian first constitution is thus the product either of revolutionary discontinuity or (highly unlikely in the modern world) of a truly first writing upon a political blank sheet.

What constitution is operative in a given country at a given time is a matter to be determined by reference to effectiveness, i.e., what constitution is actually applied. From this it would seem to follow that the *Grundnorm* cannot in Kelsen's terms truly be considered 'pure'. Effectiveness in the end rests upon all the moral, ethical, political and sociological factors which are carefully excluded from the pure theory, and yet this is the means by which the *Grundnorm*, the fountain-head of the system, is to be identified. This paradox is, however, more apparent than real. The *Grundnorm* is the assumption of the validity of the constitution and not its particular identity. The relation of the *Grundnorm* to the criterion of 'effectiveness' is simply the point at which Kelsen's hypothetical hierarchy of norms attaches to reality. Once it has been determined, through the test of effectiveness, what constitution is being assumed to be valid in a given State, the Kelsenian analysis begins to be applied to the actual substance of a real legal system. The point of contact is vitally important but it is essentially extrinsic to the pure theory itself. The doctrine of effectiveness does, however, raise a controversial issue. This arises from the treatment of a change of *Grundnorm* through a revolutionary discontinuity, that is to say when the line from a historically first constitution is broken and a new primary historical foundation is laid.

One final point requires to be made. Thus far the *Grundnorm* has been treated as the basic element of national, or municipal law, which functionally it essentially remains throughout Kelsen's thought. However, in his later writings Kelsen considered the relation between public international and national, or municipal law and was led to postulate an international *Grundnorm* ranking prior to the municipal *Grundnorms* of particular States (see 8.5). This is an important element of Kelsenian jurisprudence but it does not appear substantially to affect the role of the *Grundnorm* when viewed from a national perspective.

8.2.4 The problem of revolutionary transition

Where a revolutionary change takes place, breaking the chain of continuity from the historically first constitution then in place, the substantive, although not the hypothetical, effect of the *Grundnorm* in the given situation will change. In short, the practical efficacy of the new order will lead to the supposition of a changed *Grundnorm* authorising a revised chain of norms.

Kelsen has been criticised for omitting from his analysis of a discontinuous change in a legal order any consideration of political or moral evaluation of the revolutionary, or indeed pre-revolutionary, regime. J. W. Harris remarks that:

> Surely, it has been argued, lawyers take other things into account – such as the justice of the revolutionary cause, or the approval or disapproval of the populace – not just the fact of enforcement? Whether Kelsen, or his critics, correctly describe what lawyers do in such contexts is an issue of history. (J. W. Harris, *Legal Philosophies* (London: Butterworths, 1980), p. 71.)

The essence of this question seems to be one of context, as so often in issues of jurisprudence. It must be remembered that revolutionary regimes do not approach legal institutions as suppliants seeking their approval. A legal order of some sort will no doubt be required but if the existing institutions are unwilling to validate the new regime, they will, by one means or another, certainly be replaced by another which is more compliant.

The main stumbling-block here is the question of what exactly is meant by 'effectiveness'. The Kelsenian view of revolutionary change has from time to time been judicially considered. In a case arising from the unilateral declaration of independence by the Smith regime in Rhodesia (now Zimbabwe) in 1965, *Madzimbamuto* v *Lardner Burke* (1968) 2 SA 284, it was suggested that the effectiveness of a revolutionary regime rests to a very significant extent upon the willingness of the judiciary to implement its decrees. In relation to this and other cases, in which the Kelsenian issue of effectiveness has been judicially considered, R. W. M. Dias comments that:

> . . . it may well be that . . . pronouncements [of the illegality of a revolutionary regime] will nearly always be retrospective, since judges sitting under the power of a regime may have little alternative but to accept it as legal; those who refuse will be replaced, or their judgments will be nullified. (R. W. M. Dias, *Jurisprudence*, 5th ed. (London: Butterworths, 1985), p. 366.)

They may have 'alternatives' but they will almost certainly be profoundly unpleasant. Certainly no revolutionary regime has ever given up the power it has seized simply because the judges disapprove of it. Interestingly, the Supreme Court of Pakistan rejected the Kelsenian model in *Jilani* v *Government of Punjab* PLD 1972 SC 670, overruling a pro-Kelsenian view taken in 1958 at a time when an 'illegal' regime was in fact in power. Ultimately this question raises the same issues as those which have been most intensively debated in relation to the use of positive law in the Third Reich, albeit in a distinct context (see 3.5.1 and chapter 16).

Lawyers and others may, of course, criticise the new order and might even resist it, with whatever long-term success or failure. This, however, relates to moral, ethical, political and sociological considerations which are, *ex hypothesi*, excluded from the pure theory. Kelsen should not be understood to deny the existence or even the effect of such considerations; they are indeed inherent in the concept of 'efficacy', since successful resistance will of course render a system inefficacious whether by revolution or counter-revolution. Kelsen, however, relegates consideration of these issues to disciplines other than that of jurisprudence. In his own terms this may be accepted, but whether such limitations contribute ultimately to a distortion of analysis is, again, a serious question to be pondered.

8.3   CONCRETISATION AND THE SUBSTANCE OF NORMS

Whatever particular form they may take, legal norms ultimately have real effects, whether it be through judgments in courts or through procedures such as entering into contracts which it is hoped will not lead to litigation. The law is considered in Kelsen's model to operate at different levels of abstraction, from the hypothetical *Grundnorm*, which ultimately authorises the whole system, to the actual application of substantive norms in cases. This process of movement from the abstract to substantive application is described as one of 'concretisation'.

8.3.1   The working of concretisation

Judicial determinations represent the creation of a specific norm in the form, e.g., that the particular defendant shall pay damages to the plaintiff. In the same way persons who enter into contracts create specific norms between themselves, e.g., *x* will buy this car from *y* giving consideration therefor. The analysis of, e.g., contracts as a form of private norm creation is somewhat alien to common law thinking but much more familiar in the discourse of civilian systems. In the present context, such agreements may readily be treated as analogous with judgments in that they involve the specific application of norms in a given situation, provided, of course, that they comply with prior authorising norms.

From *Grundnorm* to judgment, contract, or other personal application, is seen as a process of progressive concretisation as the degree of abstraction of successive norms decreases to the point of direct and substantive application to the particular issue. From the presupposition of the validity of the constitution (the *Grundnorm*) to the specific purchase of, e.g., a box of apples, may be seen as a process of focusing. As one moves from the constitution, through legislation or original judicial precedent, through a descending series of norms of every increasing specificity, one finally reaches the point at which a norm is taken specifically to authorise or enable the purchase by this customer from this shopkeeper of those particular apples. If, of course, the apples turn out to be bad, the problem will be considered via a slightly different chain of norms, also originating with the *Grundnorm*, until judgment, one way or the other, is given and enforced.

8.3.2 The reality of concretisation

The analysis set out above can certainly be imposed upon such day-to-day transactions as purchase of goods and, where such transactions break down, to judicial settlement of disputes arising. The same pattern may be imposed upon the concretisation of criminal proceedings. The problem is that law is not stated, or generally appreciated, in quite this way. Does a customer in a shop really start out from the proposition, 'I assume that we are agreed, in the light of its current efficacy, that the "constitution" is valid'? All of this is 'assumed', or more accurately not considered at all. Of course Kelsen never suggested that this is the way people actually speak or think. The analysis is an explanation of what happens rather than a literalist description of it. Behind this, however, there is a more important question. The Kelsenian analysis is profoundly formalistic; it is largely concerned with the actual or potential application of sanctions by officials. Whether this is an appropriate model must be questioned.

8.4 THE OFFICIAL EMPHASIS OF KELSENIAN ANALYSIS

If the Kelsenian normative hierarchy is examined it will be seen that for the most part it is directed to official action and ultimately to the application of sanctions. Even the process of entering into a contract is truly seen as a potentially interim phase in a process of concretisation. The final point of this process would be the authorisation of force for the imposition of damages or whatever other remedy might flow from a particular breach of contract.

It is, of course, the case that where a contract, to pursue that example, does go wrong, litigation in pursuit of a remedy might result. Such litigation might, indeed, conclude with an order for a remedy which might well, in an extreme case, demand coercive implementation. Statistically, however, such an outcome is very much atypical. To return to the shop counter briefly, how many purchases of goods are expected to or actually do lead to litigation? Clearly a minute proportion. A theory which asserts not only the importance of official action, which is understandable, but also its preponderance in the operation of law would be deeply questionable. Such views are not of course unknown. Kelsen may, however, up to a point be defended against this charge. Contracts are undertaken in an 'official', in the sense of regulated, context. Even if the overwhelming majority never require 'official' intervention, that possibility is an important part of the framework of the activity. So much may be accepted but the omission from consideration of the vast majority of 'non-official' transactions which are performed according to law is a disturbing consequence of Kelsenian formalism.

8.5 THE ROLE OF PUBLIC INTERNATIONAL LAW IN PURE THEORY

The nature of public international law and its relation to municipal law have been considered problematic by a number of legal theorists. The English positivist tradition tends to take a dismissive view of the international legal order. It will be recalled that John Austin, speaking at a time when international law was institutionally much less developed than is now the case, relegated the system to the sphere of 'positive morality' (see 2.4). H. L. A. Hart, on the other hand, considers that international law approaches very close to 'legal' status, but perhaps does not quite achieve that status (see 3.4). Kelsen, ultimately, took a radically different view which led him in part to reassess the nature of his *Grundnorm* and to move it into the 'international' sphere.

8.5.1 Monism, dualism and the *Grundnorm*

There are two broad views which can be taken of the relation between public international law (assuming it to be 'law') and municipal law. They may be considered essentially separate systems in which the external obligations of a State (under international law) have only a political relation to its use of internal lawmaking powers within the national system. Thus, a State which, through its municipal law, is violating international law will be in breach of external obligations and may be made the object of sanctions. The offending municipal law will, however, be 'law' until, or rather unless, the State is forced, through sanctions or other pressures, to change it. This, crudely, is the 'dualist' view. Alternatively, it may be argued that there is only one legal order which comprises both international and municipal law, and any municipal law which violates international obligations or norms will, to a greater or lesser extent, be thereby invalidated. This, again crudely, is the 'monist' position. For a variety of reasons Kelsen ultimately took up a monist view.

The principal reason was his view that valid legal orders should not conflict and that if States were part of an international legal order, which they may generally be considered to be, then international and municipal law should be considered as part of a unified, monist system. From a Kelsenian viewpoint it follows from this proposition that international law must have a *Grundnorm*. Kelsen also took it that since the international system was the overall unity, its *Grundnorm* must rank prior to municipal *Grundnormen* and thus be the ultimate source of authority for municipal systems also.

It may be argued that this question is somewhat removed from the realities of both international and municipal law. States do have international legal obligations which do impinge upon the organisation of their municipal law. Sometimes at least quasi-monist doctrines may be found in municipal law, but ultimately in international law, perhaps even more than in municipal law, matters of morality, ethics and politics are in practice inseparable from the working of the legal order. It may be contended that in this particular issue the possibly distorting implications of the assumptions of the pure theory become very apparent.

8.5.2 The *Grundnorm* of public international law

In endeavouring to postulate an international *Grundnorm*, Kelsen followed a similar process of tracing to that which led from the particular municipal decision back to the municipal *Grundnorm*. If here the point of concretised application is a decision of the International Court, or presumably of other international bodies such as, e.g., the United Nations Security Council, then a chain of authorisation may be followed. The chain will lead back to one of the sources of public international law, as set out in art. 38 of the Statute of the International Court of Justice. That is to say, in brief summary, treaties, international custom, recognised general principles of law and, as 'subsidiary' sources, judicial decisions and academic writings. Kelsen contends that treaties, customs etc. all relate back to an essential requirement that States ought to conduct themselves in accordance with the custom established amongst them, which includes the doctrine of *pacta sunt servanda* (agreements are to be observed) which is the fundamental basis of treaty obligations. This norm of custom is then, for Kelsen, the international *Grundnorm* (see H. Kelsen, *General Theory of Law and State*, transl. A. Wedberg (Cambridge, Mass: Harvard University Press, 1949), pp. 369–70). The analysis as originally presented referred, of course, to the League of Nations rather than to the United Nations era, the translated edition being subsequent, naturally, to the original writing.

If there must indeed be an international *Grundnorm*, Kelsen's description of it is not unreasonable. However, the attempt to force international law into pure theory does seem to betoken an element of that desire for inappropriate comprehensiveness of analysis which is one of the weaknesses of much jurisprudential analysis.

8.6 THE VALUE OF PURE THEORY

Kelsenian pure theory offers a rigorously structured analysis of the working of legal systems in general, founded upon a hypothetical structure of authorising norms. In its endeavours to be scientific and to exclude all extraneous factors from consideration, it perhaps represents an extreme form of a mode of jurisprudential analysis which had roots in the 19th century and remained dominant up to the period between the First and Second World Wars. As such the theory has much of value to say about the structured working of a legal system, even granted the quite considerable shifts of emphasis which may be found in the considerable volume of jurisprudential writing which Kelsen left.

Unfortunately, like many positivist, and other, analyses, but in extreme degree, the pure theory suffers from its own self-imposed limitations. It is acceptable for purposes of a particular discourse to focus upon some aspect of the working of law, indeed doing so is almost unavoidable. When, however, an 'essence' of law is sought such limitations become problematic. Law, as an aspect of political society, may be argued to be inseparably linked, not only in its working but in its nature, with all the moral, ethical, political and sociological factors which Kelsen dismissed as 'impure'. If that is accepted, the pure theory gives only a very formalistic and partial description of the working of law. Kelsen did not deny the existence of these factors, but in excluding them from his jurisprudence he may be argued to have excluded much of the reality of law. On this basis the pure theory may be considered both interesting and useful within in its own appointed context, but that context is severely constrained.

8.7 FURTHER READING

Dias, R. W. M., *Jurisprudence*, 4th ed. (London: Butterworths, 1985), ch. 17.

Harris, J. W., 'When and why does the *Grundnorm* change?' [1971] CLJ 103.

Kelsen, H., *General Theory of Law and State*, transl. A. Wedberg (Cambridge, Mass: Harvard University Press, 1949).

Kelsen, H., *Pure Theory of Law*, transl. M. Knight (Berkeley, Calif: University of California Press, 1967).

Kelsen, H., 'The pure theory of law', transl. C. H. Wilson (1934) 50 LQR 474 and (1935) 51 LQR 517.

Lloyd, Dennis (Baron Lloyd of Hampstead), *Lloyd's Introduction to Jurisprudence*, 5th ed. (London: Sweet & Maxwell, 1985), ch. 5.

Raz, J., *The Concept of a Legal System*, 2nd ed. (Oxford: Clarendon Press, 1980), pp. 93–120.

CHAPTER NINE

Dworkin and the Rights Thesis

Ronald Dworkin succeeded H. L. A. Hart to the chair of jurisprudence at Oxford University and, to a certain extent, his theories are built on criticisms of his illustrious predecessor, just as Hart's theory starts with a critique of Austin. Dworkin's rights-based theory has two linked elements.

First he puts forward a declaratory theory of the judicial process. This is the narrow aspect of Dworkin's theory, and appears to a certain extent a throwback to an earlier, and generally discredited period of judicial decision-making in which the judges purported not to make law or to legislate but simply applied the law. This formalistic approach which was based on a strict division of competence between the judiciary and the legislature, has pervaded English jurisprudence at least since the time of Bentham and Austin, and dominated American jurisprudence at the turn of the century until the American realist movement, building on the ideas of Mr Justice Holmes, radically changed the direction of American jurisprudence (O. W. Holmes, 'The path of the law' (1897) 10 Harv L Rev 457). Despite its rather reactionary appearance, it must be said that Professor Dworkin's approach has little of the narrowness of the simple formalist approach, highlighted by the presence of a much wider liberal theory of democracy which constitutes the second element.

From the very narrow base of judicial decision-making, Dworkin then develops a very sophisticated view of democracy, arguing strongly for individual and minority rights – rights which cannot be overridden by the legislature on simple policy grounds. His theory is distinctly anti-utilitarian: the majority should not be able to ride roughshod over the minority's legal rights. This theory of democracy is linked to his view of the judicial process by the notion that judges act as the protectors of individual rights against the State as well as between individuals.

9.1 DWORKIN'S CRITICISM OF POSITIVISM
AND PRAGMATISM

9.1.1 Positivism

I want to make a general attack on positivism, and I shall use H. L. A. Hart's version as a target. . . . My strategy will be organised around the fact that when lawyers reason or dispute about legal rights and obligations, particularly in those hard cases when our problems with these concepts seem most acute, they make use of standards that do not function as rules, but operate differently as principles, policies, and other sorts of standards. Positivism, I shall argue, is a model of and for a system of rules, and its central notion of a single fundamental test for law forces us to miss the important roles of these standards that are not rules. (R. M. Dworkin, *Taking Rights Seriously* (London: Duckworth, 1977), p. 22.)

One aspect of Hart's theory examined in the course of chapter 3 was his analysis of the judicial function (see H. L. A. Hart, *The Concept of Law* (Oxford, Clarendon Press, 1961), ch. 7) although it is also implicit in his basic notion of law being a type of social rule. Hart states that in the majority of cases the rules will be clear. However, they will, at some point, become indeterminate and unclear, because they have what Hart calls an 'open texture', a defect inherent in any use of language.

We can take the simple example of a local by-law that prohibits 'vehicles' from entering public parks. In the absence of a list of vehicles, which, even if provided, would be incomplete, it would be unclear whether the by-law prohibited motorised wheelchairs, roller-skates or skateboards. At this margin of uncertainty Hart states that judges or officials must use their discretion in deciding whether a particular case comes within the rule or not. In exercising this discretion, the judge or official will look to the purposes or the social consequences of adopting a certain interpretation of the rule, for example, the competing policy arguments that, on the one hand, the park is a place of peace and quiet which would necessitate a wide interpretation of the by-law to include the controversial cases within the prohibition (with the exception of wheelchairs), and on the other hand, the contention that the park is a place of recreation and enjoyment which would lead to the by-law being interpreted restrictively so as to allow roller-skates and skateboards.

Dworkin argues against this approach which allows for the judge or official to make a *policy* decision not based on law in hard or unclear cases, stating that Hart, by seeing law solely as a system of rules, fails to take account of general principles. In a hard or unclear case the judge does not revert to policy and act as a lawmaker, but applies legal principles to produce an answer based on law.

Dworkin gives us an example of a legal principle in the case of *Riggs* v *Palmer* (1889) 22 NE 188, in which a New York court had to decide whether a murderer could inherit under the will of the grandfather he had murdered. The court held that the relevant statutes literally gave the property of the deceased to the murderer. But then the court reasoned (at p. 190):

> . . . all laws as well as all contracts may be controlled in their operation and effect by general, fundamental maxims of the common law. No one shall be permitted to profit by his own fraud, or to take advantage of his own wrong, or to found any claim upon his own iniquity, or to acquire property by his own crime.

So denying the murderer his inheritance.

Standards such as 'no man may profit from his own wrong' have, according to Dworkin, relative weight when considered judicially, and so help to determine the case in favour of one of the parties when the rules have run out. He is suggesting that, in unclear cases, the judges do not have complete discretion to make new law, instead they fall back on legal principles to make a decision based on existing law (meaning rules and principles). It is worth noting, however, that in *Riggs* v *Palmer* the rules were clear: the murderer should have inherited, and the legal principle in fact overruled the rule. It may be inferred that Dworkin is giving legal principles another role. As well as acting as the cement of the law filling in its gaps and loopholes, they are also used to prevent injustices which would arise out of a simple application of the rules. Hart himself says that rather than relying on the judges using policy to deal with unclear cases, most 'mature' legal systems lean towards certainty and predictability by stretching the rules to deal with unclear cases. However, Hart admits that the more rules are stretched the more their application becomes artificial, leading to cases of injustice (*The Concept of Law*, pp. 126–27). If the legal system is seen as being comprised of both rules and overarching principles then it is possible to avoid such injustices.

However, if Dworkin's controversial choice of examples to illustrate the basic components of his theory is ignored, it will be seen that the main thrust of his argument is that rules, whether precedents or statutes, are applicable in 'an all or nothing fashion' and so there may be cases, particularly hard ones, which are not covered by rules or if there are rules they are unclear. In a common law system it is quite possible for each party to a case to be able to marshal an equally impressive set of precedents in their favour. Positivists like Hart state that when there are such hard cases in the law, judges either have the power to make new law or, as is more likely, they stretch one line of precedents to cover the case in preference to the other line of argument. Given that they have a choice it could be argued that the reason for choosing one line of precedents over another is based not on law but on non-legal factors such as considerations of what the judges think is best for society. In this sense they act as a sort of deputy lawmaker. Dworkin states that such a role belongs to the legislature, not to the judges, not in the least because in a democracy judges have not been elected for such a job.

Dworkin is arguing that in all cases, most particularly in hard cases, judges are always constrained by the law. He paints a picture of a gapless legal universe where in every adjudication there are legal rules and standards which the judge is obliged to follow, although he does have discretion in the weak sense of weighing the standards set him by authority. What Dworkin denies is that judges have discretion in the strong sense to decide cases without being bound by precedent or statute.

9.1.2 Pragmatism

In his later works (R. M. Dworkin, *A Matter of Principle* (Oxford: Clarendon Press, 1986); R. M. Dworkin, *Law's Empire* (London: Fontana, 1986)), Dworkin expands his attack on other theories not only to cover 'conventionalism' – his new term for positivism, but also 'pragmatism' – his term for theories of legal realism and the economic approach to the law (see, for example, R. Posner, *Economic Analysis of Law*, 3rd ed. (Boston, Mass: Little, Brown & Co., 1986)) which suggests that judges, like legislators, should and do make law exclusively by reference to social goals, such as improved economic efficiency. Dworkin's own theory is restated as 'law as integrity' and he argues that it better explains how cases are decided than either conventionalism or pragmatism, and that it offers a better justification for the centralisation of sanctions found in mature legal systems.

His basic criticisms of positivism remain the same. He criticises pragmatism in terms of 'fit', how the theory 'fits' the actuality of the judicial process. Pragmatism does not fit the judicial process because of the simple but undeniable fact that judges, by and large, decide cases as if they are upholding existing rights, rather than making new law. Judges look to past decisions, whether of the courts or the legislature, to decide whether the plaintiff or the defendant is possessed of the legal right or the legal duty in a particular case, they do not look to the future and decide whether this decision will best maximise utility or some other social goal such as economic efficiency. The latter is the job of the legislature, and most judges do not purport to do it. Dworkin is stating that his is the descriptive theory whereas the pragmatists are being prescriptive: they are arguing how judges *ought* to reason. Furthermore, Dworkin claims that not only does his theory best describe the judicial process, it is the better theory for society in that it preserves the judiciary in the role of the upholders of the law and of legal rights.

Dworkin acknowledges that most pragmatists recognise the fact that there is an *apparent* discrepancy between the pragmatic theory that judges are lawmakers and the actual practice in which they seem to be applying established laws. Dworkin argues that the pragmatist says that judges appear to honour rights without regard to social welfare because overall welfare is advanced by acting as if some rights are impervious to such calculations (*Law's Empire*, pp. 154–5). Dworkin is stating that pragmatists advance the argument that judges somehow conspire to deceive citizens into thinking they have legal rights when in fact all they have are 'rules of thumb' that could be overturned by reasons of policy dressed up as another individual's legal rights.

What Dworkin is doing is providing a caricature of a pragmatist, so that it is much easier to dismiss him, a technique not uncommon among legal theorists. When we come on to look at the pragmatic theories of the realists and the critical scholars we will see that they do not subscribe to this simple view of judicial decision-making, by arguing, in the case of the critical theorists, that the judges are as much a victim of deception as the individual, in that they all believe in the ideal of the rule of law providing a neutral system of dispute resolution, when in fact it is a product of the liberal political system. The critical theorists argue that this shared belief is simply an ideology which is no better, or in many instances is worse, than alternative ideologies.

Nevertheless, Dworkin's criticism of the pragmatists is still powerful. He argues that if one accepts their view we would have law without legal rights. Law, for the pragmatists, is simply a tool to achieve political or economic goals.

> Pragmatism does not rule out any theory about what makes a community better. But it does not take legal rights seriously. It rejects what other conceptions of law accept: that people can have distinctly legal rights as trumps over what would otherwise be the best future properly understood. According to pragmatism what we call legal rights are only the servants of the best future: they are instruments we construct for that purpose and have no independent force or ground. (*Law's Empire*, p. 160.)

9.2 THE RIGHTS THESIS

Dworkin's theory of the judicial process is based on the distinction between rights (principles) and policies (goals):

> Arguments of policy justify a . . . decision by showing that the decision advances or protects some collective goal of the community as a whole. The argument in favour of a subsidy for aircraft manufacturers, that the subsidy will protect national defence, is an argument of policy. Arguments of principle justify a . . . decision by showing that the decision respects or

secures some individual or group right. The argument in favour of anti-discrimination statutes, that a minority has a right to equal respect and concern, is an argument of principle. (*Taking Rights Seriously*, p. 82.)

9.2.1 Objections to judicial decision-making on policy grounds

Dworkin's main contention is that judges do not have the discretion to decide unclear cases by reference to policy, and that in fact they decide them on the basis of principles. He raises two objections to those pragmatists who argue for judicial decision-making on policy grounds. First, judges are not elected to make policy decisions. Secondly, judges would be applying retroactive law if they made their decisions on policy grounds, whereas a principled decision means that the judge is upholding rights and duties that already exist (*Taking Rights Seriously*, p. 84; *A Matter of Principle*, pp. 18–23).

His argument that judges are not mandated to create law is certainly powerful in a democracy such as the United Kingdom, where at least part of the legislature is elected for this purpose. Nevertheless, the appointment of judges could be said to be politically motivated (see J. A. G. Griffith, *The Politics of the Judiciary*, 4th ed. (London: Fontana, 1991), pp. 20–30) and it could be said that judges are appointed so that they will apply the law in a particular way suited to the dominant political ideology of the day. This problem is even more apparent in the United States where the debate over appointments to the Supreme Court takes the form of an evaluation of the relative merits of 'conservative' and 'liberal' judges.

Dworkin's second argument goes to the issue of the unfairness of retroactive law. It is based on the concept accepted in most legal systems that law is meant as a guide to human behaviour. If judges, on occasions, simply made the law instead of applying settled law, they would be failing to allow people to act in accordance with already established rules. Individuals would be unable to plan their affairs to keep within the bounds of what is legally acceptable if there was a possibility that a judge might decide to extend a law or a line of precedents to cover marginal cases. This appears a powerful argument although, if judges were making new law in only a small number of cases, it could be argued that their decisions would not significantly undermine the ideal of certainty in the law. Furthermore, if judges occasionally decide to extend the law in marginal or hard cases, they are simply bringing certain activities clearly within the law when before they were seen as being within the margins of what was legally acceptable. It could be argued that if individuals use law as a guide they should order their affairs so that they are operating not at the margins of legality but clearly within the parameters set by the law. Finally, in many of the hard cases that Dworkin is concentrating on, a litigant is hardly likely to know that the weight of rules and principles will be in his or her favour until the judgment is actually given.

Thus even with a principled decision, that is, a decision entirely based on existing law, the litigant seems to be no better off than if subjected to a retroactive, policy-based decision. Either way the litigant's rights or duties are not known until judgment.

9.2.2 Entrenched rights

Dworkin describes policies as collective goals which encourage trade-offs of benefits and burdens within a community in order to produce some overall benefit for the community as a whole, for example, the drive for economic efficiency. Principles and individuated rights, such as the very general right to equal concern and respect, the right to freedom of speech or the right to recover damages for emotional loss in negligence claims, *may* be sacrificed to the collective welfare by the legislature but not by the judiciary (*Taking Rights Seriously*, pp. 90–6).

If this was the extent of his theory, it would seem to be very limited, and certainly could not be described as a theory going beyond the judicial process, because it would not protect rights against legislative interference. His argument that the judiciary acts as the protector of individual's rights would be hollow if the government of the day could simply take those rights away by a policy decision embodied in legislation. However, Dworkin's theory has a wider political import and as part of this he argues that rights cannot simply be overridden by governments using simple utilitarian calculations of what is best for the community or on what he calls 'consequentialist' grounds:

> But those Constitutional rights that we call fundamental like the right of free speech, are supposed to represent rights against the Government in the strong sense. . . . If citizens have a . . . right of free speech, then governments would do wrong to repeal the First Amendment [of the American Constitution] that guarantees it, even if they were persuaded that the majority would be better off if speech were curtailed.
>
> I must not overstate the point. Someone who claims that the citizens have a right against the Government need not go so far as to say that the State is *never* justified in overriding that right. He might say, for example, that although citizens have a right to free speech, the Government may override that right when necessary to protect the rights of others, or to prevent a catastrophe, or even to obtain a clear and major public benefit (though if he acknowledged this last as a possible justification he would be treating the right in question as not among the most important or fundamental). What he cannot do is to say that the Government is justified in overriding a right on the minimal grounds that would be sufficient if no such right existed. He cannot say that the Government is entitled to act on no more than a judgment that its act is likely to produce, overall, a benefit

to the community. That admission would make his claim of a right pointless, and would show him to be using some sense of 'right' other than the strong sense necessary to give his claim the political importance it is normally taken to have. (*Taking Rights Seriously*, pp. 191–2.)

Dworkin's theory involves more than simply judicial protection of established rights but also has the wider dimension of entrenching certain rights, whether they be against the government such as the right to free speech, or between individuals such as the right to recover damages for negligence. His theory is designed to give special place to rights as 'trumps' over general utilitarian justifications throughout the legal process, not merely in hard cases. He deals with hard cases by saying that they can only be decided on the basis of existing rights not policies, for the simple fact that to allow policy-making by the judiciary in these marginal cases would undermine his thesis that judges are the protectors of rights.

Rights, whether they be derived from legal rules, or from more general legal principles, protect individuals from political decisions, even if those decisions would improve collective goals. The more concrete or institutional a right is the more dramatic the general collective justification will have to be if it is to be defeated, whereas a more abstract right might be defeated by a more marginal collective justification.

It follows that in order to make this theory applicable to legal systems, it is necessary not only to be able to identify what rights an individual has against the government and against other individuals, but also to be able to identify the degree to which each right is entrenched within a given legal system. The more entrenched or institutionalised a right is the less a government is able to enact legislation which undermines that right. Dworkin provides a general distinction between abstract or background rights and institutional or concrete rights:

Any adequate theory will distinguish . . . between background rights, which are rights that provide a justification for political decisions by society in the abstract, and institutional rights, that provide a justification for a decision by some particular and specified political institution. (*Taking Rights Seriously*, p. 93.)

An abstract right is a:

. . . general political aim the statement of which does not indicate how that general aim is to be weighed or compromised in particular circumstances against other political aims. (*Taking Rights Seriously*, p. 93.)

For example, the British may talk about their right to free speech, but it is not a concrete right contained in any constitutional provision and it is overridden on collective policy grounds, such as preventing terrorist organisations from having the 'oxygen of publicity' by prohibiting media reporting of their statements, which was the purpose of the British government's 1988 ban on reporting a number of organisations, both legal and illegal, operating mainly in Northern Ireland, introduced by the Home Secretary (Parliamentary Debates (Hansard), Commons, 6th ser., vol. 138 (1987–88), cols 885–95). See further *R v Secretary of State for the Home Department, ex parte Brind* [1991] 1 AC 696. In addition, it is unclear how such abstract rights are to be weighed against other background individuated rights such as the right to privacy. The European Court of Human Rights is now making what were once abstract rights more concrete, preventing them from being easily set aside for policy reasons and weighing up the relative merits of each right against each other. Thus there is a gradual concretisation of abstract rights in the UK through the European Convention on Human Rights (213 UNTS 221, ratified by the United Kingdom in 1951, entered into force in September 1953) although it is true to say that the proper incorporation of the treaty into UK law would allow our courts to institutionalise rights rather than relying, as we do now, on the European Court's jurisprudence, not to mention the savings in time and money for litigants who want to take advantage of the European Convention.

'Concrete' or institutional rights are more precisely defined aims and, at their most concrete, grant individual rights before institutions such as the courts. Dworkin gives the rather obscure hypothetical example of a concrete right derived from the more general right of freedom of expression (*Taking Rights Seriously*, pp. 93–4). A court in deciding whether to uphold the right of a newspaper to publish secret defence plans, would weigh the newspaper's right to freedom of expression against the competing rights of the soldiers to security. The newspaper's concrete right to publish weighs more heavily than the rights of the soldiers in this particular instance because it is supported by the background right of freedom of expression, provided that the publication does not threaten the lives of individual soldiers.

9.2.3 The consequentialist theory of rights

In the example just looked at, namely, a dispute between a newspaper and the rights of soldiers to security, it could be strongly argued that the court is not balancing the competing rights of the newspaper against those of the soldiers. In reality the court will balance the newspaper's rights to publish against the *policy* argument that the interests of society are best served by maintaining secrecy as far as issues of national defence are concerned. In Dworkin's hypothetical example the court upholds the newspaper's rights, but it is more common in England for the courts to uphold the government's claims that defence documents should be kept secret in the public interest

(J. A. G. Griffiths, *The Politics of the Judiciary*, 4th ed. (London: Fontana, 1991), p. 281). If the court decides in favour of secrecy it is surely doing so on the basis of a *policy* decision, not on the basis that it is protecting the rights of soldiers, although that may be a consideration in its overall policy decision.

Dworkin attempts to deflect this argument by advising us not to confuse arguments of principle and arguments of policy with a different distinction between consequentialist and non-consequentialist theories of rights (*Taking Rights Seriously*, p. 307). A court may in fact consider the consequences of its decision in the light of its effect on future litigants' rights. In other words the court may take account of wider issues only when looking at rights. In the defence cases, Dworkin is arguing that the courts are simply balancing the alleged rights of the litigants before them against the wider rights of individuals potentially affected by their decisions. This is what Dworkin means by a consequentialist theory of rights. He claims that his theory encompasses such an approach and is not simply concerned with upholding the rights of litigants who appear before courts. This approach means that the court may decide to protect the rights of individuals even though they are not before the court, and have not had representations on their behalf heard by the court.

Dworkin briefly discusses the case of *D* v *National Society for the Prevention of Cruelty to Children* [1978] AC 171 (*Taking Rights Seriously*, pp. 308–9) as an illustration of this point. The National Society for the Prevention of Cruelty to Children (NSPCC) is an independent body which receives and investigates complaints from members of the public about cases of ill-treatment or neglect of children. The society received a complaint from an informant about the treatment of a 14-month-old girl, and an NSPCC inspector called at the parents' home. The mother subsequently brought an action against the society for damages for personal injuries alleged to have resulted from the society's negligence in failing properly to investigate the complaint and the manner and circumstances of the inspector's call which she said had caused her severe and continuing shock. The society denied negligence and applied for an order that there should be no disclosure of any documents which revealed or might reveal the identity of the complainant, on the grounds, *inter alia*, that the proper performance by the society of its duties required that the absolute confidentiality of information should be preserved, that if disclosure were ordered in the mother's action, its sources of information would dry up and that would be contrary to the public interest.

Now this appears to be a straight fight between the claimant's right to damages if she had proved negligence and the defendants' argument of public policy that the protection of children would be jeopardised if the claimant had access to information necessary for her action. However, Dworkin seems to suggest that all the court in fact was doing was undertaking a consequentialist examination of rights. In other words it was balancing the claimant's right on the one hand against the competing rights of children in general on the other.

In deciding in favour of the society the court came down in favour of the argument that disclosure could jeopardise the protection of children from abuse in future cases not for any policy reason but because the rights of children weighed more heavily than the right of the claimant in this particular case.

However, an examination of the House of Lords judgments in this case reveals scant evidence that the judges felt it necessary to find against the claimant on the ground that to uphold her right would have undue consequences for the protection of children's rights in the future. The House seemed more concerned with balancing the claimant's alleged right with the argument of public policy that disclosure would not be for the benefit of the community, and the policy argument prevailed. For example, Lord Edmund-Davies said, at p. 245:

> ... where (i) a confidential relationship exists ... *and* (ii) disclosure would be in breach of some ethical or social value involving the public interest, the court has a discretion to uphold a refusal to disclose relevant evidence provided it considers that, on balance, the public interest would be better served by excluding such evidence.

Dworkin criticised the so-called 'pragmatic' theories for not correlating with the actual judicial decision-making process in that if actual decisions are examined judges do not decide cases on grounds of policy. That may be so in the majority of cases, yet in *D v National Society for the Prevention of Cruelty to Children* and in other hard cases, judges are clearly deciding cases on policy grounds and it appears to be Dworkin who is alleging that this is merely a *cover* for rights-based arguments. It is not sufficient to argue that a court, when talking about 'discretion' and 'public interest', really means that it is weighing up competing rights. It may be that judges reason on the basis of rights most of the time, but in the hard cases they do reason and have reasoned on policy grounds. Judges appear to believe that they have the discretion to make law in these cases.

9.3   JUDICIAL DECISIONS AND THE COMMON LAW

9.3.1   The 'one right answer' thesis

Dworkin's view of judicial precedent is that judges agree that earlier decisions have gravitational force or weight. The legislature may make decisions inconsistent with earlier ones but a judge rarely has this independence, because he or she will always try to connect his or her decision with past decisions. It is because policy decisions may be inconsistent and are not individuated that a judge, when defining the particular gravitational force of a precedent must take into account only the arguments of principle that justify that precedent, ignoring arguments of policy (*Taking Rights Seriously*, pp. 110–23; *Law's Empire*, pp. 23–9, pp. 238–50). In effect judges are always looking back to precedents or statutes to justify their decisions, whilst the legislature, in formulating policy and enacting it in the form of legislation, is forward-looking. Furthermore, in looking back, the judge only looks for principles (and rules) not, for instance, at the policy that may have generated a particular piece of legislation.

Dworkin seems to admit that in practice this approach will not necessarily produce consistency in judicial decision-making, with the result that in the same case, different judges would come up with a different answer even though they were seeking the answer only in rules and principles. However, he does contend that in theory there is only one single 'right' answer to all legal questions. Unfortunately, it appears that only one person could achieve this answer every time, that person is Hercules, Dworkin's mythical judge, 'a lawyer of superhuman skill, learning, patience and acumen' (*Taking Rights Seriously*, p. 105).

[Hercules] must construct a scheme of abstract and concrete principles that provides a coherent justification for all common law precedents and, so far as these are to be justified on principle, constitutional and statutory provisions as well. (*Taking Rights Seriously*, pp. 116–17.)

The one right answer thesis has caused great debate amongst legal theorists (see, for example, A. C. Hutchinson and J. N. Wakefield, 'A hard look at "hard cases": the nightmare of a noble dreamer' (1982) 2 Oxford J Legal Stud 86) but the controversy is to a certain extent overblown in that Dworkin recognises that the requirement that judges weigh up arguments based on principles introduces a weak discretion. If judges are to make decisions at all they must be given leeway so that each judge's scheme of principles will be slightly different.

9.3.2 Integrity in practice

When dealing with a case based solely within the common law, Dworkin says that the judge relies on his interpretation of that law which produces a scheme of principles, each with a certain weight. In *Law's Empire*, Dworkin calls this approach integrity in law. That book commences with a discussion of several illustrative cases, one of which is the negligence case of *McLoughlin v O'Brian* [1983] 1 AC 410, which Dworkin uses to support his theory of common law interpretation. The case concerned the question of whether the claimant could recover damages for emotional injuries suffered away from the scene of a car crash in which her family had been injured as a result of the defendant's negligence.

The Court of Appeal [1981] QB 599 recognised that, although the defendant owed the claimant a duty of care and that her emotional injuries were reasonably foreseeable, her 'right' to recover was limited on the policy ground that liability for negligence had to stop somewhere. The House of Lords reversed that decision. Several of their lordships admitted that the policy consideration that such a precedent could open the floodgates of litigation, as taken into account by the Court of Appeal, may, in very grave circumstances, be sufficient to distinguish a line of precedent and so justify a judge's refusal to extend the principle of those cases to larger areas of liability. But such arguments must be sufficiently grave, which they were not in this case (see, for example, Lord Edmund-Davies [1983] 1 AC 410 at pp. 426–9).

Lord Scarman, on the other hand, went further, saying that once the claimant had established her right to recover, no argument of policy could take it away. Any adverse affects on the community should be dealt with by the legislature (at pp. 429–31).

Lord Scarman's judgment does correspond closely to Dworkin's approach. Nevertheless, only Lord Scarman's judgment seems to accord with Dworkin's theory; the rest of the judges seemed to believe that the judiciary could take account of policy arguments and in certain circumstances, they, not the legislature, could use them to deny a right. Although Dworkin admits that on occasions policy grounds can be used to overrule a right, that, according to Dworkin, can only be done by the legislature and not by the judges as the majority in *McLoughlin* v *O'Brian* seem to suggest. Dworkin uses the case because Lord Scarman seems to embody Hercules to a certain extent, yet overall the vast majority of judges in both the Court of Appeal and the House of Lords seemed willing to balance policy considerations against a set of precedents containing the right to recover damages for emotional injuries caused by negligence. Again Dworkin's choice of examples tends to illustrate that his theory is not descriptive of what judges actually do and that, if anything, he is describing the approach of a minority of the judiciary.

9.4 JUDICIAL DECISIONS AND STATUTES

9.4.1 Settled and hard cases

As regards the common law, Dworkin adheres to the view that judges decide cases on principle not policy, and this is the approach whether the case is difficult or straightforward. It appears that such an approach is inapplicable to cases involving, in whole or in part, the interpretation and application of statutes for the simple reason that, unlike the common law, statutes are mostly motivated by considerations of policy.

Again there are different considerations for settled and hard cases. In settled cases, the enforcement of the clear terms of some plainly valid statute is always justified on grounds of principle, even if the statute is generated by policy (*Taking Rights Seriously*, pp. 105–10). By 'principle' here, Dworkin means that the statute creates rights and duties which are recognised in individual cases even though the statute as a whole is directed towards the attainment of a policy goal.

In relation to hard cases, Dworkin states that since a judge accepts the settled practices of his legal system, then he or she must accept some theory that justifies these practices. Consequently, the judge must develop a theory of the constitution, in the shape of a complex set of principles and policies that justify the scheme of government. In interpreting statutes, the judge must use a construction, not about the mental state of the particular legislature that adopted the statute, but of a social political theory that justifies that statute.

This of course means that the judge, in interpreting unclear statutes, must take account of policy, which seems little different from the Hartian analysis of the judicial function. However, Dworkin is saying that the judge can only take account of policy considerations in a way which fits in with the rest of the legal and political system:

> Integrity requires him to construct, for each statute he is asked to enforce, some justification that fits and flows through that statute and is, if possible, consistent with other legislation in force. This means he must ask himself which combination of which principles and policies, with which assignments of relative importance when these compete, provides the best case for what the plain words of the statute plainly require. Since Hercules is now justifying a statute rather than a set of common-law precedents, the particular constraint we identified in [the common law] no longer holds: he must consider justifications of policy as well as of principle, and in some cases it might be problematic which form of justification would be more appropriate. (*Law's Empire*, pp. 338–9.)

When considering statutes with overt but conflicting policy ideals, the judge must weigh them and interpret them in accordance with the integral approach to the law.

9.4.2 Integrity in practice

Dworkin gives the example of the *Snail Darter* case in the United States (*Tennessee Valley Authority* v *Hill* (1978) 437 US 153). This was a case based on the interpretation of the American Endangered Species Act of 1973, namely, whether it should be interpreted to protect the habitat of a rare fish (the snail darter), 'a three-inch fish of no particular beauty or biological interest or general ecological importance' (*Law's Empire*, p. 21), thereby preventing the completion of an almost finished million-dollar dam, which if completed would destroy the snail darter's environment.

There are no competing rights here, either for the fish or the public authority, instead it involved the balancing of two competing policy interests, the policy of protecting endangered species and the policy that economic efficiency demands that public funds not be wasted. The Supreme Court carried out a sort of Dworkinian-type interpretation and held that the policy of protecting endangered species was paramount over other social goals, even though, if Congress had been faced with such a situation when it had enacted the Endangered Species Act, it would probably have created an exception. Dworkin's theory of interpretation places legislative intent as only one of the factors to be taken into account when judges construct a coherent, integrative legal and political theory.

9.5   THE CHESS ANALOGY

The chess analogy is a useful if somewhat simplistic way of illustrating Dworkin's theory of adjudication, particularly as regards statutory interpretation when the judges, in hard cases, must look beyond the confines of the law to attempt to fit their decision into a coherent political theory. The rules of chess are akin to the provisions of a statute, and in most cases they are fairly clear. Participants enter a chess tournament with the understanding that those chess rules apply; in other words they rely on concrete institutional rights. Dworkin then asks us to consider a hard case where the rules of chess do not directly apply, for example, where a player smiles at another in order to distract him. The referee must fit the case into the general theory of chess. Since chess is an intellectual game, the referee must apply the forfeiture rule in such a way as to protect rather than jeopardise the role of intellect in the contest.

> We have, then, in the case of the chess referee, an example of an official whose decisions about institutional rights are understood to be governed by institutional constraints even when the force of these constraints is not clear. We do not think that he is free to legislate interstitially within the 'open texture' of imprecise rules. (*Taking Rights Seriously*, p. 102.)

Similarly when weighing up the litigants' rights in each case, although possessing limited discretion in allocating weight to each, the judge does not have discretion in the strong sense of being able to reach a decision on policy or any other grounds. In cases of statutory interpretation, which do not permit the judge to decide on grounds of principle, for example, in the *Snail Darter* case considered in 9.4.2, the judge must still consider the institutions and practices that make up the legal system and fit the new case into that milieu.

Simple analogies between chess and law are illustrative but they mask the fact that law is many times more complicated and indeed it appears to miss completely the fluid nature of the law which is changing all the time as a result of legislation which is after all designed to achieve goals, not necessarily to secure rights. Furthermore, one may usefully ask whether there is the possibility in such a complicated system of reaching an objectively defensible right answer in a hard case. It is reasonable to argue that judges are primarily concerned with rights and principles in hard cases but to argue that this necessarily results in a right answer appears far-fetched. The simple fact that there is no way of measuring the relative weight of such principles destroys any pretence at complete objectivity. In the chess example it may be argued that although chess is an intellectual game, an equally strong argument would be that chess is also about mental strength and concentration, and that the player's ability to exclude all distractions is as important as pure intellect. There is in reality no 'right' answer to Dworkin's chess problem, only a range of equally plausible answers. Indeed, Dworkin seems to admit this but would argue that at least all these decisions are governed by institutional constraints. However, this misses the point that when the referee or judge chooses one answer over another, it becomes the referee's or judge's solution not *the* solution.

9.6   DEMOCRACY

9.6.1   The judge as protector of rights

Although Dworkin's theory commences as an analysis of the judicial function, it does grow into a legal and political theory of sorts. Remember that the basic division that Dworkin makes is between the legislator acting on policy considerations which are usually based on calculations of what is in the best interests of society, while the judiciary act on principle. Although there is some cross-fertilisation, for example, Parliament may enact legislation that is primarily designed to protect people's rights, and judges may in hard cases concerning statutes make decisions about competing policies, Dworkin is stating that despite this cross-fertilisation, the two processes, adjudication and legislation, are qualitatively distinct. The judge is concerned even in hard cases involving statutes with what decision best fits in with the law as a whole. The judge's job is not the same as that of the lawmakers who are elected to carry out policies which may be radically different from those of their predecessors.

However, judges, even within Dworkin's theory of integrity can make decisions which it might be argued are of a political nature and so should be left to the legislature. For example, in the *Snail Darter* case (see 9.4.2), it could be argued that Congress should have been left to decide the issue of whether environmental concerns should have been paramount over arguments of economic efficiency. Similarly, a decision that a claimant has or has not the right to recover damages away from the scene of an accident, although a question of rights, is a question of the extent of right which perhaps should be left to Parliament.

Dworkin meets this argument in the following manner:

> I shall start with the . . . argument, that legislatures . . . have some special title to make constitutional decisions. . . . One might say that the nature of this title is obvious, because it is always fairer to allow a majority to decide any issue than a minority. But that . . . ignores the fact that decisions about rights against the majority are not issues that in fairness ought to be left to the majority. Constitutionalism – the theory that the majority must be restrained to protect individual rights – may be a good or a bad political theory, but the United States has adopted that theory, and to make the majority judge in its own cause seems inconsistent and unjust. (*Taking Rights Seriously*, p. 142.)

Dworkin views judges as the preservers of rights against governmental interference, and this is particularly evident in the United States where certain fundamental rights are entrenched in the Constitution and are protected by the judiciary. This explains why the judiciary should be free to deal with issues such as that arising in *McLoughlin* v *O'Brian* (see 9.3.2), but it does not explain why the judiciary should be able to defeat legislative intent in cases concerning issues of policy not rights as found in cases like the *Snail Darter*.

9.6.2 The principle of equal concern and respect

Following from Dworkin's essentially anti-utilitarian theory of democracy, the principle of equal concern and respect could be said to be the foundation of his democratic theory. This principle signifies that people are treated as individuals by the government rather than simply as part of society as a whole. Utilitarianism favours simple calculations of what would best advance the interests of a society or more usually a section of society. In so doing it fails to treat individuals as distinct and allows the majority, or more correctly the democratically elected representatives of the majority (who in fact may not represent the majority of society as in the United Kingdom), to force decisions on the minority, not only concerning issues of policy but also permitting the government of the day to subject individual rights to policy calculations. Dworkin's approach to democracy is that the government of the day is free to take policy decisions on the basis of utilitarian calculations, but is not permitted to do so when such decisions override or deny individual or minority rights.

It is unclear whether the principle of equal concern and respect is a concrete right or an abstract right, or whether it is indeed a legal or political right. It appears too general to be institutionalised and there is no real evidence offered that it has crept into judicial calculations in hard cases. Nevertheless, the principle is so fundamental that Dworkin states that anyone who believes in rights must believe in it, more particularly in a minimum of two ideas. First, the idea of human dignity – the government must treat a person as a full member of a human community – and secondly, the idea of political equality – that every member of the community, whether weak or strong, is entitled to the same concern and respect from their government (*Taking Rights Seriously*, pp. 198–9). Dworkin does not claim these ideas to be axiomatic or self-evident but there does seem to be an assumption here rather similar to Finnis's claims of self-evidence as regards the basic goods he identifies as the foundation of a theory of natural law (see chapter 5), or the truisms that Hart identifies in arriving at his minimum content of natural law (see chapter 3). Although Dworkin does discuss the matter further elsewhere (see *A Matter of Principle*, ch. 8), one is left with the impression of a powerful theory of liberalism that one may prefer to other versions but which cannot be claimed to be objectively better than any other.

Dworkin is claiming that the protection of rights only makes sense if it is necessary to preserve an individual's rights to dignity and equal concern and respect. The principle of equal concern and respect is the background principle in a liberal society which justifies the preservation of rights:

> So if rights make sense at all, then the invasion of a relatively important right must be a very serious matter. It means treating a man as less than a man, or as less worthy of concern than other men. The institution of rights rests on the conviction that this is a grave injustice, and that it is worth paying the incremental cost in social policy or efficiency that is necessary to prevent it. (*Taking Rights Seriously*, p. 199.)

Dworkin points out that utilitarian arguments based on the external preferences of the community, which will include the worst prejudices, does not entail treating each individual with equal concern and respect. Therefore, to justify political constraints on rights, care must be taken to ensure that the utilitarian calculations on which the constraint is based focus only on internal and not external preferences. Legal restriction on homosexual behaviour, for instance, cannot be based on the prejudices of the majority who may justify their belief by saying that homosexuals are not 'real men' or 'they make me sick'. A legislator must concentrate on what is seen to be the more fundamental moral consensus in society in such a way as to exclude external prejudices from calculations and in such a way as to preserve the fundamental principle of equal concern and respect (*Taking Rights Seriously*, pp. 249–55). In this way the underlying principle of equal concern and respect preserves other individual and minority rights which will be protected against the general will, and can only be overridden in three situations according to Dworkin:

> I can think of only three sorts of grounds that can consistently be used to limit the definition of a particular right. First, the Government might show that the values protected by the original right are not really at stake in the marginal case. . . . Second, it might show that if the right is defined to include the marginal case, then some competing right, in the strong sense . . ., would be abridged. Third, it might show that if the right were so defined, then the cost to society would not be simply incremental, but would be of a degree far beyond the cost paid to grant the original right, a degree great enough to justify whatever assault on dignity or equality might be involved. (*Taking Rights Seriously*, p. 200.)

The last ground identified by Dworkin seems to allow for the overriding of rights on utilitarian grounds, but as identified earlier in this chapter (see 9.2.2) Dworkin is really identifying occasions when the whole of society is in danger from catastrophe or from war.

It is questionable whether such debate ever surrounds the limitation or removal of fundamental rights. There is little evidence to show that the 1988 order denying certain terrorist organisations media coverage in the UK was debated in terms of limiting freedom of expression (K. D. Ewing and C. A. Gearty, *Freedom under Thatcher: Civil Liberties in Modern Britain* (Oxford: Clarendon Press, 1990), pp. 241–50). The government did not introduce the ban by pointing to the extreme cost and damage to society caused by the IRA or the cost to the individual's most basic right – the right to life. It follows that, contrary to Dworkin's contention, the government did not attempt to justify the ban as coming within one of the three exceptions that he identifies, either as an attempt to preserve the right to life, so justifying a limitation on the right of freedom of expression, or as an instance of a threat to the fabric of society justifying limitations on rights.

Furthermore, even if the legislature is willing to respect those fundamental rights which Dworkin sees as reinforcing the principle of equal concern and respect, rights such as freedom of speech, it does not seem bound, according to Dworkin, to respect rights which sections of the community may view as even more important, rights such as freedom from poverty or starvation, or the right to work. Dworkin does not explore the issue whether the principle of equal concern and respect signifies that these rights may be protected from legislative interference. He seems to concentrate on those rights that have been traditionally recognised in Western societies, rights traditionally categorised as civil and political rights, as opposed to economic, social and cultural rights.

9.7 LAW AND MORALITY

9.7.1 Community morality

Throughout his exposition of the rights thesis, Dworkin sustains the view that the positivist standpoint that legal rights and moral rights are logically distinct is wrong. It is clear that Dworkin's *community* morality is not of the popular sort advocated by Devlin, nor is it akin to mainstream naturalist conceptions about a universal set of principles. For Dworkin background moral rights are derived from that abstract moral framework which is institutionalised in the community's political structures, particularly its constitutional base.

Such an *institutional* morality is not unchangeable as with natural law principles, but it is relatively stable as a product of political morality which resists the vagaries of popular sentiment:

> The community's true morality is not to be discovered by taking opinion polls about particular moral issues. It is to be discovered by asking what answer to a particular issue would fit consistently with abstract rights to which the community has already committed itself in its constitutional and institutional practices – such as rights to liberty, dignity, equality and respect. (J. W. Harris, *Legal Philosophies* (London: Butterworths, 1980), pp. 177–8.)

Background moral rights enter into the calculation of what legal rights people have when the standard materials provide uncertain guidance. A process of change from institutional morality to background moral rights to abstract legal moral rights to concrete legal rights is envisaged. For example, the right to recover damages for negligence can be traced back to background moral/Christian principle recognised in law in *Donoghue* v *Stevenson* [1932] AC 562 by Lord Atkin at p. 580:

> But acts or omissions which any moral code would censure cannot in a practical world be treated so as to give a right to every person injured by them to demand relief. In this way rules of law arise which limit the range of complainants and the extent of their remedy. The rule that you are to love your neighbour becomes in law, you must not injure your neighbour; and the lawyer's question, Who is my neighbour? receives a restricted reply. You must take reasonable care to avoid acts or omissions which you can reasonably foresee would be likely to injure your neighbour. Who, then, in law is my neighbour? The answer seems to be – persons who are so closely and directly affected by my act that I ought reasonably to have them in contemplation as being so affected when I am directing my mind to the acts or omissions which are called into question.

Simply put, Dworkin argues that in order to explain the way judges decide cases, one needs to describe the legal system as consisting of three elements: rules, principles, and the political morality that justifies the system as a whole. When there is no rule or a conflict of rules, then the judge has to resort to principles. Where there is a lack of clarity of principles then the judge resorts to the institutional morality. The uncertainty of the whole process leads Dworkin to admit that different judges will disagree (*Law's Empire*, p. 256), although theoretically Hercules would get it right every time.

9.7.2 Morality and obligation

Although Dworkin's communal morality is not to be equated with the opinion poll morality of Devlin, it may still contain principles that are objectionable in terms of general morality. A society may historically institutionalise torture or slavery so that it could be said to be part of the communal morality. Nevertheless, since his theory is backed by morality, Dworkin states that his is the better theory as regards explaining legal obligation. Thus it appears that the rights thesis not only explains judicial process, but also democracy and the obligation to obey the law:

> A community of principle, faithful to that promise, can claim the authority of a genuine associative community and can therefore claim moral legitimacy - that its collective decisions are matters of obligation and not bare power. (*Law's Empire*, p. 214.)

9.8 FURTHER READING

Cohen, M. (ed), *Ronald Dworkin and Contemporary Jurisprudence* (London: Duckworth, 1984).

Dworkin, R. M., '"Natural law" revisited' (1982) 34 U Fla L Rev 165.

Hart, H. L. A., 'American jurisprudence through English eyes: the nightmare and the noble dream' (1977) 11 Ga L Rev 969.

Hart, H. L. A., *The Concept of Law* 2nd ed. (Oxford: Clarendon Press, 1994), pp. 238–76.

Lyons, D. B., 'Principles, positivism, and legal theory' (1977) 87 Yale LJ 415.

Raz, J., 'Professor Dworkin's theory of rights' (1978) 26 Political Studies 123.

Soper, E. P., 'Legal theory and the obligation of the judge: the Hart/Dworkin dispute' (1977) 75 Mich L Rev 473.

CHAPTER TEN

Scandinavian Realism

The two nominally 'realist' schools of legal theory, Scandinavian realism and American realism (see chapter 11), have little in common apart from the claim to offer a 'realist' jurisprudence. The use of this term implies a rejection of misleading forms and theories which conceal the true nature of positive law and the adoption of an analysis which reveals law as it really operates. Of course, in one way or another almost any legal theory purports to do this, but the realist theories claim not only to demonstrate a fresh insight into law but to do so in an iconoclastic spirit sweeping away previously prevailing error. Had Jeremy Bentham (see chapter 2) written in a later age he might have claimed to be a realist.

Inevitably, the various realist theories reveal different realities, or, perhaps more accurately, different aspects of a much greater reality. American realism, deriving ultimately from the work of Oliver Wendell Holmes, approached law from the viewpoint of what courts really do. Its modern successor, in certain respects, the critical legal studies movement (see chapter 12), emphasises the obfuscatory effects of legal forms and seeks to perceive realities concealed by the formalism of conventional legal discourse. Scandinavian realism, on the other hand, sought to understand law from a psychological viewpoint, although one of the school's members, Alf Ross, came much closer to an 'American' model in his emphasis upon the realities of judicial activity.

Jurisprudence, like any other discipline, is affected by the general development of ideas in the society in which it exists and it is not very surprising that Scandinavian realism originated at the beginning of the 20th century at a time when the psychological theories of Sigmund Freud were very much in the public eye. Such influences do not devalue the consequent thought, but rather inform the intellectual climate which may, or may not, make a positive contribution to the development of disciplines such as jurisprudence.

The basic insight of Scandinavian realism is that legal concepts such as 'validity' and 'obligation' have no objective reality and rely for their real effects upon psychologically conditioned responses to given processes and uses of language. The creation of a contractual obligation, or the recognition of legal ownership is thus seen as a response upon a psychological level to formal procedures which attaches a sense of 'oughtness' to the transaction and the consequent conduct.

10.1 EARLY PSYCHOLOGICAL THEORISTS: PETRAŻYCKI AND HÄGERSTRÖM

The origins of the Scandinavian realist school of jurisprudence are traced to the work of Axel Hägerström, whose influence was undoubtedly profoundly significant. Interestingly, however, his work in the field of psychological jurisprudence was paralleled at much the same time by the Polish-Russian theorist Leon Petrażycki. Hägerström and Petrażycki do not seem to have communicated or exchanged ideas and the convergence of their work perhaps lends force to the influence of a prevailing intellectual climate suggested above. That Petrażycki is, from the viewpoint of legal theory, largely ignored today can be argued to be a misfortune deriving from political circumstance rather than intrinsic merit. Certainly, both Hägerström and Petrażycki may reasonably be thought to claim rather more attention than is conventionally now accorded to their work.

10.1.1 Petrażycki and the theory of impulsions

Leon Petrażycki (the commonly used form 'Petrazhitsky' is a transliteration of the Russian form of his Polish name) was a beneficiary of the brief reforming initiative in the Russian Empire under Tsar Alexander II (1855–81), which included a major reform of the legal system in 1864 (see 7.2.1). Born in Poland under Russian rule, he became professor of legal encyclopaedia at the University of St Petersburg until the 1917 Bolshevik Revolution and thereafter professor of law at the University of Warsaw in newly independent Poland. Petrażycki founded his legal theory upon an idea of 'impulsions' which has a general psychological importance (see L. Petrażycki, *Law and Morality*, transl. H. W. Babb (Harvard, Mass: Harvard University Press, 1956) (20th Century Legal Philosophy Series, vol. 7)). An impulsion is an experience in which a psychological response to a stimulus leads to an active response in the form of conduct. Impulsions may take a wide variety of forms, not all of which relate to legal experience.

For Petrażycki, a sense of normativity, the idea of 'rightness' or the 'ought' quality of a response or action, is the hallmark of an ethical impulsion. The stronger sense of oughtness which informs an obligation is then associated with legal impulsions as a subsidiary category of ethical impulsions. Petrażycki did not consider legal impulsions to be limited to the sphere of positive law as such, but rather to embrace the whole field of obligations. He divided these into two broad sectors:

(a)   Intuitive law, comprising all the varieties of 'moral' obligation, and
(b)   Positive law, comprising both 'law' in the strict, or lawyer's, sense (termed 'official positive law') and such social influences as public opinion and fashion (termed 'unofficial positive law').

It will be noticed that the impulsions behind a broad range of norms, including morality, positive law and popular standards, are thus treated as essentially similar. This is not, however, to say that those phenomena are in fact indistinguishable. Petrażycki was concerned with the nature of the impulsions behind compliance with normative standards and at this level the psychology of, e.g., religious, ethical, legal and social duty might indeed be considered closely comparable. The stimuli which cause an impulsion to operate in each case may of course be, and in the examples here given are, very different.

The idea of impulsions has important consequences for the understanding of legal obligations. Where a formal obligation is created at law, such as a leasehold covenant to pay rent, this is not, in Petrażycki's view, a predictive statement about the possible application of sanctions for default, as a classical positivist might argue (see chapter 2), or a manipulative disguise for some form of social domination, as a Marxist (see chapter 7) or critical legal scholar (see chapter 12) might conclude. For Petrażycki the obligation is an expression of the psychological response of the tenant to the formal stimulus of entering into a lease. The obligation has thus, upon this model, no objective reality, leaving aside the separate consideration of possible compulsion, but through its influence upon the conduct of the tenant who in fact pays rent, and the landlord's expectation of payment, it has real effects. According to Petrażycki's analysis, therefore, legal concepts such as ownership, property and rights are not in themselves real but signify psychological responses to certain formal stimuli which then, through their impact upon conduct, have real effects.

To some extent Petrażycki's work anticipated later Scandinavian realist thought and, in its recognition of the broad range of phenomena falling within the scope of legal impulsions as a source of obligation, made potentially interesting comment upon the interaction of the various types of obligation. Petrażycki did not, however, explore to any great extent the vital question of the means whereby the strong sense of oughtness associated with a legal impulsion comes to be attached to a given set of positive laws.

Petrażycki's theory did not lead to the establishment of a 'Russian realist' school of jurisprudence. After the Bolshevik Revolution of October 1917 he fled back to newly independent Poland and within the new USSR his work was denounced by Marxist-Leninist theorists such as E. B. Pashukanis (see E. B. Pashukanis, *Law and Marxism: A General Theory*, transl. B. Einhorn (London: Ink Links, 1978)), primarily by reason of the individualist, rather than class, emphasis of his jurisprudential analysis. In any event, the development of psychological jurisprudence was not ultimately founded upon the impulsions theory of Petrażycki but derived from the rather differently angled approach of Axel Hägerström.

10.1.2 Axel Hägerström: law and word magic

Like Petrażycki, Hägerström considered that ideas of 'obligation' or 'duty' represent not an objective reality but a psychological response to given stimuli, which may, of course, have 'real' effects. His particular concern was with the generation of psychological responses to legal formalities which, expressed in the discourse of 'rights', 'property', 'duties' and so on, then have a real impact upon practical conduct.

Hägerström denied that duty relates to threatened sanctions, expressions of legislative will or to the pressures of moral apprehension and public opinion. Indeed, he denied, in particular, that there actually is any simple legislative will, pointing out that the definition, and effect, of that supposed will is itself a product of 'law'. Thus:

> . . . what is a 'state' except a community organised by rules of law? Suppose, e.g., that there were no legal rules which determined the mutual relations of the citizens, and which were upheld by judges and executive authority. What would there be except a mass of . . . [people]? That being so, how can the law itself be an utterance of the State? (A. Hägerström, *Inquiries into the Nature of Law and Morals*, transl. C. D. Broad (Stockholm: Almqvist & Wiksell, 1953), p. 13.)

This is, of course, yet another attempt to wrestle with the problem of sovereign will which led Bentham and Austin into arguably unnecessary contortions in the context of classical positivism (see chapter 2), and which Hart sought to solve by reference to the formal mechanisms of a legal system. Hägerström denied the meaningful existence of such a will and, in a very different way from Hart, relied instead upon the operation of legal forms. He emphasised the importance of ritual in generating a conditioned response to norms enunciated in given ways, which therefore become a focus of obligation.

In the same way Hägerström considered that ideas of 'rights', 'duties' and 'property' rest upon psychological responses to the ritual formalities of law, in effect to a form of word magic. Thus:

. . . the notions in question [rights of property etc.] cannot be reduced to anything in reality. The reason is that in point of fact, they have their roots in traditional ideas of mystical forces and bonds. (*Inquiries into the Nature of Law and Morals*, p. 16.)

In order to investigate such psychological responses and the means of their generation Hägerström undertook a psychological study of the operation of Roman law upon the basis that it underlay much later European (civilian) jurisprudence and was also free of what Hägerström considered an undue tendency of modern theory to rationalise the operation of legal norms.

In considering the idea of 'duty' in a legal context, Hägerström denied that it arises in itself from any necessity to avoid unpleasant consequences potentially flowing from default or from any valuation of action resting upon some external structure of values such as morality. He argued instead that:

. . . we are here concerned with an impulse towards a certain action, which is felt as compulsive just because what is here determinative is not the subject's free valuation, but something which is, in that respect, external to him. The impulse imposes itself on us, no matter what evaluatory attitude we may take towards the action. That is to say . . . a feeling of being driven to act in a certain way. (*Inquiries into the Nature of Law and Morals*, p. 130.)

The creation of the impulse is then ascribed by Hägerström to a conditioned response to certain forms and contexts of linguistic usage. In this context he ascribes great significance to the ritual element of positive law in generating impulses of duty, a pattern for conduct, which might otherwise seem merely appropriate or convenient, becomes a dutiful requirement when it is presented in certain ways. The difference is that between a promise, in an informal or social sense, and a contract. In what Hägerström conceived to be the simpler jurisprudential world of early Roman law the working of legal ritual is presented as a straightforwardly magico-religious phenomenon. Thus, Hägerström remarked that:

In the older Roman legal system there was no separation between *fas*, the divine law, and *ius*, the human. Nearly all transactions seem to have taken a religious form. The administration of law was a religious concern. (*Inquiries into the Nature of Law and Morals*, p. 57.)

Something of what Hägerström meant can be seen in many of the formal rituals of Roman law, of which *mancipatio* is perhaps the most clearly illustrative. Mancipation was a form of property transference and is described by Gaius as follows:

... in the presence of not less than [five] Roman citizens of full age and also of a sixth person, . . . known as the *libripens* (scale holder), to hold a bronze scale, the party who is taking by mancipation, holding a bronze ingot, says: 'I declare that this slave is mine by quiritary right, and be he purchased to me with this bronze ingot and bronze scale'. He then strikes the scale with the ingot and gives it as a symbolic price [to the transferor]. (Gaius, *Institutes*, transl. F. De Zulueta (Oxford: Oxford University Press, 1946), 1.119.)

Mancipation could be used to transfer a variety of forms of property, including certain types of land. The description given by Gaius clearly shows the proceedings to have had their origin in some magical ritual having the effect of impressing the community, via the witnesses, with the transfer of entitlement to the property in question. The impress of this idea would then have real effects in influencing conduct by discouraging interference with the property. The whole enterprise of course rests, as Hägerström insists, upon the generation of ideas. There was no real connection between the original owner and the new one, nor would any be created by the ritual of *mancipatio*, rather, an idea of entitlement would thereby be generated which would effectively, to a greater or less extent, discourage interference with the owner's control of the property transferred.

It is not, of course, necessary to go back to Roman law to find such rituals – modern English law is replete with them. The antique robes of the judiciary do not confer upon their wearers any additional level of professional skill, the attachment of a seal (usually in fact a red adhesive wafer) to a document does not render the document any more really solemn than it was to start with and swearing an oath or affirming does not render a witness inherently any more naturally truthful. All of these, and many other, ritual observances are designed to underline the conceptual significance of what is being done and, insofar as that idea is indeed conveyed, may effectuate the intended consequence in the real world. At its simplest, when a person states, e.g., that 'This is my watch', no real relationship exists between the person and the watch, it is rather a statement of claim to entitlement which is psychologically efficacious in influencing the conduct of other persons, who, of course, similarly lay claim to 'their' watches and other property.

This is the basis of Hägerström's argument upon the nature of concepts such as 'duty', 'rights' and 'property'. They symbolise psychological reactions to ritualistic forms which have effects in the real world through their influence upon the conduct of their subject and other people. Thus, as a result of the ritual of a contract of purchase (involving the elements of offer, acceptance and consideration) the owner of the watch has a belief in an entitlement to control. The induction of acceptance of this belief by others, and therefore their refraining from interference, brings about a situation in which the owner actually does have control over the watch.

Much of this may readily be accepted. Clearly 'ownership' is an idea that exists in the minds of owners and others which leaves the owner in undisturbed enjoyment of the entitlement. The rather mechanical nature of the response to ritual and word forms implied by Hägerström is perhaps, however, over simplified and somewhat reminiscent of Pavlov's dogs. Ivan Petrovich Pavlov (1849–1936) was a Russian physiologist who showed that dogs fed when a bell rang could be conditioned so to associate the ringing of the bell with the provision of food that they were induced to salivate upon the ringing of the bell, even when no food was provided. There might seem to be some tendency to equate Hägerström's legal clients with Pavlov's unfortunate dogs, conditioned automatically to respond whenever the stimulus of legal ritual or word form is offered.

Acceptance of the presentation of legal concepts as part of the world of ideas, having real effects only through psychological impact governing conduct, should not obscure the existence of other factors, both real and psychological, which may either support or obstruct the generation of impulses of duty and so on. Legal forms in short do have a psychological effect but they are not simply a human equivalent to Pavlov's bell. They work not only through conditioning but also through the operation of moral, formal, social, political, economic and coercive factors, including, lastly but by no means least, the factor of simple convenience. It is advantageous to know how one goes about buying, e.g., a house or groceries, without having to set up a custom-made system on each occasion, quite apart from the magical effects of whatever ritual has been adopted. It may also be commented that a psychological model of law founded upon mechanisms of conditioning finds some difficulty in dealing with legal change, that is to say with reconditioning.

Some of these issues are addressed in the work of other members of the Scandinavian realist school who followed after Hägerström. This was the case for Vilhelm Lundstedt and for Karl Olivecrona. Olivecrona advanced a more detailed and in many ways a more accessible psychological theory of law than Hägerström. In particular, Olivecrona offers a much more detailed analysis of the processes of legal conditioning in a modern society than Hägerström set out to do.

10.2 VILHELM LUNDSTEDT AND THE METHOD OF SOCIAL WELFARE

Anders Vilhelm Lundstedt was very much a disciple of Hägerström and, unusually for a legal theorist, was not only an academic but also a lawmaker in his capacity as a Swedish *riksdagsman* (Member of Parliament). He was archetypically a realist in that he sought a jurisprudence based upon empirical social observation rather than value judgments or metaphysics. Like other members of the Scandinavian realist school he was dismissive of other approaches to legal theory, which he castigated as founded upon a method of justice distorted by a variety of ideological concerns. This tradition has, according to Lundstedt, been a major hindrance to the establishment of a scientific jurisprudence by reason of its reliance upon subjective evaluatory criteria. In its place he proposed a radically different and 'constructive' jurisprudence based upon a 'social welfare method' which, if not perfectly scientific insofar as it still demands the assumption of certain basic hypotheses, at least relies upon the consideration of what is in fact thought to be socially useful. The scope of Lundstedt's intention as a theorist is made clear by the title of his most important work, *Legal Thinking Revised* (Stockholm: Almqvist & Wiksell, 1956) which was published posthumously.

Whilst much of Lundstedt's argument is of interest and even importance, his claim to have 'revised' legal thinking, under the influence of Hägerström, cannot readily be accepted. The descriptive objectivity of the social welfare method is, inevitably, open to question (there is, after all, much room for debate upon what may be held to constitute social welfare in detail) and the blanket dismissal of all theory other than that inspired by Hägerström as founded upon a false justice method is, to put it mildly, rather sweeping. The exaggerated claims made by Lundstedt for his method rest in large part upon a distortion of the arguments advanced by other theorists and gain nothing from the vituperative manner of their expression. However, the extent and manner of these claims should not for the modern reader of jurisprudence be allowed to obscure what, in its proper context, is genuinely important in Lundstedt's thought.

10.2.1   The concept of social welfare

Lundstedt argued that once the observation of law has been freed from ideological and other distorting perceptions, it can be seen that legal activity must rest upon the supposition that it is 'indispensable for the existence of society' (*Legal Thinking Revised*, p. 132). This assumption might be criticised as itself an ideological perception. Such a view would, however, be somewhat unfair insofar as a functional view of law as a mechanism calculated for the performance of certain tasks, termed, in a very different context, 'law-jobs' by the American realist Karl N. Llewellyn (K. N. Llewellyn, 'The normative, the legal, and the law-jobs: the problem of juristic method' (1940) 49 Yale LJ 1355) may reasonably be accepted without reference to the specific values embodied in a given legal system.

The foundation of Lundstedt's 'constructive' investigation of the socially 'indispensable' phenomenon of law was the concept of 'social welfare'. He was careful to stress the real, rather than the metaphysical, basis of this concept, even whilst admitting that the shaping of this observed phenomenon involves influences such as ethical and religious ideas and even notions of 'justice'. The point being that while conceptions of social welfare may, indeed will, be influenced by such perceived absolutes, the outcome is not an absolute but a real social fact.

Lundstedt stated that his concept of social welfare:

> . . . involves certain *actual* evaluations of that which is best for the society concerning the enactment of a law . . . or concerning interpretation of a certain law or finally concerning . . . some maxim when an immediately applicable law is lacking. . . . In general the matter can be expressed thus: socially useful is that which is actually evaluated as a social interest. (*Legal Thinking Revised*, p. 137.)

It is difficult to dissent from this proposition as here stated, that a concept of social welfare should involve an evaluation of the welfare of society seems unavoidable and that such evaluations should be actual seems, at least, desirable. Rather more than this is, however, required if social welfare is to be accepted as a means of understanding the operation of law as a real phenomenon.

In seeking to fulfil this need Lundstedt explained that as a motivation for legal activity he conceived social welfare as encouraging the attainment of what people, having attained a certain but undefined cultural level, will actually seek from their society. These objectives are stated to comprise:

> . . . such things as suitable and well tasting food, appropriate and becoming clothes, . . . dwellings furnished in the best and most comfortable way, security of life, limb and 'property', the greatest possible freedom of action and movement . . . in brief, all conceivable material comfort as well as the protection of spiritual interests. (*Legal Thinking Revised*, p. 140.)

Lundstedt emphasised that he was not concerned with the question of whether people ought to strive for such things, merely with the fact that people in fact do seek to live and develop their lives along these lines.

This list of social welfare goals merits examination. It is, quite properly, very general in nature and wide-ranging in scope, covering food, clothing, property and personal liberties. In short, a list not dissimilar to the extended conception of 'property', the defence of which was taken by the social-contractarian John Locke to be the basis of civil society and legal order (see 4.5.2). For Lundstedt, Locke would have fallen into the despised category of metaphysical theorists. It may, however, be argued that Locke's social-contractarianism, like many other theories ultimately founded upon a percep-tion of human nature or capacities from the teleology of Aristotle (see 4.3.3) onwards, took human nature as a fact and constructed a model of what law 'ought' to be as a functional derivative from that situation. If Lundstedt's argument, not surprisingly, lacks social-contractarian rhetoric, the idea of law as a means of protecting material benefits and certain personal securities seems less distant from social-contractarian goals than might at first have been anticipated.

It might be accepted that these, very general, goals indeed describe commonly encountered social aspirations, but this does not necessarily free them from all taint of subjectivism. An immediate difficulty is encountered in the question of resolving opposed or competing securities. One person's hobby, e.g., playing loud music, might be another person's nuisance: whose interest is then to predominate? Lundstedt gives an implicit answer in his concession that it is the 'greatest possible' freedom which is to be protected. Presumably, 'possibility' for this purpose will be determined by reference to the balance to be drawn between individual aspiration and collective need which is one of the fundamental questions for any social organisation. Even if metaphysics is to be excluded, some form of value judgment seems probable here and reference to majority wish is at best an uncertain guide – what if each individual wishes to be noisy while wishing all others to be quiet? In short, social welfare itself seems inevitably to import at least some value judgments and whilst this may be less problematic than it might seem in the context of Lundstedt's thinking, it is certainly a potential problem within that context.

One value judgment which might be thought to influence the application of social welfare in such problem situations is a sense of justice. It will be recalled that Lundstedt dismissed the jurisprudential method of justice as ideologically distorting, but he still admitted that such ideas can have a powerful influence upon the shaping of actual aspirations. He therefore considered the question of ideas of justice and their psychological influence at some length.

10.2.2   The importance of ideas of justice

Lundstedt concedes that in many, if not indeed all, countries the distribution of advantage is very far from equal, but argues that this may actually serve social welfare as he conceives it. Thus:

> . . . such an order . . . is necessary for the maintenance of the social economy. With the prevailing division of . . . capable resources a legal order of this kind is requisite. . . . a varying distribution of commodities and utilities is necessary for the stimulation . . . of more highly skilled and enterprising, and consequently [more scarce] . . . sources of labour. . . . even laws . . . unfavourable for the many must . . . be influenced by social welfare. (*Legal Thinking Revised*, pp. 156–7.)

Inequality of benefit may thus be justified by the value of the highly rewarded endeavours to the society. Up to a point this may be so, although the mechanisms of valuation require debate as does the question of maximisation of opportunity within a society. Lundstedt paid very little attention to the latter question in particular.

In his analysis of unequal distribution Lundstedt primarily emphasised the beneficial consequences for the community as a whole. However, he also considered the psychological importance of a common sense of justice in the operation of law. Lundstedt treated this sense of justice in effect as an appreciation of coincidence with the interests embodied in social welfare (see *Legal Thinking Revised*, p. 161). In a very general sense this might be accepted, although the theory of justice is by no means so simple as this (see chapter 15). 'Justice' and the notions of 'right' and 'wrong', 'rights' and 'duties' which, legally expressed, flow from it, are not in this context, however, presented as objective realities. They are seen, rather, as ideas or even illusions which have real effects through the psychological or emotional feelings which then induce and which in turn underpin the efficacy of law.

This model informs the significant psychological element of Lundstedt's thought and, thus, he argued that law in action functions in many cases as a means of focusing certain psychologically efficacious emotional reactions. This point is stressed by Lundstedt especially in relation to criminal law. In so focusing emotional reactions, for or against certain types of conduct, the law is, however, understood by Lundstedt to guide, under the influence of social welfare, rather than unreflectively to be guided by a common sense of justice. Thus:

> . . . there is in reality no equity, no (natural) justice, either beside the law or opposed to it. (*Legal Thinking Revised*, p. 170.)

In reaching this conclusion Lundstedt contended that to treat law as simply conditioned by senses of justice reverses the proper order of cart and horse. However, whilst law and justice are, as Lundstedt suggested, intimately connected, it seems an undue simplification to suggest that justice is a mechanism which has no real meaning outside the machinery of law. The problem encountered here seems to be the determination to force the idea of social welfare into a role of singular objective determinant for which it is not necessarily well-suited.

10.2.3 The significance of Lundstedt's theory

Lundstedt undeviatingly rejected the metaphysical in legal theory and thus founded his model of law upon a factual observation of social welfare as the key to understanding the functioning of law. Other theorists, even within the

Scandinavian realist school, have been critical of the concept of social welfare (see, e.g., A. Ross, *On Law and Justice*, transl. M. Dutton (London: Stevens & Sons, 1958), especially at pp. 295–6; as to Ross's own theory see 10.4). Lundstedt asserts that social welfare is in fact what people seek and his statement of this ideal is so general that it might indeed be so. However, the assertions which are made in applying this model often seem to involve their own unadmitted ideology, even if not quite any metaphysics. Lundstedt's theory may ultimately be contended to be a rather extreme instance of an analysis which takes an idea which is by no means insignificant, but which is limited, and by asserting it to displace all unrelated analyses leads to distortion and even to the diminution of its own, genuine, importance.

The claimed exclusivity of Lundstedt's work should not put off the modern reader, but neither should it necessarily be accepted at its face value. A broader, and more approachable analysis of the issues arising from the psychological Hägerström tradition in jurisprudence can be found in the work of his own follower, Karl Olivecrona.

10.3 KARL OLIVECRONA: INDEPENDENT IMPERATIVES

The primary emphasis of the legal theory advanced by Olivecrona is upon the nature of the binding force which renders compliance with legal norms obligatory. In the principal statement of his theory (K. Olivecrona, *Law as Fact*, 2nd ed. (London: Stevens & Sons, 1971)), Olivecrona starts from an analysis of the so-called 'debate' between positivist and naturalist positions and concludes that both fall into essentially similar errors as voluntaristic theories, that is to say, theories which emphasise the creation and maintenance of law as an act of will to which obedience is then somehow rendered obligatory. Olivecrona contends that such approaches represent a convenient but grossly simplified and ultimately inaccurate model of a complex phenomenon. Thus:

> The [survival] . . . of the will-theory . . . may be explained partly by our natural inclination to find single causes for complex phenomena. . . .
>
> In reality [however] there is no homogenous source of the rules reckoned as legal. . . . There is no single driving force to the system; the regular application of the rules and their efficacy . . . depend on a network of psychological and material factors (ideas of rights, . . ., fear of sanctions, and so on). The will-theory substitutes an imaginary will for this infinitely complicated reality. (*Law as Fact*, p. 77.)

In place of the rejected will theory, or theories, Olivecrona seeks to examine the nature, in particular, of legislative acts on a psychological level.

10.3.1 Olivecrona and legislative efficacy

Olivecrona points out that legislating is a process by which a draft text becomes, through some process of enactment, a law and thereby acquires the characteristic of being binding upon its addressees, that is, in Olivecrona's usage, the new law changes, more or less efficaciously, people's ideas of proper and wrongful conduct. This is explained as the consequence of the acceptance by the population of the constitutional authority conferred, in the Swedish context in which Olivecrona was writing, upon the King and Diet (Parliament) to make 'law'. Olivecrona's conclusion follows simply from this proposition and is that:

> the ability to make laws with practical effect results from the general attitude among the population with regard to the constitution, this attitude being the immediate source of the lawmaking 'power' of the legislators. They are in a position to invest a text with the quality of law . . . commanding universal respect.
>   . . . It is an effect on the psychological level. (*Law as Fact*, p. 90.)

He admits that the majority of the population may have only a hazy understanding of constitutional technicality but argues that this is sufficient, granted that emphasis is placed upon the end-product, legislation, of an accepted system rather than upon the precise details of its working. One might similarly argue that it is perfectly possible to drive a car without a qualification in mechanical engineering.

Thus far Olivecrona's argument, essentially that legislative efficacy rests upon general belief in the working of certain forms of enunciation of norms, clearly relates closely, in a much more modern context, to the jurisprudence of Hägerström. Beyond the basic constitutional proposition, however, Olivecrona advances a much more subtle analysis of the attachment of obligation to legal norms. He argues that there are two main elements to be discerned in a legal rule which involve firstly an idea of a given pattern of conduct and secondly, in association, with it, the idea that such a pattern of conduct is obligatory. These elements are termed by Olivecrona, in a quasi-Latinate terminology of his own devising, respectively, the ideatum and imperantum.

10.3.2 Ideatum and imperantum: the binding quality of law

Olivecrona's 'ideatum' is the idea of conduct which a law embodies, whether to require or forbid, it is, in short, the substantive content of a legal provision. Using further quasi-Latinate terms he then subdivides the ideatum into two essential parts, the 'requisitum' and the 'agendum'. The first defines the context in which the conduct in question is to be observed; the second defines the conduct itself. In an analysis which in an oblique fashion recalls Bentham's treatment of a complete law (see 2.2.4), Olivecrona stresses that the requisitum of a legal rule is not limited to the immediate circumstances in which the conduct embodied in the agendum is to be applied. It may also involve a wide spectrum of procedures, including those of any potential adjudication upon the application of the rule in question, much of which will, of course, also be found in the requisitums (requisita?) of other rules. As Olivecrona comments:

> There is, indeed, no case where a single legal provision can be regarded in isolation by the judge or by any other person called upon to decide what sort of action conforms to the law in a given situation. Each provision is like a piece in a puzzle. Many pieces have to be put together before one can say whether an actual situation corresponds to any legal requisitum and, if this is the case, what sort of agendum is applicable. (*Law as Fact*, p. 117.)

Once the context of application and the substance of the required action, or abstinence, is set by the ideatum there remains the fundamental question of the attachment of obligation to the conclusion through the imperantum.

The making of a pattern of conduct obligatory is, for Olivecrona, the attachment of an imperative which is, by its nature, unconditional. That which is imperative is not as such an appeal to values (it would be damaging to steal from people) it is an unconditional prescription (thou shalt not steal). Such prescription may of course infer values or pragmatic counsel, but that is not an essential part of their nature. Nor, according to Olivecrona, is an imperative simply an indication of the opinion or desires of the commander (I wish you would not steal) or a prediction, in the classical positivist mode, of an unpleasant consequence attached to disobedience (if you do steal you will be punished). Again these elements may well be present but they are not essential to the nature of an imperative. The attachment of an imperative to an ideatum is for Olivecrona a function of the form of expression of the idea of conduct in question. At the simplest level:

> . . . 'You shut the door', . . . is a command if the words are uttered in a certain way with the intention of causing [a person] to shut the door. (*Law as Fact*, p. 127.)

Expressed in a different tone the same statement might of course be a suggestion or even a question ('You shut the door?' meaning, Did you do so?). Tone of voice is, of course, hardly a sufficient basis for the imperative quality of legal norms and, as Olivecrona points out, imperatives on a larger scale rest in some degree upon the preparedness and training of those to whom they are addressed, military training being advanced as an obvious, if extreme, example. This is still, however, essentially a 'form' of expression – in the military example a standard response to rank, signified by uniform, of the person giving an order. The powers of a general are, both formally and in their psychological impact, much greater than those of a private soldier. This attachment of obligation through form of expression of an ideatum is what Olivecrona means by the imperantum element of a law.

The imperative element of law, amongst other normative mechanisms, is termed by Olivecrona an 'independent imperative' because it does not rest upon the personal relationship of a face-to-face command. Thus, whereas 'You shut the door' is a demand addressed by one person directly to another, 'Thou shalt not steal' is a prescriptive standard addressed to a whole population although, naturally, particularly to those amongst them who might be inclined to theft. Olivecrona emphasises that the detailed nature of the imperantum may vary considerably from case to case, selecting out in particular the forms associated with enacted law (legislation), judge-made law and ancient customary law. In relation to legislative enactment Olivecrona states that:

> Rules of enacted law are independent imperatives that have passed through a series of formal acts. The imperantum is the whole setting in which the enactment takes place. . . . Once a constitution has been firmly established, the people respond automatically by accepting as binding the texts proclaimed as laws through . . . promulgation. Thanks to this attitude . . . the imperantum becomes effective. (*Law as Fact*, p. 130.)

Judicial decisions are treated somewhat differently since a case decision naturally relates to the issues in that particular case. However, making due allowances for the distinctions between Swedish and English, with the somewhat varied practice of other common law jurisdictions, it may be accepted that the subsequent use of judicial decisions involves in a general sense the drawing of inferences about the nature of the law from the particular application. As Olivecrona then remarks:

> . . . the practical importance of the inferences varies with the status of the persons drawing them. When a court, on the basis of previous decisions, declares that rule X belongs to the law, this is generally accepted. (*Law as Fact*, p. 132.)

In other words, the formal standing of the judge stating opinions in a court of law is the basic form of the imperantum for judge-made law. This is, however, as Olivecrona points out, a less exact process than legislation and one in which much room for debate may exist in given cases. The imperantum of ancient customary law is, by its nature, even less certain. The feeling of obligation attached to such norms is suggested by Olivecrona to derive from the whole circumstances of transition and expression of the tradition in question. Thus, the imperantum is here said to be:

> . . . everything that contributed to create the feeling that these rules were sacred and should be unconditional guides for conduct. (*Law as Fact*, p. 131.)

In all cases, therefore, Olivecrona argues that the imperative aspect of law derives from the circumstances of its expression which induce an obedient response from the addressees.

10.3.3 The problem of revolutions

Olivecrona's analysis of the obligatory characteristic of law rests to a very considerable extent upon the idea of ingrained respect for the constitutional forms of the system in question. Where a constitution is overthrown in a revolution, the old order, by definition, ceases to function and is replaced by something else which, by definition, is not the object of any ingrained respect. Most legal theorists have treated such an event as an exercise of political power which in its origin rests simply upon force, in the manner of H. L. A. Hart's hypothetical autocrat Rex I (see 3.2.3). The establishment of some form of recognisable obligation in relation to the laws made by such a ruler will then depend upon subsequent development in the community concerned. Such a situation is also problematic for the type of psychological theory advanced by Olivecrona, which tends to assume a more or less stable constitutional background or at least one that changes and evolves only through mechanisms which exist within the system.

Olivecrona deals with the problem of revolutionary discontinuity in a legal system very briefly. He remarks that in such a case:

> The ordinary source of strength for a government and a legislature, the respect for the existing constitution, is supplanted by a momentary gathering of diverse forces. But in actual fact, . . . [p]eople are . . . familiar with the idea that there must always be a government and a legislature. . . . Therefore the respect for the previous constitution may easily be transferred to the new one. (*Law as Fact*, p. 104.)

In support of this case he adds that revolutionary regimes will often imitate traditional forms to the greatest possible extent in order to ease the transition. This may be so in some cases. Some of the forms of government in the English Cromwellian Commonwealth were indeed perpetuated, although by no means all, and Oliver Cromwell was certainly driven as Lord Protector to assume, in some respects, a near monarchic presence. In many other cases it was manifestly not so. The transition from the monarchy of Louis XVI to the French First Republic displayed little, if any, continuity of constitutional form. In Russia in 1917 there was, perhaps, some degree of formal continuity from the monarchy of Nicholas II (which from 1905 had been theoretically constitutional) to the Menshevik regime which Kerensky established, with Prince Lvov as the nominal head of State, in the February Revolution. From that to the Bolshevik regime established by Lenin in the October 1917 Revolution, though, very little continuity can be detected. Examples may be multiplied but the suggestion of continuity made by Olivecrona is perhaps questionable.

This said, the argument is perhaps on surer ground in claiming that at the root of a legal order is the assumption of the existence of 'some' government. It may thus be, indeed it may be observed, that once they have become established, governments installed through revolution will make laws with as much psychological, and political, efficacy as their predecessors. The inheritance of psychological effect is not, however, necessarily a simple or immediate process. In a somewhat different context Olivecrona makes the illuminating comment that:

> When in 1688 James [II] had fled [England], . . . he was received as a king by Louis [XIV] and was [so] regarded . . . by many . . . both in England and in exile. For many years he continued to exercise some royal functions from . . . St Germain. . . . Meanwhile William and Mary were made king and queen by the Convention Parliament. . . . Were they really king and queen? Was . . . James the real king? . . . What we know is . . . that the titles of king and queen were ascribed to William and Mary, . . . the usual consequential ideas were attached to the titles, and . . . the constitutional machinery functioned on this basis, while James lost his place at the centre of the working system. (*Law as Fact*, pp. 266–7.)

Thus, an exile group, with dissidents within the country, remained loyal to the old order; the politically dominant groups and much of the population, however, adhered to the new order which thus became legitimate in practice. The forces immediately involved in revolutionary change must seem in their immediate context to be political and military rather than psychological. In the particular case of the overthrow of James II in 1688 the operative factors were the attitude of the Convention Parliament (the status of which itself raises similar jurisprudential questions, see 3.2.3) and the view taken by the military commander John Churchill, later Duke of Marlborough. In short, acceptance is a matter of political fact as Bentham specified (see 2.2.2) and as emerges clearly from the analysis of H. L. A. Hart's rule of recognition (see

3.2.3) and Kelsen's *Grundnorm* (see 8.2.1). Such processes may then refocus psychological responses to different forms through, perhaps, a residual continuity of acceptance of government as such. That an interregnum, however abbreviated, occurs seems, however, to be obvious.

It is no criticism of Olivecrona's theory to say that it describes the operation of a more or less stable order, and one that must be regenerated after any revolutionary change. In the context of his theory it is perhaps sufficient to say that the assumption of government will in the end confer psychological, in addition to other forms of, efficacy upon a newly established regime.

10.3.4 Performatory imperatives and rights

The psychological model of imperatives within a legal order still leaves open an important question in the categorisation of legal provisions. In particular, not all legal provisions are apparently imperative in any direct sense – many are facilitative in function. It will be recalled that Bentham and, particularly, Austin were forced into somewhat contorted argument in order to force facilitative laws, such as the Wills Act 1837, into a command theory (see 2.2.3). Olivecrona terms provisions of this general type 'performatory imperatives' and relates them to the basic legal concepts of rights and other legal qualities. Such imperatives raise important questions for the psychological analysis of law which Olivecrona answers by reference to ideas which are very much in the tradition established by Hägerström.

Olivecrona traces our experience of rights to childhood comprehension of property. A child will be aware of things which are 'mine' and a large other category of things which are 'other people's' and, according to Olivecrona, will derive such categorisations from the means of acquisition (this object was given to me, i.e., not to you). Similar, if more complex, understandings operate in the adult world, as in transfers of title to land. Olivecrona makes the point that at no level do the rights in terms of which such claims are expressed themselves reflect any objective reality; they are directive in nature and embody ideas of conduct in relation to, e.g., an object and its owner. This is, of course, a psychological effect which Olivecrona refers to the internal aspect of law advanced by H. L. A. Hart (see 3.2.1), that is to say that rights are an immediately comprehensible and largely, if not entirely, efficacious concept when within the context of a legal system, but quite unreal when viewed from any external context. Olivecrona also concedes that legal rights may be both complex and unclear, in which case their state requires to be declared by some authority, e.g., a court, the efficacy of such declaration resting, of course, upon the efficacy of the legal system itself.

How then are rights, of property or otherwise, created and duties established? This is done, according to Olivecrona, through performatory imperatives. These are conceived not as directing behaviour as such but as bringing about a new state of affairs, which may, indeed undoubtedly will, induce new patterns of conduct. When one buys a car the rights of the previous owner over it are extinguished and transferred to oneself. One then owns the car and both social expectation and, if necessary, the State will assist you in maintaining that claim, assuming that the transfer of ownership was in due form. These effects are not limited to transfers of ownership, they may refer to relationships or personal undertakings, e.g., a contract of employment.

Olivecrona treats the 'word magic' of legal ritual with some caution. Like Hägerström, however, he emphasises the consequential effects of word use in given contexts. Thus:

> . . . [such] words actually denote nothing. . . . Their function in our language is primarily to serve as guides to action. When used according to rules, or . . . supposed to be used in such a way, they become points of reference for consequential ideas concerning correct and obligatory behaviour. Such consequential ideas are inculcated . . . and . . . impressed . . . [and thus] real positions of power are established, real bonds are created, and certain attitudes in relations to persons and things are formed. (*Law as Fact*, p. 252.)

Olivecrona is, however, careful to distinguish these real effects from the ideal consequences supposed to be created by performatory imperatives. Having a right to property may mean that the owner is indeed left in undisturbed enjoyment of it. This aspiration may, however, fail. Consequently language as an instrument of control is backed up by many other factors, including upbringing, social habit and, ultimately, State action. The end result is that 'rights', 'duties', 'property' and other such concepts do not describe any objective reality but are instead 'directive' ideas which may, and often do, produce real effects in the shape of conduct. The orthodoxy of this conclusion in relation to the origins of Scandinavian realist thought will be apparent.

10.3.5 The value of Olivecrona's analysis

Olivecrona's psychological model of law makes a significant contribution to legal theory. It advances an account not only of a significant element of the operation of real law, but also of the means of attachment of obligation as a psychological phenomenon to legal norms within an established legal system. It is rather less satisfactory in explaining how such a psychological effect comes to be attached to a given system in the first place. Whilst a sense of governmental continuity, even through the barrier of a revolutionary, or other discontinuous, change, is undoubtedly important (consider Parliamentary rituals, coronations, presidential inaugurals and so on in established systems and the rapid development of alternatives in new systems), it is hardly a complete explanation.

Like many other theories, realist and otherwise, Olivecrona's psychological realism seems to focus upon an undoubtedly important aspect of the working of law but then to take it as superseding, rather than adding to, the contributions of other strands of thought. The dismissal of the broad spectra of positivist and naturalist legal theories as mere varieties of a 'voluntaristic' (will-based) 'heresy' largely ignores the fact that such theories can be argued to offer very important insights into law. Some of them, indeed, might be argued to contribute precisely to the psychological climate with which Olivecrona is primarily concerned. This broad methodological question feeds into an issue which also arises, e.g., in the context of the work of Hägerström (see 10.1.2). The psychological responses to the forms of expression of ideatum which for Olivecrona constitute the essential imperantum are clearly important. A lawmaking body in any system works in part because it is accepted as doing so, which is much the same thing as saying that the bulk of its subjects think that it does so.

Such a response is not, however, entirely automatic. Some do not accept laws, either because of political dissidence or simply because they are criminals (bearing in mind the intimate link between the formalities of law and what is specifically defined as 'criminal'). In a criminological context this is referred to as 'anomie', a culture opposed to mainstream values. For the majority, in most cases, who do accept the values which underlie the law, there may still be processes of judgment involved. In a reasonably stable and/or democratic society these might largely be assumed; in more extreme circumstances this may not, however, be the case. The moral, ethical and political dilemmas faced, e.g., by people living under the Third Reich, Stalinism or, most recently, the Khmer Rouge regime in Cambodia (then called Kampuchea) illustrate the point in an extreme form.

In short, the psychological analysis advanced by Olivecrona makes a most useful addition to legal theory in that it examines and elucidates a vital aspect of the functioning of positive law, and its obligatory characteristic, in a stable society. However, the claim of this theory to advance not only a new but also a comprehensive analysis, superseding voluntaristic error, seems, as with many other theories, to be excessive. The Scandinavian realism of Olivecrona is a useful resource in jurisprudential analysis, but it can hardly replace all other analyses.

10.4 ALF ROSS AND THE JUDICIAL FUNCTION

Alf Ross took as his central concern the concept of a 'valid' law and, perhaps inevitably, therefore placed great emphasis upon the judicial function. In this respect he approached a little nearer to the concerns of American realism (see chapter 11) than did other 'Scandinavian' theorists. In particular Ross emphasises the concept of 'validity' as the basic issue of the 'doctrinal' study of law, which is to say the descriptive analysis of legal norms. His starting-point is simply stated:

> . . . every proposition occurring in the doctrinal study of law contains as an integral part the concept 'valid . . . law'. For this reason it is not possible to declare . . . the meaning of any such proposition until the meaning of . . . 'valid law' is made plain. Much apparent disagreement between legal writers . . . [derives from] different assumptions as to the meaning of this concept. (A. Ross, *On Law and Justice*, transl. M. Dutton (London: Stevens & Sons, 1958), p. 11.)

The last sentence of this statement is one all too often neglected by legal theorists. To make the point expressly, when comparing different answers it is well to consider whether they result from attempts to resolve the same question. Ross's analysis of 'validity' underwent some change, but inevitably it emphasises the functioning of legal systems. This tends to place it, albeit from a 'Scandinavian' perspective in a category of theories, including those of H. L. A. Hart (see chapter 3) and Hans Kelsen (see chapter 8), which stress, perhaps unduly, the official dimension of law.

10.4.1 Validity and the chess analogy

In an extended analogy Ross considers the question of validity in the context of the game of chess. The game depends upon certain rules about how different pieces, pawns, knights, bishops, rooks, queens and kings, may be moved. Such rules exist and are operated as part of a conceptual structure which gives point to the moves and ultimately constitutes the game. The game itself then rests upon the participation and understanding of a community which in the immediate instance comprises the two players.

Ross argues that, on a much larger and more complex scale, human social life rests upon the relation of individual action to a shared perception of rules, the understanding of which renders action both comprehensible and, up to a point, predictable. Thus, as for the rules of chess in their limited relevant context:

> . . . a 'valid law' means the abstract set of normative ideas which serve as a scheme of interpretation for the phenomena of law in action, which . . . means that these norms are effectively followed, and followed because they are experienced and felt to be socially binding. (*On Law and Justice*, p. 18.)

Ross attacks metaphysical concepts of validity, as distinct from historical or sociological enquiries, as founded upon assumptions of divine or other external criteria of reference. He remarks that nobody:

. . . would ever think of tracing the valid norms of chess back to an a priori validity, a pure idea of chess, bestowed . . . by God or deduced by [human] . . . eternal reason. (*On Law and Justice*, p. 18.)

Indeed, nobody would do so but in making this implicit reference to 'naturalist' argument Ross appears to ignore his earlier assertion of the dangers of confusion inherent in the collision of differing assumptions. One might not attribute chess to a divine origin but the nature of the game certainly imposes limits upon what rules are appropriate and possible. A rule which stated that 'the establishment of checkmate will conclude the game unless one of the players chooses otherwise' would so fundamentally subvert the game as a 'game', i.e., a competition leading to a conclusion, that either it or the concept framework of chess would swiftly have to be set aside. One again returns to the proposition that legal validity, or perhaps 'law' quality, is a concept which may be approached on a number of levels. The level at which Ross is considering it is not that of moral, or naturalist, analysis (see chapters 3 and 4) and since the bases of the arguments thus differ, the confusion which he seems to suggest does not exist.

10.4.2 Norms of conduct and of competence

Ross suggests that legal norms are divisible into two broad categories, 'norms of conduct' and 'norms of competence' (*On Law and Justice*, p. 32). The former prescribe or forbid action; the latter confer powers or authority and in effect declare that norms of conduct may be set up in accordance with stated procedures. The comparison with H. L. A. Hart's primary and secondary rules as the basis of a legal system is striking (see 3.2.2). Ross, however, far from founding his concept of a legal system upon a combination of these two types of norms initially argued that in practice both categories are reducible to directions to the courts. The direction to the individual citizen thus becomes derivative in the sense that it rests upon an understanding of how a court would react to a given situation if called upon to adjudicate therein. The judgments of the court will then, potentially if not actually in all cases, rely upon the capacity of the State to enforce what has been ordered. Ross indeed defines a 'legal system' as an 'integrated set of rules' which determine when and how the State shall apply measures of force to people (*On Law and Justice*, p. 34).

Such a model joins, admittedly from a 'Scandinavian' perspective, a group of theories, including those of H. L. A. Hart and Hans Kelsen, which emphasise directions to officials rather than to people generally. This position may reasonably be questioned, especially in relation to the relative importance of officials, judges and otherwise, and the general population from the viewpoint of the operation of law.

10.4.3 Validity and the official viewpoint

The validity of a given rule which is to be enforced becomes, upon the analysis advanced by Ross, a product of the application of criteria by a judge which in turn rest upon the judge's understanding of the validity of the legal system as a whole. This is presented as a dual process involving:

> . . . partially the outward observable and regular compliance with a pattern of action [on the part of the judge], and partly the experience of this pattern of action as being a socially binding norm. (*On Law and Justice*, p. 37.)

There appears here to be some parallel with H. L. A. Hart's external and internal aspects of law (see 3.2.1). Ultimately, however, it is the predictive element that Ross emphasises in his analysis of 'validity', even though, in fairness, the 'understanding' is a necessary part of the mechanism by reference to which the prediction will be made. This is a view which raises a number of difficulties. In particular, if validity is a matter determined by the experiential reactions of judges, there arises, as with H. L. A. Hart (see 3.2.4), the problem of the relation of the general population to law.

Ross recognised this problem and sought to redress the balance by advancing a division between primary and secondary rules, which differs somewhat from that advanced by H. L. A. Hart (see 3.2.2). Ross's primary rules are norms directing conduct, in a manner somewhat similar to those of Hart, but his secondary rules define sanctions and the circumstances of their application and are directed to judges. The sanctions are not only penalties in a strict sense but would include the remedies to be applied in cases of, e.g., contract or tort. Ross concludes that logically there is in fact only one category of rule, the secondary rules, because these direct the actions of the courts which give the supposed primary rules their effect. However:

> From a psychological point of view, . . . there do exist two sets of norms. Rules addressed to citizens are felt psychologically to be independent entities which are grounds for the reactions of the authorities [and] . . . primary rules must be recognised as . . . existing . . . insofar as they are followed with regularity and experienced as being binding. (A. Ross, *Directives and Norms* (London: Routledge & Kegan Paul, 1968), p. 92.)

This admission resolves the issue to some extent, but there remains an emphasis upon official and judicial reaction which is debatable. What amounts to an emphasis upon administration rather than substance strongly implies a view which, whilst it may reflect the experience of the lawyer, at best downgrades that of the citizen subject to law. If primary rules are felt to be independent entities there seems little reason for not concluding that they are also logically so.

10.4.4 Ross in the Scandinavian realist context

Ross clearly takes a somewhat different stance from other Scandinavian realist thinkers – one which is much more closely related to the facts of court action. In some ways the emphases upon the social facts of adjudication and upon judicial behaviour may be thought problematic insofar as such a concrete model sits oddly in a school ultimately founded upon the importance of ideas. His treatment of the feelings of judges and, ultimately, the psychological reality of primary rules, however, places him clearly in a 'Scandinavian' context.

10.5 THE MESSAGE OF SCANDINAVIAN REALISM

The Scandinavian realist school considers an important element of the working of law which, however it may be defined, has at its root ideas about conduct, whether to be encouraged or discouraged. The various psychological theories which have been constructed in a tradition largely deriving from the work of Axel Hägerström offer perspectives which account for some aspects of law which other theories, indeed, underplay or ignore. Unfortunately the claim by most members of the school that all other theories are fallacious and that only psychological analyses can adequately account for legal phenomena advances an exclusivity which is highly damaging. This claim so manifestly obscures, or discounts, other important elements of law that the real importance of the psychological analyses tends itself to be devalued. In short, the question to be asked is not whether an approach is right in comparison with all others, but rather whether in its appropriate context it makes a useful contribution to understanding. It may readily be contended that Scandinavian realism indeed does so but its sometimes rather mechanistic psychological perceptions no more render a complete picture of the operation of law than does any other theory.

10.6 FURTHER READING

Hägerström, A., *Inquiries into the Nature of Law and Morals*, transl. C. D. Broad (Stockholm: Almqvist & Wiksell, 1953).
Hart, H. L. A., 'Scandinavian realism' [1959] CLJ 233.
Lundstedt, A. V., *Legal Thinking Revised* (Stockholm: Almqvist & Wiksell, 1956).
Olivecrona, K., *Law as Fact*, 2nd ed. (London: Stevens & Sons, 1971).
Ross, A., *On Law and Justice*, transl. M. Dutton (London: Stevens & Sons, 1958).
Ross, A., *Directives and Norms* (London: Routledge & Kegan Paul, 1968).

CHAPTER ELEVEN

American Realism

American realism had its core in a reaction to the 'black-letter' approach to the law which advocates the formal syllogistic application of law to the facts, an approach sometimes labelled as 'formalism' or the 'mechanical' approach to jurisprudence. The black-letter approach, although unpopular amongst theorists, is still to be found in copious quantities in the judiciary and in many traditional law schools in England and elsewhere. Students are frequently asked to apply the relevant legal rules to a hypothetical set of facts with the idea that there is one legal solution. Most academics would recognise that there might be a range of legal answers but, often as not, a particular teacher will favour one solution over the other and dismiss any others as wrong. Formalism offers us right and wrong answers, it encourages rigidity and a dismissive attitude to any analysis of the impact of non-legal factors on the law, in other words it treats law as an isolated, closed and logical system. As far as theorists are concerned, positivists such as Kelsen and Hart came the closest to this approach, but their theories are more complicated and subtle than this. The *positivist approach* of many practising lawyers, judges as well as academics, has none of the subtleties of the *positivist theories*. The black-letter approach to law is in reality a bastardisation of legal positivism, but because of its dominance in the legal establishment it has been the subject of many critical theories, including American realism.

It is not possible to see American realism as a theory as such in that its contributors tended to concentrate their attacks on formalism in different areas, and at the heart of realism, there is a fundamental difference between the rule sceptics and the fact sceptics. It is best categorised as a movement in jurisprudence united by the challenge to accepted legal philosophy. It also represented a period in American jurisprudence from about 1900–1960.

The main concern of the realist movement was the desire to discover how judicial decisions were reached in reality, which involved a playing down of the role of established rules, or the 'law in books', to discover the other factors that contributed towards a judicial decision, in order to discover the 'law in action'. Once the realists had deciphered the factors that lead to judicial decisions, both non-legal and legal, they were concerned with the prediction of future decisions. The realists were adamant that only when the 'law in action' was properly understood could a more accurate prediction of judicial decisions be made. In addition, they were of the opinion that judicial decision-making would be more amenable to the needs of society if judges were more open about the non-legal factors which had influenced their decisions, instead of instinctively trying to submerge them behind the façade of syllogistic legal reasoning.

From this brief synopsis, it can be seen that the realists were radical but they were certainly not revolutionary, unlike some of their successors. They were concerned with improving the legal system and they saw that this must emerge out of their criticisms of the courts. The realist approach was certainly court-centred and the rule sceptics, who constituted the bulk of the movement, mainly concentrated on the discovery of what the real rules were. However, the fact sceptics could be said to have a more fundamental critique of the established system by not only doubting the value of simply relying on the paper rules, but also by doubting the adequacy of the courts as fact-finding institutions. As will be seen, such a scepticism leaves little room for the improvement of the judicial system because it casts doubt on its value as a dispute-resolving mechanism, which after all is arguably one of the more important functions of a legal system.

Both rule sceptics and fact sceptics were concerned with moving away from abstract *a priori* reasoning that tends to dominate legal thinking and leads to judges looking backwards to make decisions, towards a greater concentration on the consequences of such decisions. Whereas rule sceptics advocated a more open approach as regards the real rules, which, when properly identified, included considerations of policy, the fact sceptics, because they failed to see any objectivity in fact-finding, never mind rule application, advocated that judges make decisions on the basis of fairness in the particular case. Realists were concerned that the formal approach, which, by its very nature, isolated law from other areas such as politics, economics and sociology, meant that the law was full of 'bad' decisions, 'bad' in the sense that they had a negative impact on society no matter how well they fitted into the legal system. Realists were concerned that law should not simply be separated from the society that created it and for whose benefit it should be applied.

11.1 MAJOR REALIST WRITERS

11.1.1 Oliver Wendell Holmes

Mr Justice Holmes of the United States Supreme Court was in many ways the founder of the American realist movement. He had a pragmatic approach to judicial decision-making, including a scepticism of the ability of general rules to provide the solution to particular cases:

> General propositions do not determine concrete cases. . . . I always say in conference that no case can be settled by general propositions, that I will admit any general proposition you like and decide the case either way. (O. W. Holmes cited in W. E. Rumble, *American Legal Realism: Skepticism, Reform and the Judicial Process* (Ithaca, NY: Cornell University Press, 1968), pp. 39–40. Rumble's analysis is followed to a great extent in this chapter.)

In addition to being a rule sceptic, Holmes was at the forefront of recognising the role of extra-legal factors in judicial decision-making:

> . . . the life of the law has not been logic, it has been experience. The felt necessities of the time, the prevalent moral and political theories, intuitions of public policy, avowed or unconscious, even the prejudices which judges share with their fellow men, have had a good deal more to do than the syllogism in determining the rules by which men should be governed.
>
> In substance the growth of the law is legislative . . . The very considerations which judges most rarely mention, and always with an apology, are the secret root from which the law draws all the juices of life. I mean, of course, considerations of what is expedient for the community concerned. (M. Lerner (ed.), *The Mind and Faith of Justice Holmes: His Speeches, Essays, Letters, and Judicial Opinions* (New York: Random House, 1943), pp. 51–4.)

Holmes was convinced, in complete contrast to Dworkin (see chapter 9) that the judiciary does play a legislative role. Indeed he saw it as the essence of judicial decision-making, not simply something they do in hard cases. This distances him not only from Dworkin but also from positivists such as Hart who saw judicial lawmaking as peripheral. While recognising that there are many non-legal factors which influence the law – Holmes mentioned morality, politics and prejudices – he saw 'policy' as the most fundamental element, though judges were somewhat abashed in their use of it. He advocated that the judiciary should become more open in their use of policy so that there was no longer the need to peer behind the precedents and false mechanical reasoning to see what was really going on.

Furthermore, Holmes introduced a putative predictive approach to the law. For Holmes law, or more correctly a legal duty, was simply a prediction that if a person behaved in a certain way he would be punished. This was looking at law from the perspective of the 'bad man':

> . . . if we take the view of our friend the bad man we shall find that he does not care two straws for the axioms or deductions, but that he does want to know what the Massachusetts or English courts are likely to do in fact. I am much of his mind. The prophecies of what the courts will do in fact, and nothing more pretentious, are what I mean by the law. (O. W. Holmes, 'The path of the law' (1897) 10 Harv L Rev 457 at pp. 460–1.)

For Holmes and the other realists the notions of legal duty and legal right were not to be answered by fruitless searches for the source of obligation, whether legal or moral, but by means of a simple predictive exercise. For most realists this was simply a prediction of how the courts would react to particular behaviour:

> . . . when I talk of the law I talk as a cynic. I don't care a damn if twenty professors tell me that a decision is not law if I know that the courts will enforce it. (O. W. Holmes cited in M. D. Howe (ed.), *Holmes-Laski Letters: The Correspondence of Mr Justice Holmes and Harold J. Laski* (Cambridge, Mass: Harvard University Press, 1953), vol. 1, p. 115.)

However, later realists expanded this behavioural analysis to see what sort of institutional response followed particular behaviour to cover not only a judicial response but the whole range of 'official' responses.

11.1.2 John Chipman Gray

It is not uncommon in jurisprudential works to find reference to Gray as a realist writer, and he is included here for that reason. Nevertheless, he only exhibited limited factors in common with the realists. His approach was certainly as court-oriented as the realists. Indeed, he even went as far as to say:

> The law of the State or of any organised body of men is composed of the rules which the courts, that is, the judicial organs of that body, lay down for the determination of legal rights and duties. (J. C. Gray, *The Nature and Sources of the Law*, 2nd ed. (New York: Macmillan, 1924), p. 84.)

For Gray the law was simply what the court decided. Everything else, including statutes, were simply sources of law. Until the court applies statutes they are not 'law'. This definition of law by itself was somewhat meaningless, but his intention was to show that judges act as the lawmakers by denying the existence of law until judgment. However, his unfortunate definition of judges as discoverers of the law can be interpreted to suggest that they were simply finding pre-existing and *certain* sources of law. If the sources of law are clear then the fact that the judge is converting them into real law or law in practice means that Gray was simply using different terminology to the formalists when in fact he intended to show that judges do act on public policy and do legislate. It is because of the vast array of choice that the judge has from the various sources of law (in which Gray included public policy) that it is true to say that nothing is clearly lawful or unlawful until judgment.

11.1.3 Karl Llewellyn

Llewellyn is often seen as the central figure in the American realist movement. His writings, spanning the most productive period of realism, contained within them not only the core themes for the movement, but also developed from being very critical of the judiciary to taking on a more constructive attitude. In 1931 he outlined the major themes of realism (K. N. Llewellyn, 'Some realism about realism: responding to Dean Pound' (1931) 44 Harv L Rev 1222).

He insisted upon the reality of judicial lawmaking and indeed saw it as essential in matching the law to the rapidity of social change. Law for Llewellyn was a means for the achievement of social ends and for this reason it should not be backward looking for its development but should be forward looking in terms of moulding the law to fit the current and future needs of society. Furthermore, realists should be concerned with the effects of law on society and he insisted that law should be evaluated principally in terms of its effects.

The realist's concern for the consequences of legal decisions was matched, according to Llewellyn, by their distrust of legal rules. Legal rules do not describe what the courts are purporting to do nor do they describe how individuals concerned with the law behave. Legal rules as found in books and emphasised in judicial decisions do not accord with reality. Rules, as described in books and in judicial decisions, have essentially taken on a life of their own, they have in fact become 'reified' (see the approach of the critical legal studies movement, chapter 12), and as such bear little resemblance to the actuality of the legal process. Legal rules are not the 'heavily operative factor' in producing the decisions of courts although they appear to be so on the surface. The realist should be concerned with discovering those factors that really influence judges, and judges in turn should be more open about using them. Obviously one of the problems here is, as pointed out by Dworkin (see chapter 9), an adequate explanation of why judges purport to disguise their true reasoning behind the cloak of rules and precedents.

Llewellyn also advocated a different approach to the study of law. He advocated that law be studied in far narrower categories than has been the practice in the past. He saw that the use of general rules to cover a vast array of different situations produced a distortion in the form of decisions that have adverse effects on the community. To apply the same rules to different situations is counter-productive because it ignores the fact that different considerations ought to apply. To apply the same principles of frustration in contract law to shipping cases involving the blockage of the Suez canal in 1956, to employment contracts in the 1990s serves no useful purpose except to please those formalists who insist on a false uniformity in order to satisfy their desire to see law as system isolated from the events it is purporting to control.

The requirement that law must be evaluated in terms of its consequences led to Llewellyn developing a sophisticated analysis of the purposes of law in his later works. Llewellyn described the basic functions of law as 'law-jobs' (K. N. Llewellyn, *My Philosophy of Law* (Boston, Mass: Boston Law Co., 1941), pp. 183–6). Law is an 'institution' which is necessary in society and which is comprised not only of rules but also contains an 'ideology and a body of pervasive and powerful ideals which are largely unspoken, largely implicit, and which pass unmentioned in the books'. Jurisprudence should be concerned with looking at the whole, including the important ideals, instead of merely concentrating on the rules. 'The wider view of rules-in-their-setting yields rules both righter and more effective'. Law has jobs to do within a society. These are:

1. The disposition of the trouble case: a wrong, a grievance, a dispute. This is the garage-repair work or the going concern of society, with (as case law shows) its continuous effect upon the remaking of the order of society.
2. The preventive channelling of conduct and expectation so as to avoid trouble, and together with it, the effective reorientation of conduct and expectations in similar fashion. This does not mean merely, for instance, new legislation; it is instead, what new legislation (among other things) is about, and is for.
3. The allocation of authority and the arrangement of procedures which mark action as being authoritative; which includes all of any constitution, and much more.
4. The positive side of law's work, seen as such, and seen not in detail, but as a net whole: the net organization of society as a whole so as to provide integration, direction, and incentive.
5. 'Juristic method' to use a single slogan to sum up the task of handling the legal materials and tools and people developed for the other jobs – to the end that those materials and tools and people are kept doing their law-jobs, and doing them better, until they become a source of revelation of new possibility and achievement. (K. N. Llewellyn, *My Philosophy of*

Law (Boston, Mass: Boston Law Co., 1941), pp. 186–7; see further K. N. Llewellyn, 'The normative, the legal and the law-jobs: the problem of juristic method' (1940) 49 Yale LJ 1355.)

The first three jobs ensure society's survival and continuation, whilst the latter two increase efficiency and expectations. One may disagree with Llewellyn's list of the jobs of law but they do provide a more holistic approach to lawmaking and judicial activity than others. One can contrast his jobs with Fuller's morality of duty and morality of aspiration (see chapter 5). Llewellyn's law-jobs are not simply about making law open, accessible and clear, they concern the pivotal role and function of law in society. Society, according to Llewellyn, will develop law institutions to perform these jobs. Is Llewellyn's list of tasks performed by law better than any other list? Is there any proof that the law actually does perform these jobs? His study of the Cheyenne Indians in the United States was an attempt to prove that even 'primitive' societies exhibit the first of his law-jobs (K. N. Llewellyn and E. A. Hoebel, *The Cheyenne Way* (Norman, Okla: University of Oklahoma Press, 1941)), and his contribution to and analysis of the American Uniform Commercial Code seemed to fit in with his second law-job (W. Twining, *Karl Llewellyn and the Realist Movement* (London: Weidenfeld & Nicolson, 1973), ch. 11 and 12). It seems better to view his list of law-jobs as both descriptive and prescriptive. If law is seen as a whole, as an integral and fundamental part of society, instead of looking at it in isolation simply as a set of rules to be pieced together like a legal jigsaw, then the true functions of law will be seen to be in line with his law-jobs.

11.1.4 Jerome Frank

Judge Jerome Frank, a federal judge in the United States, shared with all realists a scepticism of conventional theories but if anything his scepticism was much more fundamental. He saw that there were two categories of realists. First, the rule sceptics represented by Llewellyn, whose aim was in part to increase legal certainty or 'predictability'. Rule sceptics 'consider it socially desirable that lawyers should be able to predict to their clients the decisions in most lawsuits not yet commenced' (J. Frank, *Law and the Modern Mind* (Gloucester, Mass: Peter Smith, 1970), p. x). Rule sceptics were united in their belief that the paper rules, those formal rules found in judicial decisions and in books, were unreliable as guides in the prediction of decisions. If the real rules are discovered then a better description of uniformities in judicial decision-making is achieved and therefore reliance on the real rules will yield greater certainty.

While not disagreeing with this, Frank was dissatisfied with the narrowness of the rule sceptics' field of enquiry.

In this undertaking, the rule sceptics concentrate almost exclusively on upper-court opinions. They do not ask themselves whether their own or any other prediction device will render it possible for a lawyer or a layman to prophesy, before an ordinary suit is instituted or comes to trial in a trial court, how it will be decided. In other words, these rule sceptics seek means for making accurate guesses, not about decisions of trial courts, but about decisions of upper courts when trial-court decisions are appealed. These sceptics cold-shoulder the trial courts. Yet, in most instances, these sceptics do not inform their readers that they are writing chiefly of upper courts. (*Law and the Modern Mind*, p. xi.)

In other words rule sceptics, like many formalists, are concerned simply with the appeal courts' decisions where legal rules and precedents take on a life of their own without much regard to non-legal factors, or indeed to the question of whether the facts arrived at in the lower court were actually the *real* facts. Appeal courts generally do not debate the facts, and this, according to Frank, obscures a more fundamental problem. This led Frank to discuss the second group of realists with which he identified, namely the 'fact sceptics'.

Their primary interest is in the trial courts. No matter how precise or definite may be the formal legal rules, say these fact sceptics, no matter what the discoverable uniformities behind these formal rules, nevertheless it is impossible, and will always be impossible, because of the elusiveness of the facts on which decisions turn, to predict future decisions in most (not all) lawsuits, not yet begun or not yet tried. (*Law and the Modern Mind*, p. xi.)

It is to fact scepticism that the analysis now turns as one of the themes of the American realist movement.

11.2 MAJOR THEMES OF AMERICAN REALISM

11.2.1 Fact scepticism

As illustrated above Frank was the main fact sceptic. His point was that if we take the normal mode of judicial decision-making as the application of legal rules to the facts of a case then, even if the rules are clear, such as not parking on a double yellow line, or obeying the speed limit or driving on the left-hand side of the road, it is still not possible to predict with certainty which way the trial court will decide simply because of the elusiveness of the facts. Frank points to two main groups of elusive factors which cannot be captured by any predictive theory based on observation of the behaviour of the courts.

First, the trial judge in a non-jury trial or the jury in a jury trial must learn about the facts from the witnesses; and witnesses, being humanly fallible, frequently make mistakes in observation of what they saw and heard, or in their recollections of what they observed, or in their court-room reports of those recollections. Second, the trial judges or juries, also human, may have prejudices – often unconscious, unknown even to themselves – for or against some of the witnesses, or the parties to the suit, or the lawyers. (*Law and the Modern Mind*, pp. xii–xiii.)

Rule sceptics with their predictive models assumed that there is an ascertainable set of facts, otherwise their attempts at predicting the results of court cases by looking at the real rules would not have been possible. Frank denied that there is this certainty in the judicial process and that if his model is followed there is no way in which predictions can be made. In addition he denied that the rule sceptics could include within their real rules the second set of elusive elements he identified, which included the racial, religious, political or economic prejudices of the judge and jury. Some of these prejudices may be uniform so that it is possible to say that such a judge does not favour women, or that a juror from such and such a background will not favour blacks, but it is impossible to include all the hidden, sometimes unconscious biases of judge and jurors. Such idiosyncratic biases cannot be factored into an analysis of behavioural patterns.

Furthermore, Frank argued that in a trial court the law and the facts become intertwined – there is not a simple application of the law to the facts, instead the law emerges in an adversarial manner just as the facts do. When the jury comes to its verdict, they do not distinguish between law and fact, and in this state of confusion they decide the case on other grounds:

> Many juries in reaching their verdicts act on their emotional responses to the lawyers and witnesses; they like or dislike, not any legal rule, but they do like an artful lawyer for the plaintiff, the poor widow, the brunette with the soulful eyes, and they do dislike the big corporation, the Italian with a thick, foreign accent. (J. Frank, *Courts on Trial* (Princeton, NJ: Princeton University Press, 1949), p. 130.)

These mistakes are simply compounded in the appeal court which usually relies on the facts as adopted by the trial court. By concentrating on appeal court decisions, all lawyers, including the rule sceptics, appear to be accepting that there can be consistency and that the doctrine, of precedent and *stare decisis* are important or at least can be used to help to identify patterns of judicial behaviour. Frank denied this:

> This weakness [of the precedent doctrine] will also infect any substitute precedent system, based on 'real rules' which the rule sceptics may

discover, by way of anthropology – i.e., the mores, customs, folkways – or psychology, or statistics, or studies of the political, economic, and social backgrounds of judges, or otherwise. For no rule can be hermetically sealed against the intrusion of false or inaccurate oral testimony which the trial judge or jury may believe. (*Law and the Modern Mind*, pp. xvi–xvii.)

Although Frank's views were somewhat impressionistic, his own experience as a judge should not to be discounted. To discover whether his views have value, the law student ought perhaps to spend more time observing trial court proceedings rather than simply relying on reading appeal court judgments and their synthesis by academics, whether formalist or realist (rule sceptics).

11.2.2 Rule scepticism

As we have seen, all realists, including Frank, were sceptical of formal rules as the major deciding factor in legal cases. Traditional theory paints an ideal syllogistic picture of the judicial process where the clearly established statutes or precedents are applied to the facts with little or no discretion on the part of the judges. Judges are portrayed in this formalist conception as machine-like and totally neutral. Rule sceptics were very critical of this established position and pointed to many fallacies in the traditional approach.

Realists first of all pointed to the vast panoply of precedents that had been built up in common law systems over the centuries. Realists argued that so many precedents could not be reconciled in any logical coherent way. Since precedents were inconsistent, there was no one right answer to a legal dispute, simply a variety of answers from which the judge had to choose one. Douglas wrote that 'there are usually plenty of precedents to go around; and with the accumulation of decisions, it is no great problem for a lawyer to find legal authority for most propositions' (W. O. Douglas, '*Stare decisis*', in *Essays in Jurisprudence from the Columbia Law Review* (New York: Columbia University Press, 1963), p. 19). Law students are frequently asked to prepare an argument advising a hypothetical claimant or defendant, say in a moot court, and they usually can find a set of favourable precedents for both sides. However, when confronted with their teacher who pronounces judgment it seems to them that there is one right answer (see further chapter 9). This could be said to be because the teacher knows or ought to know more precedents than the student and so it simply *seems* that he knows the answer.

Realists not only pointed to the fact that there are numerous precedents, they also insisted that there are numerous techniques for interpreting precedents. Throughout his works Llewellyn referred to the judicial ability to be able to avoid precedents that conflict with the judge's view. A judge may simply find a different *ratio* to the case in question or may distinguish on the grounds that the *ratio* is too wide or too narrow for the facts of the instant case. In this way judges downgrade unfavourable precedents whilst boosting those that favour their particular view. Llewellyn even went on to list 64 'available, impeccable precedent techniques' used by judges and academics alike for constructing *their* scheme of legal precedents and statutes. The fact that there are many methods of interpreting precedents increases the uncertainty of the law manyfold (K. N. Llewellyn, *The Common Law Tradition* (Boston, Mass: Little, Brown & Co., 1960), pp. 75–92).

Other realists pointed to the logical indeterminacy of established rules, in that no particular proposition could be said to generate a general proposition. This is a further development on Llewellyn's idea that a *ratio* of a prior case can easily be distinguished in a current case, the idea being that the *ratio* of that prior case is particular to that case and it cannot be used as a general rule in future cases with different facts.

Oliphant illustrated this point with an example. Anne's father persuades her not to marry Brian as she has previously promised to do. Brian sues Anne's father for damages for breach of contract to marry (Oliphant was writing in the days when promises to marry were binding in law). The essence of the judge's decision is that the father is not liable to Brian. The judge's decision can be said to give rise to a number of legal principles or rules. They can be listed as:

(a) Fathers are privileged to induce their daughters to break promises to marry.

(b) Parents are privileged to induce their daughters to break promises to marry.

(c) Parents are so privileged as to both daughters and sons.

(d) All persons are so privileged as to promises to marry.

(e) Parents are so privileged as to all promises made by their children.

(f) All persons are so privileged as to all promises made by anyone.

The judge's decision that Anne's father was not liable to Brian can be subsumed under any of the above propositions. The judge may indicate what he thinks the *ratio* is and indeed he may indicate the narrowest proposition (a), although this is in itself a general proposition derived from the decision that Brian cannot recover. In a subsequent case a judge faced with different facts will probably generalise the proposition to any one of the remaining rules (b) to (f). Judges or academics looking at the past decision, ignoring the particular fact situation, will argue *ad infinitum* about how wide or narrow the *ratio* of the case is. Oliphant was critical of the usefulness of the *ratio* as a device for legal reasoning. What is more relevant is to discover the reasons why a judge will accept the third proposition but not the remainder. That choice is not based on legal logic but on reasons of policy, or morality. Oliphant himself preferred to ignore the vocal behaviour of the judge and simply advocated an analysis of judicial responses to certain fact situations (H. Oliphant, 'A return to *stare decisis*' (1928) 14 ABA J 73).

Implicit in Oliphant's arguments is the proposition that all fact situations are unique. Rodell accused classical legal theorists of assuming that fact situations fall naturally into groups, when it is clear that all cases have a unique set of facts. Placing the facts of previous cases into a particular category involves a value judgment by the judge or commentator, a judgment which can only be based on extra-legal factors. The uniqueness of the facts gives judges a large amount of leeway in determining which general principles shall apply. It is always possible to distinguish a case on the facts (F. Rodell, *Woe unto You Lawyers!*, 2nd ed. (New York: Pageant, 1957), pp. 114–15).

The aim of rule scepticism was to show that simple reliance on rules was a fallacy and that judges either consciously or unconsciously continue to play the game by paying lip-service to rule formalism. Judges and lawyers do this because they are educated in that fashion. They are not prepared to make clear the real reasons for their decisions because it would be seen as a betrayal of the ideal of the rule of law, the idea that law is neutral and objective and not dependent upon any personal factors. For the realists it was quite clear that the ideal of a logical and coherent system is impossible to achieve and in fact the judge is not bound by any antecedent rules. It follows that for the realists a judge should not feel hidebound by established precedent because there is no logical reason that dictates a choice of one precedent over another; there is in fact only the political need to respect the ideal of the rule of law, so the judge instead of being backward looking should look forwards and make policy-based decisions that are best for society. The fact that this amounted to an attack on the liberal ideal of the rule of law was not developed by the realists but has been taken on board by one of their successor movements – the critical legal scholars (see chapter 12).

11.2.3   The prediction of decisions

The realists distrusted legal rules as giving the answers to disputes, but the rule sceptics at least denied that this meant that cases were unpredictable. They were concerned with discovering uniformities in judicial decision-making so enabling the forecasting of future undecided cases as well as being concerned with making such predictions more accurate. 'The essential purpose behind the realist stress on predictivism was the promotion of certainty' (N. Duxbury, *Patterns of American Jurisprudence* (Oxford: Clarendon Press, 1995), p. 130). Formalists, of course, would explain judicial uniformity on the basis of the impact of pre-existing legal rules. The application by different judges of the same rule or principle to a similar set of facts is the main or sole reason for uniformity in judicial decision-making according to the traditional approach. Furthermore traditionalists would argue that the reason why, in a few cases, there seems to be doubt about the outcome of a particular undecided case is mainly due to a defect in the scheme of established rules they are concerned with identifying. They would argue that the law is not a perfect machine, that there are bound to be vague, inconsistent and conflicting rules, and that the only way of improving the system is to tinker with the rules, to make them compatible and clear.

The realists argued that the existence of uniformities in judicial behaviour cannot be explained simply by the examination of rules but has to be explained by an analysis of the real rules which includes legal and non-legal factors. Many of the rule sceptics agreed that there was some uniformity in judicial decision-making but it could only be explained successfully in terms of the real rules, and furthermore they played down the idea that simple intra-systemic modification of the paper rules would produce anything but a marginal improvement in judicial uniformity. Only an understanding of the real rules and more importantly a judicial recognition of, and more overt use of, these real rules would increase predictability of judicial decision-making in the future. This concern with prediction shows that far from being radical, realism is quite a conservative approach to law. As Duxbury states:

> predictivist-inspired realism treats as notionally desirable the facilitation of a formally certain, 'prediction-friendly' system of law. At the same time, the general predictivist quest for legal certainty betrays an implicit fear of judicial discretion and incertitude. And it is thus that realism, certainly in its predictivist guise, appears to attempt to replace one formalist conception of law only to replace it with another. . . . The assumption that it may be possible to predict future legal decisions with considerable, if not quite total, accuracy is hardly less formalist – is hardly less supportive of so-called slot machine justice – than the basic Langdellian belief that legal doctrine is reducible to a handful of common law principles which may be applied uncontroversially to future legal disputes. (Duxbury, *Patterns of American Jurisprudence*, p. 131.)

The realists were essentially advocating a scientific or behavioural analysis of judicial decision-making rather along the lines of an anthropologist. However, although there were many attempts at providing predictive models, some of which are outlined in this section, it is true to say that they were somewhat crude and underdeveloped. As Beutel noted, the realists' 'scientific work' on law 'reached approximately the same stage as botany would, had its efforts been devoted wholly to counting leaves on trees' (F. K. Beutel, *Some Potentialities of Experimental Jurisprudence as a New Branch of Social Science* (Lincoln, Nebr: University of Nebraska Press, 1957), p. 112). The crudity of their analysis can be explained to a certain extent by the fact that the production of a predictive model was only part of their work, indeed most spent their time on the critical aspect of realism, rule scepticism, rather than on the constructive job of forecasting and its improvement. Furthermore, those realists that did attempt a predictive model tended to concentrate on certain factors to the exclusion of others. For example, Rodell seemingly accurately predicted courts' decisions on the basis of an analysis of the personal views, characteristics, temperament, background and political views of the judges involved in cases. In order to prove the greater predictive value of the realist method, he tended to concentrate on what Dworkin would call 'hard cases' where the formalists were unable to indicate the outcome beforehand (F. Rodell, 'For every justice, judicial deference is a sometime thing' (1962) 50 Geo LJ 700).

However, a truly realist approach would have to identify all those non-legal factors such as morality, public opinion, judicial prejudice and other personal factors, issues of public policy, governmental pressure, economic, sociological and political factors, as well as the role of established rules if it was to present a totally rounded and accurate predictive model. Such a task would be mammoth, perhaps impossible. It is perhaps because of this that other realists tended to concentrate simply on judicial behaviour and eschewed any attempt to explain what the factors were that motivated judicial behaviour.

Herman Oliphant viewed patterns of regularity as characteristic of judicial decision-making but, as we have seen, his rule scepticism meant that he could not put down such regularities to simple judicial reliance on *stare decisis*. Instead, he advocated a behaviouralist approach to forecasting. He argued that attention should not be focused on the judicial decision or the vocal behaviour of the judge as this simply contained the paper rules and obscured the real rules. Realists should ignore the judicial rationalisations and concentrate on judges' non-vocal behaviour. This simply means that legal analysis should be concerned with an examination of what judges actually do when 'stimulated' by the facts of the case before them, as a scientist may examine the effect of various stimulants such as light, heat, food etc. on rats in a laboratory (H. Oliphant, 'A return to *stare decisis*' (1928) 14 ABA J 73).

Over a period of time the analyst can build up a picture of patterns of judicial behaviour not only in relation to particular disputes but also pointing to different approaches by different judges. He may find that judges are more likely to apply the rules of evidence in favour of those accused of white-collar crimes over those accused of joyriding, so that the chances of the latter being found innocent are much less than the former. In addition he may find that in those cases where both are found guilty, the likelihood is that the joyrider will be more severely punished than the white-collar criminal even though the maximum sentence for each might be the same. Such conclusions will reinforce the idea that the paper rules are simply manipulated by judges and that the real rules can only be discerned by ignoring them.

Underhill Moore developed this behaviouralist approach even further, beyond an analysis of the court's response to certain activities to looking at the overall institutional response. Like Oliphant he was a rule sceptic and instead of examining the law in accordance with the rules as enunciated by the courts he advocated an analysis based on the 'institutional patterns' of behaviour. This entails an analysis of what type of behaviour by individuals or other legal persons such as companies is met with an institutional response in the name of the law. Such institutional responses may be by the court, or by other State organs such as the police or other government bodies or a combination of these organs. In effect Moore was advocating a comparison and correlation of individual behaviour with the behaviour of State institutions. Unlike other realists, Moore tested his predictive theory with impressive results and could be said to have the most developed model for attempting to ascertain the law in action – more so than the court-based theories of his contemporaries. The law is not simply in the hands of the judiciary, although they may be the final arbiters of it. In many instances, a person's brush with the law may not go beyond the police, the local council or the tax authorities, for instance. It was with this much wider view of the law that Moore was most concerned, a view that simply could not be encompassed by the far too narrow traditionalist assertion that law was to be found in the pronouncements of judges (U. Moore and G. Sussman, 'Legal and institutional methods applied to the debiting of direct discounts – II. institutional method' (1931) 40 Yale LJ 555).

Indeed, Moore's approach was wider than most rule sceptics who, while denying a central role to paper rules, were still mainly court oriented. Llewellyn, as has been pointed out above when outlining the major themes of realism in the 1920s and 1930s, adopted a judge-centred approach. In this period Llewellyn advocated a behaviouralist approach to prediction of judicial decisions using techniques similar to those a scientist would use in analysing the behaviour of man or animals, in order to discover what the courts do as opposed to what they say. The 'legal scientist' would then be able to discover the real rules and distinguish them from the paper rules.

However, throughout his long period of writing, Llewellyn was always of the opinion that court decisions were highly predictable. In his early works he denied that this predictability, or what he called 'reckonability', was primarily due to the impact of established rules and he advocated instead a behaviouralist approach along the lines of that developed by Rodell and Oliphant. However, in his later works Llewellyn moved towards a less radical model which, while not succumbing to the formalist obsession with rules, does appear to put more weight on judicial decision-making as containing all that is required for prediction of future decisions.

This change of direction in Llewellyn's writings emerges from his 'law-jobs' theory. Remember that the fifth law-job as identified by Llewellyn was the 'juristic method', namely the traditions of handling legal materials and tools for the other law-jobs he identifies. Those concerned with the law, or the 'men of law' as Llewellyn labelled them, develop legal 'crafts' by which he meant 'advocacy, counselling, judging, law-making, administering, . . . mediation, organisation, policing, teaching, scholarship' (K. N. Llewellyn, *My Philosophy of Law* (Boston, Mass: Boston Law Co. 1941), p. 188). In relation to the judicial craft, Llewellyn was at pains to point out that this is sometimes obscured by the end-product, namely, the judicial decision which contains within it legal rules. The formalist then becomes solely concerned with the rules and ignores the craft of the judge:

[Rules] stand with such relative conspicuousness to observation, they accumulate so easily, they can be gathered so conveniently, and they are so easy to substitute for either thought or investigation, that they have drawn the attention of jurisprudes too largely to themselves; to the rules – as if the rules stood and could stand alone. A first evil has been the attribution to the rules of many results, e.g. of court decisions – which rest instead on the phases of judicial tradition. Not the least of that tradition is the ideal of justice to be reached, an ideal equipped with a whole set of *Janus-faced* techniques for the handling of rules to keep them out of the way of justice. Reckonablity of result here lies only sometimes in the rules; it lies with some consistency in the tradition. (*My Philosophy of Law*, pp. 188–9.)

The reason for the predictability of decisions in the United States appellate courts lay, according to Llewellyn, not with the rules themselves but with the common law *tradition* of the judges whose craft of decision-making ensures a conformance to a greater or lesser degree, depending on the 'period style' of the courts, of the legal rule with the needs of society.

Llewellyn saw reckonability in the appellate courts because of steadying factors in those courts as summarised by Rumble in his excellent commentary on American realism:

[Llewellyn attempts] to explain the patterns of uniformity in judicial decision-making by reference to 14 'major steadying factors in our appellate courts'. Supposedly, they furnish the basis upon which reliable predictions of future decisions can be made. The 14 are the existence of 'law-conditioned officials', personnel who are 'all trained and in the main rather experienced lawyers'; the presence of 'legal doctrine' and 'known doctrinal techniques', the responsibility of the judiciary for 'justice'; the tradition of 'one single right answer' for each case; the existence of written opinions 'which tell any interested person what the cause is and why the decision – under the authorities – is right, and perhaps why it is wise', and which may also 'show how like cases are properly to be decided in the future'; the existence of 'a frozen record from below' and the fact that the issues before the court are 'limited, sharpened, and phrased in advance';

the presentation, oral and written, of adversary argument by counsel; the practice of group decisions; the security for independent judgment which life tenure makes possible; a 'known bench'; the 'general period style and its promise'; and, finally, 'professional judicial office'. (W.E. Rumble, *American Legal Realism* (Ithaca, NY: Cornell University Press, 1968), p. 151 summarising K. N. Llewellyn, *The Common Law Tradition* (Boston, Mass: Little, Brown & Co., 1960), pp. 19–51.)

This summary of Llewellyn's later approach to judicial decision-making shows a greater respect for the legal system and the judicial office. Judicial certainty is neither a product of the simple application of rules, nor is it to be found by looking solely at extra-legal factors. It is to be discerned by understanding the tradition of the judges, and of the court process. It is to Llewellyn's ideas about tradition or what he calls 'style' that the analysis now turns.

11.2.4 Judicial reasoning

One of the 'major steadying factors' which makes judicial decision-making predictable to a significant extent is the 'period style' of judicial reasoning according to Llewellyn. Llewellyn contrasted the 'grand style' of judicial lawmaking, which uses a mixture of principle and policy to keep the law relevant and predictable, with the dry mechanical application of old-fashioned rules characteristic of what he called the 'formal style'. Llewellyn quite clearly preferred the grand style of judicial reasoning, where the judge not only tests precedents against overarching principles which 'yield patent sense as well as order' but also against policy, namely the 'prospective consequences of the rule under consideration' (contrast this with Dworkin who admits the controlling role of legal principles in his theory, but is adamant that policy has no role to play in judicial reasoning, see chapter 9). In this way the heritage of the law is constantly updated. The grand style leads to a 'functioning harmonisation of vision with tradition, of continuity with growth, of machinery with purpose, of measure with need' (*The Common Law Tradition*, p. 37). By looking to the future, judges adopting the grand style contribute to the:

. . . on-going production and improvement of rules which make sense on their face, and which can be understood and reasonably well applied even by mediocre men. *Such* rules have a fair chance to get the same results out of different judges, and so in truth to hit close to the ancient target of 'laws and not men'. (*The Common Law Tradition*, p. 38.)

Llewellyn's belief that only the grand style could produce reckonability of result is clear from this extract. The formal style, on the other hand, 'can yield reckonable results only when the rules of law are clear', which is not the case, according to Llewellyn, in the common law. He dismissed the formalistic notion that 'the rules of law decide the cases; policy is for the legislature, not for the courts, and so is change even in pure common law'. This narrow approach 'drives conscious creation all but underground' so that the law lags further and further behind the conditions and needs of society (*The Common Law Tradition*, pp. 35–45).

Llewellyn identified periods in American legal history when each style dominated, but his point was that only the grand style makes law work in the sense of fulfilling law-jobs. Not only should judges adopt the grand style but lawyers and academics as well should attempt to interpret law in a much more open way. He argued that lawyers needed to concentrate not on discovering the *ratio* of a case and fitting it into the rules relating to the area, but on examining the decision of a court for the flavour. In this way even the average lawyer can increase his or her ability to predict decisions:

> I submit that the average lawyer has only to shift his focus for a few hours from '*what* was held' in a series of opinions to what those opinions suggest or show about *what was bothering and what was helping the court* as it decided. (*The Common Law Tradition*, p. 178.)

The move away from concentrating on the *ratio* of a case to looking at it in a wider social context works best when judges are open about their use of policy and wider issues of principle rather than trying to hide them behind formal reasoning. Greater openness produces greater predictability.

Although Llewellyn's later work is reconcilable with the realist tradition that formal rules do not decide cases, it is a far cry from the radical thrust of the earlier writings of the realists which concentrated on finding the real rules in the interaction of law with society as a whole. This approach tended to play down, or even ignore, the formal judgment given by the court, whereas Llewellyn's later approach suggested that the judgment, particularly if it is adopted in the grand style of judicial decision-making, contains the real rules as well as the formal rules. The real rules can be identified by an analyst who is sufficiently skilful at reading between the lines and obtaining the flavour of the judgment. This is certainly a more conservative approach than that of Moore or of Oliphant.

The rule sceptics, including Llewellyn, who believed that it was possible to discern certainty and continuity in judicial decision-making, although they disagreed on the method for discerning this, may be contrasted with the fact sceptics such as Frank, who believing the whole system to be unstable and uncertain due to the lack of objectivity in fact finding, advocated that the only possible approach was for the judges to attempt to do justice in each individual case. For Frank the facts of each case were so different and so uncertain that there was no choice except to treat each case individually. Given the uncertainty of the facts, Frank advocated the following judicial method:

> We want judges who, thus viewing and *employing all rules as fictions*, will appreciate that, as rules are fictions 'intended for the sake of justice', it is not to be endured that they shall work injustice in any particular case, and must be moulded in furtherance of . . . equitable objects . . . . (J. Frank, *Law and the Modern Mind* (Gloucester, Mass: Peter Smith, 1970), p. 180.)

Llewellyn, on the other hand, saw judicial decisions as containing guides for the community and advocated that judges more openly decide cases on the basis of what is best for the community rather than for the individual. Community justice would best be achieved if judges adopt the grand style and so become more open about their use of policy.

11.3 THE IMPACT OF REALISM

Realism as a movement in jurisprudence passed its peak in the 1960s, and though its effects are still felt particularly in academic law, its momentum has ceased. It has helped to influence three new movements in jurisprudence, two of which, jurimetrics and behaviouralism, have had as yet a limited impact, whilst the third, the critical legal studies movement, has developed to the extent that it can be considered to be the alternative approach to positivism and formalism. Critical legal studies will be examined in chapter 12. It is pertinent here just to outline the other two movements.

11.3.1 Jurimetrics

The idea that scientific techniques for analysis of data could be used in the legal process was introduced, as was the term 'jurimetrics', by Loevinger in 1949:

> The next step forward in the long path of man's progress must be from jurisprudence (which is mere speculation about law) to *jurimetrics* – which is the scientific investigation of legal problems. In the field of social control (which is law) we must at least begin to use the same approach and the same methods that have enabled us to progress toward greater knowledge and control in every other field. The greatest problem facing mankind at this midpoint of the 20th century is the inadequacy of socio-legal methods inherited from primitive ancestors to control a society which, in all other aspects is based upon the powerful techniques of a sophisticated science. The inescapable fact is that jurisprudence bears the same relation to a

modern science of jurimetrics as astrology does to astronomy, alchemy to chemistry, or phrenology to psychology. It is based upon speculation, supposition and superstition; it is concerned with meaningless questions; and after more than two thousand years, jurisprudence has not yet offered a useful answer to any question or a workable technique for attacking any problem. (L. Loevinger, 'Jurimetrics – the next step forward' (1949) 33 Minn L Rev 455 at p. 484.)

In its more modern form jurimetrics not only involves the proposition that computers should be used increasingly to store in accessible formats legal information such as case reports and statutes – something which is now taking place in legal data storage and retrieval systems such as LEXIS – but also advocates the use of computer programs to undertake empirical analyses of judicial decisions in order to ascertain patterns of consistency and regularity, in order to help with the prediction of decisions (see, for example, F. Kort, 'Quantitative analysis of fact patterns in cases and their impact on judicial decision' (1965–6) 79 Harv L Rev 1595).

It can be seen how this aspect of jurimetrics has its origins in the realists' desire to improve the prediction of judicial-decision making. However, it must be pointed out that the use of computers can only improve the efficiency of the techniques already identified by realists such as Oliphant and Moore. Computers are tools that have the ability to make a modern-day realist's life easier but they still depend on the skill or 'craft', to use Llewellyn's terminology, of the interpreter of legal cases. The programmer must decide on the significance of the *ratio* of the case as compared to the extra-legal factors which may influence a judge's decision, as well as deciding at what level the facts are to be abstracted. The subjective element in legal interpretation is not removed from the process though it can be reduced by using a computer program.

Similar problems seem more obviously to undermine the more extreme members of the jurimetrics movement, who suggest that computers will eventually replace the judge and jury by providing a fairer and more uniform legal system (see R. Lawlor, '*Stare decisis* and electronic computers', in G. Schubert (ed.), *Judicial Behavior: A Reader in Theory and Research* (Chicago, Ill: Rand McNally, 1964), pp. 503–5). It may indeed be argued that a computer program would iron out the caprices of the jury and judge, which are manifold if Frank is to be believed, but it would be impossible to iron out the prejudices of the programmer. If somehow, in the future, a 'thinking' computer, as opposed to a very efficient mechanical device, was invented which actually established its own set of values to be used in interpreting the law, or indeed created a consistent set of laws itself, then it would be possible to state that trial by computer was possible, although given the science-fiction nightmare painted by Orwell and Huxley, there appears to be no overwhelming reason why humans should make themselves subservient to a machine and to those few people who understood it. One of the leading exponents of extreme jurimetrics conceded in 1957 that the approach could not effectively incorporate and control the subjective elements in the law. He predicted that one day scientific prediction by supercomputer would be able to encapsulate those elements to produce a system that would potentially replace the judge and jury at the very least (F. K. Beutel, *Some Potentialities of Experimental Jurisprudence as a New Branch of Science* (Lincoln, Nebr: University of Nebraska Press, 1957), p. 51).

11.3.2 Judicial behaviouralism

Behaviouralists share with the realists and the members of the jurimetrics movement the desire to improve the predictability of judicial decision-making. Unlike the realists, the behaviouralists attempt to identify and isolate the extra-legal factors that influence a court's decision by applying methods used in other social sciences, by, for instance, analysing the psychology of a small group such as the Appeal Court judges or the members of the House of Lords. The behaviouralists differ from the members of the jurimetrics group in that they do not put the computer at the centre of their scientific method, but will use a variety of empirical methods for ascertaining the 'attitudes' of judges, by looking at their backgrounds, their public statements outside the courtroom, their judicial opinions, and by asking them in interview or by questionnaire.

Being primarily social scientists or political scientists, the behaviouralists appear to believe that judges are nothing more than policy-makers and that precedent and legal rules have little relevance to the discovery of the true uniformity in judicial decision-making. Glendon Schubert, a leading exponent of behaviouralism, states:

> Social psychology, with its focus upon the attitudes of individual decision-makers, is most proximate to the empirical behaviours of judicial voting and opinion writing. One can understand and explain . . . everything about judicial decision-making on the basis of attitudinal similarities and differences of the individuals in the decision-making group. Of course, this requires a very comprehensive analysis of individual attitudes, including both attitudes toward the issues of public policy that individuals are asked to resolve and their attitudes toward each other, and toward all other participants in the decision-making process. Both legal norms and legal facts are viewed as functions of attitudes toward the public policy issues in a case.

Once the attitudes of judges are established along these lines it is possible to produce a predictive model because 'judges are expected to behave consistently with their beliefs, and the decision of the court is a linear function of the decisions of the individual members'. Schubert then suggests the factors that lead to differences in judicial attitudes. Their different 'life experiences', a product of 'political, religious, and ethnic affiliations; his wife; his economic security and his social status; the kind of education he has received. . . . His affiliations . . . will in turn be largely influenced by where he was born, and to whom, and when' (G. Schubert, *Mathematical Prediction of Judicial Behavior* (1964), pp. 445–8, extracted in *Lloyd's Introduction to Jurisprudence*, 5th ed. (London: Sweet & Maxwell, 1985), pp. 787–91).

From this very brief summary of the approach of one of the behaviouralists, it can be seen that the method develops themes found in realism, but its aim is to be more precise and less philosophical about the discovery of those extra-legal factors which the realists first identified as influencing judicial decision-making. For the behaviouralist such as Schubert, however, it is not a question of simple influence on judicial decision-making. For them the only reason for judges reaching a particular decision is to be found in their attitudes which in turn are to be found in their beliefs. A behaviouralist needs only to discover these attitudes in order to explain the mystery of the law. Clearly a formalist or indeed any lawyer who believes that there is such a thing as rational and logical legal reasoning, no matter how imperfect, would object to this type of approach. Furthermore there does seem to be a flaw in the method of the behaviouralists such as Schubert, in that it adopts 'an over-mechanical concept of causation: a judge may be a Catholic of Irish ancestry and may have consistently decided labour disputes in favour of trade unions, but neither Schubert nor any other behaviouralist has shown that he so decided *because* of his religion or his ethnic origin' (*Lloyd's Introduction to Jurisprudence*, 5th ed. (London: Sweet & Maxwell, 1985), p. 707).

11.4 FURTHER READING

Fisher, W. W., Horowitz, M. J. and Reed T. A., *American Legal Realism* (Oxford: Oxford University Press, 1993).
Gilmore, G., 'Legal realism: its cause and cure' (1961) 70 Yale LJ 1037.
McDougall, M. S., 'Fuller versus the American realists: an intervention' (1941) 50 Yale LJ 827.
Pound, R., 'Mechanical jurisprudence' (1908) 8 Colum L Rev 605.
Pound, R., 'The call for a realist jurisprudence' (1931) 44 Harv L Rev 697.
Rumble, W. E., *American Legal Realism: Skepticism, Reform and the Judicial Process* (New York: Cornell University Press, 1968).
Schlegel J. H., 'American legal realism and empirical social science: from the Yale experience' (1979) 29 Buffalo L Rev 459.
Twining, W., *Karl Llewellyn and the Realist Movement* (London: Weidenfeld & Nicolson, 1973).
White, G. E., *Patterns of American Legal Thought* (Indianapolis, Ind: Bobbs-Merrill, 1978).

CHAPTER TWELVE
Critical Legal Studies

The critical legal studies movement, which initially emerged in the United States in the 1970s in part as a successor to the American realist movement, is essentially offering a radical alternative to established legal theories. It puts forward the proposition that all other legal theories are fundamentally flawed in their belief that sense and order can be discerned from a *reasoned* analysis of law and the legal system:

> While traditional jurisprudence claims to be able to reveal through pure reason a picture of an unchanging and universal unity beneath the manifest changeability and historical variability of laws, legal institutions and practices, and thus to establish a foundation in reason for actual legal systems, critical legal theory not only denies the possibility of discovering a universal foundation for law through pure reason, but sees the whole enterprise of jurisprudence . . . as operating to confer a spurious legitimacy on law and legal systems. (A. Thomson, 'Critical approaches to law: who needs legal theory?', in I. Grigg-Spall, and P. Ireland, *The Critical Lawyers' Handbook* (London: Pluto Press, 1992), p. 2.)

The main thrust of their attack is against liberal legal theories, in which they group together as one target most of the other theories identified in this book, although their principal targets are the theories of positivism presented by Kelsen and Hart, in addition to the rights-based theories such as those put forward by Dworkin, Rawls and Finnis. The analysis below will show that the critical legal scholars characterise liberal legal thought as an ideology whose surface character hides its true nature. Furthermore, for the critical legal scholars, liberal legal theory claims to be a politically neutral and objective way to resolve conflicts. The critical legal scholars deny this and state that liberal legal thought is a conflict-ridden structure beneath its purportedly objective exterior, an exterior which also conceals the political judgments and power structures within the law.

The critical legal scholars go far beyond American realism, although they are often seen as the inheritors of the sceptical approach. While the realists rejected formalism they still saw legal reasoning as distinct. Indeed, the realists were committed to liberalism. They did not directly attempt to undermine the liberal ideal of the rule of law, and in many ways, particularly in the later writings of Llewellyn, they were trying to improve the legal system by bringing it more in line with modern social conditions. Indeed, it could be said that the urging of judges and jurists to reject formalism in favour of a realistic approach to jurisprudence was an attempt in many ways to bring law more into line with the power structures and commercial environment of the day. The critical scholars share, and indeed take further a profound scepticism of law in books, but they reject any attempt, whether realist or formalist, to present a value-free model of the law (see further J. A. Standen, 'Critical legal studies as an anti-positivist phenomenon' (1986) 79 Va L Rev 983).

In many respects, it will be seen that the major themes of the critical legal studies movement are similar to those ideas developed by the Marxists, particularly modern Marxist writers such as Gramsci and Collins (see chapter 7). Critical legal scholars appear to reject the theory of instrumentalism and the argument that law is simply a part of the superstructure of society. Indeed, they see the operations of law as being *essential* for the continuation of liberal society:

> . . . law cannot be usefully understood as . . . 'superstructural'. Legal rules the State enforces and legal concepts that permeate all aspects of social thought constitute capitalism as well as responding to the interests that operate within it. Law is an aspect of the social totality, not just the tail of the dog. (D. Kennedy, 'Legal education as training for hierarchy' in D. Kairys (ed.), *The Politics of Law. A Progressive Critique*, rev. ed. (New York: Pantheon Books, 1990), pp. 38–58 at p. 47.)

Nevertheless, this does not completely distinguish the critical legal scholars from the modern-day Marxists whose sophisticated analysis in terms of competing ideologies often appears a long way from the simple instrumentalist view of Marxism. Perhaps the more telling distinction is that critical legal studies forms part of the post-structuralist (post-modernist) phenomenon which is pervading many areas of thought, not just simply legal philosophy, whereas Marxism is essentially structuralist in its content (see further chapter 13). Whether a simple instrumentalist view is taken or whether a more sophisticated link is perceived between base and superstructure as is found in modern versions, Marxism is still a structured theory as Thomson points out:

> Politically inspired largely by the perceived failure of Marxist socialism to deliver its promise of a society that overcomes exploitation, the last two decades have witnessed a growing doubt about the Marxist project and a growing feeling that it is infected with the same weakness as the liberal capitalist system it opposes, and of which, as the counter-culture, it is arguably a part. That weakness is seen by many as the continuing faith, shared with its liberal protagonist, in the capacity of reason to realise progress. Thus many argue that domination and exploitation are not the monopoly of any one theory, but are characteristic of all theories, especially those, such as Marxism, which make claims to truth on a grand scale. (A. Thomson, 'Critical approaches to law' in I. Grigg-Spall and P. Ireland, *The Critical Lawyers' Handbook* (London: Pluto Press, 1992), p. 6.)

The overall aim of critical theory is to destroy the notion that there is one single 'truth', and that by disclosing the all-pervasive power structures and hierarchies in the law and legal system, a multitude of other possibilities will be revealed, all equally valid. Herein lies the problem for the critical legal scholars, for while they may be able to deconstruct the 'truth' of liberal legalism, they cannot, within the terms of their own methodology, put forward *the* alternative, only *an* alterative. One such alternative, indeed the only complete one, is offered by Unger's vision of a super-liberal society which will be discussed below.

To start with, however, a review of the fundamental tenets of the critical legal scholars' attack on the liberal legal tradition will be undertaken.

12.1 THE CRITIQUE OF THE LIBERAL LEGAL TRADITION

As with American realism, the critical legal scholars form part of a movement in jurisprudence, rather than offering a unified theory. The unifying feature of the realists was their attack on formalist modes of reasoning. This is indeed one of the features of the critical legal studies movement and is one that links them to early realism tradition, but it is not the common bond that unites it. Rather, the uniting feature is a profound disenchantment with liberal legalism as a whole. This encompasses not only a fundamental disbelief that the law has objective content and is neutral in its operation, but also a belief that the liberal legal tradition has used this portrayal of the legal system to mask the fundamental contradictions inherent in the law. The law is portrayed as rational, coherent, necessary and just by liberal legal scholarship, when in fact, according to the critical legal scholars, it is arbitrary, contingent, unnecessary and profoundly unjust. This constitutes a direct attack on the ideal found embedded in Western legal and political thought, the rule of law.

Furthermore, critical legal studies is an attack on Western liberal concepts of basic civil and political rights which purportedly guarantee, in a legal sense, the individual's freedom of speech, assembly, religion, and in a political sense liberal democracies are based on the concept of the freedom of the individual. These rights and freedoms are portrayed in the Western tradition as being the only true way to self-realisation and freedom of the individual. The critical legal scholars' aim is to show that these rights and freedoms, although put forward as essential to an individual's fulfilment, actually serve the political and economic requirements of liberalism. For instance, the concept of freedom of contract, though not a civil and political right in the recognised sense, is not a liberating concept but one that ties individuals to the market-place and serves the basic aims of capitalism. Contract law along with all other bodies of law in a liberal society serves political ends. Indeed, for the critical scholars they are simply politics in disguise. Why then do people accept the liberal traditions of the law?

> People do not hold to theories of the kinds I have been criticising [liberal legal theories] simply because they serve conservative ends. At least some people believe in them because they think they're true, even though it seems to them too bad that they are true. . . . For a lot of people, legitimating theories, theories that show the rationality, necessity, and (often) efficiency of things as they are, serve as a kind of defence mechanism. These theories are a way of denying, of avoiding, of closing one's eyes to the horribleness of things as they are. (D. Kennedy, 'Cost-reduction theory as legitimation' (1981) 90 Yale LJ 1275 at p. 1283.)

More will be said on this point as the specific themes of the critical legal studies movement are analysed. However, at this point it is worth noting the similarities between Kennedy's idea that people accept liberal philosophy because they think it's true, and the Marxist idea of false consciousness when the victims of capitalism embrace the ideology that is responsible for their situation. To put it in its wider context, the Western media, politicians and the Establishment in general consistently put forward as a statement of the truth that Western liberal democracy is the only natural form of society and that the freedom of the market-place is as fundamental to society as the political freedoms found in the West. This ideology has been reinforced by the defeat of communism with the West's victory in the Cold War. It is inevitable that many individuals in Western societies will believe this to be true and, given the routine of their daily lives, will not be susceptible to fundamental change or be able to perceive the fact that they are being exploited let alone be able to accept an alternative approach.

It is informative to look now at the specific criticisms that the critical legal studies movement has of liberal legalism.

12.1.1 An attack on formalism

This prong of the critical legal scholars' attack is derived from the realists' disbelief that formal rules provide an answer to a dispute. However, whereas the realists concentrated their critique of formalism on this aspect and were particularly concerned to try to find the real rules operated by the judge and jury, the critical legal scholars seem to take this element as read. They add little to the realist critique in this area apart from a few generalities. Indeed, such is the lack of detail in this area that the following criticism of the critical scholars' approach to formalism appears justified. It appears from their attack that formalism is:

> . . . the CLS [critical legal studies] caricature of the notion that law is a deductive and autonomous science that is self-contained in the sense that particular decisions follow from the application of legal principles, precedents, and rules of procedure without regard to values, social goals, or political or economic context. (L. Schwartz, 'With gun and camera through darkest CLS-land' (1984) 36 Stanf L Rev 413 at p. 431.)

As the remainder of this book reveals, traditional and modern mainstream legal theory does not simply put forward a simplistic scientific approach to the law. Theorists such as Hart, Dworkin and Finnis all recognised that law is a much more complex machine. Hart and Dworkin recognise the fact that policy in the form of social values and goals plays a role in the legal system, though they differed over whether the judge should be instrumental in its application (see chapters 3 and 9). Finnis's central thesis is more concerned with the issue of the role of morality in the definition and application of law (see chapter 5), and indeed both Hart and Dworkin also attempt to deal with the issue of morality. It appears that the critical legal scholars are too quick to condemn mainstream theory by lumping the diversity of views together as formalism (but see specific critique of theory, for example, C. Douzinas and R. Warrington, 'On the deconstruction of jurisprudence: fin(n)is philosophiae', and A. Bottomley, S. Gibson and B. Meteyard, 'Dworkin; which Dworkin? Taking feminism seriously', in P. Fitzpatrick and A. Hunt, *Critical Legal Studies* (Oxford: Basil Blackwell, 1987), p. 33 and p. 47).

Indeed, formalism in its strict black-letter sense is not to be found in legal theory, only in some law teaching and academic writing and in legal practice. It seems that the critical scholars' agenda stretches both to theory and practice, with the aim of enlightening practising lawyers as to the 'wider implications and consequences of certain courses of action, and in particular [to] reveal that unless legal actions are seen in the context of larger political action, they may well be counter-productive, at least in the long term' (A. Thomson, 'Critical approaches to law – who needs legal theory?', in

I. Grigg-Spall and P. Ireland, *The Critical Lawyers' Handbook*, (London: Pluto Press, 1992), p. 8).

However, the lack of a detailed critique of formalism may be due to the fact that the thrust of the critical lawyers' attack is on the wider issue of whether there is in fact a distinct mode of legal reasoning. If they successfully demonstrate that there is no separate mode of legal reasoning at all then it is unnecessary for them to have to deal directly with formal legal reasoning as such. Roberto Unger, one of the leading exponents of critical legal studies, indicates that this is the real point of the movement's critique of formalism.

> By formalism I do not mean what the term is usually taken to describe: belief in the availability of a deductive or quasi-deductive method capable of giving determinate solutions to particular problems of legal choice. What I mean by formalism in this context is a commitment to, and therefore also a belief in the possibility of, a method of legal justification that can clearly be contrasted to open-ended disputes about the basic terms of social life, disputes that people call ideological, philosophical, or visionary. (R. Unger, 'The critical legal studies movement' (1983) 96 Harv L Rev 563 at p. 564.)

It can be seen from this how wide and potentially destructive to established legal traditions the critical legal studies movement is. In effect it is a criticism of the positivists' idea, exemplified perhaps by Kelsen's pure theory (see chapter 8), that it is possible to separate law from other areas and that legal reasoning and exposition are essentially apolitical. From this it is clear that the aim of the movement's attack on formalism is to 'demonstrate that a doctrinal practice that puts its hope in the contrast of legal reasoning to ideology, philosophy, and political prophecy ends up as a collection of makeshift apologies' (R. Unger, 'The critical legal studies movement' (1983) 96 Harv L Rev 563 at p. 573). It is to this attack that the analysis now turns.

12.1.2   Critique of legal reasoning

The rejection of legal reasoning has already been outlined above, and it was seen that the problem for the critical legal scholars was that while they reject all the theories and practices which are dependent on the autonomy of law and legal reasoning, they do not subscribe to the equally structuralist approach of the Marxists, who, while denying the existence of legal reasoning, tend to adopt a deterministic position which presents law as simply a reflection of economic forces. The critical scholars address the problem by concentrating, as the American realists did, on the existence of external factors that operate on the judge. However, whereas the realists did recognise that legal reasoning and rules played a part, albeit a minor one, in the judge's decision, the critical legal scholars are of the opinion that these external factors are the sole operative factor in the judgment. The explanation is not put in Marxian terms of the laws simply reflecting the economic relations within society but instead is expressed in terms of judicial values and choices of a *political* nature (Hunt calls this the problem of 'relative autonomy': A. Hunt, 'The theory of critical legal studies' (1986) 6 Oxford J Legal Stud 1 at pp. 28–9).

A problem with the critical legal studies approach to legal reasoning is that, like its critique of formalism, it appears to lack any detail or precision. The following is an analysis of Kairys's examination of legal reasoning (D. Kairys, 'Legal reasoning', in D. Kairys (ed.), *The Politics of Law. A Progressive Critique* New York: Pantheon Books, 1982), pp. 11–17). Kairys concentrates on 'one of the basic elements or mechanisms of legal reasoning, *stare decisis*', the notion that judges are bound by precedent, an obligation which, according to the traditional approach, leads to the judge acting on the legal, not the political, plane. Kairys then reiterates the realists' view that:

> . . . anyone familiar with the legal system knows that some precedents are followed and some are not. . . . The important questions, largely ignored by judges, law teachers, and commentators, are: How do courts decide which precedents to follow? How do they determine the significance of ambiguous precedents? Do precedents really matter at all? Why do lawyers spend so much time talking about them?

So far Kairys's analysis does not differ from any of the early realists and indeed, if anything, seems more simplistic. He then provides a thumbnail sketch of a handful of American cases on freedom of speech which at the level of abstraction presented do appear contradictory. He then concludes his case analysis by saying:

> Unstated and lost in the mire of contradictory precedents and justifications was the central point that none of these cases was or could be decided without ultimate reference to values and choices of a *political* nature. The various justifications and precedents emphasised in the opinions serve to mask these little-discussed but unavoidable social and political judgments.
> . . .
> In short, these cases demonstrate a central deception of traditional jurisprudence: the majority claims for its social and political judgment not only the status of law . . . but also that its judgment is the product of distinctly legal reasoning, of a neutral, objective application of legal expertise. This latter claim, essential to the legitimacy and mystique of the courts, is false.

There is little attempt to assess these external factors accurately, except that they are 'a composite of social, political, institutional, experiential, and personal factors'. So far there is no difference between Kairys's critique and the realists' approach, except perhaps for a greater attempt to ascertain the exact nature of the external factors that lead to judicial decisions on the part of the realists. For the critical lawyers, however, there is no need for this because the answer is obvious and in no need of testing. Judges share social and political assumptions, in other words they share an ideology which, because of their background, leads them to make consistent decisions that reinforce the liberal order in which they operate and depend on for their livelihoods. This then distinguishes the realist from the critical lawyer.

12.1.3   Contradictions in the law

It is the critical lawyers' view that liberal legalism represents the *status quo* in society and that it seeks to mask the injustice of the system. They attempt to seek out the conflict-ridden substance that is hidden beneath that apparently smooth surface.

The descriptive portrait of mainstream liberal thought . . . is a picture of a system of thought that is simultaneously beset by internal *contradiction* (not by 'competing concerns' artfully balanced until a wise equilibrium is reached, but by irreducible, irremediable, irresolvable conflict) and by systematic *repression* of the presence of these contradictions. (M. Kelman, *A Guide to Critical Legal Studies* (Cambridge, Mass: Harvard University Press, 1987), p. 3.)

Kelman proceeds to identify the central contradictions in liberal thought that have been identified by the critical lawyers.
First Kelman identifies:

. . . the contradiction between a commitment to mechanically applicable rules as the appropriate form for resolving disputes (thought to be associated in complex ways with the political tradition of self-reliance and individualism) and a commitment to situation-sensitive, *ad hoc* standards (thought to correspond to a commitment to sharing and altruism) (*A Guide to Critical Legal Studies*, p. 3.)

The contradiction between rules and standards is one that Kelman identifies with the writings of Duncan Kennedy. Kennedy contrasts the individualism present in the dominant liberal legal thinking, in the form of the application of rigid and precise rules, with the notion of altruism or collectivism:

Altruism denies the judge the right to apply rules without looking over his shoulder at the results. Altruism also denies that the only alternative to the passive stance is the claim of total discretion as creator of the legal universe.

It asserts that we can gain an understanding of the values people have woven into their particular relationships, and of the moral tendency of their acts. These sometimes permit the judge to reach a decision, after the fact, on the basis of all the circumstances, as a person-in-society rather than as an individual. (D. Kennedy, 'Form and substance in private law adjudication' (1976) 89 Harv L Rev 1685 at p. 1773.)

There are some aspects of this approach which hark back to Jerome Frank's idea that justice should be done in each case because there is insufficient certainty and objectivity in the legal process on which to build a sustainable doctrine of precedent (see chapter 11). However, Kennedy is going further than this. The fundamental contradiction between individualism and altruism is a problem not only for a judge but is symptomatic of society in general. 'The fundamental contradiction – that relations with others are both necessary to and incompatible with our freedom . . . is not only an aspect but the very essence of the problem' (D. Kennedy, 'The structure of Blackstone's Commentaries' (1979) 28 Buffalo L Rev 205 at p. 213). In the law this fundamental contradiction can be seen in the competing and contrasting legal terminology found present, for example, in the debate between subjectivity and objectivity in such diverse areas as criminal law and international law (see further M. Tushnet, 'Legal scholarship: its causes and cures' (1981) 90 Yale LJ 1205). More specifically in the law of contract, for example, there is a clear dichotomy between those concepts which favour individualism, for example, freedom of contract which may result in a defenceless individual being taken advantage of by a more powerful individual or company, and those concepts which favour altruism, such as duress and undue influence. Within the capitalist legal order with its liberal philosophy, contract law is dominated by the former.

The second contradiction Kelman identifies in the critical lawyers' critique of liberalism is:

> . . . the contradiction between a commitment to the traditional liberal notion that values or desires are arbitrary, subjective, individual, and individuating while facts or reason are objective and universal *and* a commitment to the ideal that we can 'know' social and ethical truths objectively (through objective knowledge of true human nature) or to the hope that one can transcend the usual distinction between subjective and objective in seeking moral truth. (*A Guide to Critical Legal Studies*, p. 3. Kelman identifies a third contradiction between intentionalism and determinism, see *A Guide to Critical Legal Studies*, pp. 86–113.)

The second contradiction is pointed at one of the central tenants of positivism – the separation of law from value judgments. Nevertheless, as with the first contradiction between individualism and altruism, this aspect goes further than simply a critique of writers such as Kelsen. The main thrust is that both everyday culture and the liberal theory that supports and legitimates it downgrade values and beliefs to the extent that they are simply seen as matters of taste, peculiar to the individual, whereas reasoned analysis of facts and laws yields universal maxims which can guide any individual's behaviour.

The aim of the critical scholars is to show that these contradictions are to be found in all legal concepts and rules, even in so-called clear cases where the contradiction has simply been successfully repressed over a period of time. The assumption behind this is that within each contradiction one set of values is paramount in liberal legal theory, namely individualism over altruism and objectivism over subjectivism.

12.1.4   Deconstruction: trashing, delegitimation and dereification

These are the various techniques the critical lawyers use to reveal the underlying contradictions in the law and the deep-rooted hierarchies of power that are also hidden beneath the neutral exterior of the law. The political motivations behind these techniques must be understood for they too tend to be obscured in the dense, often incomprehensible, language of the critical lawyer. These motivations are made clear in the following extract:

> There is little systematic work on law and power despite the fact that a defining feature of law is that it operates to facilitate exploitation and discrimination. . . . We therefore need to explain how this concept of 'law' is used to justify the political order of modern society. . . . The pervasiveness of law in modern society means that law must be challenged from within by means of what we call legal insurgency. It is not enough to be critical of law and its underlying political structures; we need to move beyond mere criticism to critique and thereby expose the contradictions underpinning the principles, policies and doctrines of bourgeois law. The material effects of law and the ideological bases upon which it is manufactured must be analysed and deconstructed in order to comprehend the power of modern legal discourse as a dominant intellectual paradigm. (S. Adelman and K. Foster 'Critical legal theory: the power of law', in I. Grigg-Spall and P. Ireland (eds), *The Critical Lawyers' Handbook* (London: Pluto Press, 1992), p. 39.)

Deconstruction of law and legal language takes three main forms. 'Trashing' is essentially aimed at revealing the illegitimate hierarchies (power structures) that exist within the law and society in general. The task of the critical lawyers is to reveal those hierarchies and undermine them. The hierarchy of power is not the simple one envisaged by Marxists, who see it in terms of classes, but is much more complex and found at every level, including universities where there is a power relationship between lecturer and student (see A. Freeman, 'Truth and mystification in legal scholarship' (1981) 90 Yale LJ 1229).

Indeed, trashing or debunking the traditional methods of teaching law is an important element in critical legal studies and has led to some universities in the United States and the United Kingdom actively pursuing a critical agenda. The following extract from Kelman explains the purpose of trashing or debunking:

> We are also engaged in an *active*, transformative anarcho-syndicalist political project. . . . At the *workplace* level, debunking is one part of an explicit effort to level, to reintegrate the communities we live in along explicitly egalitarian lines rather than along the rationalised hierarchical lines that currently integrate them. We are saying: Here's what your teacher did (at you, to you) in contracts or torts. Here's what it was really about. Stripped of the mumbo-jumbo, here's a set of problems we *all* face, as equals in dealing with work, with politics, and with the world. (M. G. Kelman, 'Trashing' (1984) 36 Stanf L Rev 293 at p. 326.)

'Delegitimation' appears from the writings of the critical scholars to be a slightly different aspect of the deconstruction process. It is aimed at exposing what the scholars see as one of the most important functions of law in a liberal society, namely the legitimation of the socio-economic system of that society. To delegitimate law the scholars attempt to strip away the veneer of legitimacy to reveal the ideological underpinnings of the legal system. To many scholars the legitimacy conferred on the social system by the law is vitally important to the continuance of that system with all its unfairness and exploitation:

> The law's perceived legitimacy confers a broader legitimacy on a social system and ideology that . . . are most fairly characterised by domination by a very small, mainly corporatised elite. This perceived legitimacy of the law is primarily based on notions of technical expertise and objectivity and the idealised model of the legal process. . . . But it is also greatly enhanced by the reality that the law is, on some occasions just and sometimes serves to restrain the exercise of power. (D. Kairys, 'Introduction', in D. Kairys, (ed.), *The Politics of Law. A Progressive Critique*, rev. ed. (New York: Pantheon Books, 1990), p. 7.)

Generally speaking the law serves to mask exploitation by using the imagery of fairness, equality and justice. The summary of the critical approach to contract law given below (see 12.2.1) will illustrate this.

Finally an aspect of the deconstruction process which is firmly linked to trashing and delegitimation is 'dereification'. For critical scholars like Gabel, the law is characterised by reification, which involves a gradual process whereby abstractions, originally tied to concrete situations, are then themselves used, and operate, instead of the concrete situations. Simply put, the abstraction or concept takes on the form of a thing (P. Gabel, 'Reification in legal reasoning' (1980) 3 Research in Law and Sociology 1 at p. 2). This process can be seen in the law, which over the centuries of its development gradually becomes divorced from the actual human relations it is attempting to regulate. The process is not obvious but is clouded in legal mystification so that people both within the law, and outside the law but subject to it, mistake the abstraction for the concrete. Concepts like mortgages, consideration, trusts, wills, take on a life of their own and become totally divorced from their original conception. In so doing the purpose behind the concept becomes disguised. In the case of the legal terms listed, the purpose behind these was the facilitation of monetary exchange in a society built on the control and movement of capital. 'Legal reification is more than just distortion: it is also a form of coercion in the guise of passive acceptance of the existing world within the framework of capitalism' (J. S. Russell, 'The critical legal studies challenge to contemporary mainstream legal philosophy' (1986) 18 Ottawa L Rev 1 at p. 19). Dereification is simply the recognition and exposure of such fallacies, to reveal the law as it really is.

12.1.5 The constitutive theory of law

This final trend in the critical legal studies movement is not only part of its critique of the liberal legal tradition, but is also part of the movement's attempt to escape from the Marxist shackles of determinism.

> . . . law is not simply an armed receptacle for values and priorities determined elsewhere; it is part of a complex social totality in which it constitutes as well as is constituted, shapes as well as is shaped. (D. Kairys, 'Introduction', in D. Kairys (ed.), *The Politics of Law. A Progressive Critique*, rev. ed. (New York: Pantheon Books, 1990), p. 6.)

The idea that law plays an important role in shaping society is part of the wider post-modernist perspective that ideas, and not the economic base, constitute (form or make up) society. It follows from this that if there is to be some sort of order in society, there must be a convergence of ideas including ideas and beliefs about law, in other words a 'shared world-view'. The critical legal scholars' critique is therefore directed at 'the analysis of world-views embedded in modern legal consciousness'. The aim is to attack the shared world-view embedded in legal consciousness, to reveal its link to domination in capitalist legal societies, and to change that consciousness. This is not an easy task because the constitutive power of the dominant shared world-view in society is grounded in that world-view's claim to be the truth, and since 'every world-view is hostage to its claim to be true, its constitutive force can be undermined [only] if this claim can be refuted' (D. Trubek, 'Where the action is: critical legal studies and empiricism' (1984) 36 Stanf L Rev 575 at p. 592). The shared world-view that the liberal order is the only true and natural system can be refuted if it is shown that there is any number of alternative ways which would not result in exploitation and injustice. One suggestion of an alternative way is contained in the writings of Roberto Unger reviewed below. First, however, a more specific example of CLS work will be examined.

12.2 A SPECIFIC EXAMPLE OF THE CRITICAL APPROACH

So far in this chapter there has been an exposition of the general themes of the critical legal studies movement. In this section, the critical scholars' approach to individual legal subjects will be analysed by relating their analysis of the law of contract. As well as deconstructing contract law, it will be seen that the critical scholars advocate a new critical method of teaching the subject. This is part of the critical scholars' wider analysis of legal education as a whole which is beyond the purview of this chapter (see generally A. Thomson, 'Critical legal education in Britain' (1987) 14 J Law & Soc 183; D. Kennedy, 'Legal education as training for hierarchy' in D. Kairys (ed.), *The Politics of Law. A Progressive Critique*, rev. ed. (New York: Pantheon Books, 1990), p. 38).

12.2.1 The critical approach to contract

Contract has been chosen to illustrate the critical approach to a specific legal subject area not only for the reason that all students of law have been subjected to contract in one form or another but also because of the related reason that the critical writings in contract law are well-developed since the subject is seen as central to the liberal legal edifice. Most other areas of law receive a similar, though sometimes less convincing, treatment, and the reader should sample these in an area interest (good collections are to be found in D. Kairys (ed.), *The Politics of Law. A Progressive Critique*, rev. ed. (New York: Pantheon Books, 1990); and I. Grigg-Spall and P. Ireland (eds), *The Critical Lawyers' Handbook* (London: Pluto Press, 1992)).

Alan Thomson provides a useful introduction to the critical approach to contract law, particularly the teaching and exposition of the subject (A. Thomson, 'The law of contract' in I. Grigg-Spall and P. Ireland (eds), *The Critical Lawyers' Handbook* (London: Pluto Press, 1992), pp. 69–76). He starts by examining the assumptions behind the traditional approach to contract law found in many textbooks and many courses. These usually start by making students aware of how many contracts they had made that day, suggesting that the course will not only be practical but help to explain a central aspect of the social order:

> Yet what follows in courses based on the standard textbooks dramatically fails to fulfil . . . these expectations. Although in the student imagination the law of contract tends to become the lasting model and the measure of 'real' law, its practical relevance is extremely limited, and as for going to the heart of the social order, this is denied from the moment in those first examples when it is assumed that contract is the 'natural' form of social relations, and the only issue becomes how they are to be regulated.

> Contract introduces students into the lore and mystery of the law so that they accept from the outset that proper law does not have a social or political dimension.

> Like the reality constructed in our primary socialisation as children, the reality of law which the law of contract first constructs tends to retain for ever its massive power over us.

> The whole of the traditional contract course excludes any element which might undermine the concept of the rules as being not only neutral but natural for any social order, not just the liberal legal order. This is done in a variety of ways, for example, by attempting to construct a seamless web of precedents all logically bound together. The difficulty of applying this to practical examples of contractual situations is avoided by applying the principles to purified sets of facts which are either the hypothetical fact situations found on tutorial sheets or in exams or are the simplified set of facts to be found in leading textbooks.

> Questions of social and distributive justice, which relate to consequences and which threaten the orderly world of rules and principles, are simply outlawed from the toytown world of the contract class. . . .
>
> In this way the liberal individualist conception of injustice (which restricts justice to general rules of just conduct and ignores the fact that different people and different groups have different access to the resources of wealth, education and power), remains unchallenged as the silent underpinning of the law of contract. Just rules are conveniently conflicted with a just world. Indeed one of the features of the law of contract which appeals to students is that since it is comprehensible without any knowledge of the real world, a simple idea of justice as the-same-rules-all suffices.

It is important to recognise that this apparent comprehensibility is only possible if one excludes from sight the unequal world to which the law of contract applies.

This neutral and natural approach to contract downplays the importance of such features as undue influence, duress and unfair contract terms, which if fully understood and put in a central position in the contract curriculum would undermine the edifice by revealing contract to be an instrument of power. If this truth is revealed then it will be seen 'how contract merely serves to provide a cloak of legitimacy to the underlying structural inequalities of power in society, such as those of class, gender and race'.

Contract law thus serves the ideological function of reinforcing the conception that law is neutral, self-contained, that it cannot be challenged and that it is the product of reasoned analysis. In addition it projects an image of the law that teaches students and purveyors of the traditional approach three lessons:

The law of contract creates a master-image of the well-ordered society; a society in which law appears as the 'haven of justice', divorced from the dirtiness of business, politics, power and the conflict of interests and values; a society which rises above the uncertainties and incoherences of political and moral argument. This is the first and most general lesson which the law of contract teaches. However, it teaches two more particular ideological lessons.

First, it serves to make the contingent fact of capitalism, the appearance of social relations as market-exchange relations, look like the necessary facts of life, by concealing that the conceptualisation of social relations as contractual is not outside history but *has* a history. Secondly by creating the appearance that, through the law of contract, such relations are, or can be made, subject to universal principles of common-sense and justice, it serves to put the justice of the market-based social order beyond question.

Once the student has almost inevitably accepted the legitimacy of these lessons, the continuity of the dominant liberal legal ideology is assured. Those students as lawyers, academics or judges will perpetuate the ideology with which they have been imbued.

To undermine this reinforcement of the *status quo*, Thomson suggests that a critical contract course should diverge as much as possible from standard texts and examine the primary materials themselves to reveal the uncertainty of contract law. This means not only examining cases from the Court of Appeal, but also cases at first instance as well as looking at the formation of contracts in practice, a method which will reveal the power relationships to be found in nearly every contract. Like Karl Llewellyn (see chapter 11),

Thomson advocates an examination of the law of *contracts* not the law of contract, to reveal how it is impossible to bring employment contracts and consumer contracts under the same reasoned principles and to show that it is only by abstracting from reality that the law of contract can be maintained as a coherent whole. Cases should be viewed in terms of consequences and in terms of the moral and political attitudes which drive the judge.

> By drawing out the dominant liberal individualism and the very occasional glimpse of other views informing contract cases, one cannot avoid confronting the fact that contract law is not outside politics but part of it.

By revealing the indeterminacies and incoherence in contract, the subject is revealed not as a universal set of principles that are natural and timeless but as a product of history. It is to that history that the analysis will now turn, but before doing so it is useful to state Thomson's conclusion:

> . . . most importantly, by opening up contract law in these ways, exploring it in terms of its consequences, drawing out the political ideologies it silently expresses, revealing the historical circumstances of its development, and demonstrating the potential openness of the cases, one brings into sight exactly what the textbooks suppress, namely ideas about the expression of social relations in terms which give voice to quite different ways of conceiving living together. Thus while contract gives legal expression to society as a collection of isolated distrustful strangers, submitting only to general rules out of enlightened self-interest, to challenge contract is to struggle to conceive of and express other ways of living together, based on altruism, ideas of solidarity or on constructing norms through engaging in genuine conversation and discussion.

As Thomson states, once the superficial veneer of universality and time-lessness is stripped away from the façade of contract law, what is revealed is that contract law is a product of history and has been shaped by a combination of politics and economics to create the apparently self-sufficient set of principles that is the law of contract today. Peter Gabel and Jay Feinman provide a useful historical analysis of contract law as ideology (J. M. Feinman and P. Gabel, 'Contract law as ideology', in D. Kairys (ed.), *The Politics of Law. A Progressive Critique*, rev. ed. (New York: Pantheon Books, 1990), pp. 373–86).

They start with a brief historical survey of contract law in the 18th century, the pre-capitalist era, painting a picture of socio-economic 'reality' which appears somewhat simplistic and idyllic. The system is composed of traditional hierarchies based on ownership of land and inherited position. The ideology of contract law reflected this in that it was hostile to commercial enterprise which would threaten this system. Contract law struck down unconscionable bargains in this period and imposed contracts where justice required, for instance when there was reliance on a promise.

The 19th century or the era of capitalism witnessed a fundamental change. People were divided into classes and the working class was exploited. Society was subordinated to the market and to monetary exchange. This was accompanied by a move from an emphasis on community to individuality, with individuals being isolated and alienated.

> Within a short stretch of historical time, people experienced and were forced to adapt to the appearance of the factory and the slum, the rise of the industrial city, and a violent rupture of group life and feeling that crushed traditional forms of moral and community identity. . . . [This transformation] created that blend of aggression, paranoia, and profound emotional isolation and anguish that is known romantically as the rugged individual.

How could people be persuaded to accept such conditions?

> One vehicle of persuasion was the law of contracts, which generated a new ideological imagery that sought to give legitimacy to the new order. Contract law was one of many such forms of imagery in law, politics, religion, and other representations of social experience that concealed and denied the oppressive and alienating aspects of the new social and economic relations. Contract law denied the nature of the system by creating an imagery that made the oppression and alienation appear to be the consequences of what the people themselves desired.

Because judges and lawyers were in a privileged position in the system they naturally expressed the legitimacy of the system. Contractual legal concepts thus became reified and supposedly autonomous and objective. For example, the imagery of 'freedom of contract' developed an exterior that concealed the reality that such freedom was conditional upon that person's status, whilst the concept of consideration idealised and reified the grubby world of competition and bargaining. In other words, the imagery of the law served to deny the oppressive character of the market-place and the lack of real, personal liberty experienced by people in their private lives as well as in their workplaces.

During the 20th century capital becomes concentrated in fewer companies leading to monopolies which, combined with the development of trade unions, leads to the limited protection of workers and consumers from such great collections of capital and power, so that modern capitalism becomes characterised by varying amounts of State intervention. Law helps to maintain such a system by supplementing its previous preference for market individualism with principles based on collective welfare which results in some efforts towards redistributive justice. The ideology of law is again seeking to obscure the essentially oppressive nature of the socio-economic system. The people are still isolated and alienated. Despite the development of doctrines of duress and undue influence and wider doctrines of unconscionability of bargains, unfairness is still rampant in the market-place. The ideology of the individual and freedom of contract are still dominant.

In this reality our narrow functional roles produce isolation, passivity, unconnectedness, and impotence. Contract law, like the other images constituted by capitalism, is a denial of these painful feelings and an apology for the system that produces them.

12.3   CRITICAL LEGAL STUDIES AND FEMINIST LEGAL THEORY

Feminist legal theories represent a most important modern development in the analysis of law, concerned with the treatment of women by the legal system and the perception, or lack of perception, of women's experience and needs in legal provision. In engaging with this agenda feminist theories not only seek to identify and counter a traditionally male-oriented legal system but also to question male-oriented theories and ideologies. Part of this latter element of feminist thought emphasises a rejection of a search for objective 'truths' about law and puts in its place a contextual understanding of law as a social construct which is a product of a variety of influences, some of which are covert or even unrecognised. It is also suggested in some feminist theory that a 'male'-oriented appreciation of law emphasises individualism and 'rights' at the expense of 'female' emphases upon interaction and cooperation. This in turn demands a radical new methodology in legal theory which is, to a significant extent, found in the critical legal method.

Feminist theory is by no means limited to the context of critical legal studies; if it were, that might be seen as fundamentally inconsistent with the dynamic of the feminist approach to legal theory. Anne Bottomley, Susie Gibson and Belinda Meteyard remark that:

Feminism and critical legal studies are, of course, two entirely different creatures. Feminism is only partially and peripherally concerned with academic theorising. It is motivated by the dissatisfactions of a wide spectrum of . . . women and by the everyday experience of such women. ('Dworkin; Which Dworkin? Taking Feminism Seriously' in P. Fitzpatrick and A. Hunt, eds., *Critical Legal Studies* (Oxford: Basil Blackwell, 1987), p. 47.)

In this context, therefore, critical legal studies contribute a useful method rather than a defining context. The method is, however, important as a means of demonstrating the explicit and implicit male orientation of law and legal administration and the resulting disadvantage and marginalisation often suffered by women. Katherine T. Bartlett offers three basic elements which characterise a feminist legal theory. These are:

(a) asking the 'woman question', i.e the extent of the presence and recognition of women's experience in law;

(b) feminist practical reasoning, meaning a reasoning which proceeds from context and values difference and the experience of the unempowered; and

(c) consciousness raising, meaning an exploration of the collective experience of women through a sharing of individual experiences.

(Katherine T. Bartlett, 'Feminist Legal Method' (1970) 103 Harv L Rev, 829.) Upon these bases feminist legal theory seeks to articulate women's perspective upon law and thereby to empower women in the future development or redevelopment of law.

From a feminist perspective the expression of male domination in law may, in common with other power structures subjected to critical legal analysis, take both overt and covert, or even unrecognised, forms. Overt discrimination against women, as, for example, in certain historic and sometimes continuing employment practices, is by definition obvious when encountered. It is closely similar to race discrimination and other forms of illegitimate disadvantage and falls more into the realm of policy making than theoretical analysis. Covert or unrecognised bias presents much more difficult issues in the areas of both theory and practice.

The key question here is the extent to which an inherently 'male' legal mindset implicitly discriminates against women because it is framed in terms of male experience which does not necessarily relate to that of women. Examples may be found, significantly, even in some of the legal practices and provisions which are in principle directed towards securing gender equality. Equality is often taken to mean simply the establishment of identity in the treatment of women and men. It must first be said that in a broad range of situations the establishment of the co-equal treatment of men and women as people is, of course, precisely what gender equality does mean. However, in other issues, where the needs and experience of women and men and their respective experiences are not the same, such an approach tends to treat women 'as if' they are men with oppressive consequences. In this context Joanne Conaghan and Louise Chudleigh remark that:

Current conceptions of employment reflect a male norm: they are built upon a notion of the male worker who is full-time, long-term and unionised. Women workers tend to deviate from this norm . . . their working patterns are often interrupted and part-time. . . . Thus, labour law both embodies and conceals the gender division of labour and, by focusing exclusively on the world of paid work, ignores the differing responsibilities [of] . . . men and women . . . ('Women in Confinement: Can Labour Law Deliver the Goods?' in *Critical Legal Studies*, p. 133 at p. 137.)

Women may be disadvantaged even by legal structures which purportedly seek to take account of female needs and experience but which do so on the basis of analogy with irrelevant, and sometimes outdated, male experience. An example of this is the treatment of maternity leave as, in effect, analogous to the sick leave of a male employee, as well as the assumption that parenting is an exclusively female role, shown in the very limited provision for paternity leave. Other failures of law to deal adequately with women's experience may readily be found. The issue of domestic violence and its treatment by criminal law and law enforcement agencies is an obvious area of concern, character- ised by the recognition by English law in *R v R* [1991] 4 All ER 481 of the possibility of rape within marriage. Again in the employment sector, different retirement ages and pension entitlement for women and men, which may prejudice either men or women who might want to retire earlier or work later, has also been an issue of concern in the 1990s, with a major compensation award to three women workers in the gas industry in June 1996. The essential point in many, although not all, of these concerns has been put shortly by Katherine T. Bartlett in her statement that the essential 'woman question' in law is:

> how the law fails to take into account the experiences and values that seem more typical of women than of men, for whatever reason, or how existing legal standards and concepts might disadvantage women. ('Feminist Legal Methods' (1970) 103 Harv L Rev, p. 829 at p. 837.)

The value of critical methodologies in the display and analysis of such gender distortions in law and legal administration should be evident. The point to be emphasised is perhaps that of the disadvantaging effect of concealed and frequently unrealised bias in a legal order which has for the most part developed from male rather than female experience. This is not to assert a 'conspiracy theory' or to claim that all law discriminates against women. It is also not necessary to assert a gender-exclusive model in which there are claimed to be wholly incompatible 'individualist' male and 'collectivist' female viewpoints. This latter claim is also sometimes made in relation to different human cultures and in both cases it can unwisely be forgotten that we are, in an Aristotelian sense (see 4.3.3), social individuals, i.e. each person, woman or man, is an individual who lives in association with others in a social structure. The key endeavour of feminist legal theory may rather be to identify a fact of social, political and legal history which in many important respects fails adequately to take account of the experience of somewhat more than half of the human population. This is expressly a failure to afford mutuality and recognition not only to women as members of society but, in fact, a failure to recognise the mutuality of all society's members, women and men. Such failures, based upon whatever form of improper discriminatory selectivity, generate alienation and, ultimately, disfunctionality in the working of a legal order. The ways in which this has happened and the present real extent of the problem are the issues central to the interface between feminist legal theory and critical legal studies. This then opens the question of deconstructive and positive agendas. Much of the critical legal endeavour is concerned with the identification of defects and concealed agendas in law; feminism is at least as much concerned with establishing proper recognition of women's experience in society and law. Nonetheless, the identification of the sources of marginalisation and alienation may be seen as at least an important stage in a process of response.

12.4   THE ROLE OF ROBERTO UNGER

It is to these feelings of isolation and disenchantment with society, that are often felt but misunderstood by individuals, that Roberto Unger's often highly abstract and sometimes impenetrable analysis of law and society turns.

12.4.1   Contextuality

Whereas traditional perspectives on law and society view the present system found in Western liberal societies as the only one capable of marrying individual freedom with social order, Unger views a legal system that does not have any profound understanding of *personality* and society as simply being a 'brutal and amoral conflict' that only benefits the rich and powerful operating under the benevolent cloak of the rule of law (R. M. Unger, *Passion: An Essay on Personality* (New York: Free Press, 1984), p. 47).

Unger shares with the rest of the critical legal studies movement a desire to deconstruct, dereify and trash the liberal legal order. For him legal adjudication is purely arbitrary and used for political purposes to further the needs of the powerful and the persuasive in society (*Passion: An Essay on Personality*, p. 47). In addition, the legal process, with its surface of neutrality and fairness, serves to slow down any process of change that there may be in society. In other words the legal system with its inherent backward-looking nature simply reinforces the status quo and stymies any type of revolution, whether violent or not within society. Unger is of the opinion that such a blanketing effect is bad for society because it is against human nature. As well as advocating that adjudication in legal decisions should be concerned with an open-ended debate about values instead of a narrow doctrinal discussion of precedent, he goes much further by arguing that the whole concept of fixity in society, embodied in the legal system by the concept of *stare decisis*, is contrary to fundamental human needs (R. M. Unger, 'The critical legal studies movement' (1983) 96 Harv L Rev 561 at pp. 564–76).

Unger's very complex analysis of human nature (clearly greatly simplified here) leads him to discern a fundamental contradiction between, on the one hand, our longing for other people, and on the other our fear of other people. Individuals need each other in order to become fulfilled, but in so doing they are made vulnerable to those others, who, if they are so minded, can make use of this vulnerability to exploit them. This contradiction not only goes to personal and family relationships but is as important when individuals interact to gain the necessities of life, when other people may seize the opportunity to use the exchange of goods or labour to subjugate the individual in 'an entrenched hierarchy of power and wealth' (*Passion: An Essay on Personality*, p. 96).

Unger then analyses the contradiction between our altruistic and individualistic desires using the modernist approach to 'contexts'. He shares the belief that both our mental and social lives are shaped by 'institutional and imaginative assumptions' known as 'contexts'. He further believes that it is impossible to think or act in a way that is completely free from all conceptual or social contexts. He expresses the view that all conceptual or social contexts can be broken or revised. In this way new contexts may be created which in turn will be broken or revised. This allows for change in society and for the individuals in it. The more rigid a context is then the more difficult it is to change or to revise it. On the other hand the more 'plastic' a context is the greater the flexibility and potential for change.

The point appears to be that rigid contexts lead to individuals being categorised in terms of the *roles* they play in society, rather than as individuals, who, if they choose, may decide to play a variety of roles and feel free to move between them. Rigid contexts, in part produced by the pseudo-fixity of the legal system, lead to people being categorised *only* or at least *mainly* in terms of the role they play such as spouse, employee, woman or lawyer. The self-perpetuating rigidity of the system entrenches people in these roles and prevents them from attempting any form of self-assertion by trying any context-breaking or context-changing acts which might upset the social order and the status quo. Furthermore, once individuals are fully programmed into their roles they can then be exploited.

It follows that individuals are more likely to be treated as persons rather than as roles in a society that is comprised of plastic contexts rather than rigid ones. Plastic societies are more amenable to self-assertion and to reconciling the apparent contradiction between a person's altruistic and individualistic desires by preventing exploitation. To make society more plastic, individuals must reject rigid contexts, which in the case of law involves a rejection of rigid hierarchies of rigid rules which lead to exploitation of individuals in their assigned roles, and instead enter into an open-ended debate about politics (*Passion: An Essay on Personality*, pp. 7-27). Unger also suggests other methods involving a change in the structure of society whereby an individual's narrow functional role in that society can be changed for the better.

12.4.2 Empowered democracy

Hugh Collins gives us a simple example of the problem that Unger's critical societal theory attempts to surmount. He asks the reader to imagine that he or she wants to be a creative writer. The problems facing such a person are virtually insurmountable even in a developed Western country. The need to survive and to look after any dependants stifles such an ambition primarily because that choice is not a free one but is dependent on the prospective writer finding a *market* for his or her work. Faced with this unforgiving and rigid context so prevalent in liberal societies, and maintained by their legal systems, namely the primacy of the market-place, the writer's ambitions become thwarted and instead he or she opts for a second-best career or job.

> In the spirit of critical social theory, Unger argues for the possibility of establishing social conditions more suitable for satisfying this quest for self-fulfilment. Not everyone could become a creative writer, of course, but then probably few would find this option attractive. The point is not to establish a community of literati, but rather social conditions which empower individuals to explore successfully the myriad ways in which they may imagine their lives will flourish and have meaning or purpose. (H. Collins, 'Roberto Unger and the critical legal studies movement' (1987) 14 J Law & Soc 387 at p. 389.)

Unger argues from the basis of contextuality for the need to establish a super-liberal society within the terms of the 'programme of empowered democracy' (R. M. Unger, *Politics, a Work in Constructive Social Theory*, vol. 2, *False Necessity. Anti-Necessitarian Social Theory in the Service of Radical Democracy* (Cambridge: Cambridge University Press, 1987), p. 341). This programme contains Unger's vision of society and has three main elements, namely a new and radically different system of legal rights, a reorganisation of the constitution and government and finally a reconstruction of the economy.

Unger's system of rights differs greatly from the established system of civil and political rights found in Western liberal democracies. He proposes to replace that system, which simply serves the strictures of the market economy, with four types of super-liberal rights, namely 'market rights', 'immunity rights', 'destabilisation rights', and 'solidarity rights', all designed to produce a plastic society, where individuals will be able to seek and achieve self-fulfilment. Market rights are 'the rights employed for economic exchange in the trading sector of society' and are dependent on his vision of a radically reconstructed economy. Immunity rights 'protect the individual against oppression by concentrations of public or private power, against exclusion from the important collective decisions that influence his life, and against the extremes of economic and cultural deprivation'. If individuals are to be encouraged to engage in the transformation of society they must have not only negative freedom from interference but also positive freedom from want. The third group of rights identified by Unger allow the individual to venture further in his or her attempts to transform society. Destabilisation rights 'protect the citizen's interest in breaking open the large-scale organisations or the extended areas of social practice that remain closed to the destabilising effects of ordinary conflict and thereby sustain insulated hierarchies of power and advantage'. Finally solidarity rights 'give legal form to relations of reliance and trust . . . Solidarity rights form part of a set of social relations enabling people to enact a more defensible version of the communal ideal than any version currently available to them' (*Politics, a Work in Constructive Social Theory*, vol. 2, pp. 520–36).

Unger is somewhat unclear about the exact nature, extent and protection of these rights. What is clear is that they are dependent on the second and third elements of his programme for empowered democracy.

Unger's programme for the remodelling of government is based on the premise that the present variety of constitutional structures within societies are far too rigid, so promoting confrontation and alienation. His basic argument is that instead of having an entrenched 'stifling and perverse institutional logic' there should be a 'multiplication of overlapping powers and functions'. A multiplication of the number of branches of government with greater decentralisation leads to the diffusion of power to all individuals instead of to a class of powerful individuals at the top of the existing hierarchies within society. This in turn will increase the opportunities for individuals to engage in transformative activities and so change society from being based on individuality to being based on community. The reorganisation of government would further involve the abolition of the traditional doctrine of separation of powers into the executive, the judiciary and the legislature. These would not only overlap but would be virtually unrecognisable when compared to the existing institutions. For example, Unger suggests that the judiciary 'may forge complex interventionist remedies allowing for the destabilisation and reorganisation of large-scale institutions or major areas of social practice, even though such remedies may be irreconcilable with the received view about the appropriate institutional role of the judiciary (or of any other branch of government)'.

Unger does propose a system of priority with his scheme based on the principle of 'the absolute restraint one power may impose on another'. In the case of a constitutional deadlock he proposes a system of referenda and elections and in particular he proposes immediate elections when the government is not receiving popular support. The legitimately elected government would be supervised by the 'decisional centre' encompassing the roles traditionally allocated to the judiciary and the legislature. Further principles in Unger's complex vision of society (greatly simplified here) include the concepts of 'miniconstitutions' 'for limited contexts and aims'; 'subsidiarity' requiring that 'power to set rules and policies be transferred from a lower and closer authority to a higher and more distant one only when the former cannot adequately perform the responsibility in question'; and 'antigovernment' such as trade unions and neighbourhood organisations to form 'restraining social counterweights' which will diminish 'the risk of despotic perversion' (*Politics, a Work in Constructive Social Theory*, vol. 2, pp. 444–80, p. 551).

Central to Unger's proposals for the reconstruction of the economy in his post-modernist society is the rejection of the current 'private-rights complex of the advanced Western countries', in particular the central concept of 'the consolidated property right: a more or less absolute entitlement to a divisible portion of social capital'. Inequalities are inherent in such a system and any attempts at reforming the present system will be inadequate since they will still be based on the concept of the 'consolidated property right'. Instead of this present iniquitous system, Unger proposes 'a perpetual innovation machine', the primary example of which is a 'rotating capital fund' (*Politics, a Work in Constructive Social Theory*, vol. 2, pp. 480–508). Collins gives a useful summary of this element and the way that it fits into Unger's wider theory:

Unger claims that contemporary politics possesses a disabled institutional imagination. In other words, it fails to recognise that markets and democracies can be organised in a huge variety of ways. For example, liberalism (and, for that matter, Marxism) has always assumed that exclusive ownership of the means of production must constitute a cornerstone of market economy. Unger suggests, however, that instead of the means of production being owned either by the State or individuals, it should be possible to create a rotating capital fund through which the State would make loans of capital to entrepreneurs for a fixed period of time, and then, having permitted the entrepreneur to reap sufficient profit to provide the necessary incentive for efficient production, the State should reclaim the balance of the funds in order to make fresh loans. This scheme of a rotating capital fund avoids the excesses of domination involved in either communism or capitalism through control over the means of production, yet preserves incentives for efficient production. Unger offers further illustrations of the [current] disabled institutional imagination. . . . In each case, by a recombination of familiar ideas into novel institutional arrangements, Unger seeks to demonstrate how practical reforms could enable us to transcend the formative context of our society. (H. Collins, 'Roberto Unger and the critical legal studies movement' (1987) 14 J Law & Soc 387 at p. 401.)

An attempt has been made to give the reader a flavour of Unger's alternative society. The summary by its nature tends to exaggerate the flaws in his scheme such as the exact nature and protection of his new legal rights, the danger that his system may create an overelaborate and ever-changing bureaucracy that may not necessarily transform society, and finally the fact that his rotating capital fund, for instance, will not remove domination only reduce it. An attempt by the reader to analyse the detail of his proposals will offset many of these criticisms. Furthermore, what Unger is doing above all is making the reader think of a different society which will overcome the contradictions and unfairness of current Western society. He is offering *an* alternative not necessarily *the* alternative to current structures in society and in philosophy (for a liberal philosophical critique of Unger's philosophy see W. Ewald, 'Unger's philosophy: a critical legal study' (1988) 97 Yale LJ 665). He is in many ways attempting to introduce into philosophy and politics an open debate about society by offering a vision of there being much wider choices than the ones offered in so-called liberal democracies.

12.5 FURTHER READING

Bartlett, K. T., 'Feminist Legal Method' (1970) 103 Harv L Rev 829.

Boyle, J., *Critical Legal Studies* (Aldershot: Dartmouth, 1992).

Douzinas, C., Goodrich, P. and Hachamovitch, Y., *Politics, Postmodernity and Critical Legal Studies* (London: Routledge, 1994).

Fitzpatrick, P., and Hunt, A. (eds), *Critical Legal Studies* (Oxford: Basil Blackwell, 1987).

Goodrich, P., *Reading the Law* (Oxford: Basil Blackwell, 1986).

Harris, J. W., 'Unger's critique of formalism in legal reasoning: Hero, Hercules, and Humdrum' (1989) 52 MLR 42.

Hunt, A., 'The theory of critical legal studies' (1986) 6 Oxford Journal of Legal Studies 1.

Price, D. A., 'Taking rights cynically: a review of critical legal studies' [1989] CLJ 271.

Smart, C., *Feminism and the Power of Law* (London: Routledge, 1989).

CHAPTER THIRTEEN
Postmodern Legal Theory

Postmodern legal theory is the latest radical theory to challenge the liberal orthodoxies that society has a natural structure and that history is simply a process of evolution towards that truth. Grand claims made by Fukuyama, for instance, that history has come to an end 'since the entire world – or those parts of it that counted for anything – had converted to free market capitalism and liberal democracy', are ridiculed by the postmodernists (C. Norris, *The Truth about Postmodernism* (Oxford: Blackwell, 1993), p. 1. See F. Fukuyama, *The End of Liberty and the Last Man* (London: Hamish Hamilton, 1992)). Liberalism and capitalism are not the end of the road but are simply the major components of what the postmodernists call 'modernity'. Modernity's structures, its laws, its literature, its architecture, its art, in fact any of its products, are all subject to 'deconstruction', a process which reveals numerous alternatives. An inherent aspect of this process is a recognition that society is simply made up of a complex network of subjectivities and contains no objective truths or natural laws upon which it can be grounded.

Developing the radical critique promulgated by the Critical Legal Studies movement in the 1980s, postmodern legal theory offers a more profound, indeed more disturbing vision of law and society in the 1990s.

13.1 A CRITIQUE OF THE ENLIGHTENMENT

Postmodernism groups 'progressive' versions of history under the label 'Enlightenment'. Followers of these versions believe that the 'Enlightenment brings "light", and modernity's task is to finish the task that the Enlightenment began. The progressives, the Lockeans, Benthamites, Millians, Social-Darwinists and most Marxists see the Enlightenment as the unleashing of a great potential for good'. 'The shackles' of superstition 'that held back political organisation, thought, individual liberty, and production were overthrown' by the Enlightenment (C. Douzinas and R. Warrington, *Postmodern Jurisprudence* (London: Routledge, 1991), pp. 6–7). Followers of modernity deride the postmodern as 'chaotic, catastrophic, nihilistic' and 'the end of good order'. Postmodernists, on the other hand, characterise modernity as 'an iron cage of bureaucratization, centralisation and infinite manipulation of the psyche by the "culture industry" and the disciplinary regimes of power and knowledge', while portraying postmodernism as 'an exhilarating moment of rapture'.

> It defies the system, suspects all totalising thought and homogeneity and opens space for the marginal, the different and the 'other'. Postmodernism is here presented as the celebration of flux, dispersal, plurality and localism. (Douzinas and Warrington, *Postmodern Jurisprudence*, p. 15.)

The post-Enlightenment concept of progress, of constant modernisation, with its overriding sense of movement towards the truth or 'meta-narratives' (J. F. Lyotard, *The Post Modern Condition: A Report on Knowledge* (Manchester: Manchester University Press, 1984), p. xxiv) is rejected. In law, modernist theories such as those presented by Hart, Kelsen, Dworkin and Finnis try to portray law as a unified whole, and posit the rule of law as the method of 'neutral, non-subjectivist resolution of value disagreement and social conflict' (Douzinas and Warrington, *Postmodern Jurisprudence*, p. 14). However, in the reality of the postmodern world where such rigid homogeneity is recognised as being imposed arbitrarily, 'the panglossia of statutes, delegated legislation, administrative legislation and adjudication, judicial and quasi-judicial decision-making; the multiform institutions and personnel; and the plural non-formal methods of dispute avoidance and resolution cannot be seen any longer as a coherent, closed ensemble of rules or values' (Douzinas and Warrington, *Postmodern Jurisprudence*, p. 27). Despite this, modernist theories still attempt to legitimate the idea of a closed, logical legal order.

The lineage of postmodernism in law can be traced back to Legal Realism's fundamental tenet that law is an instrument of policy, which was amplified by the Critical Legal Studies movement's statement that all law is politics. However, the postmodernist disenchantment with the rationalist desire to make sense of the world is much more wide ranging than either of its predecessors. Its targets are everything from art to science and beyond. Indeed, its scepticism is so profound that it inherently knows no bounds, for there are none, only 'flux, dispersal, plurality and localism' (Douzinas and Warrington, *Postmodern Jurisprudence*, p. 15).

> Postmodernism, then, is the rejection of . . . faith in rationalism, and a recognition that any argument, no matter how perfectly logical, is only as

good as its presuppositions. Thus the postmodernist proclaims the death of western 'meta-narratives' such as capitalism, liberalism, and marxism. But along with their rejection of rationality comes the rejection of the possibility of truth. (M. Donaldson, 'Some Reservations About Law and Postmodernism' (1995) 40 *American Journal of Jurisprudence*, p. 335 at p. 336.)

Nevertheless, there is the possibility that postmodernism, by rejecting many aspects of modern society, does have a positive agenda. Postmodernism, as shall be seen, has an image problem of its own in the sense that it is viewed as nihilistic, having no purpose except to undermine. As shall be seen, though many proponents seem to offer no solutions, others hold out a more positive agenda. This is revealed in Balkin's rejection of the Enlightenment:

The Enlightenment sought to free humanity from the chains of unthinking tradition and religious bigotry. It sought to master the world through science and remake the world according to the dictates of reason. It sought to understand and recast society in rational and scientific terms, and it was confident about the ability of the human intellect to do this. Two centuries later, humanity is imprisoned by new chains that the Enlightenment forged for us. These are the chains created by science, technology, and rationality, which in the course of liberating us subjected us to new forms of control, bureaucracy, mediaization, suburbanization, and surveillance. We still need liberation, we still need emancipation, but now it is from the products of our previous emancipation – from computer data bases, sound bites, political action committees, voodoo economics, electronic surveillance, commodified video images, and the industrialization of professional culture. The emancipation we now require cannot be on the same terms as those proposed by the Enlightenment. It must, at least in part, be a rejection of the terms by which we freed ourselves from pre-Enlightenment thinking. (J. M. Balkin, 'What is Postmodern Constitutionalism?' (1992) 90 *Michigan Law Review* p. 1966 at p. 1989.)

13.2 LYOTARD AND FOUCAULT

The postmodernist dialectic is perhaps too narrowly portrayed as simply a recipe for relativism when in fact it is a positive method of forcing individuals to confront and change the rigid contexts and structures (including laws) within which they have arbitrarily confined themselves. In this sense it is a liberating philosophy. This can be understood by Lyotard's depiction of the world of the painter and the writer:

If they do not wish to become supporters (of minor importance) of what exists, the painter and the writer must refuse to lend themselves to such therapeutic uses. They must question the rules of the art of painting or of narrative as they have learned and received them from their predecessors. Soon those rules must appear to them as a means to deceive, to seduce, and to reassure, which makes it impossible for them to be 'true'. Under the common name of painting and literature, an unprecedented split is taking place. Those who refuse to reexamine the rules of art pursue successful careers in mass conformism by communicating, by means of the 'correct rules', the endemic desire for reality with objects and situations capable of gratifying it. (Lyotard, *The Postmodern Condition*, pp. 74–75.)

While those painters and writers who do not conform to the accepted rules struggle to get their works seen or read, for they are not accepted as 'real' artists. However, a realisation that those rules will have originated in a context breaking piece of art or literature shows the falsity of the belief in the truth as represented by those rules. Those rules in fact just represent one view or approach, they have no superior or prior claim than any other view or approach. A context breaking writer may start a literary school which becomes so established that it eventually becomes the orthodoxy. The mistake is then made to elevate the orthodoxy to the level of a received truth.

A postmodernist painter or writer is in the position of a philosopher: the text he writes, the work he produces are not in principle governed by pre-established rules, and they cannot be judged according to a determining judgment, by applying familiar categories to the text or to the work. Those rules and categories are what the work of art itself is looking for. The artist and the writer, then, are working without rules in order to formulate the rules of what *will have been done*. Hence the fact that work and text have the characters of an *event*; hence also, they always come too late for their author, or, what amounts to the same thing, their being put into work, their realization (*mise en oeuvre*) always begin too soon. *Post modern* would have to be understood according to the paradox of the future (*post*) anterior (*modo*). (Lyotard, *The Postmodern Condition*, p. 81.)

In essence, postmodernism is not anti-modernism, for as Lyotard's example illustrates 'a work can only become modern if it is first postmodern', so that postmodernism is definitely 'a part of the modern', not a historical period beyond modernity.

In some ways it is better to view postmodernism as post-structuralism or post-positivism – a rejection of the structured, logical and internally consistent picture of society and law exemplified in legal theory by Hart's union of primary and secondary rules, or Kelsen's pyramid of norms. 'Positivist structuralism . . . treats the given order as the natural order' (R. Ashley, 'The Poverty of Neorealism', in R. O. Keohane (ed.), *Neo-Realism and its Critics*

(New York: Columbia University Press), p. 255 at p. 258) when in reality 'all
truths are, in fact, products of past practices' (T. L. Knutsen, *A History of
International Relations Theory* (Manchester: Manchester University Press,
1997), p. 275). Those past practices are founded upon power (F. Nietzsche,
'Aus dem Nachlass der Achtzigerjahre', Werke, Vol. III (Munich: Carl
Hansen Verlag, 1960), p. 917), particularly if power is seen as something
much more than repressive coercion. As Michel Foucault points out:

> . . . power is not to be taken as a phenomenon of one individual's
> consolidated and homogenous domination over others, or that of one
> group or class over others. What, by contrast, should always be kept in
> mind is that power, if we do not take too distant a view of it, is not that
> which makes the difference between those who exclusively possess it and
> retain it, and those who do not have it and submit to it. Power must be
> analysed as something which circulates, or rather something which only
> functions in the form of a chain. It is never localised here or there, never
> in anybody's hands, never appropriated as a commodity or a piece of
> wealth. Power is employed and exercised through a net-like organisation.
> And not only do individuals circulate between its threads; they are always
> in the position of simultaneously undergoing and exercising this power.
> They are not only its inert or consenting target; they are also the elements
> of its articulation. In other words, individuals are the vehicles of power not
> the points of application. (M. Foucault, 'Two Lectures' in C. Gordon
> (ed.), *Power/Knowledge* (New York: Harvester, 1980), p. 96.)

Foucault's neo-Marxism shares with postmodernism an emphasis on the
'shifting relationships between self and Other' (C. Douzinas and R. Warrington, '"A Well Founded Fear of Justice": Law and Ethics in Postmodernity'
(1991) II(2) *Law and Critique*, p. 115 at p. 118), in that at one point a person
is exercising power and in another instance she or he is subject to it.

13.3   IDENTITY AND THE 'OTHER'

The postmodernist concern with the 'other' combats to a certain extent the
perception that it has no ethical content. In simple terms the 'other' appears
to be the individual who is outside the system, who is disadvantaged by it,
though with Foucault in mind this categorisation must necessarily take place
at a macro level, for at a micro level we are both powerful and powerless. In
the legal sphere the 'other' cannot assert that the law is on their side within
the current structures since the system alienates them. Postmodernism
recognises that they have an equal claim to consideration since their assertions are no less valid than those who are advantaged by the system, indeed
no less valid than the views of lawyers, judges or politicians. The concept of

the 'other' is important in postmodernism, given that much of our traditional thinking is based on presumptions, what the postmodern feminist would label white, male, and middle class, thereby excluding lots of other groups and individuals from the structures of society (see for example M. J. Frug, 'Rescuing Impossibility Doctrine: A Postmodern Feminist Analysis of Contract Law', (1992) 140 *University of Pennsylvania Law Review* 1029). In essence postmodernism is inclusive in that it purports to embrace the 'other'. Indeed, following Foucault, by embracing the 'other' we are also embracing ourselves.

Take for example the case of *R* v *Bentley* (11 December 1952. The original trial is recounted by the Court of Appeal on 30 July 1998 when Bentley's conviction was quashed. The judgment can be found at http//www.courtservice.gov.uk/bentley.htm). Bentley, aged 19, but with a much lower mental age, was convicted of murdering a police constable after he was in a struggle with another officer. He shouted to his younger friend, who had a gun, 'Let him have it Chris'. What does that mean? The prosecution argued it meant 'shoot him', whereas Bentley's defence counsel argued 'let him have the gun'. Bentley was convicted and hanged. It could be strongly argued that Bentley was only guilty of 'using ambiguous language' (B. Chigara, *The Process of Custom and the Legitimacy of Norms of Customary International Law: A Deconstructionist Perspective* (Unpublished Ph.D thesis, The University of Nottingham, 1998), p. 153). He did not shoot the officer, but he was a victim of the system that needed to find someone guilty and to execute them, particularly when the murder involved an attack on the representatives of order, and the individual who fired the gun was too young to be sentenced to death. The law was simply a reflection of society's attitudes. Postmodernism considers such cases, and given the inherent absence of 'truth' in any case, recognises the plight of the defendant as well as the victim.

However, clearly the case of *R* v *Bentley* is a hard case in terms of establishing intent. In the case of someone who in a similar case shouts 'shoot him dead', then the positivist would contend that there is no ambiguity in language and the defendant is clearly guilty. The postmodernist, however, would contest the rigid invocation of the issue of intent by the courts (J. Wicke, 'Postmodern Identity and the Legal Subject' (1991) 62 *University of Colorado Law Review* 455). A parallel can be drawn with Camus' discussion of suicide (A. Camus, *The Myth of Sisyphus* (London: Penguin, 1981), p. 13). Camus states that there are multiple explanations for why a person commits suicide including the fact that the individual's friend addresses him indifferently on the day in question. Similarly, there are multiple explanations for why the defendant uttered those words, including the possibility that he feared for his own life.

In essence there is no truth, only versions of it. Presumably, for the postmodernist, the court should cease to apply rigid rules of law on intention for instance and widen its doors to let in an open-ended discussion about the responsibility of other individuals and the wider community for the crime. In essence this was the end result of the inquiry into the death of the London teenager, Stephen Lawrence (Report of Sir William MacPherson, *The Stephen Lawrence Inquiry*, Cm 4262–I (London: The Stationery Office, 24 February 1999)), where responsibility for the death of the black teenager was widened beyond the five suspected of the stabbing to the police, and then to society as a whole where there is clearly still a high level of racism. However, this 'postmodernist' conclusion seems to have been forced only because institutional racism in the police led to the failure to prosecute the five suspects. If a 'proper' case had been mounted against them, then responsibility would have stopped at the five individuals.

The rigid structures of the law have been variously used to provide an artificial definition of a 'tribe' and of 'native title' thus denying land rights to the Mashpee Indians of Cape Cod in the United States (J. Wicke, 'Postmodern Identity and Legal Subject', p. 465), and the Yorta Yorta people of Australia (*Guardian Weekly*, 21 March 1999, p. 13). Although it is inherently unclear as to what a postmodernist 'result' would be in these cases, it is contended that the coming together of 'postmodernism and the Law, with its stern capital "L" intact, promises to be a dynamic coupling, postmodernism offering to put its delirious spin on the rigor and fixity of the body of the law' (J. Wicke, 'Postmodern Identity and Legal Subject', p. 455). Presumably then, given postmodernist concern with the 'other', the law should seek to accommodate their claims but to what extent and in what manner cannot be determined until we have a truly fluid postmodernist debate in such disputes.

13.4 POSTMODERNISM AND FUNDAMENTAL VALUES

There appears to be a contradiction at the heart of the postmodernist concern with the 'other', at least if this concern results in the elevation of certain 'truths' over other contrasting ones. In many societies women and racial minorities have been disadvantaged, there is no doubt about that, but the question remains whether postmodernism can embrace these 'others' over their oppressors, namely the sexists and racists still found in great numbers in society. Hilaire Barnett recognised that postmodernism presents a problem for feminism:

> The implications of the postmodern critique for feminist jurisprudence are profound. If 'grand theory' is no longer sufficient to explain women's condition, concepts such as patriarchy and gender, the public and the private, lose their explanatory force, and throw doubt on the potential for a convincing coherent theoretical understanding of women's lives and conditions. In place of grand theory, there must be developed critiques

which concentrate on the reality of the diversity of individual women's lives and conditions, critiques which reject the universalist, foundationalist philosophical and political understanding offered by modernism. With the 'age of innocence' lost, in its place there exists diversity, plurality, competing rationalities, competing perspectives and uncertainty as to the potentiality of theory. (H. Barnett, *Introduction to Feminist Theory* (London: Cavendish Publishers, 1998), p. 180.)

This certainly challenges the different branches of feminist thought, from liberal through to cultural and radical, to re-think their generalisations over the condition of women in society (Barnett, *Introduction to Feminist Jurisprudence*, pp. 121–76. On radical feminism see C. MacKinnon, *Towards a Feminist Theory of the State* (Cambridge Mass.: Harvard University Press, 1989)).

Inherent in the postmodernist tradition is what Foucault has labelled the 'death of the Subject' (M. Foucault, *Power/Knowledge* (New York: Pantheon Books, 1972), p. 117), which simply means 'recognising the multiplicity of subjectivities, identities, which inhere in the individual and recognising that each individual is comprised of multiple subjectivities. The postmodern Subject has multiple identities as he or she moves in and out of differing milieux' (H. Barnett, *Introduction to Feminist Jurisprudence*, pp. 1179–80). The question, in the radical tradition, is why a particular individual is oppressed or is the oppressor. For women the answer is not always because of male dominance, or at least that is the implication of postmodernism (see further S. Bordo, 'Feminism, postmodernism and gender-scepticism' in L. Nicholson (ed.), *Feminism/Postmodernism* (London: Routledge, 1990)). Hilaire Barnett, provides a way forward for feminism if it is to embrace the latest radicalism:

Feminist theory which fails to identify the differences between women, and the impact which those differences have on women's lives, fails to be inclusive. The scepticism with gender may be helpful in so far as it obliges feminist scholarship to 'demote' gender as an organising concept, in so far as it has been the *dominant* concept in feminist modernist theory, and to set gender alongside crucial other factors such as race, class, age, sexual orientation, the local and specific (as opposed to the universalising and general) and so forth. Thus a postmodern feminism must focus on the specificities of women's lives, rather than assuming the commonality of all women's lives. Feminist pluralism must replace feminist modernism. (Barnett, *Introduction to Feminist Jurisprudence*, p. 197.)

Nevertheless, within the all pervading relativism of postmodernism there appears to be no grand theory which explains why feminism is to be preferred to sexism. What makes sexist attitudes wrong? What makes racist attitudes wrong? The extent to which postmodernism can recognise, however fleetingly, a shared morality within society is questionable. Certainly postmodernists have been heavily critical of liberal attempts to overcome the subjectivity inherent in moral discourse. Liberal appeals to 'We the People' (Ackerman), 'the Interpretive Community' (Fiss), 'Persons in the Original Position' (Rawls), or even 'Hercules' (Dworkin), are simply conveniently abstracted 'supra-individual subjects' with no base in the world of real individuals. They represent the 'mythical fashioning of supra-individual subject identities' with the sole purpose of legitimating liberalism (P. Schlag, 'The Empty Circles of Liberal Justification' (1997) 96 *Michigan Law Review* 1 at p. 13. Schlag is deconstructing, B. Ackerman, *We the People – Foundations* (Cambridge Mass.: Harvard University Press, 1991), pp. 6–7; R. Dworkin, *Law's Empire* (London: Fontana, 1986), pp. 238–40; J. Rawls, *A Theory of Justice* (Cambridge Mass.: Harvard University Press, 1971), p. 11; O. Fiss, 'Objectivity and Interpretation' (1982) 34 *Stanford Law Review* 739 at p. 745). The refusal of liberalism to enforce even what appears to be shared morality in favour of an elitist academic representation of that morality is perhaps evidence of the force of the postmodernist critique. Even Lord Devlin's shared morality, criticised by many for coming too close to opinion poll morality, is based on the hypothetical *man* on the Clapham omnibus (see 3.5.2). Modernity's denial that society's 'values' are based on a shifting, prejudiced, majoritarian morality is unconvincing. The moral relativism revealed by postmodernism may be nearer to reality but its potential reduction of the views of Martin Luther King to the same level as those of the Grand Wizard of the Ku Klux Klan is, to say the least, deeply disturbing.

13.5 DERRIDA AND DECONSTRUCTION

Poststructuralism is at the heart of postmodernism, and Jaques Derrida is commonly seen as its founder. Derrida, Foucault and Lyotard are not academic lawyers, but their postmodernist/poststructuralist writing in the areas of literary criticism, history, and philosophy respectively, have made their impact. Derrida's deconstruction, in particular, has been tremendously influential, since law is like literature:

Language is a complex web of signs and, for Derrida, is metaphorical. Metaphor is a figure of speech in which a word or a phrase is applied to an object or action that it does not literally denote in order to imply a resemblance, as in *he is a lion in battle*. Language can never mean literally what it says – language is made up of metaphors and symbolisms. (Hilaire Barnett, *Introduction to Feminist Jurisprudence*, p. 185.)

In the use of language, modernism posits the belief that language discloses the relationship between the word and the world – the principal function of language is representational – it depicts the way things are. The proposition depicts reality. 'This is a chair' is a statement of truth. However, even modernists admit that some statements are simply statements of opinion – this chair is beautiful'. The postmodern approach is that there is no division of language into fact and opinion, all statements are opinions. How can this be? How can a challenge be made to the basic proposition that 'this is a chair'? The answer is because language is inherently indeterminate. The postmodernist would argue that there is no true meaning to the concept of chair – even what appear to be factual statements are open to debate and deconstruction.

This is all the more so in law in which the language is already an abstraction from reality – the concepts of 'family' or 'property' in law are removed from the ones in 'reality' – and the debates revolve around them. Nevertheless, the question to be asked is if there is no meaning in legal language, why do postmodernists concern themselves with it? The answer lies within semiotics which aims at an understanding of 'the system of signs which creates meaning within a culture' (M. D. A. Freeman, *Lloyd's Introduction to Jurisprudence*, 6th ed. (London: Sweet & Maxwell, 1994), p. 1155). Language is all there is. 'There is nothing outside the text' – that is the postmodernist message – language has to be examined to see what it reveals about the person using it or the class of persons using it (see J. M. Balkin, 'Being Just with Deconstruction' (1994) 3(3) *Social and Legal Studies* 393 at p. 394). Statements in law are assertions – assertions of the truth but simply assertions. In choosing between competing assertions, an individual will favour those which clash least with everything else that person takes to be true. In legal terms the law is self-reinforcing since individuals agree with the 'right' legal propositions because they fit into the legal system which is presumed to be 'right' – the whole system is based on dominant assertions which must ultimately be built on pure ideology or power. In this way the law and the legal system are self-perpetuating hierarchies.

The overriding postmodernist message is that the truth is, there is no truth. If everything is subjective, there are no meta-narratives, no overriding values, then is deconstruction simply painting a desperate picture of society in the late twentieth century – a cultural and moral wasteland? Binder's evaluation of Derrida is that 'probably no one has contributed more to the . . . disenchantment with cultural identity than this Algerian born post-structuralist' (G. Binder, 'Representing Nazism: Advocacy and Identity at the Trial of Klaus Barbie' (1989) 98 *Yale Law Journal* 1321 at p. 1373). Furthermore, Binder points to the inherent problem with post-structuralism – its valuelessness. There is no measure by which we can evaluate the Holocaust, nor any other inherently evil act such as the genocide in Rwanda in 1994. Derrida was clearly aware of this consequence when trying to defend another deconstructive theorist, Paul de Man, who had been accused of pro-Nazism (Binder, 'Representing Nazism', p. 1377, see J. Derrida, 'Like the Sound of the Sea Deep Within a Shell: Paul de Man's War' (1988) 14 *Critical Inquiry* 590) Although Derrida tried to define 'deconstruction as opposition to Nazism, he employs the very logic he condemns. In so doing, he unacceptably implicates those who identify with Judaism in their own persecution' (Binder, 'Representing Nazism', p. 1373). Binder expands on this conclusion:

> First because deconstruction shows every argument to contain its opposite, it seems nihilistic. Second because deconstruction is said to 'annihilate the subject' – to deny the individual identities of authors and of characters – it seems to deny individual responsibility for evil. Third, because it exposes the futility of efforts to deny loss, contradiction and violence, deconstruction seems to urge acceptance of their necessity. Perhaps an 'antihumanist' philosophy that attempts to annihilate the subject sees no great loss in the annihilation of subjects. (Binder, 'Representing Nazism', p. 1377.)

Derrida denies that an individual, group or culture can be identified by adherence to scripture or moral code, because such codes will always be contradictory (Binder, 'Representing Nazism', p. 1374). It might be supposed that the deconstruction of identity in this way may lead to a better world, in the sense that a realisation that such identities are meaningless may result in a world where individuals do not define themselves and identify others in terms of race, ethnicity, religion, or sex, thereby making persecution of individuals or groups of individuals on these bases less likely. However, that (possibly hypothetical) gain may be argued to be outweighed by the fact that deconstruction actually seems to legitimate the beliefs or codes of the persecutors by placing them at the same level as those beliefs of the persecuted. Indeed, Derrida seems to argue that 'like Nazism, all creeds define themselves by their antipathies' (Binder, 'Representing Nazism', p. 1373). Thus 'Derrida is . . . driven to the unacceptable conclusion that one cannot claim a Jewish identity as authentically one's own without becoming a Nazi' (Binder, 'Representing Nazism', p. 1324).

The question then is whether cultures and minorities will disappear because of possible post-structuralist 'enlightenment', or because Nazism or a similar ideology has already 'cleansed' them. Individuals within ethnic, religious or other minorities, whatever our views of their creed, deserve better protection from persecution than this – one such form of protection is the law, for instance the rights of minorities contained in Article 27 of the International Covenant on Civil and Political Rights, and its accompanying mechanisms. International law is not posited as a panacea, but at least it provides a universal, concrete, and in many ways 'moral' code – a form of *jus gentium*. Of course, though the texts of international laws are equally susceptible to the pens of the deconstructionists (see M. Koskenniemi, *From Apology to Utopia: The Structure of International Legal Argument* (Helsinki: Finnish

Lawyers' Publishing Co., 1989), p. 475. But see I. Scobbie, 'Towards the Elimination of International Law: Some Radical Scepticism about Sceptical Radicalism' (1991) 61 *British Yearbook of International Law* 339).

Nevertheless, postmodernism contains within it what has been labelled 'affirmative postmodernism', where 'not all socio-political action is decried, not all values are rejected', as well as 'sceptical postmodernism' which focuses 'on the negative: the uncertainties and ambiguities of existence' (Barnett, *Introduction to Feminist Jurisprudence*, p. 187). Representing the former stream, Balkin, for instance, makes the following statement:

> The deconstruction of legal concepts, or of the social vision that informs them, is not nihilistic. *Deconstruction is not a call for us to forget moral certainty*, but to remember aspects of human life that were pushed into the background by the necessities of the dominant legal conception we call into question. Deconstruction is not a denial of the legitimacy of rules and principles; it is an affirmation of human possibilities that have been overlooked or forgotten in the privileging of particular legal ideas . . . By recalling the elements of human life relegated to the margin in a given social theory, deconstructive readings challenge us to remake the dominant conceptions of our society. (J. M. Balkin, 'Deconstructive Practice and Legal Theory' (1987) 96 *Yale Law Journal* 743 at p. 763. Emphasis added.)

The question remains as to where those moral certainties can be found. That it is wrong to kill a person for no reason – killing for killing's sake – is a moral certainty for affirmative postmodernists as well as natural lawyers, but while the latter can point to their universal, unchanging, rational moral code, all the former has is a *conviction* that it is wrong: 'the point is that morality is not a matter of truth or logical demonstration. It is a matter of conviction based on experience, emotion and conversation' (J. W. Singer, 'The Player and the Cards: Nihilism and Legal Theory' (1984) 94 *Yale Law Journal* 1 at p. 39).

Nevertheless, 'the positive ethical thrust of deconstructive theory' is inherent in its challenges to the dominant conceptions which govern liberal (legal) orders (N. Duxbury, *Patterns of American Jurisprudence* (Oxford: Clarendon Press, 1995), p. 483). Deconstruction reveals the law's inadequacies. Often legal language is clearly indeterminate. Thus a deconstruction of how it is used to control and to oppress is clearly ethical. Deconstruction helps individuals towards liberation upon realisation that the system or society they are part of has no superior claim than a system or society they might prefer. Deconstruction may appear anarchical but it does reveal the coercive, arbitrary and contingent nature of the legal system, and the broader societal structures (see J. Derrida, 'Force of Law: The "Mystical Foundation of Authority"' in D. Cornell, M. Rosenfeld and D. G. Carlson, *Deconstruction and the Possibility of Justice* (London: Routledge, 1992), p. 3).

Although Derrida himself makes the claim that 'deconstruction is justice', and that justice itself is not susceptible to deconstruction (which implies that deconstruction has become the meta-narrative) (Derrida, 'Force of Law', p. 15), the logic of deconstruction does not simply apply to legitimating legal concepts such as the Rule of Law, or the constitution, but to much more basic 'truths', whereby good is given priority over evil, and life over death. Derrida's analysis of these dichotomies or polarities is intended to reveal that there is no rational process whereby one is given priority over the other (J. Derrida, *Dissemination* (Chicago: Chicago University Press, 1981), p. 233).

It may be because of deconstruction's lack of any limits – there are no concepts that are protected from its application – that Norris, while attracted by deconstruction, states that 'deconstruction is . . . an activity of thought which cannot be consistently acted on – that way madness lies – but which yet possesses an inescapable rigour of its own' (C. Norris, *Deconstruction: Theory and Practice* (London: Methuen, 1982), p. xii). Personal moral convictions may not be enough to stop a general descent into the heart of darkness. Is it enough for deconstructionists to state that '[p]eople do not want to be beastly to each other . . . The evidence is all around us that people are often caring, supporting, loving, and altruistic, both in their family lives and in their relations with strangers' (Singer, 'The Player and the Cards', p. 54)? From the killing fields of Cambodia of the 1970s, the genocide in Rwanda in 1994, to the indiscriminate shootings occurring within the United States and other developed States on a regular basis, there does appear to be plenty of evidence of inhumanity. Postmodernism does not provide any answers to this, any criteria for universalising the clear wrongness of these acts, indeed its reduction of all 'positive' values to the same level as all 'negative' values, may be said to condone, even encourage it. At most all that Derridian deconstruction seems to provide is stated by its chief proponent in drawing conclusions on the Holocaust:

> I do not know whether from this nameless thing called the final solution one can draw something which still deserves the name of a lesson. But if there were a lesson to be drawn, a unique lesson among the always singular lessons of murder, from even a singular murder, from all the collective exterminations of history (because each individual murder and each collective murder is singular, thus infinite and incommensurable) the lesson that we can draw today – and if we can do so then we must – is that we must think, know, represent for ourselves, formalize, judge the possible complicity between all these discourses and the worst (here the final solution). (J. Derrida, 'Force of Law', pp. 62–3.)

It may be because of this sort of equivocation that 'most liberals . . . are utterly repelled by postmodernism's more extravagant visions, which are cognitively relativist, morally nihilistic, and politically anarchistic' (M. Osiel, *Mass Atrocity, Collective Memory, and the Law* (New Brunswick: Transaction, 1997), p. 294).

13.6 DECONSTRUCTION AND JUSTICE

Balkin, of all postmodernists, makes a greater effort to analyse the relationship between deconstruction and justice. He recognises the problem 'that deconstructive techniques do not seem to support any particular vision of justice; indeed they appear to preclude the possibility of any stable conception of the just or the good that could provide the basis for political belief or the authority for political action' (J. M. Balkin, 'Being Just with Deconstruction' (1994) 3(3) *Social and Legal Studies* 393 at p. 393). However, Balkin clearly believes that deconstruction, if it is to have any purpose or value, must be capable of being used to reveal injustice. Deconstruction, in a strict Derridian sense, seems to be engaging in an endless round of word play, the purpose of which is to reveal various alternative meanings and 'truths', leaving it up to the interpreter to choose on the basis of that individual's own moral convictions. This might be sufficient in the world of literary criticism, and it is perfectly acceptable at one level to treat legal texts in the same way. Nevertheless, 'if deconstruction merely discovers instability and incoherence in all texts, then it cannot help us decide that one interpretation is better than another, or that one conceptual scheme is more just than another' (Balkin, 'Being Just with Deconstruction', p. 395). Derridian deconstruction lacks relevance when turning to the legal and social order, where it is essential to take the debate a step further:

> Why might anyone want to deconstruct law or legal doctrine? One reason has to do with the pursuit of justice. We might want to demonstrate that the law or some part of the law is unjust. Alternatively, we might want to show that the law or some part of the law conceals aspects of social life we believe to be important, and that its failure adequately to deal with these aspects leads to injustice. This is a 'critical' use of deconstruction in a very ordinary sense of that word – it involves pointing out that something is wrong and arguing that it could and should be made better or done better. (Balkin, 'Being Just with Deconstruction', p. 394.)

However, it is not sufficient simply to *assume* that deconstruction can be used to reveal injustice, it must be justified. The answer lies in the reason why individuals (including Derrida) undertake deconstruction. They do so because they believe that 'there is a better way of looking at things, even if this is in turn subject to further deconstruction' (Balkin, 'Being Just with Deconstruction', p. 395).

For Balkin deconstruction is not simply to reverse the hierarchy between conceptual opposites such as 'racial equality' and 'apartheid', rather the deconstructive argument becomes the 'careful and patient analysis of the grounds of similarity and difference between conceptual opposition in shifting historical and practical contexts of judgment'. Balkin argues that 'one deconstructs a conceptual opposition by showing that it is really a *nested opposition*. A nested opposition is a conceptual opposition in which the two terms "contain" each other; that is they possess simultaneous relationships of difference and similarity which are manifested as we consider them in different contexts of judgment'. 'To analyze this opposition as a nested opposition, we might ask whether there are certain features of apartheid that have unexpected commonalities with particular theories of racial equality, and whether discovery of these similarities can assist in our legal and social critiques' (Balkin, 'Being Just with Deconstruction', p. 398. See further J. M. Balkin, 'Nested Oppositions' (1990) 99 *Yale Law Journal* 1669).

For instance, if apartheid is defined, initially, by governmental distinctions based on race, it has similarities with one conception of racial equality which, for example through programmes of positive discrimination, is also based on similar governmental decisions. Thus this forces the interpreter to look for a better distinction between these two 'opposites', for example one based on 'the presence of racial subordination, or the state's decision to replicate or foster beliefs about white supremacy and black inferiority'. 'The goal of this analysis is to change our view of the real issues involved, by discovering relevant grounds of similarity and difference. Such an analysis, in turn, will lead to new concepts, categories and distinctions that can be further deconstructed'. '[D]o some conceptions of racial equality produce or maintain racial subordination by other means? If so, then they have important similarities to systems of apartheid, and these similarities can serve as the basis of a critique' (Balkin, 'Being Just with Deconstruction', pp. 398–9). Thus the process of deconstruction continues, seeking a better explanation or conception of 'racial equality' by looking at what is supposed to be its conceptual opposite. Each reinterpretation brings a better understanding, though each in turn can be deconstructed. There is no absolute truth, though there are relative truths. Nevertheless, the process of deconstruction is not a scientific one – 'it is informed by the values and commitments of the individual deconstructor, and the directions she chooses to investigate'. Thus although theoretically deconstruction is 'potentially endless, our own deconstructive arguments must come to an end at some point', unless our underlying political and moral values are themselves deconstructed (Balkin, 'Being Just with Deconstruction', p. 399). Balkin thus concludes at this point that although deconstructive argument will not lead 'inexorably to justice' it can 'used rightly . . . assist us in our critical endeavors' (Balkin, 'Being Just with Deconstruction', p. 400).

This does not really seem to take the argument any further in establishing a firm link between deconstruction and justice. Clearly with these inadequacies in mind, Balkin attempts to make a link between deconstructive argument and the 'transcendental value of justice', by positing law and justice as conceptual opposites:

> We deconstruct law for critical purposes because of a perceived inadequation between law and justice – because we seek a justice yet unrealized in law. Thus our deconstruction of law assumes a conceptual opposition between law and justice. However, deconstruction asks us to reconceptualize every conceptual opposition as a nested opposition. When we reconceptualize the opposition between law and justice as a nested opposition, we discover that there is in fact a complex relationship of mutual dependence and differentiation between the two. (Balkin, 'Being Just with Deconstruction', pp. 400–1.)

'Law is always, to some extent and to some degree, unjust'. However, the only way of articulating a person's conceptions of justice is through imperfect laws. Such laws will be inadequate leading to a deconstruction and a modified law, and so the process continues. Balkin states that:

> [W]e must think of our value of justice as an insatiable demand that can never be fulfilled by human law. In short, we must postulate a human value of justice which transcends each and every example of justice in human law, culture and convention. In this way our deconstructive argument brings us to a transcendental value of justice. Thus the normative use of deconstruction becomes what I call 'transcendental' deconstruction, because it must presume the existence of transcendental human values articulated in culture but never adequately captured by culture. (Balkin, 'Being Just with Deconstruction', p. 402.)

Nevertheless Balkin is not approaching Plato's transcendental values, simply 'the insatiable yearning or longing for justice lodged in the human heart'. 'Hence, our laws are imperfect not because they are bad copies of a determinate Form of justice, but because we must articulate our insatiable longing for justice in concrete institutions, and our constructions can never be identical with the longings that inspire them' (Balkin, 'Being Just with Deconstruction', p. 402. See further J. M. Balkin, 'Transcendental Deconstruction, Transcendent Justice' (1994) 92 *Michigan Law Review* 1131). Despite Balkin's valiant attempt to drag deconstruction away 'from the abyss of normative nihilism' (Balkin, 'Being Just with Deconstruction', p. 403), towards the pursuit of justice, the interpreter of Balkin is still left with the sense that since justice lacks any definable content, the analysis has taken us no further than justice simply being an individual's (including Balkin's) assertions or convictions. Having aligned themselves with Hume's scepticism (see 2.1; but see P. Foot, 'Does Moral Subjectivism Rest on a Mistake?' (1995) *Oxford Journal of Legal Studies* 1), postmodernists cannot accept any notion of there being 'basic goods' or a 'minimum content of natural law', as posited by modernists in the 'opposing' traditions of naturalism and positivism (see 5.2.2 (Finnis) and 3.5.3 (Hart)).

13.7 DECONSTRUCTION AND THE LIBERAL CONSTITUTION

The application of the deconstructive technique to the liberal constitution is not only a useful illustration of how postmodernism is applied to legal texts or more accurately legal concepts, but also how postmodernists use this technique to dejustify or delegitimate the liberal constitution. Indeed, many modernist legal theories are forms of constitutionalism, in that they reinforce the idea of a society governed by the rule of law with the supreme law or the constitution at the top of the pyramid of laws. Mention need only be made of Hart, Kelsen or Rawls. The recognition of law as the key to the exercise of power facilitates the legitimation of the exercise of such political power. Thus constitutional jurisprudence is one of the 'grand narrative[s] of modernity' (Douzinas and Warrington, *Postmodern Jurisprudence*, p. 28) which, when deconstructed, will reveal the inadequacy of its claim to the truth. Clear links can be seen here between postmodernism and critical legal studies in this respect.

Schlag looks at the practice of liberal justification, which he sees as premised upon a 'popular constitutional mythology' (P. Schlag, 'The Empty Circles of Liberal Justification' (1997) 96(1) *Michigan Law Review* 1 at p. 3).

The popular *narrative* recounts the story of a sovereign people who in a foundational moment established their own state by setting forth in a written constitution the powers and limitations of their government. The very identity, content, and character of this government is established by the Constitution itself. In turn, the authority of this Constitution stems from the consent of the governed – their acquiescence in a limited surrender of their sovereign power in return for the benefits of a limited, representative government. (Schlag, 'The Empty Circles', p. 3.)

The key concepts for liberal constitutionalists are 'The Constitution', 'The Founding', 'The People' and 'The Consent of the People'. The Constitution is the 'authoritative paramount norm' which is invoked in a variety of ways 'as icon, symbol, plan, rule, argument, text, spirit – to perform a variety of actions – constitute, organize, control, regulate, inspire, justify'. The Founding is 'an origin that signals a discontinuity between all that has happened before and all that will happen after that moment'. 'The People also occupy a special place in the popular constitutional mythology. From the high school civics classroom to the most intellectualized law school seminar, the people is held to be Sovereign'. 'Flowing from this is that the legitimacy of the Constitution depends upon the Consent of the People' (Schlag, 'The Empty Circles', pp. 3–5).

These concepts are so deeply embedded in American culture that it rarely seems to be an issue of what gave the generation of 1787 the authority to delimit freedom for all subsequent generations who in reality have not been consulted despite the mythology of consent. Liberal jurists tend to obscure these problems by 'rendering the key ontological identities and narratives more capacious and appealing than the historical originals'. Rawls' principles of justice, Hart's rule of recognition, or Dworkin's principle of integrity give us 'the kind of norm that will allow each of us to read into it whatever we wish to find there. The more abstract, mystical, or capacious the paramount norm, the less it will exhibit concrete features that might trigger the objection of any particular reader'. The problems of the founding moment being simply a point in history is removed by Rawls' 'timeless' original position or Hart's mythical transition from pre-legal to legal world (a step from the pre-modern to the modern). The problem of lack of consultation with the real subjects of the constitution is removed by the invention of 'grand supra-individual subjects', such as Dworkin's Hercules or Rawls' persons in the original position, who clearly give their consent to the constitution (Schlag, 'The Empty Circles', pp. 12–17).

Schlag is concerned not simply to reveal the myths of liberal constitutionalism, for myths by themselves are perhaps inherent in any conception of society. He believes that it is necessary to take the deconstruction further. The overall myth of liberalism offers the individual (interpreter) a stark choice:

Choose the myth or face perdition. Within the circle there is something good, appealing, admirable, necessary, sensible, reasonable (this is liberalism), while on the outside there is something bad, unappealing, contemptible, unavoidable, senseless, and unreasonable (this is the antithesis of liberalism and goes by names such as chaos, tyranny, totalitarianism, and so on). (Schlag, 'The Empty Circles', pp. 24–25.)

The individual has to choose the whole system or nothing else. Once consent to the paramount norm is established this 'necessarily entails consent to a whole series of institutions and practices that are authorized by the paramount norm. Once the paramount norm is accepted, it is as if the entire liberal pinball machine lights up' (Schlag, 'The Empty Circles', p. 25). Despite liberal myths of rational free choice in the original contract between

State and government, individuals in reality choose liberalism for emotional reasons such as fear of dictatorship or anarchy (see Hobbes at 4.5.1). In reality the element of choice is not available to the liberal consumer, given that they live within a political world 'already mapped out in liberal categories'. The only benchmarks given to the individual within such a world are liberal ones and these benchmarks themselves are not subject to criticism – 'the liberal thinker approaches a category such as "rights" with the same degree of credulity that a medieval scholar approaches the category of "angels", or a communist apparatchik the category of "bourgeoisie"' (Schlag, 'The Empty Circles', pp. 32–4).

What Schlag is pointing to is that liberalism is not a rational choice, it is an emotional one and thus does not have a superior claim to acceptance than other visions of society. Schlag reveals this by deconstructing the language of liberal constitutionalism, revealing it simply to be a legitimation of a political choice that was made by certain individuals centuries ago. The use of 'metalanguage' such as the 'rule of recognition' (Hart) or the 'original position' (Rawls), is an abstraction from the US constitution of 1787 and the founding fathers (Madison, Hamilton etc.) in order to represent liberalism as timeless and rational. Furthermore, the system is self-perpetuating, in that interpretation of law within the liberal system, according to liberal jurists (see for example Dworkin, chapter 8), is undertaken by reference to these meta-narratives. The point of deconstruction though is that those meta-narratives themselves, as Schlag has shown, are themselves deconstructible revealing a clearer, less mythological, interpretation. Thus the 'Constitution' is represented as the 'Paramount Norm' or words to that effect by liberal thinkers, but further deconstruction will reveal it to be 'Ultimate *Authority*' and so on (Schlag, 'The Empty Circles', pp. 43–6).

13.7.1 Postmodern constitutional theory

Postmodernism may be successful in deconstructing the rigid, arbitrary normative structure of the liberal legal system but, as with Critical Legal Studies, the issue is whether it can offer an alternative without falling into the trap of constructing another legal leviathan. Postmodernists recognise the importance of the constitution to the liberal legal order, but would they retain it within a postmodern society? Ladeur offers a post-modern constitutional theory, based on what he calls a 'self-organising society' (K. H. Ladeur, 'Post-Modern Constitutional Theory: A Prospect for the Self-Organising Society' (1997) 60 *Modern Law Review* 617).

As with those visions offered by Unger (see 12.4.2), the propositions are essentially based on an improvement of liberalism. Liberalism based on a rigid and illegitimate constitution, though, is clearly inadequate. There needs to be a transformation of the system because of the 'growth of complexity', namely the recognition that there is uncertainty and indeterminacy in every aspect of law and life. This forces the 'legal system to reintroduce more flexibility, more capacity for self-description and more learning capability into the range of its operations' (Ladeur, 'Post-Modern Constitutional Theory', p. 620). However, an 'experimenting society' is still linked to 'the liberal principle that a constitution must always be based on a kind of pre-constituted order' for without it there lies the path towards chaos. Despite this attempted reconciliation of the old order with the new flexibility, it is difficult to see any justification beyond the pragmatic for the retention of the old order as the following extract illustrates:

A post-modern society cannot be integrated by common shared beliefs but rather by overlapping networks of practical differentiated political and social interactions. These generate a kind of implicit knowledge which functions as the raw material for setting up explicit conventions. Civilised society should be based on the possibility of the pursuit of self-interest, a strategy from which much more learning capability and universality can be generated than by an abstract discourse of justice which is not adapted to the description of constraints imposed on networks of collective actors, and, at the same time, this permits it to take advantage of its inherent productive potential to permit greater differentiation and innovation. This approach could introduce new life into the a-centric distributed order of rights and competencies of the liberal system. (Ladeur, 'Post-Modern Constitutional Theory', pp. 626–7.)

A possible deconstruction of this language suggests that the vision is a depressing one where, because of the lack of accepted values, pragmatics dominate, where individualism no longer predominates but fluctuating 'organisational networks of relationships' built on self-interest. The collapse of any distinctions upon which modern liberal society is built – particularly the distinction between 'public' and 'private' sectors – results in an unstructured, self-regulating society, where liberal justice discourse may form a background but has little relevance. 'The stress of this conception is laid on a paradoxical eternal determination of internal self-determination of organisational networks of interrelationships, leading towards a new legal order of a "self-organising" society which is distinguished from the primary liberal society of individuals by its characteristic that its self-modification comprises of its own rules.' Rather than substantive rights, a post-modern society would be based more squarely on 'procedural rules stressing flexibility, innovation, experimentation'. Although a rights-based individualistic society has been relatively successful in managing indeterminacy, the constitutional system now needs to be remodelled to take account of indeterminacy leading to a 'more complex, more rapidly self-modifying and self-organising society' (Ladeur, 'Post-Modern Constitutional Theory', pp. 627–9).

13.8 RECONSTRUCTION

While Ladeur perhaps shows that postmodernism can be allied to capitalism, the more natural bent of postmodernism is left-leaning. Capitalism is equated with liberalism and modernity and only continues its domination through a combination of inertia and hegemony. Bonaventura de Sousa Santos has provided a vision of a postmodernist transition to a new alternative. As with all postmodernism, Santos recognises the 'increasingly complex network of subjectivities' enmeshing each individual. Correspondingly there is a 'proliferation of political and legal interpretive communities' whose activities will result in a decanonisation and trivialisation of the law. While recognising that 'modern men and women are configurations or networks of different subjectivities', Santos depicts four, later six, prevalent 'structural subjectivities' arising out of the four dominant 'structural places' found in contemporary capitalist society: 'the householdplace', 'the workplace', 'the citizen place', the 'world place' (B. de Sousa Santos, 'The Postmodern Transition: Law and Politics' in A. Sarat and T. R. Kearns (eds.), *The Fate of the Law* (Ann Arbor: Michigan University Press, 1991), 79 at pp. 105–7), and later the 'marketplace' and 'communityplace' (B. de Sousa Santos, *Towards a New Common Sense* (Routledge: New York, 1995), p. 485).

While providing for more focus on particular subjectivities than is normal in postmodernism, de Sousa Santos also narrows down the dominant forms of power in capitalist society, thus distinguishing himself from Foucault:

> But again I think, and now contrary to Foucault, that we cannot go to the extreme of giving up the task of structuring and grading forms and power relations. If power is everywhere, it is nowhere. In my view, the four structural places . . . are the loci of four major power forms circulating in our society. These power forms are: Patriarchy, corresponding to the householdplace; exploitation corresponding to the workplace; domination, corresponding to the citizenplace; and unequal exchange, corresponding to the worldplace. There are other forms of power but these are the basic ones . . . Of all four forms of power, only one, domination, is democratic, and even so in a limited degree and in a small group of countries in which the advanced capitalist societies are included. *The political aim of postmodern critical theory is to extend the democratic ideal to all other forms of power.* (de Sousa Santos, 'The Postmodern Transition', p. 108. Emphasis added.)

Thus in the *householdplace*, the contradiction and competition is between the dominant paradigm of the 'patriarchal family' and the emergent paradigm of the 'cooperative domestic community' which includes 'all alternative forms of domestic sociability and sexuality'. In the *workplace* the competition is between the dominant paradigm of 'capitalist expansionism, and the emergent paradigm of eco-socialist sustainability' which involves 'free associations of producers, geared towards the democratic production of use-values, without degrading nature'. In the *marketplace* the contradiction is between the paradigm of 'individualistic consumerism', and the paradigm of 'human needs' in which 'the satisfiers are at the service of needs' and the 'market is but one of many forms of consumption'. In de Sousa Santos's other additional structure, the *communityplace*, the competition is between 'fortress-communities' and 'amoeba-communities'. Within the latter 'identity is always multiple, unfinished, undergoing a process of reconstruction and reinvention that is, in fact, a process of ongoing identification'. In the *citzenplace*, where the competition is between 'authoritarian democracy' and 'radical democracy' with the latter as the emergent paradigm, 'the democratic process is furthered by the transformation of relations of power into relations of shared authority, despotic law into democratic law, regulatory common sense into emancipatory common sense'. In the *worldplace* the transition is away from unequal development and exclusive sovereignty towards 'democratically sustainable development and reciprocally permeable sovereignty'. The latter will abolish the North-South hierarchy and thus will result in the emergence of a 'new system of international and transnational relations guided by the principles of cosmopolitanism and common heritage of mankind' (de Sousa Santos, *Towards a New Common Sense*, pp. 484–9).

As with Roberto Unger in the field of Critical Legal Studies, de Sousa Santos is prepared to make presumptions, to offer structure although of an intensely flexible nature. De Sousa Santos does this by looking at the established paradigms on which capitalist societies are built and then offering opposites or rather alternatives. The technique is typically postmodern, though the willingness to make choices from multiple subjectivities is not.

Santos's distillation of the basic structures in society flows down into the law. For instance domestic law reflects the householdplace and so on. The undemocratic and rigid nature of these laws is under attack as there emerge 'forms of law that are explicitly liquid, ephemeral, ever negotiable, and renegotiable, in sum disposable'. It is perhaps controversially that de Sousa Santos gives EC legislation as an example of the new law. The new law is an 'antiauratic law, an interstitial, almost colloquial law, which repeats social relations instead of modelling them, and in such a way that the distinction between professional and non-professional legal knowledge (as much as the discrepancy between the law in books and the law in action) ceases to make sense' (de Sousa Santos, 'The Postmodern Transition', pp. 112–13).

Santos recognises that for postmodernism to move away from mere deconstruction towards reconstruction it is necessary 'to reinvent the future by opening up new horizons of possibility mapped out by radical new alternatives. Merely to criticize the dominant paradigm, though crucial, is not enough. We must also define the emergent paradigm, this being the really important and difficult task'. De Sousa Santos urges a return to utopian thinking on the basis that modernity is generally hostile to such thinking. De Sousa Santos is arguing against the alternatives offered by liberalism of either 'modernity or barbarity'. The seeds of the utopian alternatives are found within the margins and within the 'other' of modernity (Santos, *Towards a New Common Sense*, pp. 479–82). For inspiration de Sousa Santos looks to innovative, somewhat chaotic, 'frontier' societies where authority and power have not been channelled and centralised, as well as baroque subjectivity which 'lives comfortably with the temporary suspension of order and canons' investing instead in 'the local, the particular, the momentary, the ephemeral and the transitory'; and above all 'The South' which 'signifies the form of human suffering caused by capitalist modernity'. Praising the notions of community and solidarity which draw on all three inspirations of frontier, baroque and the South, and found clearly expressed in the writings and thoughts of Chomsky and Gandhi, de Sousa Santos's methods of paradigmatic contradiction and competition between the structures of modernity and the emerging radical paradigms are powerful and compelling. As with Unger this is not 'the blueprint of a new order' but evidence that the 'collapse of the existing order . . . does not entail barbarism at all'. 'It means, rather, an opportunity to reinvent a commitment to authentic emancipation, a commitment, moreover, which, rather than being a product of enlightened vanguardist thought, unfolds as sheer common sense' (Santos, *Towards a New Common Sense*, pp. 491–519).

13.9 CONCLUSION

There appears to be a paradox at the heart of postmodernism which undermines its own claim to the truth, that is between its commitment to radical and absolute pluralism and a commitment to the 'other'. As Donald-son points out:

> Tolerance is the supreme postmodern virtue, yet the question that needs to be asked is, 'How should we tolerate? Are we to tolerate the murder of six million Jews, racism, poverty, or homophobia?' These are the very evils which lead to the rejection of modernism; are we now to allow them to continue? Few postmodernists would argue that we should, but a commit-ment to absolute pluralism cannot allow anything else. It is somehow assumed that 'true' pluralism does not allow for these things, but to make this claim is to admit reference to some external and universally valid standard. Unless we are willing to accept absolutely anything, such an external reference must eventually be made. What this tells us is that postmodernists, just like everybody else, make use of and reference to a worldview. (Donaldson, 'Some Reservations About Law and Postmodern-ism', pp. 338–9.)

Clearly genocide and other human actions are wrong, this is a truth that even postmodernists seem to accept. Postmodernists though seem to accept it on the basis of pure conviction whereas most modernists would base such truths on objective foundations, symbolised by Hart's minimum content of natural law. If the law is founded upon these basic axioms then the question arises as to whether it is immune from postmodernist deconstruction. If deconstruction is applied to every single law then the question arises as to whether law becomes largely irrelevant. Critics of postmodernism believe so: '[o]nce relativism is accepted into the law, there is no basis upon which to justify legal prohibition or action' (Donaldson, 'Some Reservations about Law and Postmodernism', p. 244). It may well be that the judge's or the legislator's attempts at putting these basic axioms into the law are faulty and require deconstruction so that a better law can be enacted, but this deconstruction must come to a halt when all the layers of meaning have been peeled back to reveal the truth. That there must be an end point is clear if the core provisions of the law are going to survive the postmodernist assault. It appears essential that such provisions do have this core immunity if a society is to have legal safeguards against a descent into chaos and violence.

However, while it may be argued that certain laws have a core meaning which remain intact in the face of deconstruction, it is not clear that this can be said about all, if not most, laws which are built on presuppositions rather than unshakeable moral foundations. Such laws may be given 'meaning' in practice where public opinion as well as the views of judges will have an influence but they are susceptible to potentially endless deconstruction. The question then is whether this destroys the law. Is the law about absolutes and certainty or can it cope with, indeed, benefit from the extreme fluidity and change that postmodernism brings? Is the law on the edge of the abyss of indeterminacy or on the brink of a golden age of justice?

Postmodernism makes us think about these questions, though it does not, perhaps cannot, provide answers to them. However, the use of opposing paradigms as employed by Santos does give an insight into a possible, fairer, alternative. De Sousa Santos employs the postmodernist technique of opposition – of the structures of modernity with their postmodernist counterparts drawn from the margins of society. The alternative modes of domesticity, productivity and democracy, and the fluid and disposable laws which accompany them, do seem to give postmodernism that element of reconstruction it so desperately needs if it is to move beyond the negative.

13.10   FURTHER READING

Balkin, J. M., 'Understanding Legal Understanding: The Legal Subject and the Problem of Legal Coherence' (1993) 103 *Yale Law Journal* 105.

Boyle, J., 'Is Subjectivity Possible?: The Postmodern Subject in Legal Theory' (1991) 62 *University of Colorado Law Review* 489.

Carty, A. (ed.), *Post-Modern Law* (Edinburgh: Edinburgh University Press, 1994).

Davies, M., *Delimiting the Law: 'Postmodernism' and the Politics of Law* (London: Pluto Press, 1996).

Doherty T., (ed.), *Postmodernism: A Reader* (London: Harvester Wheatsheaf, 1993).

Douzinas, C., Goodrich P. and Hachamovitch, Y., *Politics, Postmodernity and Critical Legal Studies* (London: Routledge, 1994).

Frug, M. J., 'A Postmodern Feminist Manifesto (An Unfinished Draft)' (1992) 105 *Harvard Law Review* 1045.

McGowan, J., *Postmodernism and its Critics* (London: Cornell University Press, 1991).

Mootz, F. J., 'Is the Rule of Law Possible in a Postmodern World?' (1993) 68 *Washington Law Review* 249.

Patterson, D., 'Postmodernism/Feminism/Law' (1992) 77 *Cornell Law Review* 254.

Patterson, D., *Postmodernism and Law* (Aldershot: Dartmouth, 1994).

Schlag, P., 'Normativity and the Politics of Form' (1991) 139 *University of Pennsylvania Law Review* 801.

Silverman, H. J., *Derrida and Deconstruction* (London: Routledge, 1989).

Weed, E., 'Reading at the Limit' (1994) 15 *Cardozo Law Review* 1671.

CHAPTER FOURTEEN

The Economic Analysis of Law

Should law be primarily concerned with promoting economic efficiency? The answer to this question will depend upon the political leanings of the reader. The believer in the free market and *laissez-faire* economics will answer in the affirmative, whereas the more left-leaning individual will counter that law should be more about justice, rights and redistribution. *Is* the law mainly concerned about the promotion of economic efficiency? The two different answers already given may be repeated, but the former probably with less conviction than before. Even the most avid free marketeer will admit that the law has a central concern to protect rights and uphold justice, although certain parts of it will be concerned with promoting and protecting market transactions. Nevertheless, despite the fact that judges, lawyers and individuals appear to view the law in terms of rights and justice, there is a school of legal thought which not only advocates that the law ought to be concerned with economic efficiency, but also claims to put forward a descriptive theory in which law is simply and straightforwardly concerned with promotion of economic efficiency and the protection of wealth as a value.

14.1 THE ANTECEDENTS OF THE ECONOMIC APPROACH

There have been many claims as to the origins of the economic approach to the law, which grew out of the United States in the early 1960s with work by Ronald Coase, Guido Calabresi and Richard Posner. As with many theories, the so-called Chicago school can trace its inspirations from an amalgam of previous approaches.

14.1.1   Realism

In some ways the economic approach grew out of American realism which, you will remember, was desirous to better explain law in terms of non-legal factors such as economics. Indeed, with its precision and scientific underpinnings, economics is more attractive than other social sciences for lawyers wishing to point to links between law and non-legal factors:

> . . . whatever its deficiencies, the economic theory of law seems, to this biased observer anyway, the best positive theory of law extant. It is true that anthropologists, sociologists, psychologists, political scientists, and other social scientists besides economists also do positive analyses of the legal system. But their work is thus far insufficiently rich in theoretical and empirical content to afford serious competition to the economist. My impression, for what it is worth, is that these fields have produced neither systematic, empirical research on the legal system nor plausible, coherent, and empirically verifiable theories of the system. (R Posner, 'The Economic Approach to the Law' (1975) 53 Texas Law Review 757 at pp. 774–5.)

However, the fact that the economic approach concentrates on one non-legal area to the exclusion of others is where law and economics and realism start to diverge.

14.1.2   Critical legal studies

In the discussion of the critical school (chapter 12) it has already been pointed out that critical legal studies can also trace its roots back to American Realism. This has led to somewhat superficial comparisons between law and economics and critical legal studies in that 'both treat law as a political phenomenon; and both undermine the image of law as an autonomous discipline'. However, this comparison ignores the obvious differences between the formalism (in economic terms) of the economic approach and the anti-formalism of the critical school as well as the divergent political directions of the two schools. The conclusion is that both the economic and critical schools have 'sprung from the same well' (N. Duxbury, *Patterns of American Jurisprudence* (Oxford: Clarendon Press, 1995), pp. 301–309).

14.1.3   Utilitarianism

Another way of looking at the economic approach to the law is to view it as an improved model of utilitarianism. Bentham's utilitarianism was based on the 'felicific calculus', the greatest happiness to the greatest number (see chapter 2). The inherent uncertainty of lawmaking within this method is remedied to a large extent by the economic analysis of law. J. W. Harris explains how the remedy works.

> The felicific calculus is difficult because one cannot be sure how people will react to alternative measures. The answer of economic analysis is to make an assumption. Man is a rational maximiser of his satisfactions. The entire theory is premised on this definition. If he will achieve more of what he wants to achieve by taking step X rather than step Y, *homo economicus* will, by definition, take step X; to do otherwise would, by definition, be acting irrationally. The felicific calculus is also problematic because of the empirical difficulties in finding out what people do in fact want. No problem! For the economic analysis of law, what I want is, by definition, what I am willing to pay for - either in money, or by the deployment of some other resource that I have such as time and effort. (J.W. Harris, *Legal Philosophies* (London: Butterworths, 1980), p. 42.)

Richard Posner, in explaining the meaning of 'wealth maximization', states that 'wealth' refers

> to the sum of all tangible and intangible goods and services. . . . If A would be willing to pay up to $100 for B's stamp collection, it is worth $100 to A. If B would be willing to sell the stamp collection for any price above $90, it is worth $90 to B. So if B sells the stamp collection to A say for $100 . . . the wealth of society will rise by $10,

in that A has a stamp collection worth $100 and B has $100, whereas before the transaction A had $100 and B had a stamp collection worth $90. As Posner says, the transaction 'will not raise measured wealth . . . by $10 but the real addition to social wealth consists of the $10 increment in non-pecuniary satisfaction that A derives from the purchase, compared with that of B'. Posner is illustrating that wealth in the economist's sense is 'not a simple monetary measure', and it is this definition of wealth we must use when looking at the law, for Posner asserts that the 'common law facilitates wealth-maximising transactions in a variety of ways' (R. A. Posner, *The Problems of Jurisprudence* (Cambridge, Mass.: Harvard University Press, 1990), pp. 356–7).

However, a fundamental defect can be seen in the basic assumptions of the economic school - that man is a rational maximiser of his satisfactions. The reader will have seen how such basic assumptions about the nature of man have led to different conceptions of law even within the same school - the pessimism of Plato need only be contrasted with the optimistic view of human nature held by Aristotle, similar differences can be seen between Augustine and Aquinas, and Hobbes and Locke. Economists and accountants may be rational maximisers but are the rest of us? Do social workers, nurses, teachers, to name but a few, act in such a rational self-interested manner, or do they in fact act out of altruistic motives rather than individualistic ones?

However, the economic approach seems to avoid this problem by making an assumption that human beings are rational. This allows the economic school to view human behaviour as always so motivated. This makes the economic approach 'basically circular; it argues that since people are rationally self-interested, what they do shows what they value, and their willingness to pay for what they value is the ultimate proof of their rational self-interest' (W. Z. Hirsch, *Law and Economics* (New York: Academic Press, 1979), p. 4). The point is that once this assumption is made then all human actions are rational in the economic sense - the approach is essentially self-justifying due to the fact that it is impossible to say that a particular human action did not satisfy the individuals concerned in a 'non-pecuniary' way. Professor Hirsch further asks the question of 'whether human value is indeed determined by people's willingness to pay or whether it is determined rather by people's ability to pay for the good or service' (Hirsch, *Law and Economics*, p. 5).

A related problem is that the economists' assumption of the rational man is not the same as the reasonable man so often central to legal doctrine. 'The reasonable man, according to the traditional tort literature, will ordinarily behave in a reasonable, prudent manner. Thus he will act with fair regard to the welfare of others.' . . . 'The rational man, according to traditional economic theory, seeks to maximise his own self-interest: he shows only limited concern for the well-being of others' (Hirsch, *Law and Economics*, p. 7).

14.2 DIFFERENT CONCEPTIONS WITHIN THE SCHOOL

The work of Richard Posner, so often viewed as the greatest contributor to the Chicago school of thought, will be examined later in the chapter. In this section, the works of Coase and Calabresi will be outlined to give the reader an insight into their writings, and also to highlight the fact that there are significant differences in approach within the school, despite the fact that the application of economic principles to the law is portrayed as purely scientific, and therefore more universally acceptable than other approaches. It must be noted though that the claim to have science on its side is not unique to the Chicago school. The reader will have witnessed such claims in many of the other schools of thought considered in this book.

14.2.1 The Coase theorem

Many of the ideas put forward by the Chicago school are derived from an article by Ronald Coase (R. H. Coase, 'The Problem of Social Costs' (1960) 3 *Journal of Law and Economics* 1). A good explanation of the theorem is to be found in A. M. Polinsky's work (*An Introduction to Law and Economics* (Boston, Mass.: Little Brown and Co., 1983), pp. 11–14). He posits the problem of a factory which is emitting smoke, thereby damaging the laundry hung out at five nearby houses. In legal terms the question is whether the residents have the right to clean air or whether the factory has the right to pollute in these circumstances. Our natural instinct is to favour the residents in that it is the factory causing the damage. However, for the economists the issue is not one of causation in that, although the factory has caused the damage, that damage would not have occurred if the houses were not so close to the factory. 'If we are to discuss the problem in terms of causation, both parties cause the damage' (R. Coase, 'The Problem of Social Cost' (1960) 3 *Journal of Law and Economics* 13).

For the Chicago school the issue is not one of causation or justice but of efficiency. In Polinsky's example each of the residents suffers $75 in damages, a total of $375. The smoke damage can be eliminated in two ways - either by installing a smokescreen in the chimney of the factory at a cost of $150 or by providing each of the residents with a tumble dryer at a cost of $50 per resident (total cost $250). 'The efficient solution is clearly to install the smokescreen since it eliminates total damages of $375 for an outlay of only $150, and it is cheaper than purchasing five dryers for $250' (Polinsky, *An Introduction to Law and Economics*, p. 11). But who is to purchase the smokescreen? Our automatic assumption that the factory should pay is not dictated by efficiency but by our own instincts for justice – embodied in one of the fundamental principles of environmental law, whether municipal or international, namely the polluter pays (see, for example, P. W. Birnie and A. E. Boyle, *International Law and the Environment* (Oxford: Clarendon Press, 1992), pp. 109–111).

The efficient solution depends on whether there are transaction costs or not. 'Transaction costs include the costs of identifying the parties with whom one has to bargain, the costs of getting together with them, the costs of the bargaining process itself, and the costs of enforcing any bargain reached' (Polinsky, *An Introduction to Law and Economics*, p. 12). If there are zero transaction costs then for an efficient solution it does not matter whether we have a legal rule saying that the polluter pays or whether we have a legal rule allowing the right to pollute, i.e. whether the factory or the residents pays the $150. Presumably in these conditions of zero transaction costs then the judge may fall back on notions of justice apart from the requirements of efficiency.

However, it is rare for there to be zero transaction costs. If there are positive transaction costs then there is a more sophisticated version of the Coase theorem.

If there are positive transaction costs, the efficient outcome may not occur under every legal rule. In these circumstances, the preferred legal rule is the rule that minimizes the effects of transaction costs. These effects include the actual incurring of transaction costs and the inefficient choices induced by a desire to avoid transaction costs. (Polinsky, *An Introduction to Law and Economics*, p. 13.)

In the above example the residents would have to incur transaction costs of $60 each, in the form of 'transportation costs and the value attached to time', to buy a smokescreen for the factory. This would then render the right to pollute inefficient and the right to clean air efficient. The law should then favour the residents and make the factory, whose transaction costs are, let us assume, zero or less than the residents' pay for the smokescreen (Polinsky, *An Introduction to Law and Economics*, p. 12).

14.2.2 Efficiency and equity

As with most schools of legal philosophy, there are significant variations on the central theme. In the situation where transaction costs are not zero, Calabresi not only addresses the 'narrow' issue of efficiency in his analysis, he also looks at the nature of a right and the issue of its distribution as well (G. Calabresi and A. D. Melamed, 'Property Rules, Liability Rules and Inalienability: One View of the Cathedral' (1972) 85 Harv L Rev 1089–1128). The premise on which this branch of the Chicago school is based is that society has to make 'first order legal decisions' as to which entitlements prevail over others – for example, between the right to clean air and the right to pollute. In the absence of such decisions, 'life itself will be decided on the basis of might makes right'. Calabresi then lists three groups of reasons for deciding in favour of one entitlement over another: 'economic efficiency, distributional preferences, and other justice considerations'.

On the first, Calabresi states that:

> economic efficiency asks that we choose the set of entitlements which would lead to the allocation of resources which could not be improved in the sense that a further change would not so improve the condition of those who gained by it that they could compensate those who lost from it and still be better off than before. This is often called Pareto optimality.

However, in addition to this traditional definition of efficiency, Calabresi then notes that Pareto optimality will differ with the starting distribution of wealth. 'Pareto optimality is optimal *given* a distribution of wealth, but different distributions of wealth imply their own Pareto optimal allocation of resources'. A person's right to silence may be secured because he is willing to pay more for it than his neighbour is prepared to pay for the right to make noise. On a wider scale the wealth and power of industrialists will result in a general right to pollute.

So far, despite his initial warnings against the powerful and rich prevailing unless there are first-order legal decisions which allocate entitlements, this seems to be meaningless if a party or interest group can force the allocation in their favour. However, Calabresi's approach differs from that of Coase and Posner, who tend to base their theories on the efficient outcome of a dispute between two parties, in that he looks at the decisions society has to make. A society (i.e. the legislature) chooses the initial entitlements on whatever basis it wishes. Some of these entitlements may then be renegotiated by individuals (i.e. those protected by a simple property rule), others may be bought and sold but only at a price determined by the State (governed by so-called liability rules), whilst others may not be sold at any cost or only under certain conditions (governed by inalienability rules). Entitlements governed by liability rules, and even more so by inalienability rules, involve a high degree of State intervention, and seem to fly in the face of the dictates of efficiency - at least in the free-market sense.

Calabresi asks this very question:

Why cannot a society simply decide . . . who should receive any given entitlement, and then its transfer occur through a voluntary negotiation? Why, in other words, cannot society limit itself to the property rule? To do this it would only need to protect and enforce the initial entitlements from all attacks, perhaps through criminal sanctions, and to enforce voluntary contracts for their transfer. Why do we need liability rules at all?

The answer is simple enough in efficiency terms:

Often the cost of establishing the value of an initial entitlement by negotiation is so great than even though a transfer of the entitlement would benefit all concerned, such transfer will not occur. If a collective determination of the value were available instead, the beneficial transfer would quickly come about.

He gives the rather extreme example of a tract of land owned by 1,000 owners in 1,000 parcels. As parkland, the tract of land would benefit a neighbouring town of 100,000 people. Each citizen of the town would be willing to pay an average of £100 to have it. 'The park is Pareto desirable if the owners of the tracts of land . . . . actually value their entitlements at less than $10,000,000 or an average of $10,000 a tract'. The owners in fact value them at $8,000 each. Economic efficiency dictates that the transaction should occur but this may well not happen because 'there is no reason to believe that a market, a decentralized system of valuing, will cause people to express their true valuations and hence yield results which all would *in fact* agree are desirable'. In such situations where negotiations are so complex, involving many individuals, an efficient result may never emerge, and so it is in fact much more efficient for the State to impose the market valuation.

Davies and Holdcroft provide this evaluation of Calabresi and Melamed's approach:

> Calabresi and Melamed's distinctions between different kinds of entitlements is an important one. One advantage of an entitlement protected by a property rule is, of course, that since it can be sold voluntarily, its value is determined by that transaction; whereas the value of an entitlement protected by a liability rule may be much harder to determine if others may breach it and then compensate for the breach. The possibility of both over- and under-compensation is obvious, either of which would, of course, be inefficient. Moreover, the conditions of the Coase theorem are significantly relaxed since bargaining need not have taken place. And though the result may be more efficient, there may well be a feeling that the loss of the right to bargain is itself an important loss, and that the outcome does not have the same legitimacy, since it is the process gone through, not the actual outcome, that makes it legitimate. Even so, Calabresi and Melamed's reasons for claiming that entitlements protected by liability rules rather than property rules are the most efficient in some cases are convincing; so the issue is not about the efficiency of such rules in these cases, but about their justice. (H. Davies and D. Holdcroft, *Jurisprudence: Texts and Commentary* (London: Butterworths, 1995), p. 406.)

This modification of the economic approach does allow aspects of justice into the equation, in terms of the distribution of entitlements and the designation of which of the entitlements are to be protected by liability and inalienability rules. Having said that, however, the goal of the approach is still to produce economic efficiency; distributional issues are simply built in recognition of the greater acceptability, and reality, of such an approach. Issues of justice and distribution are clearly subject to the overriding aim of efficiency. In addition, there is a lack of clarity on the relationship between the distribution on the original entitlements and the concept of efficiency. A point made more generally by Burrows and Viljanovski:

> A disappointing feature of the economic approach to law to date has been the tendency of many studies to ignore the relationship between *social efficiency* and the distribution of income and wealth. If a perfectly competitive market is to operate we require . . . a clearly defined initial distribution of income and wealth which is legally protected by a set of property rights . . . The desirability of social efficiency as a goal requires value judgement as to the justness of the underlying distribution of income and property rights. (P. Burrows and C. J. Viljanovski, *The Economic Approach to the Law* (London: Butterworths, 1981), p. 12.)

Furthermore, other members of the Chicago school reject the idea that the economic approach should take account of these wider issues - that the introduction of wider issues, even in a subsidiary fashion, in fact undermines efficiency (see Polinsky, *An Introduction to Law and Economics*, p. 115). Indeed, it could be argued that the approach undermines justice as well, in that it is possible to argue that facilitating transactions voluntarily arrived at is just (Davies and Holdcroft, *Jurisprudence: Texts and Commentary*, p. 407). Furthermore, to allow the court to impose liability on a party when, if that situation was left to voluntary negotiation, the opposite result would have been achieved, produces an inefficient outcome, in that the party made liable, a manufacturer for instance, will simply pass the cost on to its customers.

However, one criticism of both approaches - Coase's and Calabresi's - is that, whether the court is applying liability rules or property rules, it is in both instances simply mimicking the market place, thereby allowing inefficiencies to creep in. Posner defends the role of the court in these instances by stating that 'the purist would insist that the relevant values are unknowable since they have not been revealed in a market transaction, but I believe that in many cases a court can make a reasonably accurate guess as to the allocation of resources that would maximise wealth' (R. A. Posner, *The Economics of Justice* (Cambridge, Mass.: Harvard University Press, 1981), p. 62). However, the concept of a court guessing what value parties place on a transaction reveals a serious flaw at the centre of the Chicago approach. The scientific analysis of the economist is subject to the vagaries of a courtroom in which none of the participants has formal training in economics but is steeped in a tradition of rights and justice based not on efficiency principles but on precedents, which may admittedly have been formulated in a time of free-market economics, but have long since developed in a peculiarly legal fashion.

Posner argues further that the art of legislation is not about the allocation of entitlements, but is simply about the improvement of economic efficiency.

14.3 POSNER'S ECONOMIC ANALYSIS

14.3.1 The economic approach and legislation

As well as arguing that much of the common law is explicable in terms of the promotion of economic efficiency, i.e. it is purporting to be a descriptive theory, the Chicago school also claims it has a normative aspect which wields the economic analysis of law as a means of evaluating new rules, in particular those found in legislation (Davies and Holdcroft, *Jurisprudence: Texts and Commentary*, p. 393).

The Chicago school is also of the opinion that not only can legislation be simply evaluated by the economic approach, but also that the whole process of legislation is based on the fundamental assumption that 'legislators are rational maximisers of their satisfactions just like anyone else'. This leads to the rather depressing conclusion that 'nothing they do is motivated by public interest as such'. The desire for election leads legislators to make deals with organised interest groups for votes, the bargain being that the interest groups will provide votes and money for the campaign in return for favourable legislation. 'Such legislation will normally take the form of a statute transferring wealth from unorganised taxpayers (for example, consumers) to the interest group'. Only organised collective action will work in this way, 'the rational individual knows that his contribution is likely to make little difference' (R. Posner, *The Problems of Jurisprudence* (Cambridge, Mass.: Harvard University Press, 1990), pp. 354–5).

Nevertheless, a statute is an imperfect deal in terms of efficiency because of its generality and because of the compromise which has gone into it. Legislation needs to be interpreted and applied by the courts. For Posner judges have 'a dual role: to interpret the interest group deals embodied in legislation and to provide the basic public service of authoritative dispute resolution' (Posner, *The Problems of Jurisprudence*, p. 355). The importance of the judge, not only in applying common law rules but in interpreting legislation in a way which promotes economic efficiency, is thus demonstrated.

14.3.2 The economic approach and the common law

The economic analysts insist that most of the common law can be explained in economic terms.

> Although few judicial opinions contain explicit references to economic concepts, often the true grounds of legal decision are concealed rather than illuminated by the characteristic rhetoric of opinions. Indeed, legal education consists primarily of learning to dig beneath the rhetorical surface to find those grounds, many of which turn out to have an economic character. (R. Posner, *Economic Analysis of Law*, 3rd ed., (Boston: Little, Brown and Company, 1986), p. 21.)

The Chicago school admits that most judges only arrive at these results by intuition of what is best for the market, subconsciously if you like, although occasionally this reasoning does hit the surface, even in cases before that approach was first advocated by theorists. The most famous of these judicial statements is by Judge Learned Hand in *United States v Carroll Towing Company* (1947) 159 F 2d 169 (2nd Cir) in formulating a test for the tort of negligence:

The defendant is guilty of negligence if the loss caused by the accident, multiplied by the probability of the accident's occurring, exceeds the burden of precautions that the defendant might have taken to avert it.

The proponents of this approach recognise that the reasons for the judicial promotion of efficiency lies in the nature of the Western economic system. In other words an economic system which is based on free-market principles with the aim of wealth maximisation will have a legal system which reflects this – in many ways a recognition of the correctness of the Marxist approach. As Posner states:

> The common law facilitates wealth maximizing transactions in a variety of ways. It recognizes property rights, and these facilitate exchange. It also protects property rights, through tort and criminal law . . . Through contract law it protects the process of exchange. And it establishes procedural rules for resolving disputes in those various fields as efficiently as possible. (Posner, *The Problems of Jurisprudence*, p. 357.)

The economic approach does not simply make general claims about the central role of efficiency in the common law. Posner provides a non-exhaustive list of the areas of law where reasonable attempts have been made to explain the rules in terms of efficiency.

> The wealth maximizing properties of the common law have been elucidated at considerable length in the literature of the economic analysis of law. Such doctrines as conspiracy, general average (admiralty), contributory negligence, equitable servitudes, employment at will, the standard for granting preliminary injunctions, entrapment, the contract defence of impossibility, the collateral-benefits rule, the expectation measures of damages, assumption of risk, attempt, invasion of privacy, wrongful interference with contract rights, the availability of punitive damages in some cases but not in others, privilege in the law of evidence, official immunity, and the doctrine of moral consideration have been found ... to conform to the dictates of wealth-maximization. (Posner, *The Problems of Jurisprudence*, p. 358.)

While it is relatively straightforward to apply the economic analysis to contract law, property law, and tort law, which are, after all, central to a capitalist economy, it is more difficulty to apply the approach to other areas. In these areas the reader is sometimes reminded of the stilted attempts of the crude materialist school of Marxist writers such as Pashukanis (see chapter 7) whose analysis of areas such as family, criminal and constitutional law was a simple attempt to explain them as based on contractual principles.

While the economic approach is quite thorough in its analysis and explanation of most areas of law in terms of efficiency, it is less strong when it comes to offering reasons why judges decide cases on this basis rather than the more obvious. Posner offers only general explanations of 'what drives judges to decide common law cases in accordance with the dictates of wealth maximization'. He argues that prosperity is a relatively uncontroversial policy for judges to aim at, enabling them to operate within their naturally conservative parameters. In addition, the influence of the *laissez-faire* philosophy of the 19th century on the formation of many common law doctrines must not be forgotten. So far the reasons given for the judicial preference for efficiency are fairly obvious, and would not be disputed by other schools of thought, the critical approach, for instance.

However, Posner adds more specific arguments such as the fact that judges are particularly well equipped to promote prosperity:

> The rules of the common law that they promulgate attach prices to socially undesirable conduct. . . . By doing this the rules create incentives to avoid such conduct, and these incentives foster prosperity. In contrast judges can, despite appearances, do little to redistribute wealth. A rule that makes it easy for poor tenants to break leases with landlords, for example, will induce landlords to raise rents in order to offset the costs that such a rule imposes, and tenants will bear the brunt of these higher costs. Indeed, the principal redistribution accomplished by such a rule may be from the prudent, responsible tenant, who may derive little or no benefit from having additional legal rights to use against the landlord – rights that enable a tenant to avoid or postpone eviction for nonpayment of rental – to the feckless tenant. That is a capricious redistribution. Legislatures, however, have, by virtue of their taxing and spending powers, powerful tools for redistributing wealth. So an efficient division of labour between the legislative and judicial branches has the legislative branch concentrate on catering to interest-group demands for wealth distribution and the judicial group, on meeting the broad-based social demand for efficient rules governing safety, property, and transactions. (Posner, *The Problems of Jurisprudence*, pp. 359–60.)

Judges are also driven to be efficient by the fact that inefficient decisions will impose greater social costs than efficient ones. Those litigants losing from an inefficient judicial decision will have a much greater incentive to appeal than would be the case if they had lost by reason of an efficient decision. The proliferation of appeals and further legal costs will act as a disincentive for the judge to act beyond the confines of efficiency in reaching a decision.

However, the case for the common law being based on the concept of efficiency is not overstated by Posner, who admits that wealth maximisation is built into the law but due to the independence of the judiciary the law does not achieve perfect efficiency (Posner, *The Problems of Jurisprudence*, p. 360). This is also presumably exacerbated by the judicial preference for basing decisions on precedents rather than overtly on economic considerations. The precedents may themselves be based on considerations of efficiency and wealth maximisation, but the judicial reliance on the precedent rather than the economic considerations may mean that the economic considerations may not be truly applicable to the case. Economic considerations may have been particularly influential in the 19th century but the modern judge is applying those principles not directly but through a long line of cases which may have divorced the rule from the policy consideration underlying it.

The economic approach to the law recognises that there is a gap between the common law and the logical economic doctrines which ought to dictate judicial decisions:

> The efficiency theory of the common law is not that *every* common law doctrine and decision is efficient. That would be completely unlikely, given the difficulty of the questions that the law wrestles with and the nature of judges' incentives. The theory is that the common law is best (not perfectly) explained as a system for maximizing the wealth of society. Statutory or constitutional as distinct from common law fields are less likely to promote efficiency, yet even they as we shall see are permeated by economic concerns and illuminated by economic analysis. (Posner, *Economic Analysis of Law*, p. 21.)

Although the Chicago school perhaps underestimates the gap that exists between law and economics there is no denying that the level of research and economic analysis of law is much more thorough than, say, the American realist analysis of non-judicial factors or perhaps even the critical analysis of fundamental contradictions. The theory is challenging and radical. Posner makes the claim that the underlying project is to reduce the hundreds and thousands of cases 'to a handful of mathematical formula', in that 'much of the doctrinal luxuriance of common law is seen to be superficial once the essentially economic nature of the common law is understood'. Furthermore, 'a few principles, such as cost-benefit analysis, the prevention of free riding, decision under uncertainty, risk aversion, and the promotion of mutually beneficial exchanges, can explain most doctrines and decisions' (Posner, *Problems of Jurisprudence*, pp. 360-1). The role of the economic analyst is twofold — to reduce law to economic formulae and to criticise judges who are failing to maximise wealth fully. Before moving on to an evaluation of whether the Chicago school is right to advocate wealth as a value, some examples of the economic analysis will be given. It is not possible in a work of this size to go through the economic approach to all sectors of the law, although, as with the critical school, no area of the law has been left untouched by the economic approach.

14.3.3 Contract law

With the law of contract at the centre of a free-market economy, being based on transactions voluntarily agreed between individuals, the economic approach to the law is readily able to explain this area of the law in terms of efficiency. Contractual transactions are the fundamental mechanisms for wealth maximisation. Yet why is there a need for a *law* governing these voluntary transactions? Why does the law have to intervene in this, arguably 'natural', process of exchange? Posner argues that there is no need for legal intervention when the parties perform their parts of the bargain simultaneously. This is rare according to Posner because, there is usually a gap between the executory stage and the executed stage of a contract. It is because of this lapse of time that the law of contract has developed. In the period between agreement and performance, one party is usually at the mercy of the other, and so requires legal protection:

> Thus the fundamental function of contract law (and recognised as such at least since Hobbes' day) is to deter people from behaving opportunistically towards their contracting parties, in order to encourage the optimal timing of economic activity and make costly self-protective measures unnecessary (Posner, *Economic Analysis of Law*, p. 81, referring to Hobbes' *Leviathan*, pp. 70–71).

It may be pointed out that this 'two-stage' view of contract law in which there is a delay between agreement and performance is a little too traditional for many modern contract lawyers. Indeed, it has the hallmarks of the classical bilateral executory contract made between businessmen since the advent of the industrial revolution at a time when the free market was being forged. Contract law has had to change (and sometimes without conviction) a great deal since then to cope with modern consumer transactions where there is no delay between agreement and performance. According to Posner such 'rare' simultaneous transactions do not require the intervention of the law, but consumer protection is probably one of the biggest growth areas in the law since the Second World War. The Chicago school might claim that such legislation does not produce efficiency, but this would again be a denial of the reality of the economic approach. The fact is that consumer contracts are by far the most common form of contract in modern society, and that such contracts are heavily policed by the law, even in the 1980s when, in the United Kingdom at least, there had been a concerted effort to return to a free-market economy, and to move away from social justice concerns.

Posner is readily able to explain the basic tenets of contract law in terms of efficiency. Consideration, for instance, promotes the need for economic exchange. Contract damages protect a party's expectations. Furthermore, he provides convincing examples of how contract law has coped with atypical contracts such as unilateral contracts:

> I offer $10 for the return of my lost cat. There is no negotiation with potential finders, no acceptance of my offer in the conventional sense. Yet someone who hears of the reward and returns my cat has a legally enforceable claim to the reward; his compliance with the terms of the offer is treated as acceptance. The result is correct because it promotes a value-maximizing transaction: The cat is worth more than $10 to me and less than $10 to the finder, so the exchange of money for the cat increases social welfare yet would not be so likely to occur if the finder did not have a legally enforceable claim to the reward. (Posner, *Economic Analysis of Law*, p. 89.)

Students of contract law will be familiar with the example but will not have thought about a unilateral contract in this way. Posner is thus able to show that his analysis is not solely concerned with the paradigm – the bilateral, executory contract. However, it must be remembered that unilateral contracts, unlike consumer contracts, are not simply of recent origin. They were assimilated into the law of contract at a very early stage when contract law was the dominant form of intervention (all students will remember *Carlill* v *Carbolic Smoke Ball Co.* [1893] 1 QB 256). The point is that, although the Chicago school is very adept at reformulating contract law in terms of efficiency, its fundamental assumptions about contract law are too general and sweeping.

14.3.4 Criminal law

The Chicago school has also developed economic explanations for areas of law that on the surface appear to be outside the bounds of efficiency. Here the reader is introduced to the economic analysis of criminal law (see also the economic analysis of constitutional law, for example in Posner, *Economic Analysis of Law*, ch. 24). The economic rationale behind criminal law

> views crime, with the exception of crimes of passion, as an economic activity with rational participants. A person commits a criminal offence if his expected utility exceeds the level of utility he could derive from alternative (legal) activities. He may choose to be a criminal, therefore, not because his basic motivation differs from that of other persons, but because his options and the valuation of their benefits and costs differ. The criminal

law seeks to influence human behaviour by imposing costs on criminal activities, thereby providing the individual with an economic incentive to choose *not* to commit a criminal offence; that is, a deterrent incentive. (W. Z. Hirsch, *Law and Economics* (New York: Academic Press, 1979), p. 200, citing G. Becker, 'Crime and Punishment: An Economic Approach' (1968) 78 Journal of Political Economy 169.)

In essence, massive State intervention in the form of criminal law is required to coerce rational maximisers away from operating outside the market place. Individuals are thus rational maximisers under the paternal guidance of the State. This appears to be a subversion of the economic school's presumption that market transactions are somehow 'natural' and do not require the heavy hand of the State to encourage them.

Criminal law represents a problem for the law and economics school in a different, but related, way, in that the right of action is taken away from the individual victim and put in the hands of the State. In simple terms this seems to be moving the law away from the economics of the market place, where the principles of contract law, and tort law as formulated by the famous Hand formula, mimic the responses of individuals as rational maximisers. If the Chicago school is meant to be a descriptive as well as normative theory how can the central role given to criminal law in most States be explained? Furthermore, given the significant element of overlap between tort and criminal law, it could be argued that an efficient legal system would leave most of the acts which are currently categorised as crimes to the law of tort.

Intentional torts . . . represent a pure coercive transfer either of wealth or utility from victim to wrongdoer. Murder, robbery, burglary, larceny, rape, assault and battery, mayhem, false pretences, and most other common law crimes . . . are essentially instances of such intentional torts as assault, battery, trespass, and conversion . . . (Posner, *Economic Analysis of Law*, p. 201.)

Despite this significant hurdle which seems to give the economic analysis of criminal law an artificial air (see, for example, the apparently ludicrous statement that 'the prevention of rape is essential to protect the marriage market' - Posner, *The Economic Analysis of Law*, p. 202), the Chicago school persists in rewriting criminal law in economic terms. To go back to the original economic underpinnings of criminal law as identified by the economic school Posner gives a useful illustration:

To illustrate, suppose B has a jewel worth $1,000 to him but $10,000 to A, who steals it ('converts' it, in tort parlance). We want to channel transactions in jewellery into the market, and can do this by making sure that the coerced transfer is a losing proposition to A. Making A liable to pay damages of $10,000 will almost do this, but not quite; A will be indifferent between stealing and buying, so he might as well steal as buy. (How will attitude to risk affect his choice?) So let us add something on, and make the damages $11,000. But of course the jewel might be worth less to A than to B (A is not planning to pay for it after all), in which event a smaller fine would do the trick of deterring A. If the jewel is worth only $500 to him, damages of $501 should be enough. But as a court can't determine subjective values, it probably will want to base damages on the market value of the thing in question and then add on a hefty bonus . . . to take account of the possibility that the thief may place a higher subjective value on the thing. (Posner, *Economic Analysis of Law*, pp. 203–4.)

The problem with simply allowing the victim to sue for damages in tort is that 'once the damages in the pure coercive transfer case are adjusted upward to discourage efforts to bypass the market . . . it becomes apparent that the optimal damages will often be very great – greater in many cases, than the tortfeasor's ability to pay'.

Three responses are possible, all of which society uses. One is to impose disutility in non-monetary forms, such as imprisonment or death. Another is to reduce the possibility of concealment by maintaining a police force to investigate crimes. A third, which involves both the maintenance of a police force and the punishment of preparatory acts . . . is to prevent criminal activity before it occurs. If . . . public policing is more efficient than private, the State is in the enforcement picture and has a claim to any monetary penalties imposed. Hence these penalties are paid to the State as fines, rather than to the victims of crime as damages. The victim can seek damages if the crime is also a tort. (Posner, *Economic Analysis of Law*, pp. 204–5.)

Where the defendant has the ability to pay 'there is no need to invoke criminal penalties'. The victim's action in tort and the heavy fine imposed will deter the criminal/tortious conduct.

This means that the criminal law is designed primarily for the non-affluent; the affluent are kept in line by tort law. This suggestion is not refuted by the fact that fines are a common criminal penalty. Fines are much lower than the corresponding tort damage judgments, and this for two reasons. The government invests resources in raising the probability of criminal punishment above that of a tort suit, which makes the optimal fine lower than the punitive damages that would be optimal in the absence of such an

investment. Every criminal punishment imposes some non-pecuniary disutility in the form of a stigma, enhanced by such rules as forbidding a
convicted felon to vote. There is no corresponding stigma to a tort
judgment. (Posner, *Economic Analysis of Law*, p. 205.)

Convinced? Posner attempts to explain the rationale behind criminal law as
a method of deterring non-market transactions. No regard is paid to any
other justification for the criminal law, based on morality, retribution, the
harm principle, etc. The presumption is made that criminal law has purely
an economic purpose, and from that point a reasonably convincing attempt
is made to explain why crime is in the hands of the State and its relationship
to tort law. Like the analysis of contract the superstructure of the theory
appears reasonable, though not wholly convincing; the foundations, however,
are too narrow. Once that fundamental presumption is made then of course
the rest of the examination will follow logically.

Furthermore, the more distance there is between the economic approach
and commercially based laws, the less convincing the superstructure of the
theory becomes. Posner's assertions that there is no stigma attached to a
tortfeasor is surely overstated. If it were the case then no stigma is attached
to rich people who commit unlawful conduct, while poor people who commit
the same conduct are punished, possibly locked up, and have a stigma
attached. If this is so then the economic analysis of law does indeed represent
a Marxist caricature of the capitalist system – with every aspect of law, indeed
life, being based on the market, and a totally hierarchical system in which the
well-off, protected no doubt by insurance, can commit wrongs without real
punishment, while the lower classes are kept in order, and kept within the
market place which exploits them, by the criminal law. Critical lawyers may
well say that, stripped of its economic jargon, this is exactly the picture the
Chicago school is painting and, furthermore, is an accurate picture of a
Western society. Although it may be argued that society does approach this
bleak vision, in many ways there are flaws in many of the points Posner
makes. For example, when an act is committed which is both a crime and a
tort, is there a deliberate decision, or a market-induced decision, by the State
or the individual victim (or both?) that since the wrongdoer, say, is a rich
person, the law of tort applies?

Again the economic analysis makes sweeping assumptions about the nature
and function of law. By isolating the economic factors, which no one can
doubt do play a significant role in the law, and explaining their influence or
more accurately their total dominance, the Chicago school has simply ignored
the myriad of other factors which shape the law. What can be a useful tool in
helping to explain the workings of the law, more useful in some areas of the
law than others, becomes a straitjacket into which every aspect of the law is
forced, in many cases kicking and screaming.

14.4   WEALTH AS A VALUE

The law and economics movement is unashamedly based around the concept of wealth maximisation. It is seen as an improvement on utility because 'the pursuit of wealth, based as it is on the model of the voluntary market transaction, involves greater respect for individual choice than in classical utilitarianism', with its concern simply to increase the happiness of the greatest number. The concept of 'economic liberty' is grounded in wealth maximisation which can only be achieved in a free market. Furthermore, 'the wealth-maximization principle encourages and rewards the traditional "Calvinist" or "Protestant" virtues and capacities associated with economic progress' (Posner, *The Economics of Justice*, pp. 66–8).

The claim that wealth is a value has come under considerable criticism from several authors (see, for example, J. L. Coleman, 'Efficiency, Utility, and Wealth Maximization' (1980) 8 *Hofstra L Rev* 509; A. T. Kronman, 'Wealth Maximization as a Normative Principle' (1980) 9 Journal of Legal Studies 227; E. J. Weinrib, 'Utilitarianism, Economics, and Legal Theory' (1980) 30 University of Toronto Law Journal 307; J. M. Steiner, 'Economics, Morality and the Law of Torts' (1976) 26 University of Toronto Law Journal 227). An outline of the arguments of Ronald Dworkin and the responses of Richard Posner will be examined here. Dworkin makes the following preliminary statement about the economic analysis of law:

> The economic analysis of law has a descriptive and a normative limb. It argues that common law judges, at least, have on the whole decided hard cases to maximize social wealth, and that they ought to decide such cases in that way . . . I shall argue that the normative failures of the theory are so great that they cast doubt on its descriptive claims. . . . (R. M. Dworkin, *A Matter of Principle* (Oxford: Clarendon Press, 1986), p. 237.)

His main point is that the Chicago school has not proven that wealth is a social value — 'why a society with more wealth is, for this reason alone, better or better off than a society with less'. The arguments between Dworkin and Posner focus on one example given by Dworkin. Dworkin states that the economic school defines wealth maximisation as being 'achieved when goods and other resources are in the hands of those who value them the most, and someone values a good more if he is both willing and able to pay more in money (or the equivalent of money) to have it' (Dworkin, *A Matter of Principle*, p. 237). The flaw in an approach based on such a goal is illustrated by Dworkin:

> Derek has a book Amartya wants. Derek would sell the book to Amartya for $2 and Amartya would pay $3 for it. T (the tyrant in charge) takes the

book from Derek and gives it to Amartya with less waste of money or its equivalent than would be consumed in transaction costs if the two were to haggle over the distribution of the $1 surplus value. The forced transfer from Derek to Amartya produces a gain in social wealth, even though Derek has lost something he values with no compensation. Let us call the situation before the forced transfer takes place 'Society 1' and the situation after it takes place 'Society 2'. Is Society 2 *in any respect* superior to Society 1? I do not mean whether the gain in wealth is overridden by the cost of justice, or in equal treatment, or in anything else, but whether the gain in wealth is, considered in itself, any gain at all. I should say, and I think most people would agree, that Society 2 is not better in any respect. (Dworkin, *A Matter of Principle*, p. 242.)

Posner seems to agree with Dworkin's premises and with his example stating that 'it is difficult to see how society is better off as a result. But suppose we change the figures. Let the book be worth $3,000 to Amartya and $2 to Derek. Then the transfer probably will increase the amount of happiness in society, even if Derek is not compensated. This is especially likely if Derek might receive one of these delicious windfalls sometime'. Despite the fact that Posner has suggested that wealth maximisation is a better value than utility maximisation, he now is willing to hitch the two together because 'happiness is one of the ultimate goods to which wealth maximization is conducive' (Posner, *The Economics of Justice*, p. 108).

The second objection Posner has to Dworkin's example is 'the absence of a plausible reason for taking the transaction away from the market place and putting it into the hands of a "tyrant"'. Further:

Suppose we change the example as follows. Derek owns a home, and Amartya owns an airline. An airport is built near Derek's home, and Amartya's airline produces noise that reduces the value of the home by $2,000. Derek sues the airline, alleging nuisance. The evidence developed at trial shows that it would cost the airline $3,000 to eliminate the noise and thereby restore Derek's home to its previous value; on these facts the court holds that there is no nuisance. This example is analytically the same as Dworkin's, but it illustrates more realistically than his how a system of wealth maximisation would operate in a common law setting, and it makes less plausible his argument that wealth is not a 'component of social value'. (Posner, *The Economics of Justice*, pp. 168–69.)

Dworkin realises that his example has bypassed the market place but he makes the point that Posner *recommends* market transactions 'for their *evidentiary* value' only. If transaction costs are high or the transaction is impossible to carry out, the economic school recommends the 'mimicking' of the market, 'which means imposing the result which they believe a market would have reached'. All Dworkin is doing in his example is enforcing a transaction which will produce a gain in social wealth – a result the market would have reached according to the economic school (Dworkin, *A Matter of Principle*, p. 243). Furthermore, there is no real difference between the example of the book argued over by Dworkin and Posner, and the example of the airport given by Posner; in both cases the transaction is not voluntary but enforced, in the first case by a tyrant and in the second case by the court. To base a theory on voluntary market transactions would be convincing if it was clear that in Posner's second example the court is simply arriving at the result the parties would have come to as rational maximisers. However, the fact that they ended up in court undermines this assumption about human nature.

Furthermore, even if the reader still felt, in the example of the book, that Society 2 is better because the book is in the hands of the party willing to pay the most, thereby increasing overall utility as well as wealth, Dworkin counters that this argument fails to take account of the relative wealth of the parties. What if Derek is poor and sick and is willing to sell his favourite book for $2 because he needs medicine, whereas Amartya is rich and content and is willing to spend $3 on the off-chance that he might read it some day. 'If the tyrant makes the transfer with no compensation, total utility will sharply fall. But wealth, as specifically defined, will improve'. The fact that the goods are in the hands of the person willing to pay the most 'is as morally irrelevant as the book's being in the hands of the alphabetically prior party. . . . Once social wealth is divorced from utility, at least, it loses all plausibility as a component of value. It loses even that spurious appeal given to utilitarianism by the personification of society' (Dworkin, *A Matter of Principle*, p. 245).

Dworkin's example of the tyrant, although obscure, is meant to show that, stripped of all the appealing outward trappings of the voluntarily entered into market place, the economic approach is no different from a tyrant imposing guessed-at market solutions. Rights, except as derived from the goal of maximising wealth, justice and fairness, even considerations of utility, are simply to be ignored if social wealth is increased. Clearly such a 'pragmatic approach' is the antithesis of Dworkin's rights-based approach. However, even if the reader is not prepared to accept that judges do not take account of wealth maximisation in making individual decisions, the Realists would argue that such considerations are simply one of the extra-judicial factors taken into account by certain judges in certain cases.

14.5 AN ASSESSMENT OF THE CHICAGO SCHOOL

The failure of the law with economics movement (with the limited and unsatisfactory attempt by Calabresi) to examine the initial distribution of goods and rights within society, and the sheer relentlessness with which the school applies the logic of the market to the law raises many questions about the reality of the approach (Burrows and Viljanovski, *The Economic Approach to Law*, p. 13). In many ways, it appears to be an economists' model of how a totally efficient (in a free-market sense) legal system should operate. The proposition that wealth maximisation is the sole social value and that individuals are all rational maximisers are both unproven foundations on which a very impressive edifice is built. The appeal to the 'fairness' of the market place illustrates the political bent of the theory but is also suspect, given that the courts are required to mimic the market place. Having said that, the movement has made an impressive attempt to prove that the law is indeed based on economics. In many ways it has been much more thorough than some of the other schools which tend to rely more on the simple application of general principles than a detailed exposition of the fundamental tenets of contract law or criminal law or any other field of law. Furthermore, the Chicago school has one tremendous advantage in that there is no doubt that large parts of the law are based on the concept of wealth maximisation within a free market, since that is the political and economic environment within which the law operates and which the law facilitates.

In the end, the reader may be left with the feeling that the Chicago school and the critical legal studies movement both see the law in terms of the free market and wealth maximisation – while the former school supports such a system, the latter school has the aim of undermining it and eventually replacing it. The two schools, one on the left and one on the right of the political spectrum, both agree on the nature of the law, they just disagree as to whether it is a good thing or not.

14.6 FURTHER READING

Coleman, J. L., 'Efficiency, Utility and Wealth Maximization', (1980) 8 *Hofstra L Rev* 509.
Hirsch, W. Z., *Law and Economics: An Introductory Analysis* (New York: Academic Press, 1979).
Goetz, C. J., *Law and Economics: Cases and Materials* (St Paul, Minn.: West Publishing, 1984).
Michelman, F. I., 'Norms and Normativity in the Economic Theory of Law' (1978) 62 *Minn L Rev* 1015.
Posner, R., 'Utilitarianism, Economics and Legal Theory' (1979) 8 *Journal of Legal Studies* 103.
Siegan, B. H., (ed.), *The Interaction of Economics and Law* (Lexington, Mass.: Lexington Books, 1977).

CHAPTER FIFTEEN
Justice Theory

'Justice' is a commonly encountered term of legal rhetoric and to deal 'justly' is held out as a fundamental aspiration of a legal system. At the same time, the intention which this rhetoric supposedly reflects is often less than clear. In practice a distinction is drawn between 'justice according to the law' and 'justice' as an ideal form of dealing. In the former case little more is meant than the proper operation of a given system, albeit subject to some very basic expectations of due process. In the latter case an external standard is being advanced by reference to which the operation of the legal system may be evaluated.

Within the operation of law, 'justice' is often a claim essentially made for procedure. The law may also, however, contain, or have imposed upon it, some form of resort to a 'justice' beyond the rules. This can be seen in a number of situations. Historically in English law the rules and principles of equity, originally administered by the Court of Chancery at a time when the Lord Chancellor was almost invariably an ecclesiastic, were developed as a means of circumventing the inflexibility of contemporary common law upon a basis of 'conscience'. It has been said that:

In the Middle Ages the Chancellor's . . . powers were . . . coextensive only with the necessity that evoked them [and were exercised] . . . on the ground of conscience. The principle [became] secularised . . . and the Chancellor was designated the Keeper of the Queen's Conscience. Yet this . . . did not prevent the cynical gibe voiced by Selden . . . about the standards varying with each Chancellor, even as his foot. (P. V. Baker and P. StJ. Langan, *Snell's Equity*, 29th ed. (London: Sweet & Maxwell, 1990), p. 8.)

This relates more or less directly to the question of judicial discretion which is an important issue in modern jurisprudence (see in particular chapter 9). It is an inevitable question whether a means of avoiding a potentially damaging application of a given system will simply create new problems, including those of uncertainty. By the 19th century equity had in fact become at least as constrainingly rigid, not to say dilatory, as the common law, a depressing picture of the system at this time will be found in Charles Dickens's novel *Bleak House* (1853). With the fusion of the common law and equitable jurisdictions (not their rules and remedies, the modern English superior courts implement both structures, not strictly a combination) in the Judicature Acts 1873 to 1875 and the Appellate Jurisdiction Act 1876, this problem was to a large extent mitigated. It is of interest in the present context, however, that even an attempt to correct the faults of a legal system by some external reference rapidly became itself a part of the system and one tending to the same faults.

'Justice' as perceived from within a legal system is subject to considerable limits. In this context a plea that a particular law is 'unjust' will be doomed to failure if it is indeed a 'law'. The claim, explicit and implicit, of a system to be 'just' is, however, ultimately a claim to comply with a standard of evaluation standing outside the forms of law as such. It may indeed be argued that the 'justice discourse' of formal legal language is an attempt, properly or otherwise, to endow legal proceedings with the aura of an external standard of justice. Here, the standard of justice is not something bound within the law but a criterion according to which the operation of law, amongst other social mechanisms, might be judged. The distinction drawn is somewhat similar to that found between positivist and naturalist approaches to legal analysis. The division is, however, less sharp. To call a judge 'Lord Justice' suggests more than a formally correct application of law, it implies that the system itself will render a 'just' result.

If it is accepted that even 'justice according to law' is a claim referring indirectly to an expectation of absolute justice, ill-founded as that expectation may sometimes be, there still remains a significant problem of definition. 'Justice' is usually contrasted with 'injustice' as an opposite condition. The distinction may crudely be illustrated by a hypothetical example. Assume that two persons with identical, high and appropriate qualifications apply for a job where there can only be one appointment made. After an interview at which each candidate performs identically, the issue is determined by the flick of a coin. Has the person not appointed been unjustly treated? Such a person has certainly been unlucky but it is difficult to give a good reason why actual injustice should be alleged. If, however, out of two unequally qualified candidates the less qualified is appointed by reason of being a relative of the managing director, one might more clearly argue that an injustice has been done. The distinction is that in the one case a Gordian knot was cut by admittedly arbitrary means, whereas in the other a new and irrelevant qualification was suddenly demanded which, so to speak, unfairly shifted the goalposts (see chapter 16).

Such simple examples do not of course adequately define or even describe 'justice'. A further question arises in the nature of the relation between 'justice' and 'injustice'. Is the latter simply the absence of the former? Alternatively, is there an evaluative spectrum with 'justice' and 'injustice' as opposed polar extremes with a large intermediate grey area? This is a question best considered by reference to specific examples in the light of modern analyses of the concept of 'justice'. Consideration of this final issue will therefore be deferred (see 15.4).

In the course of development of jurisprudential theory a number of approaches have been adopted and this background merits brief consideration. Not unnaturally many of these concerns have arisen in the context of other theories considered in preceding chapters which were not necessarily specifically focused upon a justice theory.

15.1 PERSPECTIVES UPON JUSTICE THEORY

The relationship between law and justice has, not very surprisingly, been a major question in legal theory over the years. Ideas of an external standard of justice, whether derived from divine command or from human nature, or both, have played an important part in the development of jurisprudential analysis, whether or not expressed in quite such terms. The different uses of the term 'justice' within a legal system or as an external criterion of evaluation of its functioning have been indicated above. But for jurisprudence the important question is, again, the viability of the claims made for law and this in the end rests upon some analysis of the substantial claim which is implicitly made by formal justice rhetoric in legal discourse.

The substance of justice is as much, if not more, a question of political philosophy as of jurisprudence. It is ultimately a question of perceptions of the relations of human beings in society. Ideas of 'justice' have, not surprisingly, played an important part in the development of naturalist legal theory (see chapters 4 and 5). A legal order held to conform to the criteria of evaluation advanced by the varieties of naturalist theory was held, in some degree at least, to be 'just' in nature. This should not be taken to mean that naturalists have generally argued that a perfectly just society can be attained through legal mechanisms alone. To take one particular example, St Augustine of Hippo argued that positive law can never be more than a corrective for wrongdoing and that a just society can result only from a quite different and much higher order. So far as the role of law as such is concerned, similarly dismissive views can be found in such diverse sources as classical Confucian doctrine and Marxist thought. None the less, ideas of justice, whether more or less closely associated with law, play an important part in naturalist thinking. However it is expressed, justice is for these theorists a matter of equitable relations between people in society. Such ideas are implicit in Aristotle's concept of human beings as social or political animals (see 4.3.3) and was stated very clearly by St Thomas Aquinas in his view that justice is concerned with maintenance of the common welfare in a society composed of interactive individuals (*Summa Theologica* 2a2ae, 58.5). The same idea may be argued implicitly to underlie the general Social Contractarian notion of social order which fundamentally concerns the jointure between individual claims and collective entitlements.

It would be quite false to claim that there is any singular or uniform concept of 'justice' to be found in classical or indeed modern naturalist theories. There is, however, an identifiable concern with human relations in a social order and the need to balance their particular needs and wishes with the claims of the collective order in which they live. That is to say that justice in one way or another is concerned with issues of *distribution*. In modern discourse this is a concept which has tended to be treated largely as a matter of distribution of wealth and material goods and whether this should be 'rights' or *laissez-faire* based. These are important political arguments, but it is clear that a properly ordered society must involve some principles by which the relations of its members *inter se* and with the society itself will be regulated. It must also be remembered that the focus of concern is not only upon the distribution of material goods. When a theorist such as John Locke in the 17th century (see 4.5.2) referred to security of 'property' as a social goal, he included not only material goods but also entitlements which we might now classify as human rights. This is, or should be, no less a concern in the context of modern justice theories. We are, then, concerned with concepts of individual relations in a social order. The isolated individual upon the hypothetical desert island has, so far as existence on the island is concerned, little concern with justice unless theological debates are to be opened. If the one and only coconut tree fails to fruit that is a disaster but hardly an injustice. If, on the other hand, there are two castaways, the tree does fruit and one of the castaways keeps all the coconuts denying the other all access to them, a question of justice clearly does arise. That is to say, questions of distribution arise and with them the questions both of distributive justice and of whether or not distribution is itself a relevant criterion of 'justice' in social and political analysis. In modern writing, contrasting views of this question have been set out by John Rawls and Robert Nozick.

15.2 JOHN RAWLS AND A LIBERAL DISTRIBUTIVE THEORY OF JUSTICE

In his major work, *A Theory of Justice* (London: Oxford University Press, 1973), John Rawls, professor of philosophy at Harvard University, sets out

principles of justice which derive from a form of argument, in a rather
different context, very similar to that variously used by the social contractarian thinkers of the 17th century (see 4.5). Rawls's starting-point is an idea of
'justice as fairness' (for an early view see J. Rawls, 'Justice as fairness' (1958)
67 *Philos Rev* 164). From this he developed a detailed analysis of principles
of justice including their priority of application and the nature of the
considerations which feed into both their content and interpretation. This
argument is set out in a generally social-contractarian form, although the
form of argument should not be permitted to obscure the substance of the
conclusions.

15.2.1 The original actors and the veil of ignorance

In order to discover principles which may be considered objectively fair, i.e.,
not a rationalisation of particular wants, Rawls employs the device of 'original
actors' placed behind a 'veil of ignorance'. This rather picturesque presentation represents quite a simple point. The basic principle is that the choice of
just principles for social organisation is to be made by persons who do not
know what actual position they are to occupy in society, nor what their
particular interests and inclinations will be. They are, thus, precluded from
shaping their principles by reference to personal advantage and can only
proceed upon the basis of securing, to the greatest possible degree, fairness
for all, including themselves. The purpose of this procedure as Rawls
expresses it is:

> . . . to set up a fair procedure so that any principles agreed to will be just.
> . . . Somehow we must nullify the effects of specific contingencies . . .
> [tempting the original actors] to exploit social and natural circumstances to
> their own advantage. . . . the parties are situated behind a veil of ignorance.
> They do not know how the various alternatives will affect their own
> particular case and they are obliged to evaluate principles solely on the
> basis of general considerations. (*A Theory of Justice*, pp. 136–7.)

The specific deprivations of knowledge imposed by the 'veil of ignorance' are
of (a) place in society, (b) class or social status, (c) natural assets or abilities
such as intelligence and strength, (d) personal conception of 'good',
(e) personal life plan, (f) psychological inclination, (g) the economic and
political situation of their society, (h) the level of civilisation and culture
attained by their society, and (i) the generation to which they belong (*A
Theory of Justice*, p. 137).

It will be noticed at once that there are two broad types of knowledge of
which the actors are deprived behind their veil of ignorance. These are first
knowledge of personal characteristics and secondly of the condition of the

society for which a standard of justice is to be devised. Rawls, however, presents one list and since the unified intention is to screen out particular preferences and advantages this may be seen as reasonable enough. It is, however, necessary to know a little more about the original actors. Something must be known about their general psychology, even though they themselves are denied knowledge of their individual psychology. Granted that the hypothetical actors are to set up principles of justice for a society of which they have no particular knowledge, it is reasonable to ask whether they are, e.g., generally to be taken as optimistic or pessimistic. The original actors are not idealists, they are intended to act in a spirit of rational self-interest, and the nature of their expectations about the unknown society thus becomes important. The actors, being deprived of particular knowledge, cannot assess the probabilities of their own position and are therefore argued by Rawls to work for the optimum opportunity for attainment of the most extensive goods, but also to maximise the minimum condition in which they might find themselves in the real society. Rawls states that his principles of justice are:

. . . those a person would choose for the design of a society in which his enemy is to assign him his place. (*A Theory of Justice*, p. 152.)

The actors may thus be seen, crudely, as hopeful pessimists. They seek the best but prepare for the worst in designing their principles of justice.

The psychology imposed by Rawls upon his original actors has been criticised (see, e.g., R. P. Wolff, *Understanding Rawls* (Princeton, NJ: Princeton University Press, 1977), pp. 129–32) particularly in relation to the suppositions about general human psychology which the original actors are made to make. Wolff suggests in particular that Sigmund Freud's work is left out of the account by Rawls. The problem here appears to be that both the actors and their position are hypothetical constructs and neither are, nor are supposed to be, real. The whole structure of the veil of ignorance shielding the original actors is essentially a rhetorical device used to present the reasoning by which Rawls's principles of justice are supported. It is ultimately the value of those principles which must be assessed rather than the mechanics of what is an inherently impossible original position.

15.2.2 Distribution and the thin theory of good

The original actors are concerned to secure the optimum system of distribution of benefit for their own advantage. Although the hypothetical actors are denied specific knowledge of their own position they necessarily have a conception of the good which underlies the distribution to be undertaken. Each person will have, upon emerging from behind the veil of ignorance, an individual conception of good in the shape of a rational life plan. Whatever this may be, it is argued by Rawls that it will involve, in varying degrees, certain primary goods. These are taken to be rights and liberties, powers and opportunities, income and wealth, with, very importantly, self-respect (*A Theory of Justice*, p. 62). Rawls admits that in addition to these 'social' goods there are 'natural' goods such as health and vigour, intelligence and imagination. These are, however, much less at the disposal of society in terms of their distribution, even if they may be affected by social conditions.

The starting-point for the working out of principles for just distribution is thus set out in a 'thin theory of good' which Rawls states is limited to 'essentials' and the function of which is in effect to establish the premises about what a just system is to distribute (see *A Theory of Justice*, p. 396). Once objective principles of justice have been worked out, they can, of course, be related to a much more detailed sense of goodness in society which Rawls terms a 'full theory of good' (*A Theory of Justice*, p. 398). The principles of justice thus rest upon the assumptions underlying the 'thin theory of good' but then feed into a 'full theory of good'.

15.2.3 The principles of justice

Upon the basis of his argument from the position of rationally self-interested actors in the original position Rawls sets out two principles of justice (*A Theory of Justice*, p. 302). The first is that:

Each person is to have an equal right to the most extensive total system of equal basic liberties compatible with a similar system of liberty for all.

The second is that:

Social and economic inequalities are to be arranged so that they are both:

(a) to the greatest benefit of the least advantaged, consistent with the just savings principle, and
(b) attached to offices and positions open to all under conditions of fair equality of opportunity.

These principles are then 'lexically' ordered in application, so that the first principle, that of liberty, always has priority, and liberty may only be curtailed in order to defend liberties. The first principle will therefore always have priority over the second, but the second is always prior to 'efficiency', maximisation of advantage and the 'difference' principle (i.e., the acceptance of inequality).

Two things are immediately apparent about this scheme. First the priority given to liberty and secondly the fact that, subject to certain basic caveats, it is accepted that society will contain significant inequalities as between the circumstances of its members. The priority of liberty is explained by Rawls as an inevitable consequence of the rational self-interest of his original actors. Although they know that certain goods will be desirable to all, they do not know what their own circumstances or particular predilections will be. It would thus be rational to maximise liberty because this will be the route to the maximisation of their own ultimate attainment, whatever their actual situation may turn out to be. Rawls argues that the value of liberty is proportional to the ability of individuals and groups to advance their goals within the system concerned (*A Theory of Justice*, p. 204). Even those least enabled will, however, value liberty as affording the best chance for self-improvement.

The acceptance of inequality, the 'difference principle', also relates to the supposed rational self-interest of the original actors. One might imagine that if the actors know nothing of their actual social situation they might opt for equality on the basis that they would then at least be no worse off than anyone else. Rawls excludes this possibility by denying that the original actors are motivated by comparisons with others or, in particular, by envy. They aim individually for the best for themselves and therefore seek to maximise their own potential position whilst, in the light of their cautious psychology building in a safety net in case they are in fact in a situation of disadvantage. In other words they are high-jumpers who nonetheless ensure that a safety net is provided. Rawls would seem here to be considering primarily material benefit, i.e., wealth, but it may also be added that the general aspirations of real people vary considerably, and equality in the sense of sameness might indeed conflict with the self-interest of the original actors. Liberty is equal and so is fair equality of opportunity in competition for jobs, but this does not mean that Rawls therefore urges positive discrimination as a means of redressing past social injustice. The argument is rather for bolstering opportunity through the operation of the 'maximin' principle of maximising the position of the least benefited.

It is interesting to note that Rawls also argues that the principles of justice which he advances and, in particular, the priority of liberty, only become operative beyond a certain basic stage of social development. His essential argument is that in the course of the development of a society, as basic needs are more and more effectively satisfied, the emphasis will shift from such needs to concerns with liberties as their exercise becomes viable with improving material conditions (*A Theory of Justice*, p. 542). Prior to this point, when basic material needs are not being met, Rawls suggests that equality would in general be preferred. This can be argued to be a somewhat curious proposition. If liberty is preferred, as a 'total basic system', because it affords the best-protected route to maximisation of position, it would seem highly relevant to people denied even essential needs. Liberty, and with it justice, seem to lose credibility if they become luxuries to be enjoyed only beyond a certain point of affluence.

15.2.4 Generational equity and the just savings principle

The rational self-interest of the original actors is taken by Rawls to require the placing of a form of social safety net to mitigate the effects of the difference principle at its lower end of operation. It will be recalled that in the principles of justice, principle 2(a) requires the arrangement of social and economic inequalities, 'to the greatest benefit of the least advantaged, consistent with the just savings principle' (*A Theory of Justice*, p. 302). The qualification of the accepted inequality implicit in the difference principle by reference to the advantage of the disadvantaged is thus itself qualified by the just savings principle. This refers to human concern for at least the generation next following, which may impose limits upon the use of resources by any given generation. It also implies an investment by each generation for those who will follow. Thus, as Rawls explains the point, whilst the first principle of justice and the principle of fair opportunity moderate the impact of the difference principle in application between people at a given time, the just savings principle limits its impact as between generations (*A Theory of Justice*, pp. 292–3).

This form of justice between generations cannot rest upon the greatest benefit of the least advantaged since earlier generations can hardly be retrospectively benefited. Later generations may however be advantaged, or at least protected from disadvantage, by the wise investments of their predecessors. In the context of the concerns of the late 20th century, energy policy serves as an obvious instance for the operation of the just savings principle. The use of natural resources and some of the associated environmental effects raise serious questions for both the present and the future and these may readily be expressed in terms of the inter-generational justice which is the essential concern of the principle.

15.2.5 Application of the principles of justice

Principles of justice are in themselves of great theoretical interest but are of little more concern without some indication of the ways in which they are to be applied. Rawls sets out a 'four-stage sequence' for the attainment of a just society. The stages, of which the first is the original position, are all hypothetical constructs designed to facilitate consideration of the questions arising in the creation of a just society. Rawls admits that these stages are to some extent modelled on the processes of constitutional development in his own country, the USA (*A Theory of Justice*, p. 196, n. 1; referring to K. J. Arrow, *Social Choice and Individual Values*, 2nd ed. (New York: John Wiley and Sons, 1963), pp. 89–91).

The four stages in sequence are:

(a)   The enunciation of the principles of justice from the original position.

(b)   A partial lifting of the veil of ignorance so far as the general circumstances of the society but not the individual circumstances of the actors, the devising of a constitutional system dealing with powers of government and the rights of citizens. This process must, amongst other factors, cope with different and possibly opposed political viewpoints. Granted the priority of liberty, the outcome is assumed to be some form of constitutional democracy (*A Theory of Justice*, p. 198).

(c)   Having established a constitution, the next step is legislation in accordance with the principles of justice as well as the constitutional procedures. The legislators are intended to act in the light of general interest rather than to their personal advantage. It is admitted that judging whether or not a law is just may be difficult, especially in the context of the inequalities of the difference principle, and that it may be easier simply to determine whether a law is not unjust. This proposition, of course, raises the question of the interface between concepts of justice and injustice (see 15.4).

(d)   The final stage is that of application of the laws and rules by judges and administrators and their working in the actions of people generally, at which point, of course, the veil of ignorance is wholly removed.

The original veil of ignorance may be accepted as a rhetorical device used for the presentation of the arguments leading to the two principles of justice. It is used similarly but decreasingly in the presentation of the constitutional and legislative stages but not at all in relation to the stage of application. Beyond the fact that the constitution is to be democratic, whilst, in the light of the principles of justice, presumably, protecting minorities from majority oppression, the second, third and fourth stages seem curiously insubstantial. It is true that different societies will demand different particular responses but the conclusion that in a just society legislation might at most be judged not unjust must seem rather tentative.

Rawls's theory of justice has been criticised in detail from a number of points of view. The general psychology with which he endows his original actors has been criticised by Wolff (see R. P. Wolff, *Understanding Rawls* (Princeton, NJ: Princeton University Press, 1977) and Barry questions the individualistic emphasis of Rawls's analysis (see B. Barry, *The Liberal Theory of Justice* (Oxford: Clarendon Press, 1973)). One of the most sustained attacks has, however, come through the presentation of quite a different theory of justice by Robert Nozick.

15.3   ROBERT NOZICK AND JUST ENTITLEMENTS

Robert Nozick's theory, set out in *Anarchy, State and Utopia* (Oxford: Basil Blackwell, 1974), rejects not only the concept of distributive justice but also the elaborate mechanisms of State that go with it. To this extent Rawls and Nozick stand on opposite sides of a dichotomy which became prominent in political debate in both the United Kingdom and the United States, and in varying degrees in a number of other countries in the 1980s. It would, however, be a gross simplification to suggest that the distinction between the two theories is simply an expression of these points of view. The difference in reality raises fundamental questions about the general concept of justice in society.

15.3.1 The idea of the minimal State

In analysing the role of the State and the extent of its legitimacy, Nozick, like Rawls but with different intent, commences from a form of social-contractarian argument, in this case John Locke's formulation of a hypothetical state of nature (see 4.5.2). In such a condition, according to Locke, individuals would have natural rights but not efficient or adequate means of enforcing them. The necessity for the performance of this function in a viable social order becomes for Locke the basis for the existence of the State. Nozick takes a similar view and analyses the state essentially as a 'dominant protective association' (*Anarchy, State and Utopia*, pp. 15–17).

At this point the 'protective association' is seen very much as a contractual factor which, wielding a force much greater than that of any individual, protects the rights of 'clients' as between themselves and, subject to a number of complicating factors, as between clients and non-clients. This, of course, would hardly amount to a 'State' but rather to a form of modified contractual vigilantism with the strong probability of there being several competing protective associations. Such a system would tend to be highly inefficient, even if the actual international order is in effect a group of uneasily relating protective associations albeit not, usually, competing in the same territory. There is thus the need for a single and efficient protective association in a territory and this, for Nozick, is the basis of the State.

The State, as compared with a mere protective association, must, according to Nozick, meet two essential conditions. These are (a) an appropriate monopoly of force in the territory and (b) the protection of everyone in the territory rather than a limited client base (*Anarchy, State and Utopia*, p. 113). If these are accepted as criteria for an efficient rights-protecting 'State', there remains a debate characterised by Nozick in terms of 'ultra-minimal' and 'minimal' ideas of the State (see *Anarchy, State and Utopia*, ch. 3). The former is voluntary and extends its protection, and its cost, only to those who expressly opt for it. As a voluntary system this is not, compulsorily, redistributive (obviously any financial transaction is redistributive in a general sense), but it would tend towards inefficiency in exactly the same way as a structure of competing protective associations. The question becomes, at root, that of whether one can properly be required to pay for policing only in cases of personal need or for the armed forces only if one requires one's own life or property to be directly protected from enemy action.

Voluntarism on this scale would be self-defeating since it would ultimately deny the basic prerequisites for a social order in which individual rights can effectively be maintained. Nozick thus emphasises the 'minimal State' which is monopolistic and general in application in the performance of its legitimate functions within its territory. The cost of this 'minimal State' is then properly borne by all since, in effect, it is the necessary foundation for the protection of the rights which might be violated by State exactions going beyond such legitimate levels.

What, then, are the legitimate functions of the 'minimal State'? In Nozick's theory these functions are all 'protective' in nature and involve the means of protective force and what may loosely be considered mechanisms of adjudication for the identification and ascertainment of rights.

15.3.2 Minimalism, tax and the free market

If people are to pay for the general protective function of the minimal State, it must be asked why they should not pay, compulsorily, for other benefits, including benefits to others through redistribution of wealth and resources by taxation. Nozick contends that society, and thus the State, has no proper concern with the distribution of wealth, or poverty, as between individuals or groups. Consequently, in his view, the State has no legitimate capacity for exaction beyond what is necessary for the performance of its minimal protective functions. Upon this basis Nozick states an extreme opposition to general taxation, which he equates with forced labour (*Anarchy, State and Utopia*, pp. 169–72).

The argument advanced by Nozick is that if a person works for income and pays tax thereon at a percentage rate, that percentage of the working day is spent, in effect, in forced labour for the State. He makes the point that a person who chooses to work less and take more leisure time would not be forced to spend part of that time on compulsory activity directed by the State.

Nozick's argument in opposition to tax shades into a more general argument against redistributivism which is illustrated by his analysis of high earnings made by a baseball star (*Anarchy, State and Utopia*, pp. 160–6). Nozick asks why the choice of supporters to pay a high ticket price for attendance at games, including a hypothetical extra levy for the presence of the star, should be interfered with through tax levies upon the star's earnings. If the supporters thus choose to pay, Nozick argues that it can hardly be unfair for the star to gain the extra income and that there is no case for its redistribution, through tax, to other people who are not skilled, or lucky, enough to be baseball stars. This is a superficially persuasive argument in that the status and earnings of the star do indeed rest upon some combination of ability and luck which should not obviously attract a penalty. The argument contains, however, a defect in the flawed assumption that in such a situation a free market is truly operating. What in fact operates is a very tightly controlled monopoly on the part of the owners of the baseball stadium in association with the team. If the supporters are to see the game at all they have no choice but to pay whatever price is demanded and whilst it may truly be said that they may choose to go or not to go, this hardly amounts to market competition. In the light of this it may be wondered whether recontrol, through redistributive taxation, of the proceeds of what is already a very tightly constrained market is quite so outrageous as Nozick seems to suggest.

For Nozick, however, the free market analysis is not properly open to such criticism and it becomes for him the linchpin of a radical revision of the model of 'justice'. This leads to an analysis founded not upon 'distribution' as between individuals or groups but upon the concept of 'just entitlements'.

15.3.3   The concept of just entitlements

Nozick's theory of justice is concerned not with the distribution of wealth or benefits as between individuals, but with the material holdings of each individual. His fundamental question is, therefore, not the pattern of comparative holdings but whether each individual is 'justly' entitled to his or her actual holdings, at whatever level they may be.

The justice of entitlements is considered in terms of (a) justice in acquisition and (b) justice in transfer, with, on a rather different level, (c) just rectification in the case of 'unjust' holdings (*Anarchy, State and Utopia*, pp. 150–3). The first two are concerned with various forms of acquisition of assets, whereas the third is a corrective mechanism operating where either of the first two basic principles have been breached. 'Justice in acquisition' is treated as the obtaining of ownership over an asset formerly unowned, in the simplest case a *res nullius* such as a natural object found which is subject to no prior claims. Nozick dismisses Locke's analysis of this type of acquisition as operating through the addition of labour to an object as subject to too many ambiguities, but gives little clearer indication of how the principle is to operate. He emphasises, however, the importance of the issue of the worsening of the position of others, through deprivation of the opportunity of acquisition, and the need, therefore, for justification of such acquisition.

Upon the assumption that all things were once unowned but many have since become owned, the issue of justice in transfer becomes a matter of vital importance, and especially so in the market context emphasised by Nozick. Purchase, gift, inheritance and so on would all, in Nozick's scheme, be just modes of transfer. Theft, on the other hand, would not. Nozick's minimal State would be expected to interfere with the free operation of the former but its protective power would be essential in the event of the latter.

For Nozick's scheme the third element, that of 'rectification', presents some difficulty. What is to happen if a person purchases, 'justly' in terms of immediate transfer, a holding from someone who in fact stole it? The dispossession of the original owner was patently unjust, the acquisition by the new owner was prima facie just, although not actually founded upon good title. More generally, what, if anything, is to be done about, e.g., large inherited holdings which were acquired in some historically unjust fashion to the arguable detriment of persons now living? Nozick admits this as an issue and even, interestingly, suggests that some redistributive patterning might in extreme cases be necessary as a 'rough rule of thumb' in applying the principle of rectification (*Anarchy, State and Utopia*, p. 231). It is, however, to be noted that this is not an admission of redistributivism in principle. The central issue is the justice of the acquisition and not the relative wealth or deprivation of individuals or groups as such. As Nozick admits, much detail would need to be worked out for the elucidation of the operation of the principles of justice in acquisition, transfer and rectification, but the implications of the analysis are clear enough.

The free market model of just entitlements advanced by Nozick represents in extreme degree an individualistic analysis in which the social collective becomes no more than the setting for the operation of individual aptitude or good fortune. This differs from Rawls notably in that an individual who is not either able or lucky is not permitted to rely upon the support of others who are so advantaged. The fundamental question is one of the relation of individuals to groups, and most particularly to the large group of a national society. Whether, in seeking a position upon this vital issue, modern justice theories take adequate account of the nature of the balance to be sought is a point which may reasonably be questioned.

15.4 JUSTICE, INDIVIDUALS AND SOCIETY

Aristotle argued that human beings are *politikon zōon*, political or, more accurately, social animals (see 4.3.3), that is to say individuals who are inclined by their nature to live in groups and ultimately in societies. There arises from this an inevitable conflict between individual wishes and collective interests, symbolised in a crude way by the person who wishes to play music to the irritation of neighbouring individuals. Playing music is a perfectly reasonable individual aspiration, so is the wish to get some rest. So whilst some music playing is reasonable, very loud music at 3.00 a.m. is clearly unreasonable. In short, a compromise is necessary between the conflicting aspirations of neighbouring individuals in a social setting. Much of the argument upon justice turns precisely upon the nature of the balance which is here to be drawn. In such a situation any emphasis which is so individualistic as to deny the collective, or so collectivist as to deny individuality will omit half the terms of the equation. The question to be asked, it may be urged, is less whether the answer is to be 'individualistic' or 'collectivist' and rather one of the values which groups of individuals are seeking to enshrine in their social organisation.

This, of course, invites the form of qualified social-contractarian investigations from which, in different ways, both Rawls and Nozick start. Justice ultimately, however, is about a concept of 'right relations' in society and the choice is not *between* individualism and cooperation, but rather a choice to be made for the expression of the individualism of human beings as social creatures.

15.5 FURTHER READING

Barry, B., *The Liberal Theory of Justice* (Oxford: Oxford University Press, 1973).

McCoubrey, H. *The Development of Naturalist Legal Theory* (London: Croom Helm, 1987), ch. 7.

Nozick, R., *Anarchy, State and Utopia* (Oxford: Basil Blackwell, 1974).

Rawls, J., *A Theory of Justice* (London: Oxford University Press, 1972).

Rawls, J., 'Justice as fairness' (1958) 67 *Philos Rev* 164.

Wolff, R. P., *Understanding Rawls* (Princeton, NJ: Princeton University Press, 1977).

CHAPTER SIXTEEN

The Concept of Injustice

'Justice' is commonly contrasted with 'injustice' as, in effect, its opposite or, at least, a negative condition defined by its absence. Whatever model or definition of 'justice' may be favoured, and it has been indicated in the preceding chapter that there is some room for debate in this area, it must clearly in some sense be in opposition to a condition which might be considered 'unjust'. It does not, however, follow from this that social or legal phenomenon can simply be categorised as 'just' or 'unjust' by reference to some simply applied criterion or criteria. It may be argued in the first place that most legal provisions are not absolutely just or unjust but rather vary across a considerable intermediate spectrum both in their substance and in their application. It is, of course, entirely possible for a law which may be just in principle to be very dubious or even unjust in particular applications, a phenomenon which demands at least some flexibility of interpretation in processes of adjudication. This is not a new question, it was, indeed, addressed by St Thomas Aquinas in the 13th century. Aquinas gave the hypothetical example of a medieval walled city under siege in which the governor had, sensibly, ordered that the gates be kept closed in order to exclude the enemy. He then asked what was to be done if a group of citizens fleeing to escape the enemy sought admission to the city in circumstances where an instant decision had to be made whether to admit them or not, without time to refer the matter to the Governor. Aquinas answered that the citizens should be admitted, presumably if this could be done without imperilling the city, as an emergency action displacing the normal and proper authority of the Governor's order (see St Thomas Aquinas, *Summa Theologica*, 1a2ae, 96.6). The point here is that the regulation is in itself entirely unexceptionable but its inflexible application in the given case would be both harsh and unjust to the citizens seeking refuge. However, even if most practical questions in relation to injustice tend to arise in an intermediate grey area rather than in the realm of absolutes, the qualities which may be taken to render a provision or action 'unjust' still call for investigation and definition.

It is necessary first to determine whether injustice is simply an absence of justice or a polar negative having its own distinctive criteria of identification. In the latter case it must also be considered whether injustice is a quality which can be objectively discerned or merely an expression of subjective disapprobation. Take as an example the case of two hypothetical job interviews. In each case there is only one appointment to be made and there are two applicants. In the first, rather unlikely, case there are two applicants who are entirely indistinguishable one from the other in their qualifications, experience and aptitude. The interviewing panel make their decision by flicking a coin and so appoint one and reject the other. In the second case one candidate is very well qualified and has demonstrated marked aptitude in the course of significant work experience. The other candidate is unqualified, has little experience and even that was disastrous. This candidate is, however, a cousin of the Personnel Manager and so is appointed to the job. In each case the rejected candidate will not be pleased by the result, but is it possible to say that either has been treated 'unjustly'? In the first case it can be argued that the unsuccessful applicant was essentially unlucky on the day, granted the unlikely absence of any distinguishing elements upon which a more rational decision could have been based. In the second case the rejected, and clearly much better qualified, applicant could clearly argue that he or she has been unfairly or unjustly treated in so far as the decision was made upon the basis of a demand for an additional and irrelevant quality – being related to the Personnel Manager. It is, of course, precisely upon this type of reasoning, in rather more likely contexts, that provision is made against, e.g., race or sex discrimination in employment practice.

Investigation of these issues is most effectively pursued in the context of a system which may generally be accepted to have been in some high degree pernicious in either or both of its substance and application. Sadly the history of the 20th century offers all too many possible examples. To cite but a few, the Stalinist regime in the former USSR, the Nazi Third Reich in Germany, the Khmer Rouge regime in Cambodia (then Kampuchea), the Ceausescu regime in Romania, the processes of 'ethnic cleansing' (the term has gained popular currency although it is both offensive and inaccurate) in former Yugoslavia or the genocidal oppression carried out in Rwanda might all be considered in this context. It is important to emphasise the number of possible examples in order to be aware that none of them can be seen as a unique abuse of power and that the problem is not confined to any particular shading of the political spectrum. However, as a result of the exigencies of military defeat, the best known and documented example is to be found in the Third Reich, although with the opening of former Soviet and Soviet bloc archives and the proceedings before the International Criminal Tribunals for former Yugoslavia and Rwanda, more information on other areas may very well come to light. The Third Reich cannot be considered unique, even in its practice of genocide, other than in terms of its sheer scale, but its stark example cannot safely be forgotten or wisely be ignored.

For the present purpose the focus is not upon the external military conquests of the Third Reich or upon the occupation regimes set up by it in the conquered territories. The central issue is rather that of the treatment of German citizens by their own government in the period from 1933 to 1945.

16.1 LAW IN THE THIRD REICH

German Nazism, like European Fascism more generally, had a core ideology which is often misrepresented in modern political debate. Fascism emphasised the corporate State as a hierarchy of authoritarian structures organising every aspect of national life and culminating in a single party with, at its head, a 'leader'. To this basic model, found, e.g., in Mussolini's Italy, Hitler and the Nazis added an overtly racist element which was largely, but not exclusively, anti-Semitic and which was not found to any great extent in the Italian Fascist regime. The Nazi State was organised upon a 'leadership principle', the *Führerprinzip*, according to which each level in the hierarchy was 'led' by the next above and the whole structure led by Hitler himself. The will of the leader was not admitted to be subject to any institutional constraint and in such a system, inevitably, positive law was seen simply as one amongst several instruments for the implementation of the will of the leader and the Party.

It is possible to debate whether the Third Reich was in any real sense a *Rechtsstaat*, a State ruled by law, but there was a thin, but clear, pedigree linking it legally with the preceding Weimar Republic and, before that, Imperial Germany. Adolf Hitler was elected Reichskanzler in 1933 in accordance with the Weimar Constitution, even if the election was far from free of implicit and some explicit coercion. On 28 February 1933 the aged President von Hindenburg was persuaded by Hitler that the country faced a national emergency of imminent subversion and disorder, a claim given colour by the burning of the Reichstag (Parliament) building in Berlin on the previous day. Quite who was ultimately responsible for this, apart from the actual arsonist, and whether the Nazis themselves had any hand in it or merely grasped at the incident as a most convenient opportunity, is still to some extent a matter for debate. It is clear, however, that the only real threat of subversion at that time in Germany came from the Nazi Party. Be that as it may, on 28 February the

President, acting under art. 30 of the Weimar Constitution, granted to Hitler as Reichskanzler powers of government by emergency decree. These powers were confirmed and consolidated by the Reichstag in a vote on 24 March 1933 and were thereafter renewed at four-year intervals until the end of the Third Reich. The votes were not, of course, in doubt between 1933 and 1945. It may, however, be noted that in Italy the Fascist Grand Council on 24–25 July 1943 resolved that the constitution which Mussolini had abrogated be restored and requested King Vittorio Emanuele II to appoint a ministry with policies designed to extract Italy from the military and national crises with which it was beset. In Italy it was possible for a constitutional order unexpectedly to revive. In Nazi Germany this did not happen, partly because there was no source of authority beyond Hitler by which or whom such a transition could have been effected without an overt *coup d'état* such as was attempted unsuccessfully by Count von Stauffenberg and the other July Plotters in 1944. In practice, therefore, Hitler ruled Germany under powers of emergency decree duly renewed by a completely subservient Reichstag and his dictatorship was on this basis just about 'constitutional' from a narrowly positivist viewpoint.

Legislation continued to be enacted and courts continued to sit, but the law and its operation were at all times manipulated and sometimes grossly so in order to serve the Party's interests. William L. Shirer comments upon the Nazi political police, the Gestapo, that:

> The basic Gestapo law promulgated . . . on February 10, 1936, put the secret police organisation above the law. The courts were not allowed to interfere with its activities in any way. As Dr Werner Best . . . explained, 'As long as the police carries out the will of the leadership, it is acting legally'. (W. L. Shirer, *The Rise and Fall of the Third Reich* (London: Pan Books, 1964), p. 337.)

Wherever courts reached conclusions displeasing to the Party, proceedings might be quashed or defendants who had been acquitted, such as Pastor Niemöller, might be seized by the Gestapo and incarcerated in concentration camps without any possibility of appeal or review. For cases which were considered to be of special political sensitivity and for which the regular courts were thought to be 'unreliable' special political courts, the *Sondergericht*, were set up by a law of 21 March 1933 and a Supreme Political Court, the *Volksgerichtshof*, was established by a law of 24 April 1934. Judges and counsel were vetted for their political commitment and those acting for the defence were unwise greatly to exert themselves. Of proceedings before the Supreme Political Court, which he witnessed as a foreign journalist, William L. Shirer remarks,

> [They were more like] a drumhead court-martial than a civil-court trial. The proceedings were finished in a day, there was practically no opportunity to present defence witnesses . . . and the argument of the defence

lawyers who were 'qualified' Nazis, seemed weak to the point of ludicrousness. (*The Rise and Fall of the Third Reich*, p. 335.)

In reality, although the outward shell of a *Rechtsstaat* and the bare shell of due process was maintained, law in the Third Reich had indeed become simply one amongst many means for the political application of the *Führerprinzip* and Nazi ideology.

The gross abuse of State power in Nazi Germany, as in the commission of genocide and in the almost unlimited persecution of all opposition voices, tempts one to say that law under the Nazis was an institution so perverted and misused from any 'proper' purpose that it must be considered to have been unjust to such a degree that it merits no further consideration as a formal prescription. This, however, will not suffice as a response. Much of the law in the Third Reich was not in fact much different from that found in most States. In general, traffic regulation is dictated by a certain logic which is near universal, and, although even in this area gross abuses did occur under the aegis of Nazi racism, it would be impossible to say that German road traffic law as such between 1933 and 1945 was much distinguishable from that found in other countries. In a more contentious area such as marriage law, in which an 'Aryan' ancestry had to be proved for a given number of generations with arbitrary and very oppressive consequences in some cases, it is still not possible to reach sweeping conclusions in so far as many marriages were entered into in Germany under these laws between 1933 and 1945 to which no possible exception could reasonably be taken. It is, in short, necessary to approach the problems of Nazi law, as of other legal systems which might be considered iniquitous, upon a more cautious and principled basis than that of sweeping and comprehensive condemnation. To do this a principled concept of 'injustice' is necessary and, to remain with the particular, but let it be remembered not unique, example of the Third Reich, a starting point is afforded by the various post-World War II judicial considerations of the effects of Nazi legal administration both in Germany and beyond.

16.2 POST-1945 JUDICIAL CONSIDERATION OF NAZI LAW

After the collapse of the Third Reich in military defeat in 1945 both the Allied Occupation and the post-war German authorities were left with a difficult task in disentangling some of the consequences of Nazi legal administration, as indeed were some jurisdictions operating outside Germany. The approaches variously adopted to abuses of law were significantly different in various jurisdictions and shed a useful, if sometimes indirect, light upon ideas of 'injustice'.

In what was then West German jurisdiction the most interesting decisions were those made in the so-called 'grudge informer cases'. Two cases in particular, each arising upon very similar facts, call for comment. In each case a German soldier who was home on leave had made critical remarks about Hitler and the Nazi regime to his spouse who had then reported him to the Party in the expectation that he would be severely punished and probably killed. As a result charges were brought against both the husbands under a law of 20 December 1934 which forbade statements critical of the Nazi regime and one of 17 August 1938 forbidding all actions damaging to military morale. These prosecutions could not proceed, even in the Third Reich, without the evidence of the spouses of the soldiers and, despite strong contrary advice in one of the cases, this evidence was duly rendered. In each case the soldier was convicted and condemned to death but 'reprieved' and sent to the Russian front where, to everyone's surprise, both survived. After the war both soldiers sought to bring action against the spouse and the judge who had tried the original case.

In the first case (see H. O. Pappe, 'On the Validity of Judicial Decisions in the Nazi Era' 23 *Modern L Rev* 260), brought under para. 239 of the 1871 Penal Code claiming unlawful deprivation of liberty, the court agreed that the Nazi provisions in question had generally been considered harsh and repressive and their use for the satisfaction of personal malice strongly disapproved of, but held that the laws themselves were properly applicable by a court called upon to hear a case arising upon relevant facts. The judge in the original case was therefore acquitted but the informer was convicted of an abuse of process in using a repressive law for malicious ends. This seems a most curious decision. Since the law, however objectionable, was held to have been correctly applied it is difficult to see what offence the informer had committed, however objectionable her conduct may have been. It may be added that her action in informing upon her husband was not only not unlawful at the time but actually encouraged by some elements of the State, although not by all and so the question of retrospective criminalisation is also implicitly raised.

The second 'grudge informer case', decided by the (West) German Federal Supreme Court in 1952 (see Pappe, 'On the validity of Judicial Decisions in the Nazi Era', at p. 264) may be considered very much more satisfactory. The facts were almost identical to those of the first case considered above and after the war charges of unlawful deprivation of liberty and attempted murder were brought against the informing spouse and the original trial judge. The Federal Supreme Court here decided that either the judge and the informer must be guilty on the basis of the illegality of the proceedings or neither could be so. In order to determine this question the Federal Supreme Court examined the original prosecution from the viewpoint of criminal procedure and found it to have been grossly defective. It was pointed out that the Nazi laws under which the prosecution had been brought were broadly concerned with 'public' subversion and damage to morale and however the term 'public'

might be construed it seemed unlikely that it could include discreet communication between spouses in their own house. It was further noted that the
laws provided for a wide range of penalties covering a spectrum from short
custodial terms to death. Even if the soldier in this case could properly be
held to have committed an offence at all, it must have been at the most trivial
end of this spectrum. It was therefore held that the judge in the original case
had been guilty, at least, of a culpable neglect to exercise his judicial
discretion and that the informer, who had sought and procured this very
result, had participated in the offence. The case was therefore referred back
for reconsideration upon the basis of conviction of both the judge in the
original case and the informer for unlawful deprivation of liberty and
attempted murder.

It will be observed that in the first case the emphasis of the post-war trial
was upon the objectionability of the Nazi enactment as such, whereas in the
second case the post-war court examined the Nazi proceedings and in essence
condemned them for culpable denial of due process even in their own terms.
The latter case avoided the logical difficulties found in the first decision and
emphasised the importance of process, in so far as the Third Reich court had
not properly applied the enactments actually before it. This has some
affinities with the 'procedural natural law' advanced by Lon L. Fuller (see
chapter 5) and sets out one important aspect of the idea of 'injustice' in the
need for the correct application of stated law, with proper capacity for
defence and response and guarantees of freedom from arbitrary or oppressive
maladministration or variation of effect. Failures of process are not, however,
the only components of injustice. There remains the problem of laws which
are inherently unjust in their substance even when 'correctly' applied. In the
context of Nazi law two cases decided outside Germany relate in somewhat
different ways to this question. These are the conjoined English decisions in
Oppenheimer v *Cattermole* and *Nothmann* v *Cooper* [1976] AC 249 and the
decision in the USA in *Leidmann* v *Reisenthal* 57 NY St. Reps. (2d) 875.

Oppenheimer v *Cattermole*, conjoined on very similar facts with *Nothmann* v
Cooper, concerned Meir Oppenheimer who had been born a German citizen
and had until 1933, when the Nazis came to power, worked as a teacher in
a Jewish orphanage. He was incarcerated as a Jew by the Nazis but was
eventually allowed to go into exile abroad on condition of leaving all his assets
and property behind in Germany. He was deprived of his citizenship and all
property claims by a decree of 25 November 1941 which deprived all German
Jews living abroad of their legal claims and entitlements. He settled in the
United Kingdom and in 1948 he became a British citizen by naturalisation.
In 1953 the Federal Republic of West Germany granted him a reparationary
pension. The case arose upon the question of the assessment to income tax
of this pension. Under the applicable double taxation conventions of 1954
and 1964 it was assessable to English tax if the recipient had only United

Kingdom citizenship, as compared with dual UK and German citizenship. This question turned upon the effects of the 1913 German Nationality Law, the 1941 Nazi decree and the Basic Law of the then Federal Republic of West Germany. The House of Lords finally determined that Oppenheimer had lost his German citizenship, irrespective of the Nazi decree, under the 1913 Nationality Law by taking British citizenship in 1948 and by not having opted for the offer of restored (West) German citizenship under the post-war Basic Law. He was therefore held to be only a United Kingdom citizen and liable to UK tax upon his reparationary pension.

In the present context, however, the comments of the House of Lords in relation to the 1941 decree, *obiter dicta* as they are, are of very considerable interest. The majority of the House of Lords decided, on slightly differing grounds, that the Nazi decree could neither be recognised as 'law' nor applied by an English court. The two essential grounds advanced for this view were, first, that the 1941 decree was invalidated by reason of its violation of basic human rights norms set out by public international law and secondly, that it failed by reason of its simple moral turpitude. The first ground is much stronger now than it would have been in 1941, subject to the question of the historic applicability of the proscription of laws enacted in pursuance of genocide *stricto sensu*. It must, of course, be remembered, that the case was decided in the 1970s and not in the 1940s and the application of the 1941 law in an English court would indeed have been extremely dubious. The second ground of objection comes as close as an English court ever has to a simple assertion of the principle that '*lex iniusta non est lex*' (an unjust law is no law) in the literal sense which was not intended by St Augustine of Hippo (see 4.4.1). Whatever view may be taken of the comparative merits of these two approaches, the essential conclusion of the House of Lords was set out concisely by Lord Cross of Chelsea in his statement at p. 278, that:

> . . . legislation which takes away without compensation from a section of the citizen body singled out on racial grounds all their property . . . and . . . deprives them of their citizenship ... constitutes so grave an infringement of their human rights that the courts of this country ought to refuse to recognise it as a law at all.

Here there may be seen set out clearly a fundamental objection to the substance and impact of the 1941 decree. The root of the objection seems to lie in the arbitrary quality of a deprivation inflicted not by reference to the conduct of the person affected but to a quality, racial identity, wholly beyond the control of the individuals thus singled out. This is, of course, a fundamental objection even before consideration of the murderous impact of the race laws of the Third Reich.

Leidmann v *Reisenthal* raised somewhat different questions which found a distinct solution. The plaintiffs had sought to escape racist persecution in

Vichy France during the Second World War, including possible deportation to a death camp. In order to achieve this they had paid over to the defendant substantial sums of money and had handed over valuable jewellery in return for a promise that he would assist them in escaping into a safe country. In fact the defendant took the money and jewellery and abandoned the plaintiffs to their fate. They ultimately succeeded in escaping by other means and later re-encountered their plunderer in New York where they brought an action against him for money had and received. The defendant claimed that under the relevant national law, that of Vichy France, the original contract to aid the plaintiffs in their escape attempt had been illegal and that the New York court therefore had no jurisdiction to grant the recovery which was sought. Hooley J held that in the circumstances of the case, where the contract for escape had been entered into *in terrorem*, the formal illegality of the contract under Vichy law could not act as a bar to an action for restitution. In this case, therefore, the status of the law in Vichy France in the Second World War was not as such discussed, but the attempt to secure its application by a United States court *ex post facto* was held in effect to be an abuse of process. That is to say that, whatever its original status in its territory of enactment, it was not such a law of which a US court *now* would take cognisance.

16.3   CONCEPTS OF INJUSTICE IN THE POST-WAR CASES

Post-1945 judicial decisions arising upon the effects of Nazi laws and judicial decisions have not been uniquely or even directly concerned with jurisprudential questions of 'injustice' *stricto sensu*. Important issues of the validity of laws have been central to these cases (for discussion see H. McCoubrey, *The Obligation to Obey in Legal Theory* (Aldershot: Dartmouth, 1996), ch. 7), but the question of injustice as a vitiating element in legal provisions and decisions is implicit in all of them. From this background it is possible to derive much of value and instruction in the analysis of the perceived nature of injustice as a defect in law. The discernible elements may, crudely if usefully, be divided into 'positivist' and 'quasi-naturalist' categories. The principal approach of post-1945 courts to this question has, not surprisingly, been of a 'positivist' nature. The most satisfactory of the 'grudge informer case' decisions adopted an essentially procedural approach in which the Nazi proceedings were impugned upon the basis of their inherent defectiveness even in their own terms. In the US, *Leidmann v Reisenthal* was essentially determined upon the basis of a possible abuse of process in the context of US law. This type of approach, and especially in the latter case, combines elements of both a positivist analysis *stricto sensu* and of the type of 'procedural naturalism' advanced by Lon L. Fuller (see 5.1). It may be recalled that in *The Morality of Law* Fuller included amongst the eight defects which might call into question the procedural status of a purported 'legal' system, the making of rules with which compliance is impossible and discontinuity between the stated rules and their administration in practice. The latter clearly goes to the root of the objection made to the second of the two 'grudge cases' considered above and may more generally be seen in the extraordinary levels of political interference which typified the administration of 'justice' in the Third Reich. The first of Fuller's negatives referred to above raises a fundamental objection *inter alia* to the Nazi race laws, as to any other race laws such as the former South African *Apartheid* regulations, in that deleterious consequences attached to race in effect demand that an individual make the physically impossible response of changing his or her racial identity. These 'positivist' and associated 'procedural naturalist' approaches go a considerable way towards defining and dealing with the fundamental problem of injustice in the laws of the Third Reich and other parallel systems of various ideological hues. Indeed, in the particular context of race oppression they also supply a solution to the questions raised in *Oppenheimer* v *Cattermole* for the reasons set out above. The excursion of the House of Lords into a somewhat over-simplified strict naturalism in that case, however, raises other matters of considerable importance. It raises in particular the fundamental limitation of both positivism and procedural naturalism in dealing with 'injustice'. That is to say, what is to be done where a procedurally adequate means of enacting and applying abominable law has been found ?

Here indeed the concerns of classical naturalism become matters of central concern. It will be recalled that St Thomas Aquinas in his *Summa Theologica* defined law as a rational ordinance made for the good of the community by whoever has the governance of it and promulgated (see 4.4.2). For the present purpose the 'naturalist' elements of this portmanteau definition, those of rationality and action for the communal good, are of paramount importance. The questions of individual conscience and the limits of the 'obligation' to obey law have been considered above in chapter 4, but in the present context the foundational question is that of the proper and legitimate expectations of the members of a society. In the course of the development of naturalist thought these concerns have been explored and expressed in a number of different, but not necessarily incompatible, ways. In the second half of the 20th century the proper expectations which people may entertain of the society in which they find themselves have been expressed formally in the law of human rights. This sprang originally from the horrors disclosed at the fall of the Third Reich and its development and importance has been sustained by the horrors of many subsequent and present regimes. The law of human rights as such is contained in a number of international treaties, including the 1948 Universal Declaration of Human Rights and the European Convention on Human Rights. Such treaties have to some extent codified certain basic expectations which a human being may legitimately expect of the society in which he lives, meaning the expectations which each person may properly have of other people around them. These provisions are important but are in themselves also positive law and open to the same critical analyses as any other such provisions.

In opening the question of the minimum standards of social and political conduct beneath which a system could be said to be or become 'unjust', much broader questions are raised than those of definition of specific human rights. The basic nature of injustice as a defect of a society and its organisation calls for broad statement as well as corrective provision specific to particular abuses. To return to the type example of the Third Reich, whilst again emphasising that this is sadly far from a unique case, two principal defects may be pointed out in its 'legal' structures. Some of the laws themselves were profoundly cruel and arbitrary in their substance, including the race laws which savagely penalised not conduct but personal identity. The application of all laws, whether or not they were objectionable in substance, was also subjected to a degree of political interference which denied all effective procedural guarantees. In short, in its dealings with the people subject to it, Nazi law to a very significant extent not only failed to respect, but was precisely calculated to deny, their status as participating members of a human society. This might be differently expressed as a conclusion that law and its administration in the Third Reich to a considerable extent contravened the Kantian categorical imperative and principle of right (see 4.6). It will be recalled that these respectively argue that any maxim for particular should be capable of being used as a general maxim and that humanity should always be respected as an end in itself and not treated as a means to some other end. Violation of these basic naturalist principles is perhaps the best available general definition of 'injustice', bearing in mind that, as in the case of the law and legal administration of the Third Reich, much more complex interpretation may be demanded in analysing the content and application of particular provisions. It must also be remembered that questions of injustice arise not only in the context of the quality of whole legal systems but also in relation to given provisions or their application in systems which may be otherwise unobjectionable. This, of course, is the point essentially made by Aquinas in his assessment of the closure of the gates in the city under siege (*Summa Theologica* 1a2ae, 96.6).

16.4 JUSTICE AND INJUSTICE: THE LINK

'Justice' and 'injustice' may now be suggested to be distinctively different concepts rather than the latter being simply an absence of the former. The two concepts also differ from the point of view of the value and purpose of determining their existence or otherwise in a given situation. As it was suggested in the preceding chapter, justice is a condition in which the optimum balance is achieved between individual aspiration and collective need (which may be seen as a sum total of the combined individual aspirations of the members of a society). As such it is an aspiration which may be more or less closely approached by given societies but is unlikely ever to be perfectly attained in any human endeavour. Injustice, in contrast, is a condition of society in which the humanity of the people living in it, both as individuals and as social creatures, is fundamentally denied. It is not directly associated with aspiration, it is rather a definition of the point at which a social order fails to attain or maintain a minimum acceptable standard and at which its 'legitimacy' is fundamentally called into question either in general or in some particular respect. In some cases legal rules and principles, or general social organisation, may reasonably be termed 'just' or 'unjust' without qualification. In most instances, however, the situation will be much less clear. Rules or principles, which are required to be applied over a spectrum of situations some of which may well not have been anticipated by those who enacted or determined them, will rarely be either perfectly 'just' or absolutely 'unjust'. In most cases they will lie in a large centre ground and the determination of their quality will rest upon their tendency towards justice or injustice. Their acceptability or otherwise, and the highly significant consequences which might flow therefrom, will then rest upon the point at which they are found upon a broad spectrum between the two absolutes.

16.5   FURTHER READING

Fuller, Lon L., *The Morality of Law*, revised edn. (New Haven: Yale University Press, 1969), Appendix: The Problem of the Grudge Informer.
Koch, H.W., *In the Name of the Volk: Political Justice in Hitler's Germany* (I. B. Tauris & Co., 1989).
McCoubrey, H., *The Development of Naturalist Legal Theory* (London: Croom Helm, 1987), ch. 7.
Stone, J., 'Theories of Law and Justice in Fascist Italy' (1937-38) 1 MLR 177.

Index

Abstract rights 164–5
  concretisation 165
Abuse of power 78
Accountability 104
Adjudication
  rule of 38, 40
  theory 171–2
Advantage distribution 187–8
Affirmative postmodernism 261
Agendum 190
Alluring motives 21, 22
Ambiguity 255
American realism 5, 202–23
  behaviourism 222–3
  economic analysis and 276
  fact sceptics 209–11
  Frank 208–9, 219–20, 232
  Gray 205–6
  Holmes 204–5
  impact of realism 220–3
  judicial reasoning 218–20
  jurimetrics 220–2
  law in books and in action 203
  Llewellyn 206–8, 216–17
  prediction of decisions 213–18
  rule sceptics 204, 208–9, 211–13,
    219–20
  see also Critical legal studies
Analytical positivism 12
Anarchy
  avoidance of 60–1
  social contractarian response 77–9
Anarchy, State and Utopia (Nozick) 306–10
Apartheid 264
Apology (Plato) 64–5, 66
Aquinas, Thomas (Saint) 60, 61, 94, 101,
    312, 321
  Christian Aristotelianism 72–6
  concept of good 95–6

Aristotle 7, 61, 310
  Christian Aristotelianism 72–6
  teleological analysis 67–9, 73
Aspiration, morality of 88–9
Ataturk, Kemal 113
Augustine of Hippo (Saint) 33, 124
  Christian platonism 70–2
  very narrow definition of terms 72
Austin, John 13, 22, 25–6, 50, 100–1

'Bad man' perspective 205
Balkin, J. M. 252, 261, 263–6
Bankowski, Z. 141
Barnett, Hilaire 256–7, 258
Bartlett, Katherine T. 242
Behaviour identification 39
Behaviourism 222–3
  behaviourist approach 215–16
  Holmes behavioural analysis 205
  institutional patterns 216
Bentham, Jeremy 12–13, 25–6, 59, 60, 73
  censorial jurisprudence 28–31
  complete law 23–4
  see also Command theory
Beyleveld, Deryck 102–7
Bill of Right (1689) 43
Binder, G. 259–60
Black letter approach to law 202, 228
Blackstone, Sir William 12, 60
Bodde, Derk 137
Bolsheviks 128
Bottomley, Anne 241
Bourgeois revolution 122, 124
Brownsword, Roger 102–7
Butler, W. E. 130

Calabresi, Guido 275, 278
  efficiency and equity 280–3
Caliphate 112–13

Calvin, John   76
Capitalism   240, 270
  capitalist encirclement of Soviet Union
      129, 132
Censorial jurisprudence   13, 21
  Bentham   28–31
  good of greatest number   30
  'mischievous' tendency   29
  utility principle   30
Change, rule of   38, 40
Chicago School   275, 295–6
  see also Economic analysis
China (Imperial China)   135–7
  Ch'ing dynasty law code   137
China (Nationalist)   137–8
China (People's Republic)   120
  Cultural Revolution   135, 138
  Gang of Four   135, 139
  Hong Kong and   140
  law in   138–40
  Red Guards   135, 138–9
  socialist legality   139, 140
  Tienanmen Square incident   135, 140
  see also Chinese legal theory
Chinese legal theory   134–40
  Cultural Revolution   135, 138–9
  socialist legality idea   135, 139, 140
  Stalinist model   135
  see also China (People's Republic)
Christian Aristotelianism   72–6
Christian Platonism   70–2
Christianity   70
Chudleigh, Louise   242–3
Cicero   68–9, 72
Claim-rights   100
Class and Marxism   122, 123
Classical naturalism   60–84
  age of reason   76–83
  Greek   61–9
    see also Aristotle; Plato
  Hobbes   12, 77–9
  'is' and 'ought' distinction   12–13
  Judaeo-Christian impact   69–76
    see also Aquinas, Thomas (Saint);
      Augustine of Hippo (Saint)
  Kant   83–4
  Locke see Locke, John
  objectivity   83–4
  Roman Empire   68–9
  Rousseau see Rousseau, Jean-Jacques
  social contract see Social contractarianism
  standing of   84
  theories   13
Classical positivism   11–31
  modified by Hart see Hart's positivism
  public international law   26–8
Coase, Richard   275

Coase theorem   278–80
Coercion   4–5, 94
  command theory   15
  motives   22
  see also Sanctions
Coercive power   142
Collins, Hugh   141–2, 225, 246
Command theory   13–26
  coercion   15
  command   14–17, 33
    adoptive   16, 17
    pre-adoption   16
    recognition   17
    suspension   16
    tacit   17
  complete law   23–4
  critique by Hart   33–4, 37
  employment contract   17
  express conventions   19
  military orders   16–17
  sanctions   13, 17, 21–3, 33
    punitive   25
  sovereign   13, 15, 17–20
  viability   24–6
Common law, economic analysis and
      284–8
Commonwealth of Independent States   130
Commonwealth period   77, 193–4
  political discontinuity   42–3
  rule establishing   42
Community morality   176–7
Complete law theory   23–4
Comrades' courts   130
Conaghan, Joanne   242–3
Concept of Law, The (Hart)   158, 159
Confucian thought   62–3, 136–7
Confucius (K'ung-Fu-tzu)   136
Consequentialist theory of rights   165–7
Constantine the Great   69
Contextuality   244–6
Contract
  command theory   17
  critical approach   236–41
  economic analysis   288–9
  voluntary residence   65
Conventionalism   160
Conventions   19
Coplestone, F. C.   73
Coulson, N. J.108–9   111
Courts on Trial (Frank)   210
Criminal law, economic analysis and
      289–92
Critical legal studies   224–49
  aim   226
  constitutive theory of law   235–6
  contextuality   244–6
  contract   236–41

Critical legal studies – *continued*
  contradictions in law 231–3
  deconstruction 233–5
  delegitimation 234
  dereification 235
  economic analysis and 276
  economic reconstruction 248
  empowered democracy 246–9
  feminist legal theory 241–4
  formalism, attack on 228–9
  legal reasoning critique 229–31
  liberal legal tradition critique 226–36
  property rights 248
  referenda and elections 248
  roles 245–6
  rotating capital fund 248–9
  trashing 233–4
  Unger 244–9
    rights system 246–7
  world views 236
  see also Postmodern legal theory
Critical reflective attitude 36
  changing 43
Critique of Practical Reason (Kant) 83
Crito (Plato) 64, 65, 66
Cromwell, Oliver 42
Cultural Revolution 135, 138–9

De Civitate Dei (St Augustine) 71
De Libero Arbitrio (St Augustine) 71
De Regimine Principum (Thomas Aquinas) 75
De Sousa Santos, Bonaventura 270–2, 273
Declaration of Right (1688) 43
Declaratory theory 157
Deconstruction
  critical legal studies 233–5
  postmodern legal theory 258–63
  justice and 263–6
  liberal constitution and 266–9
Democracy
  Dworkin on 172–5
  empowered 246–9
  equal concern and respect 173–5
  judge as protector of rights 172–3
D'Entrèaves, A. P. 75–6
Derrida, Jacques 258–63
Devlin, P. 53–5
Dialectic social development (Hegel) 121
Dialectical materialism 121
Dias, R. W. M. 56
Distribution of advantage 187–8
Doi, Abdur Rahman I. 116
Domitian (Emperor) 75
Donaldson, M. 252, 272–3
Douzinas, C. 251
Du Contrat Social (Rousseau) 81

Duty, morality of 88–9
Dworkin, Ronald 35, 47, 116, 157, 228, 267
  adjudication theory 171–2
  community morality 176–7
  criticism of positivism 158–60
  criticism of pragmatism 160–1
  declaratory theory 157
  democracy 172–5
  hard cases 215
  institutional morality 176
  rights thesis 100
  see also Rights thesis

Economic analysis
  antecedents of economic approach 275–8
  causation 279
  Chicago School 275
    assessment of 295–6
  Coase theorem 278–80
  common law 284–8
  contract law 288–9
  criminal law 289–92
  critical legal studies and 276
  efficiency and equity 280–3
  legislation 283–4
  Posner's analysis 283–92
  rational man assumption 278
  realism and 276
  transaction costs 279–80
  utilitarianism and 276–8
  wealth maximization 277
  wealth as value 293–5
Economy, tax and free market 308–9
Edgeworth, Brendan 45
Elections 248
Employment contract, command theory 17
Enforcement of morality, Hart's positivism 52–5
Engels, Friedrich 121
Enlightenment, postmodern legal theory critique 250–2
Entrenched rights 163–5
Equity, generational 305
European Communities, express conventions 19
European Convention on Human Rights 321
European Court of Human Rights 165
Expositorial analysis, command theory 15, 16
Expository jurisprudence 26
Express conventions 19

Fact sceptics 46, 203, 209–11
Fei Hsiao Tung 139

Feinman, Jay 239
Feminist legal theory 241–4
  employment 242–3
  male domination in law 241, 242
  parenting 243
  postmodern legal theory and 256–8
Finnis, John 94, 174, 228
  defence of naturalism 95–6
  importance of theory 102
  obligation to obey 100–2
  see also Natural rights theory
Formalism 46, 202, 225
  critical legal studies movement attack on
    228–9
Foucault, Michel 254, 257, 270
Frank, Jerome 208–9, 219–20, 232
Free market 308–9, 310
French Revolution 83
Fukuyama, Francis 250
Fuller, Lon L. 87, 99, 320–1
  Third Reich 50–2
  see also Procedural naturalism
Fundamental values, postmodern legal
    theory and 256–8

Gabel, Peter 239
Gaius 182–3
Gang of Four 135, 139
Generational equity 305
Generic consistency 103, 104
Gestapo 315
Gibson, Susie 241
Glasnost 130
Glorious Revolution (1688) 43, 194
  bad government 79
God, social contract with 70
Good
  basic forms of human good 96–7
  definition 95–6
  of greatest number 30
  thin theory of good 302–3
'Good' life 95
'Good will', Kantian 83
Gorbachev, M. 130
Government
  John Locke on 79–81
  limits on rights of 60
Gramsci, Antonio 225
Gray, John Chipman 205–6
Grotius 27
Groundwork of the Metaphysic of Morals
    (Kant) 83
Grundnorm 41, 145, 147–50, 154
  public international law 155

Hägerström, Axel 179, 181–4, 200
Hanafi school 111–12

Hanbali school 111–12
Harm, absence of 53
Harris, D. J. 27
Harris, J. W. 151
Hart, H. L. A. 228, 267
Hart's positivism 32–58
  command, tacit and adoptive 17
  command theory critique 33–4, 37
  critical reflective attitude 36
  judicial discretion 160
  legal systems 44–6
  minimum content of natural law 55–7
  morality 50
    enforcement 52–5
  officials 44–6
  public international law 48–50
  rules 25
    adjudication 38, 40
    change 38, 40
    importance of 34–46
    internal aspects 35–7
    legal systems and officials 44–6
    primary 37–40, 44
    recognition 38, 40–4, 94
    rule scepticism 46–8
    secondary 37–40, 44, 45
    truisms 56, 57
    ultimate rule 41
  significance 57–8
  Third Reich 50–2, 58
  totalitarianism 50–2
  truisms 56, 57, 174
Hegel, G. W. F. 121
Hermeneutic method 36
Hobbes, Thomas 12, 56, 77–9
Holmes, Oliver Wendell 157, 178, 204–5
Hong Kong 140
Human rights 321
  Islam and 115–16
Hume, David 12–13, 59, 74, 95
Hussein, Saddam 119

'Ideal' prison 13
Idealism, platonic 62–4
Identity and the 'other' in postmodern legal
    theory 254–5
Images of Law (Bankowski and Mungham)
    141–2
Imperatives see Independent imperatives
Imperial Russia
  code 126
  duma period 127
  law in 125–8
  liberation of serfs 126
  Mensheviks 127, 128, 194
  peace jurisdiction 126
  socio-democratic republic 127–8

Imperial Russia – *continued*
  see also Soviet legal theory
Impulsions, theory of   179–81, 182
Independent imperatives   189–97
  agendum   190
  conduct which law embodies   190–1
  ideatum   190–1
  imperantum element   192–3
  judicial decisions   192–3
  legislative efficiency   190
  performatory imperatives and rights
    195–6
  requisitum   190–1
  revolutions   193–4
  value of analysis   196–7
  will-theory   189
Individualism   310–11
Inequalities   303, 304
  of benefit   187–8
Institutional morality   176
Instrumental theory   225
International law *see* Public international law
International treaties   99–100
'Is' and 'ought' separation   59
  Bentham on   12–13
  classical naturalism   12–13, 84
  Finnis   95, 96
  Kant   146
  Kelsen   145, 147
  Rousseau   81
Islamic jurisprudence   70, 106–19
  Caliphate   112–13
  human rights and   115–16
  ijma   108, 109–10
  ijtahad   108, 110–11
  international law and   117–19
  interpretation   108, 110–11
  jihad   118–19
  naturalism   106–7
  qiyas   108, 110, 112
  rights of non-Muslims   116
  schools   111–12
  secular law and   113–15
  Shiah Islam   113
  state and   112–16
  structure   107–11
  Sunnah   108, 109
  ummah   109, 118
Ius gentium   69

Jihad   118–19
Judaic tradition   69–70
Judges
  external factors operating on   229–31
  integrity   168–9
  lawmakers   206
  political appointment   162

Judges – *continued*
  prediction of decisions   213–18
  protectors of individual   157
  protectors of rights   172–3
  see also Judicial decisions
Judicial decisions
  Dworkin   158–60
  Hart   47–8, 158
  independent imperatives   192–3
  integrity   168–9
    statutes   170–1
  objections on policy grounds   162–3
  'one right answer' thesis   167–8
  precedent   167–8
  prediction of   213–18
  rights thesis   162–3
  settled and hard cases   169–70
  statutes and   169–71
  see also Judges
Judicial reasoning, American realism
    218–20
Juries, emotional response   210
Jurimetrics   220–2
Jurisprudence
  censorial   13, 21
  censorial *see* Censorial jurisprudence
  expository   26
  meaning   3–10
  method problems   6–9
  national law and   9–10
  practitioner   11
  value of   10
  variety of issues   2–3
  see also individual aspects
Juristic method   216–17
Just entitlements   306–10
  concept of   309–10
  minimal state   307–8
  tax and free market   308–9
  transfers   310
Just savings principle   305
Justice   297–311
  according to law   298
  between generations   305
  concept   299–300, 312–23
    grudge informer cases   316–18
    post-1945 cases   320–2
    post-1945 judicial consideration
      316–22
  deconstruction and   263–6
  historically   297–8
  individuals and society   310–11
  injustice and   298–9, 322–3
  just entitlements   306–10
  law and   299
  liberal distributive theory   300–6
  limits   298

Justice – *continued*
  minimalism, tax and free market 308–9
  Nozick 306–10
  Rawls 300–6
  Third Reich, under 313–22
  totalitarianism and 313–22

Kairys, D. 230, 235
Kant, Immanuel 83–4, 121, 145
  moral theory 77
Kelman, M. 231
Kelsen, Hans 40, 144, 146–7, 199
  see also Pure theory
Kennedy, Duncan 231–2
Khmer Rouge 197
  justice under 313
Khrushchev, Nikita 130
Koran (Qu'ran) 106, 107–8, 118
Korner, S. 83

Ladeur, K. H. 268–9, 270
Last Days of Socrates (Plato) 64, 65
Law
  binding effect 4, 5, 6
  black-letter approach 202
  command theory *see* Command theory
  complete law theory 23–4
  constitutive theory 235–6
  contradictions in 231–3
  in populum 20
  in principem 20
  as integrity 160
  international *see* Public international law
  jurisprudence and national law 9–10
  justice and 299
  nature of 3–4
  primitive 28, 39–40, 49
  proximate subsidiary 24
  remote subsidiary 24
  as rules 25
  subsidiary 24
  value judgments and 232–3
Law jobs 185, 207–8, 216–17, 219
Law and Marxism: A General Theory
  (Pashukanis) 131–2
Law and the Modern Mind (Frank) 210,
  211
Law as a Moral Judgment (Beyleveld and
  Brownsword) 102–3
Law of nations *see* Public international law
Law of the Soviet State, The (Vyshinsky)
  132
Lawmaking
  imperantum for 192
  judges as lawmakers 160–1, 206
  procedural naturalist criteria 89–91
  proper purposes doctrine 60

Lawrence, Stephen 256
Law's Empire (Dworkin) 161
Laws (Plato) 63
Legal Thinking Revised (Lundstedt) 185
Legalism, platonic 62–4
Legislation, economic analysis and 283–4
Lenin, V. I. 128
Leviathan (Hobbes) 77, 78
Lex aeterna 71, 73, 74
Lex caelestis 69
Lex divina 74
Lex humana 74
Lex iniusta non est lex 71, 319
Lex naturae 69
Lex naturalis 74
Lex temporalis 71
Lex vulgus 68–9
LEXIS 221
Liberal constitution, deconstruction
  and 266–9
Liberal distributive theory 300–6
  distribution and thin theory of
    good 302–3
  generational equity 305
  just savings principle 305
  original actors 301–2
  principles of justice 303–5
    application 305–6
  veil of ignorance 301–2, 306
Liberal legal tradition, critical legal studies
  critique 226–36
Llewellyn, Karl N. 47, 185, 206–8, 216–17
  judicial reasoning 218–20
  reckonability of result 218
Locke, John 43, 186, 307
  bad governments 79–81
  social contractarianism 79–80
Lundstedt, Anders Vilhelm 184–9
  constructive investigation 185
  distribution of advantage 187–8
  inequality of benefit 187–8
  motivation for legal activity 186
  significance of theory 188–9
  social welfare concept 185–7
  social welfare goals 186
  social welfare method 184–9
Lyotard, J. F. 251, 252–3

MacCormick, N. 36
Mackenzie Wallace, D. 126–7
Majority, tyranny of 81–2
Maliki school 111–12
Mancipation 182–3
Mandate of heaven rule 62
Marx, Karl 121
Marxism 72, 120–43
  Bankowski and Mungham 141–2

Marxism – *continued*
  bourgeois revolution   122, 124
  China *see* China (People's Republic);
       Chinese legal theory
  class antagonism   122
  class domination   122, 124
  class reductionism   123
  classical theory   121–5
  Collins   141–2
  consensual ordering   142
  determinism   235
  form and function contrast   140–2
  law in classical theory   123–5
  modern-day   225–6
  proletarian revolution   122
  Renner   140–2
  revolutionary realignment   122
  as scientific model   122, 123
  show trials   133–4
  significance of analyses   142
  social understanding   121
  in Soviet Union *see* Soviet legal theory
  superstructure   121, 123–4, 225
  thesis, antithesis and synthesis   121
  transition from theory to practice   125
  Vyshinsky   132–4
  Western marxist jurisprudence   140–2
  see also Critical legal studies; Soviet legal
       theory
Materialism, dialectical   121
Matter of Principle, A (Dworkin)   160
Melamed, A. D.   280–3
Mencius (Meng K'e)   63, 75, 136, 137
Mensheviks   127, 128, 194
Meta-narratives   251
Meteyard, Belinda   241
Mill, John Stuart   52–3, 81–2
Minimal state   307–8
Minimalism   308–9
'Mischievous' tendency   29
Moore, Underhill   215–16
Moral obligation   3, 4
Morality
  of aspiration   88–9
  community   176–7
  of duty   88–9
  generation of rights from morality
       99–100
  Hart's positivism   50
       enforcement of morality   52–5
  higher than good laws   67–8
  institutional   177
  internal   91–2, 93
  Islamic law and   108–9
  'jurybox' morality   53
  Kantian   84
  naturalism and   102–7

Morality – *continued*
  law as moral phenomenon   102–3
  obligation   103–4
  obligation and   177
  procedural   91–3
  right as end in itself   84
  right minded citizen   53
  substance of laws and   91–3
Morality of Law, The (Fuller)   87, 88, 89
Morris, Clarence   137
Motivation
  alluring motives   21, 22
  coercive motives   22
  compliance with command   21–2
  reward   22
Muhammad, Prophet   106, 107, 117,
       118
Mungham, G.   141

National Society for the Prevention of
       Cruelty to Children   166
Native title   256
Natural law, minimum content   55–7, 93
Natural rights theory   94–102
  Finnis defence of naturalism   95–6
  generation of rights from morality
       99–100
  importance of Finnis's theory   102
  Locke   80
  practical reasonableness tests   98–9
Naturalism
  Bentham attack on   12
  Beyleveld and Brownsword   104–7
  central concerns   60–1
  classical *see* Classical naturalism
  continuing role   105
  Finnis *see* Natural rights theory
  Islamic jurisprudence and   106–7
  moral nature   102–7
       law as moral phenomenon   102–3
       obligation   103–4
       natural rights   94–102
       see also Natural rights theory
  procedural *see* Procedural naturalism
  revival   86–105
Naturalist-positivist debate   59–60
Nazism *see* Third Reich
Nichomachean Ethics (Aristotle)   67–8
Nozick, Robert   306–10

Obedience obligation   3–4, 7, 8
  Aristotle   68
  bad governments   80
  changing political circumstances   42–4
  'collateral' moral obligation   101
  expository jurisprudence   26
  external collateral obligation   104

Obedience obligation – *continued*
external synthetic collateral obligation 104
Finnis's theory 100–2
habit of obedience 19
Hart 33–4
Hobbes 78–9
impulsions 180, 182
internal collateral obligation 104
internal obligation 104
limitations of 60
Locke 80
moral view 3, 4, 101, 103–4
motivation for compliance 21
Plato 64–7
revolutionary change 44
Rousseau 82
social pressure 35
to society not government 82
subjectivity 104
word magic 181
Obligation
being obliged and being under obligation 33–4
Hart's positivism 33–4
internal aspect of rules 35–7
to obey *see* Obedience obligation
October Revolution 128, 194
Oliphant, Herman 212–13
Olivecrona, Karl 189–97
legislative efficiency 190
see also Independent imperatives
On the Free Choice of the Will (St Augustine) 71
'One right answer thesis' 167–8
Original actors 301–2
'Other', identity and the 'other' in postmodern legal theory 254–5

Pacta regalia 20
Panopticon 13
Pashukanis, E. B. 131–2
Peace, compelling 77
Perestroika 130
Petrazycki (Petrazhitsky), Leon 179–81
Philosopher king 62, 63, 67
Plato 61–7, 77, 265
Christian platonism 71–2
idealism and legalism 62–4
obligation to obey 64–7
philosopher king 62, 63, 67
Pobedonostsev, Konstantin 126
Polinsky, A. M. 279
Political discontinuity 42–3, 44
see also Revolutionary change
Positivism 11
amoral stance 94

Positivism – *continued*
analytical 12
Austin 13
Bentham concept 12–13
see also Command theory
classical *see* Classical positivism
Dworkin criticism 158–60
Kelsen *see* Pure theory
limitations 11
modified by Hart *see* Hart's positivism
naturalist-positivist debate' 59–60
pure theory *see* Pure theory
'time-frames' 56
Posner, Richard 275, 277
common law 284–8
contract law 288–9
criminal law 289–92
economic analysis 283–92
legislation 283–4
Postmodern legal theory 250–73
critique of Enlightenment 250–2
deconstruction 258–63
justice and 263–6
liberal constitution and 266–9
Derrida 258–63
feminism and 256–8
Foucault 254, 257, 270
fundamental values and 256–8
identity and the 'other' 254–5
Lyotard 251, 252–3
reconstruction 270–1
Poststructuralism 258
Practical reasonableness tests 98–9
good citizen reasoning 101
Practitioner jurisprudence 11
Praemiary laws 22
Pragmatism, Dworkin criticism 160–1
'Pre-legal' societies 39
Precedent 167–8
American realists and 210–11
Primitive law 28, 39–40, 49
Primitive societies 39, 208, 256
Princess Sophia Naturalisation Act 1705 47–8
Principle of utility 30
Procedural naturalism 87–94, 320–1
lawmaking criteria 89–91
morality
of aspiration 88–9
of duty 88–9
internal 91–2, 93
and substance of laws 91–3
naturalist analysis 93–4
retroactivity 90–1
Proletarian revolution 122
Proper purposes doctrine 60
Property 80

Proximate subsidiary law 24
Public international law
  Austin 26
  classical positivism 26–8
  Hart's positivism 48–50
  Islamic jurisprudence and 117–19
  postmodern legal theory and 260–1
  pure theory 49, 154–5
    Grundnorm 155
  sources 27–8
Public opinion 82
Public policy 166–7
Pure theory 144–56
  concretisation
    reality of 153
    working of 152–3
  definition of subject matter 144
  discontinuous change 150–1
  distance from real legal systems 146
  dualism 154–5
  grundnorm 41, 145, 147–50, 154, 155
  hierarchy of norms 147–52
    Grundnorm 145, 147–50, 154
    structure of norms 147–50
    validation in 148, 149
  Kantian theory of knowledge and 145–6
  monism 154–5
  official emphasis 153–4
  public international law 49, 154–5
  purity meaning 146–7
  revolutionary transition problem 150–2
  scientific analysis claim 144
  value 155–6
Purges 90, 133–4

Qu'ran 106, 107–8, 118

Racism 256, 257–8, 264
Rawls, John 267
  application of principles of justice 305–6
  distribution and thin theory of
    good 302–3
  generational equity 305
  just savings principle 305
  liberal distributive theory 300–6
  original actors 301–2
  principles of justice 303–5
  veil of ignorance 301–2, 306
Realism
  American *see* American realism
  economic analysis and 276
  impact in America 220–3
  postmodern legal theory and 251
  Scandinavia *see* Scandinavian realism
  social *see* Social realism
Reciprocity 94
Reckonability 217

Recognition, rule of 38, 40–4
Reconstruction
  economic 248
  postmodern legal theory 270–1
Red Guards 135, 138–9
Referenda 248
Remote subsidiary law 24
Republic (Plato) 62
Requisitum 190–1
Residence, voluntary 65, 66
Restoration, The 42–3, 44
Restraint 104
Retroactivity 90–1, 162
Revolutionary change 42–4
  independent imperatives 193–5
  political discontinuity 42–3
  pure theory 150–2
  realignment 122
Reward, as motive for compliance 22
Right as end in itself 84
Rights
  Dworkin rights thesis 100
  establishment 195–6
  exceptionless claim rights 100
  generation from morality 99–100
  Islam and human rights 115–16
  natural *see* Natural rights theory
  performatory imperatives and rights
    195–6
  Unger system 246–7
Rights thesis 100, 161–7
  abstract rights 164–5
  community morality 177
  concrete or institutional rights 165
  consequentialist theory of rights 165–7
  distinction between rights and policies
    159
  entrenched rights 163–5
  equal concern and respect 173–5
  individual and minority rights 157
  institutional morality 176
  integrity 168–9, 170–1, 172
  judicial decisions
    chess analogy 171–2
    judge as protector of rights 172–3
    'one right answer' thesis 167–8
    policy ground objections 162–3
    precedent 167–8
    statutes 169–71
  judicial precedent 167–8
  morality
    community 176–7
    institutional 176
    obligation and 177
  policies as collective goals 163
  public policy 166–7
Roberts, Simon 39

Roman Empire 68–9, 76
Ross, Alf 178
  chess analogy 198–9
  judicial function 197–201
  norms of conduct and competence 199
  validity of rule 198–9
Rotating capital fund 248–9
Rousseau, Jean-Jacques 81–3
Rule sceptics 46–8, 203, 204, 208–9,
    211–13, 219–20
Rules
  distrust of 206
  grundnorm 41, 145, 147–50, 154, 155
  Hart's positivism
    adjudication 38, 40
    change 38, 40
    importance of rules 34–46
    internal aspects of rules 35–7
    legal systems and officials 44–6
    primary rules 37–40, 44
    recognition 38, 40–4, 94
    rule scepticism 46–8
    secondary rules 37–40, 44, 45
    truisms 56, 57
    ultimate rule 41
  law as 25
  primary and secondary 200
  Ross norms of conduct and competence
    199
  validity 198–9
Russia see Imperial Russia; Soviet legal
    theory

Saddam Hussein 119
Sanctions 100, 181
  command theory 13, 17, 21–3, 33
  punitive 25
  United Nations and 27
Santos, Bonaventura de Sousa 270–2,
    273
Scandinavian realism 5, 178–201
  constructive jurisprudence 185
  early psychological theorists 179–84
  Hägerström 179, 181–4, 201
  impulsions 179–81, 182
  Lundstedt 184–9
  mancipation 182–3
  normativity 180
  Olivecrona see Independent imperatives
  ownership 184
  Petrazycki (Petrazhitsky) 179–81
  Ross 197–201
  scientific jurisprudence 185
  social welfare method 184–9
  word magic 181–4
Scepticism
  fact sceptics 46

Scepticism – continued
  rule sceptics 46–8, 203, 204, 208–9,
    211–13, 219–20
Schlag, P. 266–8
Schubert, Glendon 222–3
Secular law, Islamic jurisprudence and
    113–15
Secularisation 12
ash-Shafi'i, Muhammad ibn-Idris 107–8,
    112
Shafi'i school 111–12
Shaming 130
Shariah see Islamic jurisprudence
Shirer, W. L. 315–16
Social contractarianism 65, 77, 186
  compelling peace 77
  contract with society not government
    81–3
  Hobbes 77–9
  humans in groups 78
  Locke 79–80
  reaction to anarchy 77–9
  Rousseau 81–3
Social living 78
Social order 103
Social pressure 35
Social realism 23
Social welfare method 184–9
  concept 185–7
  constructive investigation 185
  distribution of advantage 187–8
  goals 186
  ideas of justice 187–8
  inequality of benefit 187–8
  motivation for legal activity 186
  significance of theory 188–9
Socialist legality 133, 135, 139, 140
Socrates 61, 64–5
Sovereign
  abuse of power 78
  command theory 13, 17–20
  continuity 15
  Crown in parliament 41
  definition 17–18
  express conventions 19
  limit by constitutional laws 18–20
  Princess Sophia Naturalisation Act 1705
    47–8
  surrender of power of individuals to 77
Soviet legal theory 125–34
  Bolsheviks 128
  capitalist encirclement 129, 132
  collapse of state 130
  comrades' courts 130
  dictatorship of proletariat 128
  five year plans 129
  glasnost 130

Soviet legal theory – *continued*
  Imperial Russia 125–8
  marxism 120
    see also Marxism
  Mensheviks 127, 128, 194
  new economic policy 129
  October Revolution 128, 194
  perestroika 130
  shaming 130
  show trials 133–4
  socialist legality 129
  socio-democratic republic 127–8
  war communism 129
  see also Imperial Russia
Stalin, Joseph 129
Stalinism 50, 86, 129, 197
  capitalist encirclement 129, 132
  justice under 313
  model for China 135
  show trials 133–4
Stare decisis 213, 215
State
  dominant protective association 307
  Islamic jurisprudence and 112–16
  minimal 307–8
  voluntarism 308
Stephen, Sir James Fitzjames 53, 54
Stoic philosophy 68
Stuchka, P. I. 128–9
Subjectivity 104
Subsidiary law 24
Summa Theologica (Thomas Aquinas) 72, 73, 74, 75, 312, 321
Summers, Robert S 93
Sunnah 108, 109
Szeftel, Marc 127

Tarquinius Superbus 14, 75
Tax 308–9
Teleological analysis of Aristotle 67–9, 73
Theory of Justice, A (Rawls) 301–6
Third Reich 86, 87, 197
  Gestapo 315
  Hart's positivism and 50–2, 58
  justice under 313–22
  leadership principle 314
  nature of injustice 316
  Nuremburg race laws 90
  post–1945 judicial consideration 316–22
    grudge informer cases 316–18
  postmodern legal theory and 259–60
  purges 90
  will of society and 82
Thomson, Alan 224, 236–9
Tienanmen Square incident 135, 140
Totalitarianism 50, 86, 90, 92, 197
  justice under 313–22

Transaction costs 279–80
Treaties 99–100
Trevelyan, GM 42
Trotsky, Leon 129
Two Treatises on Government (Locke) 79
Tyranny 92
  deposed tyrants 75
  of majority 81–2
  tyrannical governments 79

Ummah 109, 118
Uncertainty, Hart's positivism 40, 46, 47
Unger, Roberto 229, 236, 244–9, 268
  contextuality 244–6
  economic reconstruction 248
  empowered democracy 246–9
  government remodelling 247–8
  referenda and elections 248
  rights system 246–7
  roles 245–6
  rotating capital fund 248–9
United Nations sanctions 27
Universal Declaration of Human Rights 99–100, 321
Unjust government
  Locke and 79–81
  St Augustine 71–2
  Thomas Aquinas 74
  see also Tyranny
Utilitarianism
  economic analysis and 276–8
  utility principle 30

Values
  postmodern legal theory and fundamental values 256–8
  value judgments 232–3
  wealth as value 293–5
Veil of ignorance 301–2, 306
Vietnam War protests 66
Volonté générale of Rousseau 81–2
Voluntarism 308
Voluntary residence 65, 66
Vyshinsky, A. Ia. 129, 132–4

Warrington, R. 251
Western marxist jurisprudence
  Bankowski and Mungham 141–2
  Collins 141–2
  form and function contrast 140–2
  Renner 140–2
Will of society 81–2
Will theory 189, 197
Wolfenden Report 53
Woozley, A. D. 65–6
Word magic 181–4, 196
Wu Min Aun 115